A Guidance Approach for the Encouraging Classroom

2nd Edition

In Memory of Two Education Professors

Ben Thompson of Antioch College,
Yellow Springs, Ohio

and

Maurice Lucas of the
University of North Dakota,
Grand Forks

A Guidance Approach for the Encouraging Classroom

2nd Edition

Daniel Gartrell, Ed.D.
Bemidji State University

1-800-487-5510

Delmar Publishers

I(T)P® **International Thomson Publishing**

Albany • Bonn • Boston • Cincinnati • Detroit • London • Madrid
Melbourne • Mexico City • New York • Pacific Grove • Paris • San Francisco
Singapore • Tokyo • Toronto • Washington

Cover Design: Brucie Rosch

Cover Illustrator: Alexander Piejko

Delmar Staff
Publisher: William Brottmiller
Senior Editor: Jay S. Whitney
Associate Editor: Erin J. O'Connor

Production Coordinator: Sandra Woods
Art and Design Coordinator: Carol Keohane

Printed in the United States of America
6 7 8 9 10 XXX 02 01 00

For more information, contact Delmar, 3 Columbia Circle, PO Box 15015, Albany, NY 12212-0515;
or find us on the World Wide Web at http://www.westlegalstudies.com

International Division List

Japan:
Thomson Learning
Palaceside Building 5F
1-1-1 Hitotsubashi, Chiyoda-ku
Tokyo 100 0003 Japan
Tel: 813 5218 6544
Fax: 813 5218 6551

Australia/New Zealand
Nelson/Thomson Learning
102 Dodds Street
South Melbourne, Victoria 3205
Australia
Tel: 61 39 685 4111
Fax: 61 39 685 4199

UK/Europe/Middle East:
Thomson Learning
Berkshire House
168-173 High Holborn
London
WC1V 7AA United Kingdom
Tel: 44 171 497 1422
Fax: 44 171 497 1426

Latin America:
Thomson Learning
Seneca, 53
Colonia Polanco
11560 Mexico D.F. Mexico
Tel: 525-281-2906
Fax: 525-281-2656

Canada:
Nelson/Thomson Learning
1120 Birchmount Road
Scarborough, Ontario
Canada M1K 5G4
Tel: 416-752-9100
Fax: 416-752-8102

Asia:
Thomson Learning
60 Albert Street, #15-01
Albert Complex
Singapore 189969
Tel: 65 336 6411
Fax: 65 336 7411

Library of Congress Cataloging-in-Publication Data
Gartrell, Daniel.
A guidance approach for the encouraging classroom / Daniel Gartrell. — 2nd ed.
p. cm.
Rev. ed. of: A guidance approach to discipline © 1994.
Includes bibliographical references and index.
ISBN 0-8273-7617-0
1. School discipline—United States. 2. Child psychology—United States. 3. Problem solving in children. 4. Interpersonal relations in children—United States. I. Gartrell, Daniel. Guidance approach to discipline. II. Title.
LB3012.2.G37 1997 97-16706
371.5'0973—dc21 CIP

Contents

Preface

This is the second edition of a text originally published as *A Guidance Approach to Discipline*. The purpose of the new edition remains the same; the text provides a comprehensive, caring, developmentally appropriate approach to guiding children's personal and social development. *A Guidance Approach for the Encouraging Classroom* is about *management and discipline* in early childhood. Yet, instead of traditional management and discipline practices, the text focuses on the use of **guidance** with children, individually and in groups, in order to build the **encouraging classroom.**

In the first edition, I wrote that many in the early childhood field have come to regard the term *discipline* as controversial. Because of the connotation of punishment associated with it, i.e., to "discipline" a child, early childhood educators are embracing instead the term *guidance.* I agree with this trend, but was reluctant to change the title for the new edition. This text addresses teaching children at both the preschool and early elementary grade levels. Because many elementary educators still use the term "discipline," I did not want to confuse these readers.

Perhaps the deciding factor was my decision to include more information on *conflict management* in the second edition. The functions of the teacher are clearly different when instead of punishing misbehavior, the teacher resolves *mistaken behavior* through mediation and teaching negotiation skills. Through the guidance techniques of conflict management, the teacher helps children learn to solve their problems, rather than punishing children for having problems they cannot solve. The intent of the text has always been to assist the teacher to build *an encouraging classroom*—one where problems of learning and social interaction can be resolved in mutually beneficial ways—and the means for building the encouraging classroom has always been guidance. The decrease in emphasis on "a guidance approach to discipline," and the increase in "guidance for the encouraging classroom" is the main conceptual change from the first edition to the second.

New Features

The encouraging classroom is a place where children feel they belong, can learn, and can solve social problems peacefully. In this context, of course, *classroom* refers to more than a physical structure in a school or center. It is the home away from home for children and the adults who work with them. The education program of the encouraging classroom is developmentally appropriate. The social atmosphere is supportive, mutually respectful, and culturally responsive. Leadership in the encouraging classroom is not by the teacher alone, but by the teacher in cooperation with the other adults of differing backgrounds, and most especially the parent. The encouraging classroom is a new strand in the second edition, woven throughout the text and given expression in several chapters.

A second strand is a new focus emphasis on *conflict management,* a central tool of guidance. Conflict management refers to the ability to prevent and resolve disputes peacefully in the everyday affairs of the classroom. In the second edition, the text takes the position that conflict management must not be an "add on" intervention strategy, but must be a human priority integral to the program. As an element of *peace education,* as well as guidance, conflict management is given distinct discussion in several chapters and full exploration in a new Chapter 9, Guiding Children to Solve Social Problems.

A second change from the first edition is the reworking of Chapter 7 into two new chapters, Leadership Communication with the Group (Chapter 7) and Leadership Communication with the Individual (Chapter 8). I believe the term *leadership communication* works well to define the communication style necessary for the adult who is an "adult friend" to children in the encouraging classroom.

In deference to the current literature, references and recommended resources at the end of each chapter have been updated. Additionally, a reflection activity has been added to the follow-up activities to encourage students to integrate their experiences with text ideas. References to terms like *resiliency, peace education,* and *character education* have been added to the pool of guidance terms from the first edition, including *levels of mistaken behavior* and *liberation teaching*. In the second edition, each term appearing in boldface in the text is defined in the Glossary at the back of the book.

Text Organization

Unit One traces the guidance tradition in progressive educational thought, develops the concept of mistaken behavior, and spells out "bottom line" principles for the use of guidance. Unit Two makes the case that a major component of guidance is *prevention,* reducing the need for mistaken behavior. The focus is on how the adult can use a knowledge of child development, developmentally appropriate practice, and leadership communication to build the encouraging classroom in which *democratic life skills* can be learned.

Unit Three retains its emphasis on solving problems in the classroom. This unit provides methods for guiding children to resolve problems themselves and provides techniques for solving problems that are too large for children to solve on their own. As in the first edition, the book concludes with a discussion of the unifying concept of *liberation teaching,* now including sections on resiliency and peace education.

Developmentally appropriate practice (DAP) continues to define the educational program at the core of the guidance approach. The 1997 edition of the National Association for the Education of Young Children's (NAEYC) *Developmentally Appropriate Practice in Programs Serving Young Children*—is frequently cited in the text. Current references to DAP, including at the primary level, appear in various chapters. Constructivist education, at its current zenith in the Reggio Emilia approach, continues the progressive education tradition so compatible with guidance and the encouraging classroom. To illustrate practices both of DAP and guidance, I particularly enjoyed again using anecdotes and captioned photos to illustrate important concepts. (New anecdotes and photos have been added.)

Each chapter ends with a section on building and maintaining productive relations with parents. Parent-teacher partnerships are vital for sustaining the effects of the encouraging classroom: growing self-esteem, confidence in one's ability to learn, and the capacity to accept and get along with others. The teacher who realizes that the child is an extension of the family respects the culture of the family and the importance of family members to the child. *Respecting cultural diversity is thus a key concept in the text.* To recall a line from the first edition, "The parent is the primary educator of the child; teachers only help."

The concept of *mistaken behavior* is gaining acceptance in the field, but likely remains the most controversial element of the text. I continue to believe that whether readers grow comfortable with the concept or simply use the term *misbehavior* more consciously, **guidance for the encouraging classroom** will stand on its own merits.

In keeping with the spirit of *inclusion,* or teaching children with different abilities in the integrated classroom, I again have avoided separate sections to address these children's needs. Disabled children either may show mistaken behavior because of unmet needs and still developing social skills; or they may be the victims of mistaken behavior due to their circumstances. Chapter 3 develops the concept of unconditional positive regard, which certainly pertains to young children with disabilities. Chapter 12 discusses liberation teaching, which is teaching that empowers children toward *resiliency,* the ability to overcome one's vulnerabilities, whatever their cause. I am confident that other chapters as well address skills teachers use to meet the needs of special populations.

Finally, throughout the text I have continued the practice of referring to many other authors. I've done so to illustrate the broad base of agreement in the literature about guidance ideas. Even exciting new ideas about social and personal development build from a tradition in the early childhood field, a longstanding commitment to the potential and worth of the developing child. Going back to Froebel and Montessori and moving forward to the efforts of NAEYC, the Association for Childhood Education International (ACEI), and the proponents of Reggio Emilia, early childhood educators always have been in the forefront of progressive educational thought. My hope is that this second edition continues that tradition.

Dan Gartrell
Bemidji State University, Bemidji, Minnesota

Acknowledgments

Many persons have helped make this text possible. First, deep appreciation goes to my mother, Beth Goff, for raising me this way, and to my wife, Julie Jochum, for her love and unending assistance. Thanks are due to the many teachers I have worked over the years and who practice guidance. I wish I could recognize them all, but a few who have contributed anecdotes and case studies are Pat Sanford, Sue Bailey, Vicki Wangberg, Teresa Galloway, Lynn Hart, Diane Lerberg, Ina Rambo, Nellie Cameron, John Ostby, Dee Bretti, and staff members of Bi-County Head Start, Bemidji Early Childhood Family Education, and Paul Bunyan School of Bemidji.

From the first edition, special acknowledgment is given to Dr. Steven Harlow for permission to duplicate his important discussion of "relational patterns" from the monograph, "Special Education: The Meeting of Differences"; the material forms a basis of the discussion in Chapter 2. Thanks go to four local readers: Diane Lerberg, who offered major encouragement early on, Julie Jochum, Cathy McCartney, and Joan Miller of Bemidji State University. Also at Bemidji State, assistance with inputting the first edition was contributed by Cherry Brouwer of the Child Development Training Program.

Special appreciation is extended to numerous teachers, children, and parents who permitted their photos to be included in the second edition. Programs and schools where photos were taken include Blackduck and Bemidji classrooms of Bi-County Head Start, Bemidji, Minnesota; Paul Bunyan School, J. W. Smith School, and St. Philip's School, Bemidji, Minnesota; Onigum Center of Leech Lake Head Start; Centers of Kootasca Head Start, Grand Rapids, Minnesota; Shirley G. Moore Laboratory Nursery School at the University of Minnesota; classrooms of Audubon School in Minneapolis; and the Riverside School of St. Louis Park, Minnesota.

Monte Draper of Bemidji's newspaper, *The Pioneer,* again has provided appreciated technical assistance with photography for the text. In the second edition photos are used courtesy of *The Pioneer.* Also, Lin Wahlberg, Michael Crowley, and Richard Faulkner contributed photos carried through to the second edition.

Student teachers have contributed several perceptive anecdotes that appear in the second edition, including: Julie Curb, Cindy Cronemiller, Sharon Hoverson, Heather Johnson, Jenny Oulman, Karen Palubici, Carol Pelton, Jen Stratton, and Sandra Weiland. Thanks to these undergraduate and graduate early childhood students. Names have been changed in the anecdotes, and classrooms have not been identified.

Thanks go to Chapter 9 contributors Sue Liedl and Sarah Pirtle and to reviewers Susan Smith, Marilyn Grave, and Maggie Carlson. For assistance with the Chapter 9 case study, appreciation is expressed to the staff, children, and families of St. Philip's School in Bemidji. Especially, gratitude is expressed to principal Carol Rettinger and parent and conflict management coordinator, Sue Liedl.

My appreciation is extended to the reviewers enlisted through Delmar for the constructive criticism and helpful suggestions. They include:

Janet Baggett
Auburn University
Montgomery, AL

Lois Burnes
Minot State University
Minot, ND

Jeffrey I. Gelfer, Ph.D.
University of Nevada-Las Vegas
Las Vegas, NV

Robin Christine Hasslen, Ph.D.
St. Cloud State University
St. Cloud, MN

Kathy Head
Lorain County Community College
Elyria, OH

Jann James, Ed.D.
Troy State University
Goshen, AL

Marie Keeling
Tidewater Community College
Portsmouth, VA

Jennifer Perkins
Terra Community College
Fremont, OH

Olivia N. Saracho, Ph.D.
University of Maryland at College Park
College Park, MD

Sharon T. Willis
North Harris Community College
Houston, TX

The entire editorial staff at Delmar, headed by Erin O'Connor Traylor, have been supportive, professional, and efficient. They made the task easier. Special thanks go to Erin for her leadership with the second edition and to Genne Gault of Book-Masters, Inc.

ABOUT THE AUTHOR

During the 1960s, Dan Gartrell was a teacher at an inner city elementary school in Ohio and the Head Start Program of the Red Lake Band of Ojibwe in Minnesota. In the early 1970s Dan earned a Masters Degree at Bemidji State University in northern Minnesota. At Bemidji State, Dan became a field advisor, CDA trainer, and then director for the Child Development Training Program. Dan completed his doctorate at the University of North Dakota's Center for Teaching and Learning in 1977. He is currently Professor of Early Childhood and Elementary Education and Director of the Child Development Training Program at Bemidji State University. As a teacher, CDA trainer, and student teaching supervisor, Dan has been working with students in early childhood classrooms for more than 30 years.

Dan has led over 100 presentations on guidance in five midwestern states; California; Washington, D.C.; and Alaska. Additionally, he has written articles on this subject, including four for *Young Children*. Dan is an amateur photographer who enjoyed taking many of the photos that appear in the text. He is a member of a blended family that includes his wife, Dr. Julie Jochum, five children in their twenties and thirties—Jesse, Kateri, Adam, Sara, Angie—and special Granddaughter, Julia. Dan comments that his family has added much to his understanding about guidance.

Unit One

Foundations of a Guidance Approach

CHAPTER OVERVIEW

1 The Guidance Tradition

Chapter 1 provides historical overview of the guidance tradition. Direct quotes by pioneers in the field are included to document their own thoughts about education and the role of guidance. Mid-20th century influences of the developmental and self psychologists are traced. The trend away from punishment and toward guidance in the 1980s and 1990s is presented. The tradition of parent-teacher partnerships within the guidance approach is explored.

2 Mistaken Behavior

Chapter 2 presents a concept in line with the work of the self psychologists for understanding young children's behavior: that behavior traditionally considered as *misbehavior* is more constructively viewed as **mistaken behavior.** Three levels of mistaken behavior are analyzed. Considerations for acquainting parents with the concept of mistaken behavior are discussed.

3 Guidance: The Bottom Line

Chapter 3 develops four principles of a guidance approach: that it builds from positive teacher-child relations; reduces the need for mistaken behavior; takes a solution-orientation; and involves teamwork with other adults—particularly parents—on behalf of the child.

1

The Guidance Tradition

GUIDING QUESTIONS

As you read chapter one, you will discover answers to the following questions:

- **Who were the pioneers of the guidance tradition?**
- **Who were mid-20th century influences on the guidance tradition?**
- **What was the significance of discipline trends in the 1980s?**
- **What is the state of the guidance tradition today?**
- **What is the role of parents in the guidance tradition?**

As we enter the 21st century, we want citizens to be able to think intelligently and ethically and to solve problems by the use of civil words. Through a comprehensive examination of the areas traditionally called **discipline** and **group management,** *A Guidance Approach for the Encouraging Classroom* explores the teaching and learning of these life skills in early childhood education.

The **guidance approach** has its roots in the history of western education and is tied to the thoughts of progressive educators over the last two centuries. The basis of guidance, the empowering of productive human activity, lies in the view that human nature, in the embodiment of the child, has the potential for good. In this view, the role of the adult is not to "discipline the child away from evil" but to guide the child to develop the personal strength and understanding necessary to make ethical, intelligent decisions. This capacity, which Piaget (1932/1960) termed **autonomy** and current educators refer to as **character education,** is a primary goal in the guidance approach. A companion goal, related and no less important, is to guide children in the use of **conflict management,** the ability in the every day business of life to prevent and, if necessary, peaceably resolve conflicts. These two goals serve as themes that are interwoven throughout the text, sometimes directly addressed and sometimes implicit in the discussion, but always there.

In recent years a growing number of educators have come to believe that the term *discipline* is controversial. For these educators discipline implies punishment, a practice precluded in the use of guidance (Gartrell, 1997). In the guidance tradition, the purpose of discipline is clear: to teach children the **life skills** of getting along with others, expressing strong feelings in acceptable ways, and managing conflicts peaceably. For this reason, the guidance approach transcends the function of **conventional discipline,** the use of rewards and punishments to keep children under the teacher's control (Gartrell, 1995; Greenberg, 1988; Kohn, 1993). Guidance is education for democracy, and a guidance approach is a teaching approach—the teaching of democratic life skills through all classroom situations.

The classroom environment through which children are empowered to learn democratic life skills is the **encouraging classroom.** In the encouraging classroom, all students feel that they are able learners and worthy members of the class. The teacher builds the encouraging classroom through active leadership with the children, their families, and the community. In the encouraging classroom, positive discipline practices merge with developmentally appropriate practices and become part of the everyday curriculum. For the teacher in the encouraging classroom, human differences—differing abilities, cultural backgrounds, appearances, and behavioral styles—become sources of mutual affirmation and respect. With both the individual and the group, the teaching approach for the encouraging classroom is guidance.

Unit One provides the foundations of the guidance approach. This first chapter documents that over the years progressive educators consistently have called for an integrative education model, one that links the positive potential of the child, the interactive nature of an appropriate curriculum, and the guiding role of the teacher as democratic leader. Chapter 1 traces the guidance tradition in western educational thought.

PIONEERS OF THE GUIDANCE TRADITION

A principle in the guidance tradition is that discipline cannot be separated from the curriculum used, and that both are tied to views of human nature (Gartrell, 1992). This three-way relationship is no recent occurrence and can be seen in the seventeenth century in the writings of the educators of the time—the clergy. Osborn's informative chronology, *Early Childhood Education in Historical Perspective,* frames a fundamental disagreement about the nature of childhood that still impacts education and discipline practice today (1980). Osborn documents that within the clergy two contrasting reasons were given for the importance of education. The 1621 treatise, *A Godly Form of Household Government,* states:

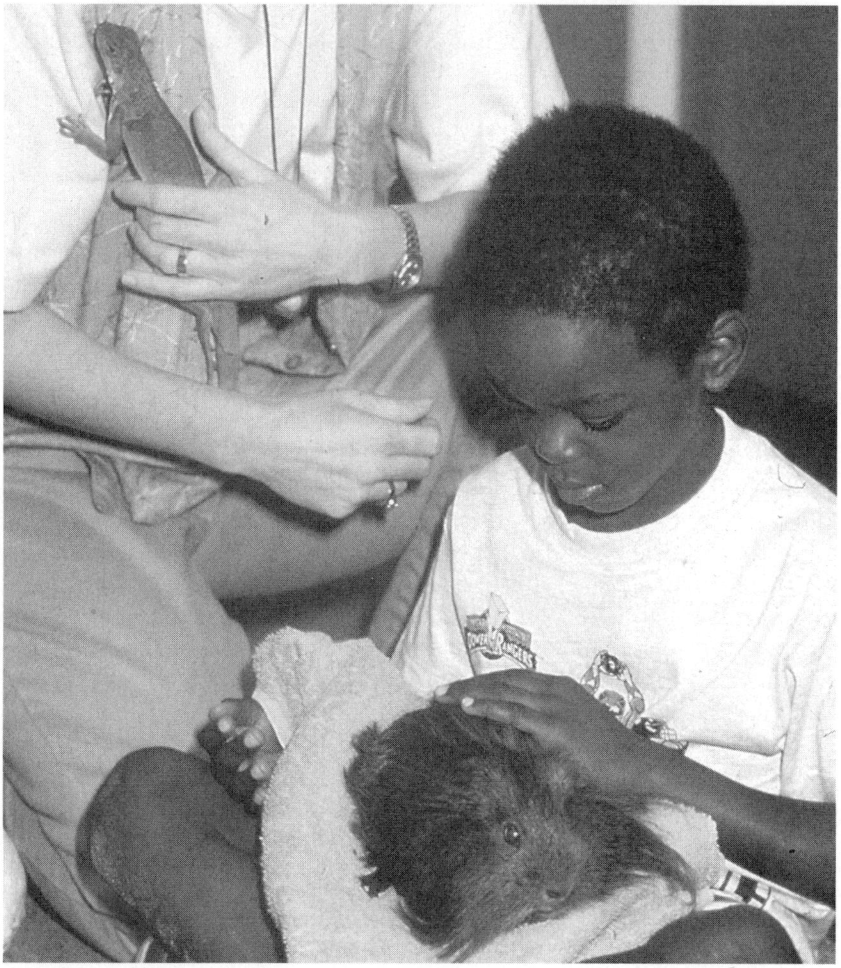

Guidance is based on the view that human nature has the potential for good.

Believing that children tended toward evil, school masters of previous times "beat the devil" out of children—corporal punishment that would be considered child abuse today. (Courtesy, Corbis-Bettman, *The developing person through childhood and adolescence,* New York: Worth Publishers, Inc.)

> The young child which lieth in the cradle is both wayward and full of affection; and though his* body be small, yet he hath a wrongdoing heart and is inclined to evil . . . . If this spark be suffered to increase, it will rage over and burn down the whole house. For we are changed and become good, not by birth, but by education (p. 24)."

An opposing point of view portrayed the child as a *tabulae rasae* (blank slate). This point of view can be seen in Earle's *Microcosmography* (1628):

> The child is a small letter, yet the best copy of Adam. . . . His soul is yet a white paper unscribbled with observations . . . and he knows no evil (p. 24).

Among western cultures, the prevalence of the first view meant that strict discipline based on obedience and corporal punishment has been widely practiced into the twentieth century (Berger, 1991; deMause, 1974). Corporal punishment as an issue is still unresolved in the nation's schools. Progress toward humane educational practice has been made, however, and some teachers of the attitude expressed by Earle always have used the tenets of guidance.

During the nineteenth century such European educators as Herbart, Pestalozzi, and Froebel fundamentally reformed educational practice, in no small part as a result of their views about human nature. Herbart and Pestalozzi recognized that children learned best through real experiences rather than through the rote recitation of facts. Pestalozzi put into practice schools for the "less well-to-do" and so modeled the beginning of universal education. He also co-wrote *Manual for Mothers,* which provided guidance for mothers of very young children and inspired Friedrich

---

* For purposes of accuracy, masculine pronouns are retained in quotes. Otherwise, the author has sought to reduce and balance gender-specific pronoun use.

Froebel's interest in early childhood education (Lilley, 1967). Herbart wrote effectively about the importance of motivating students to take an interest in learning, a fundamental **preventive guidance** strategy (Osborn, 1980).

Friedrich Froebel

Froebel was the originator of the kindergarten, at the time intended to serve children aged three to six. The purpose of the kindergarten was to provide an extension of the family life that Froebel thought all children should have. Education for Froebel was guidance so that the "innate impulses of the child" could be harmoniously developed through creative activity. In line with his views about the role of development in education, Froebel believed that the nature of the child was essentially good and that "faults" were the product of particular experiences. In *Friedrich Froebel: A Selection From His Writings* (1967), Lilley quotes the educator:

> There are many faults . . . which arise simply through carelessness. When children act on an impulse which in itself may be harmless or even praiseworthy, they can become so entirely absorbed that they have no thought for the consequences, and indeed from their own limited experience can have no knowledge of them. . . .
>
> Moreover, it is certainly true that as a rule the child is first made bad by some other person, often by the educator himself. This can happen when everything which the child does out of ignorance or thoughtlessness or even from a keen sense of right and wrong is attributed to an intention to do evil. Unhappily there are among teachers those who always see children as mischievous, spiteful . . . whereas others see at most an overexuberant sense of life or a situation which has got out of hand (Lilley, p. 135).

In these views about children and their behavior, Froebel showed clear understanding of the need for a guidance approach to discipline.

Maria Montessori

As a transition figure between a pedagogy dominated by the philosophy of 19th century and the psychology of the 20th, Maria Montessori was the first woman psychiatrist in modern Italy as well as the leading authority in early childhood education. Similar to Froebel, Montessori maintained that a fundamental principle in "scientific pedagogy" was that "the child is in a continual state of growth and metamorphosis, whereas the adult has reached the norm of the species." (Standing, 1962).

Montessori—as well as her American contemporary, John Dewey—abhorred traditional didactic practices, with children planted behind desks and expected to recite lessons of little meaning in their lives. Both criticized approaches to discipline based on this pervasive schooling practice. In her comprehensive, *The Montessori Method* (1912/1964), the educator asserted:

> We know only too well the sorry spectacle of the teacher who, in the ordinary schoolroom, must pour certain cut and dried facts into the heads of the scholars. In order to succeed in this barren task, she finds it necessary to discipline her pupils into

> immobility and to force their attention. Prizes and punishments are ever-ready and efficient aids to the master who must force into a given attitude of mind and body those who are condemned to be his listeners (1964, p. 21).

Montessori went on to devote an entire chapter of her text to an alternative discipline methodology that was more respectful of the child's development. For Montessori the purpose of education and discipline is the same: to encourage the development of responsible decision-making (1964).

John Dewey

John Dewey is considered the architect of progressive education in the United States. Over a sixty-year period, Dewey raised the nation's consciousness about the kind of education needed in an industrial society. Like Montessori, Dewey viewed discipline as differing in method depending on the curriculum followed. In the 1900 monograph, *The School and Society,* Dewey commented:

> If you have the end in view of forty or fifty children learning certain set lessons, to be recited to the teacher, your discipline must be devoted to securing that result. But if the end in view is the development of a spirit of social co-operation and community life, discipline must grow out of and be relative to such an aim . . . There is a certain disorder in any busy workshop; there is not silence; persons are not engaged in maintaining certain fixed physical postures; their arms are not folded; they are not holding their books thus and so. They are doing a variety of things, and there is the confusion, the bustle that results from activity. Out of the occupation, out of doing things that are to produce results, and out of doing these in a social and co-operative way, there is born a discipline of its own kind and type. Our whole conception of discipline changes when we get this point of view (pp. 16–17).

Through Dewey's achievements in the advent of progressive education, guidance began to be established in American educational thought.

MID-20TH CENTURY INFLUENCES: THE DEVELOPMENTAL AND SELF PSYCHOLOGISTS

In the 20th century two distinct branches of psychology contributed to the progressive education movement and to the guidance tradition. In Europe, Jean Piaget brought together his distinct scholarship in the fields of biology and child study to provide the foundations of modern developmental psychology. In the United States, a group of psychologists integrated neo-Freudian thought and American humanistic psychology into a new branch of study, *self-concept* psychology, shortened in the text to **self psychology.**

These two distinct psychological fields gave articulation to many of the practices of today's guidance approach. Piaget's influence is introduced here and returned to in Chapter 4. The contributors of the self psychologists are also highlighted.

When the classroom becomes a "busy workshop," our conception of discipline changes.

Perhaps the most noted self psychologist, Erik Erikson, is discussed in more detail in Chapter 4.

Jean Piaget

Decidedly clinical in his orientation, Jean Piaget was the pre-eminent developmental psychologist of the 20th century. Writing in French, the Swiss psychologist shared with Montessori the precept that the developing child learns most effectively by interacting with the environment. Further, Piaget shared with Dewey a basic regard for the social context of learning—that peer interaction is essential for healthy development. Piaget agreed with both that education must be a cooperative endeavor and that discipline must respect and respond to this fact. In his landmark work, *The Moral Judgement of the Child* (1932/1960), Piaget stated:

> The essence of democracy resides in its attitude towards law as a product of the collective will, and not as some thing emanating from a transcendent will or from the authority established by divine right. It is therefore the essence of democracy to replace the unilateral respect of authority by the mutual respect of autonomous wills. So that the problem is to know what will best prepare the child for the task of citizenship. Is it the habit of external discipline gained under the influence of unilateral respect and of adult constraint, or is it the habit of internal discipline, of mutual respect and of "self government"? . . . If one thinks of the systematic resistance offered by pupils to the authoritarian method, and the admirable ingenuity employed by children the world over to evade disciplinary constraint, one cannot help regarding as defective a system which allows so much effort to be wasted instead of using it in cooperation (pp. 366–367).

Subsequent generations of psychologists and educators have been influenced by Piaget's studies of how children develop. In the last few years, many of these "Neo-

Figure 1.1
Pioneers of the Guidance Tradition

Frederich Froebel 1782–1852	Generally, the child is first made "bad" by some other person, often by the educator himself through confusion of the natural exuberance of childhood with an intention to do evil.
Maria Montessori 1870–1952	In the ordinary classroom the master [teacher] must use prizes and punishments to pour certain cut-and-dried facts into the heads of the scholars.
John Dewey 1859–1952	Out of the occupation, out of doing things that are to produce results, and out of doing these things in a social and cooperative way, there is born a discipline of its own kind and type.
Jean Piaget 1896–1980	If one thinks of the admirable ingenuity employed by children the world over to evade disciplinary constraint, one cannot help regarding as defective a system which allows so much effort to be wasted instead of using it in cooperation.

Piagetian" writers have focused on **constructivist education.** (See Recommended Resources.) In the constructivist educational model, the child builds knowledge by interacting with the social and physical environment. A foremost expression of the constructivist viewpoint is found in the acclaimed schools of the city of Reggio Emilia in Italy (Gandini, 1993). The schools have taken to new heights the idea of the child's innate ability to create meaning through expressive activity. The multimedia creations of even the very young at the schools are causing teachers the world over to rethink the creative and problem-solving potential of children in the classroom.

By redefining education from a *constructivist* perspective, developmental educators are changing the way professionals in the field look at teaching, learning, the curriculum, and discipline. This developmental and interactive view of the educational process blends well with the guidance tradition.

A synopsis of the views of the pioneers in the guidance tradition, including Piaget, is provided in Figure 1.1, closely paraphrasing the full quotes already cited.

The Self Psychologists

During the 1960s the writing of such psychologists as Erikson (1963), Rogers (1961), Maslow (1962), and Combs (1962) focused on the developing self as the primary dynamic in human behavior. These theorists suggested that to the extent children felt safe in their circumstances and valued as members of the group, they would see themselves positively and not need to act out against the world. Numerous studies of self-image (the collection of feelings about who one is) and self-concept (the conscious picture of who one is) were conducted. Collected in works by Purkey (1970) and Hamacheck (1971), the trend in these studies was that children who felt better about themselves got along better with others and did better in school. Moreover, the studies found a high correlation between schooling practices and heightened or lowered self-esteem. Purkey stated:

> The indications seem to be that success or failure in school significantly influence the ways in which students view themselves. Students who experience repeated success in school are likely to develop positive feelings about their abilities, while those who encounter failure tend to develop negative views of themselves (p. 26).

Purkey discussed schooling practices that reinforced failure and frustration:

> Traditionally, the child is expected to adjust to the school rather than the school adjusting to the child. To ensure this process, the school is prepared to dispense rewards and punishments, successes and failures on a massive scale. The child is expected to learn to live in a new environment and to compete for the rewards of obedience and scholarship . . . Unfortunately a large number of schools employ a punitive approach to education. Punishment, failure, and depreciation are characteristic. In fact, Deutsch argues that it is often in the school that highly charged negative attitudes toward learning evolve. The principle that negative self-concepts should be prevented is ignored by many schools (p. 40).

The **self psychologists** provided insights that assisted educators with learners of all ages. Their ideas were valued especially in schools practicing "open education" and programs serving preschool children. Such writers as Dreikurs (1968, 1982) and Ginott (1972) adapted principles from self psychology into general models of discipline, still studied and utilized today.

Theodore Dreikurs

Theodore Dreikurs (1968, 1982) made a substantial contribution to educators' understanding of the "goals" of misbehavior. Building on his background in Adlerian theory, Dreikurs emphasized that all behavior is goal-directed and that the preeminent goal of behavior is social acceptance.

> Behavior is purposive or goal-directed. . . . Humans are social beings with the overriding goal of belonging or finding a place in society. . . . The child's behavior indicates the ways and means by which he tries to be significant. If these ways and means are antisocial and disturbing, then the child did not develop the right idea about how to find his place. The antisocial ways or "mistaken goals" . . . reflect an error in the child's judgment and in his comprehension of life and the necessities of social living. To understand a child, we must understand the child's purpose of behavior, a purpose of which the child may be unaware (1982, p. 9).

In such books as *Psychology in the Classroom* (1968), Dreikurs developed a theory, using four levels, for why children misbehave. A clear synopsis of the "four

Repeated success experiences help children build positive feelings about their abilities.

mistaken goals of misbehavior" is provided in *Building Classroom Discipline* (1996) by C. M. Charles:

> Dreikurs identifies four mistaken goals to which students turn when unable to satisfy the genuine goal [of social acceptance]: (1) getting attention, (2) seeking power, (3) seeking revenge, and (4) displaying inadequacy. . . . The goals are usually, though not always, sought in the order listed. If unable to feel accepted, individuals are likely to try to get attention. If they fail in that effort, they turn to seeking power. If thwarted there, they attempt to get revenge. And if that fails, they withdraw into themselves and try to show that they are inadequate to accomplish what is expected of them (pp. 90–91).

As important as Dreikurs' theories are, they have not been correlated with recent understandings about the development of the young child. Neither have they received scrutiny for consistency with ideas about personality development contributed by the self psychologists. Stated in Dreikurs' writings, the "overriding goal" of student behavior is acceptance by important others. This view differs from theory based on developmental research and the writing of psychologists like Maslow and Combs. In the view of developmental and self psychologists, social acceptance *is* a significant factor in children's behavior, but it is regarded more as a foundation for healthy personal development than an end in itself (Gartrell, 1995). Between three and eight years, children make tremendous strides in brain development and thinking processes, the communication of ideas and feelings, perceptual-motor skills, self-concept development, cultural identity, and social responsiveness. They are engaged in a process of *total development.* Yet with the natural insecurities of childhood and limited ability to understand the needs of others, children make mistakes. Social acceptance of each child even while addressing mistaken behavior, sustains *healthy personal development,* the primary goal in human behavior (Maslow, 1962; Rogers, 1961).

In his insistence that adults can understand the purposes of unacceptable behavior, Dreikurs nonetheless has made a vital contribution to the guidance tradition in educational thought (Charles, 1996). Dreikurs' writings argue persuasively that unacceptable behavior is a result of mistakes that children make in the "purposeful" goal of getting along with others (1968, 1982). By placing misbehavior in the context of social acceptance, Dreikurs raised the discussion of discipline from judgments about children's morality to strategies for helping children learn acceptable behavioral alternatives.

Haim Ginott

If Dreikurs has contributed to the theory of the guidance tradition, Ginott has contributed to its language. The opening lines from the chapter, "Congruent Communication" in his classic book, *Teacher and Child* (1972), illustrate the eloquent phrasing that typify Ginott's "psychology of acceptance":

> Where do we start if we are to improve life in the classroom? By examining how we respond to children. How a teacher communicates is of decisive importance. It affects a child's life for good or for bad. Usually we are not overly concerned about whether

one's response conveys acceptance or rejection. Yet to a child this difference is fateful, if not fatal.

Teachers who want to improve relations with children need to unlearn their habitual language of rejection and acquire a new language of acceptance. To reach a child's mind a teacher must capture his heart. Only if a child feels right can he think right (p. 69).

Virtually all early childhood education texts written in the last twenty years have emphasized a need for discipline methods that respect the feelings and dignity of the individual child. Although Ginott's writings do not address the early childhood age group per se, they speak to adult-child relations at all levels and are in agreement with the tone and philosophy of the guidance approach. Ginott's words are cited frequently in chapters to come. His writings nurture the caring spirit that infuses the guidance tradition.

THE 1980s: GUIDANCE, OR OBEDIENCE-BASED DISCIPLINE

Since the very first public school kindergartens in the 19th century, there has been much debate on what proper educational practice for young children entails. Traditional minded educators clung to an academic emphasis, countered by the progressive views of associations such as the National Association for the Education of Young Children (NAEYC) and the Association for Childhood Education International (ACEI). During the 1980s, the educational pendulum swung in the direction of academics, even in early childhood education. With the need to keep normally active young learners in their seats and on-task, new, obedience-driven discipline systems became popular.

The Push-Down of Academics

During the 1980s, many of the criticisms of traditional education made by Froebel, Montessori, Dewey, Piaget, Ginott and others took on a new urgency. With the "back to the basics" emphasis and the "educational reform" of the late 1970s and 1980s, curriculum and teaching methods became more prescribed. Though the emphasis clashed directly with increased understanding about how young children learn (Bredekamp, 1997), the prescriptive academic influence meant increasing numbers of young children at school spending long hours in their seats, following directions passively, and completing endless numbers of work sheets. Teacher-directed education again had come to the fore.

In some kindergarten and many primary classrooms the prescribed academic program was not new—classrooms had always been run this way. However, on a broad scale, kindergarten programs were expected to become academic, and preschool programs felt pressures to "get children ready for kindergarten." The emphasis on academic programming with younger children lent itself to tightly controlled classrooms (Elkind, 1987). Except for the occasional teacher who made human relations a priority, the interactive nature of the guidance approach did not fit the regimen of the prescribed, academic classroom. Suffice it to say that with the shift in educational priorities, discipline systems changed as well.

Assertive Discipline

Looking for methods to increase student compliance, administrators and teachers embraced new, "more effective" **obedience-based** discipline systems. Predominant among these programs was Canter's assertive discipline, "a take-charge approach for today's educator" (1976). Developed in a clinical setting for emotionally disturbed students, assertive discipline gained rapid acceptance in school systems across the country (Canter, 1989). Although its effects were regarded by many educators as controversial, assertive discipline was widely used with kindergarten children and high school students, and even in some prekindergarten programs.

As followed in the 1980s, common practices under assertive discipline included:

- making rules and establishing consequences and rewards with children;
- obtaining consent agreements from parents for use of the system;
- recording names, often publicly, of children who break rules;
- issuing "disciplinary referral slips" to repeat offenders—which commonly include trips to the principal, telephone calls home, and "in-school suspensions";
- holding periodic popcorn parties or class outings as rewards for children who have complied with the system—and excluding those who have not.

To reach a child's mind, a teacher must capture his/her heart. (Courtesy, Lin Wahlberg, Early Childhood Family Education Program, Bemidji, Minnesota)

By the end of the 1980s, debate about the effects of assertive discipline had become heated and ongoing (Canter, 1988, 1989; Curwin & Mendler, 1988, 1989; Gartrell, 1987; Hitz, 1988; Render, Padilla, & Krank, 1989).

Canter (1989) points out that assertive discipline clearly establishes the authority of the teacher and the role of the student. The model teaches students to choose between the rewards of compliance and the consequences of disobedience. It provides a consistent system of rewards and punishments for teachers within a classroom and across a school or district. It involves parents. In the eyes of Canter and his adherents, his system "works."

Critics, including Brewer (1995), Curwin & Mendler (1989), Gartrell (1987), and Hitz (1988), argue that assertive discipline has negative implications for children and for teachers.

Effects on Children

Because rules and their consequences are cut in stone, the model does not allow for individual circumstances. Children who may make innocent mistakes suffer. The tendency toward public identification of "culprits" causes humiliation and begins a process of negative self-fulfilling prophecy. Students frequently identified and punished grow immune to the system and become stigmatized as "outgroups" in the classroom and school (Render, Padilla, & Krank, 1989).

Although the system includes positive recognition for compliance, even the public rewards set up "winners" and "losers" within the class. Classrooms in which teachers have become entrenched in the negative aspects of the system are unpleasant, anxious places to be. The emphasis on obedience in the assertive discipline classroom inadequately prepares children to function in a democracy (Curwin & Mendler, 1989; Render, Padilla, & Krank, 1989). Directing their comments to early childhood, Gartrell (1987) and Hitz (1988) assert that the Canter model is inappropriate for use with children during their most impressionable years.

Effects on Teachers

A second criticism is that the system seriously reduces the teacher's ability to use professional judgment (Gartrell, 1987). Because of the "obedience or consequences" emphasis, the teacher cannot react to the uniqueness of individual situations or individual children's needs. Neither can the teacher accommodate background, developmental, or learning style differences that manifest themselves in behaviors outside of acceptable limits (Hitz, 1988). Because the model is essentially authoritarian, it cannot adapt to democratic, interactive teaching styles necessary for developmentally appropriate practice; the system pressures the teacher to be an authoritarian. Where schools or districts have mandated the system, teachers are expected to use it even if they are uncomfortable with it; the danger is that teachers may become technicians rather than professionals (Curwin & Mendler, 1989; Gartrell, 1987; Render, Padilla, & Krank, 1989). In some situations, parents who object to use of the system may find themselves at odds with teachers and administrators charged with soliciting parental compliance. Often, parents who object are the very ones who might otherwise become productively involved (unpublished correspondence of parents with the author).

In their text, *Discipline With Dignity,* Curwin and Mendler say this about the "obedience models of discipline," such as assertive discipline of the 1980s:

> It is ironic that the current mood of education is in some ways behind the past. The 1980s might someday be remembered as the decade when admiration was reserved for principals, cast as folk heroes, walking around schools with baseball bats, and for teachers and whole schools that systematically embarrassed students by writing their names on the chalkboard. But we do have hope that the pendulum will once again swing to the rational position of treating children as people with needs and feelings that are not that different from adults. Once we begin to understand how obedience is contrary to the goals of our culture and education, the momentum will begin to shift. Our view is that the highest virtue of education is to teach students to be self-responsible and fully functional. In all but extreme cases, obedience contradicts these goals (p. 24).

The very term "discipline with dignity" supports and reinforces the guidance approach.

THE TRANSITION FROM DISCIPLINE TO GUIDANCE

During the 1980s, pressures to sustain and renew an emphasis on the use of guidance were strong within two separate fields: early childhood and the growing field of conflict management education. The guidance tradition in early childhood had always been strong. By the end of the 1980s, this tradition was receiving renewed attention by writers who spoke directly about it and by new emphasis from NAEYC on the use of **developmentally appropriate practice (DAP).**

The Contribution of Early Childhood Education

At the same time that obedience-based discipline systems were taking hold in many school systems, other forces were at work. Inspired by the nursery school movement earlier in the century and the work of the developmental psychologists, writers at the preschool level were declaring their independence from the conventional role and functions of classroom discipline. Textbooks in the nursery school tradition, such as Read (1950, ninth edition—1993), phrased the setting of the preschool as a "human relations laboratory" in which the teacher models positive guidance skills. In the writings of Stone (1978), Shickendanz & Shickendanz (1981), Cherry (1983), Marion (1995), Clewett (1988), and Greenberg (1988), careful distinction was drawn between positive and negative discipline practices. Teachers using negative discipline relied on punishment to enforce compliance or impose retribution (Clewett, 1988). Teachers using positive discipline, in contrast, worked to prevent problems and, when they occurred, intervened in ways respectful of the child's self-esteem (Gartrell, 1987b; Greenberg, 1988; Wickert, 1989).

Significantly, after the debate about obedience-based discipline systems began, textbooks not specific to early childhood education have renewed the need for positive discipline practices. Albert's *A Teacher's Guide to Cooperative Discipline* (1995) features the subtitle: "How to Manage Your Classroom and Promote Self-Esteem." Based on the theories of Dreikurs, the book stresses diagnostic and communication skills to build cooperative relations not just between teacher and student, "but also between teacher and parent, teacher and teacher, and teacher and administrator" (1995, p. 3). Two other discipline texts, *Discipline with Dignity* (Curwin & Mendler, 1988) and *A Guide to Positive Discipline* (Keating, Pickering, Slack, & White, 1990), are guidebooks that present specific classroom management approaches. Each offers a coordinated system that can be used school-wide but still allows the teacher room for professional judgment while respecting the integrity of the learner.

In early childhood literature, discomfort with the very term *discipline* emerged. Despite the claim that discipline is "value neutral" and an "umbrella term" (Marion, 1995), *discipline* still carries the baggage of negative connotations. The term to *discipline a child* suggests punishment, a practice unacceptable in the guidance approach. Gartrell (1997) points out that in problem situations, teachers tend to blur the distinction between punishment and discipline, and not to think about "guidance" at all. He comments that unless handled so that a logical consequence

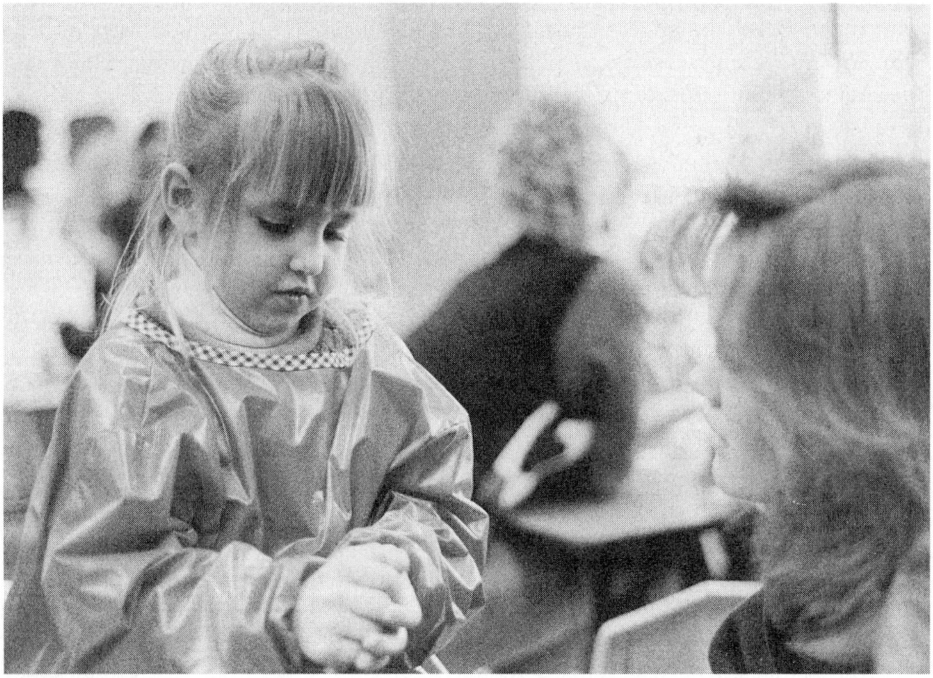

The guidance approach addresses children's behaviors in ways that support self-esteem.

is logical from the child's point of view, the child tends to perceive the act of discipline as punishment. For this reason, the teacher needs to emphasize guidance, which involves carefully teaching children about consequences and behavior alternatives (1997).

In *Guiding Young Children* (1996), Reynolds provides a problem-solving approach that begins with setting up the environment and includes specific communication and problem-solving strategies and techniques. Reynolds argues that the problem-solving approach precludes the necessity of the term *discipline.* She does not use the term in her text "in order to avoid confusion and misinterpretation" (1996, p. 3). In fact, the term **discipline** generally is fading from early childhood literature, supplanted by *guidance.* For some teachers, unless the connection between the two terms is made, they may tend to think of *guidance* in one set of circumstances and *discipline,* perhaps lapsing into punishment, in another. The second edition of the present text takes the position that one can address any situation with the use of guidance. The term *discipline* is used sparingly and has been dropped from the title.

The Contribution of Developmentally Appropriate Practice

In 1987, the National Association for the Education of Young Children (NAEYC) published *Developmentally Appropriate Practice in Early Childhood Programs Serving Children From Birth Through Age 8* (Bredekamp & Copple). This now updated (1997) NAEYC policy statement* has synthesized prevailing trends in research and theory pertaining to the education of young children. Significant is the fact that chapters in the work are supported by 600 separate references to authorities in the child development and early childhood fields. The position statement advocates educational practices that allow for an interactive approach to learning and teacher-child relations. Developmentally appropriate practices discussed reflect the guidance-oriented approach to discipline advocated by Froebel, Montessori, Dewey, Piaget, and the self psychologists. Clearly espousing the guidance tradition, the NAEYC document cites positive guidance techniques that encourage the teacher to: establish routines and expectations understandable to children; use methods such as modeling and encouraging expected behavior; redirect behavior toward acceptable activity; and set clear limits (1997, p. 129). "Teachers' expectations match and respect children's developing capabilities" (1997, p. 129). In addition:

> Teachers ensure that classrooms or groups of young children function as caring communities. They help children learn how to establish positive, constructive relationships with adults and other children (1997, p. 123).
>
> Teachers provide many opportunities for children to learn to work collaboratively with others and to socially construct knowledge as well as develop social skills, such as cooperating, helping, negotiating, and talking with others to solve problems (1997, p. 129).

* *Retitled Developmentally Appropriate Practice in Early Childhood Programs.*

According to the NAEYC document, *inappropriate* discipline practices are these:

> Teachers spend a great deal of time punishing unacceptable behavior, demeaning children who misbehave, repeatedly putting the same children who misbehave in time-out or some other punishment unrelated to the action. . . . Teachers do not set clear limits and do not hold children accountable to standards of behavior. . . . Teachers do not help children set and learn important rules of group behavior and responsibility (1997, p. 129).

Guidance Defined

This important document, pertaining to children birth to eight, concretely contrasts guidance with developmentally inappropriate discipline practices based on rewards and punishments. Building from DAP, a definition of guidance emerges.

In summary, guidance discipline goes beyond the traditional goal of classroom discipline: to induce student compliance toward the authority of the teacher and the expectations of the educational program (Gartrell, 1997). A guidance approach teaches the skills children need to get along with others, express strong feelings in acceptable ways, and solve problems with words—in short, to function as citizens of a democracy (Gartrell, 1997, Greenberg, 1992). Guidance facilitates an interactive learning environment in which the adult functions as democratic leader and the child constructs meaning through developmentally appropriate activities (Greenberg, 1992). A guidance approach assists children to take pride in their developing personal and cultural identities and to view differing human qualities as sources of affirmation and learning. The approach links together teacher, parent, and child as an interactive team.

Teachers facilitate the development of positive social skills at all times.

Guidance and the Conflict Management Movement

From the country's beginnings, a peace tradition has been part of American religious thought, most often associated with the views of the Quakers. During the Vietnam Conflict, peace groups such as the Fellowship of Reconciliation in Nyack, New York, assumed a higher profile in the society. Following the conflict, in response to growing social awareness of what the Surgeon General termed "the epidemic of violence," such groups began to turn attention to child rearing and the schools.

As early as 1973, the Children's Creative Response to Conflict Program trained teachers in the New York City area both to teach conflict resolution skills to children and to create a classroom atmosphere modeling the friendly community (Prutzman, 1988). In Miami, the Grace Contrino Abrams [Peace Education] Foundation also began working with teachers at about this time. Other groups followed, including the Community Board Program in San Francisco; Educators for Social Responsibility in Cambridge, Massachusetts; and School Mediation Associates in Belmont, California. The National Institute for Dispute Resolution, now merged with the National Association for Mediation in Education, has become a national clearinghouse for conflict management materials.

Over the first half of the 20th century, John Dewey (1900, 1944) fundamentally altered views about education by advocating that the society should manifest its democratic ideals by making the classroom a "microcosm" of democracy. Democratic practice in the classroom (with the teacher as leader) remains a goal of educators who espouse the guidance tradition. Using a similar pragmatic philosophy, groups working for a nonviolent society see the **peaceable classroom** as an important first step. In the book, *The Friendly Classroom for a Small Planet,* Prutzman (1988), states:

> We find that children develop positive self-concepts and learn to be open, sharing, and cooperative much more effectively when they become part of a [classroom] community in which these attributes are the norm (p. 2).

During the 1980s, the conflict management movement in American schools took root and established these important principles still gaining in acceptance today:

1. Each individual in the classroom, both child and adult, is to be treated with friendly respect;
2. All individuals, including young children, can learn to prevent and resolve problems by using words in peaceable ways;
3. Teachers create friendly classrooms both by modeling and teaching conflict management and by a philosophy of peace education throughout the entire school program.

With these principles and active training programs built around them during the 1980s, the peace organizations served as a counter trend to the practice of obedience-based discipline. Today, the conflict management movement continues to complement the practice of guidance. Perhaps the movement's foremost contribution is its friendly reminder that the primary vehicle for learning democratic life skills by the child is interaction with other children, facilitated by the teacher in the encouraging classroom.

PARENTS AND THE GUIDANCE TRADITION

A full history of parents and the guidance tradition would document events that have perpetuated both cooperative and adversarial trends in parent-teacher relations. Noted here are a few major events that have supported each trend. Significantly, parent-teacher partnerships have a tradition in early childhood education going back to the last century. Positive parent-teacher relations contribute at a fundamental level to the success of the guidance approach.

Froebel's Kindergartens

Froebel's first kindergartens in 19th century Germany called for cooperation between parents and teachers. As Lilley indicates, Froebel recognized the importance of the family in the education of the child:

> The child fully develops his driving need for creative activity only if the family, which is the vehicle of his existence, makes it possible for him to do so (1967, p. 94).

Home visits were a part of the first kindergarten programs, and Froebel included parents in his vision of early childhood education:

> The plan [for the kindergarten] is primarily to provide games and means of occupation such as meet the needs of parent and child, educator and pupil, and possess interest and meaning for adults as they share children's play or observe children sympathetically and intelligently (1967, p. 98).

In his writing Froebel called upon the mothers of Germany to take leadership in organizing kindergartens nationwide (Lilley, 1967). The original kindergartens, in Germany and then other countries, relied on parent involvement and began a practice that has continued in early childhood education ever since. The first kindergartens in America were run by immigrant parents who wanted the kindergarten experience for their own children. As the beginning point for K–12 education, kindergartens traditionally have enjoyed high levels of parent interest, allowing the opportunity for productive parent-teacher relations to this day.

Montessori's Children's Houses

Montessori (1964) no less than Froebel, encouraged parent involvement in the Children's Houses of Italy. Perhaps due to her standing as doctor, psychiatrist, and educator, Montessori saw the directress (teacher) as a consummate professional, providing a model for children and parents alike. Montessori's "Children's Houses" were located in tenement buildings and were attended by the children of the residents. Directresses lived in the tenements in which they worked. In the translation of her definitive work, *The Montessori Method* (1964) Montessori described the "modeling" role of the directress:

> The directress is always at the disposition of the mothers, and her life, as cultured and educated person, is a constant example to the inhabitants of the house, for she is obliged to live in the tenement and to be therefore a co-habitant with the families of all her little pupils. This is a fact of immense importance (pp. 61–62).

Despite a professional-client emphasis in the relationship, an element of partnership was also present. The parent and directress met each week to discuss the child's progress at school and home. Moreover, Montessori reported that the parents felt a sense of "collective ownership" toward the Children's Houses which she discussed this way:

> The parents know that the "Children's House" is their property, and is maintained by a portion of the rent they pay. The mothers may go at any hour of the day to watch, to admire, or to meditate upon the life there (pp. 63–64).

The Nursery School Movement

Between 1890 and the 1930s, the child study movement, along with the growing influence of Freudian psychology, sparked new interest in humane child-rearing practices and child-oriented education. The nursery school movement in Britain and the U.S. was an expression of these values. Cooperative nursery schools, administered by parents, began in Chicago in 1916 and continue on a nationwide basis today (Osborn, 1980). The nursery school model, with parent governing boards and close parent-teacher relations, has proven popular in other types of early childhood programs and private "alternative" schools as well.

Head Start

By the 1960s new knowledge about the importance of the early years in development began to infuse government policy. In 1965 Project Head Start began and parent involvement became an integral part of its operations. Head Start encourages cooperative parent involvement at several levels. In the home-based option, home visitors work with individual parents and children on a regular basis. In the center-based option, besides regular conferences with teachers and periodic home visits, parents are encouraged to volunteer in the classroom. Under both options, parents are given active policy roles on a local, agencywide and regional basis. Many trained Head Start staff began as parents with children in the program. Because the families served by Head Start are predominantly low-income, the contribution of Head Start to parent involvement in American education is significant (Gage & Workman, 1994).

The Public Schools

Notably, early childhood programs have had a positive influence on parent-teacher relations both in the areas of special and regular education. In many states early childhood special education teachers now establish contact with parents before the infant has left the hospital. Teachers in early childhood special education work with families in some cases for years before a child with a disability begins kindergarten. Parent-teacher collaboration is a hallmark of successful special education at all levels; the foundation often is being set by early childhood special education teachers.

In the last 20 years, a new generation of parent and child programs run through public schools are beginning to change the face of parent involvement. One national model is a state-wide program in Minnesota that features weekly parenting classes held in conjunction with preschool activities. Minnesota's Early Childhood Family Education, is available at no or low cost in virtually every school district in Minnesota, and last year served nearly 300,000 children and parents. Another model for bringing parents and teachers together is Georgia's school-based program for all four-year-olds, funded by the Lottery, and similar "even start" and "learning readiness" programs now beginning in other states.

Historically, many parents, especially from low income and minority group backgrounds, have felt ill at ease at building and maintaining relationships with educators. Head Start, early childhood special education, and the new school-based child and parent programs are helping to raise parent-confidence at communicating with teachers and increasing the amount of parent involvement in their children's education and in the school system.

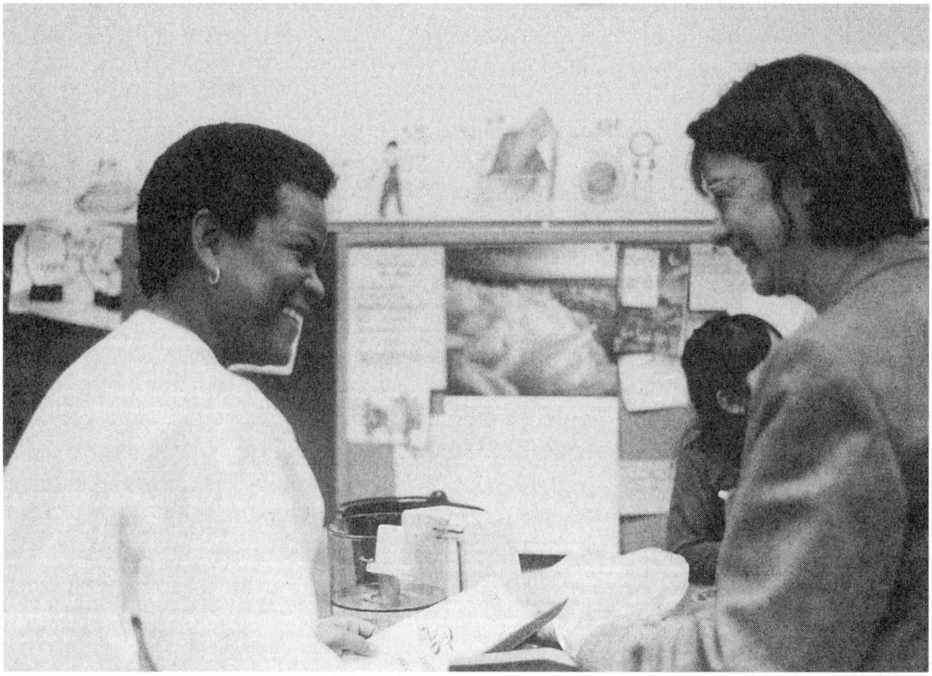

Parent-teacher partnerships are accepted practice in Head Start, as are early childhood family education, and other types of preschool programs.

Public school personnel traditionally have assumed an authority-client relationship with parents. Between the end of the Civil War and 1920, the population of the United States more than doubled with many new citizens being non-English speaking immigrants. Universal education got its start during this time. To "Americanize the aliens," kindergarten teachers especially were requested to make home visits and start mothers' group (Weber, 1919). The practice of the Bureau of Education in the Department of the Interior (with the encouragement of business leaders) was to reach children in the school and mothers in the home so that immigrant and other non-mainstream families could be made "good citizens" (Locke, 1919). Although now somewhat outdated, this "melting pot" idea long was a part of American education.

With the advent of compulsory attendance laws, over time American schools have assumed a powerful role in their communities, as the institutions charged with socializing children to American society. One result of the schools' growing institutional power is that the opportunity for real parent input has become limited, especially for parents "out of the mainstream" (Greenberg, 1989). Although the parents of children with disabilities have led the way, the determination and confidence necessary to advocate for one's child at school remains for many a daunting task. In most school districts, the individual teacher must build cooperative parent-teacher relations, largely on his own time. Indeed, individual teachers can make a difference, and teachers and parents together can change school policy. From the perspective of the guidance approach, the situation will improve as schools give more recognition and resources to parent-teacher conferences, home visits, and innovative programs that help parents feel that they are valued partners in the education of their children.

Parents and Developmentally Appropriate Practice

The NAEYC position document (1997) is significant because it ties together research about child development and appropriate teaching practice. As shown, the discipline methods are those in the guidance tradition. A dimension of the guidance approach is close, cooperative relations between parents and teachers. As discussed, Froebel and Montessori each recognized parents as the primary educators of their children. They involved parents in their programs to ensure that differences in values and lifestyle did not negate the purposes of their programs. Following through to today, NAEYC's "Developmentally Appropriate Practices" identifies characteristics of parent-teacher relations that continue the guidance tradition:

> Teachers work in partnerships with parents, communicating regularly to build mutual understanding and ensure that children's learning and developmental needs are met. Teachers listen to parents, seek to understand their goals and preferences for their children, and respect cultural and family differences. . . . Teachers and parents work together to make decisions about how best to support children's development and learning. . . . Parents are always welcome in the program and home visits are encouraged (p. 134).

For the guidance approach to be effective, the teacher develops a team relationship that includes the teacher, the parent, and the child. The parent-teacher partnership is part of a developmentally appropriate practice, and of the guidance tradition.

SUMMARY

Who were the pioneers of the guidance tradition?

Guidance has its roots in the history of western education and is tied to the thoughts of progressive educators over the last two hundred years. During the 19th century, Froebel considered the child to be "unfolding" toward goodness but vulnerable to the negative influences of others. He believed that the purpose of education was to guide the child along the path of wholesome development. Maria Montessori held that a mistaken practice of traditional education was to force obedience to the authority of the teacher. In her view discipline is an extension of education itself—the purpose of which is to provide for the development of responsible decision-making on the part of the child.

Like Montessori, Dewey believed that schooling practices of the day were outmoded and dependent on negative discipline. For Dewey, the classroom should be "a busy workshop," with teachers not enforcing silence, but teaching cooperation. The function of discipline is fundamentally changed when education becomes no longer prescriptive but interactive in nature.

Who were mid-20th century influences in the guidance tradition?

The guidance tradition has been reinforced by many psychologists of the last forty years, notably from two fields of study. As the foremost developmental theorist of the 20th century, Piaget wrote that children construct the ability for intelligent, moral thought through social interactions. He argued that only when authority is shared by all members of the group can autonomous moral thought develop. Building on Piaget's work, developmental psychologists established the importance of the child's construction of knowledge in the interactive classroom.

The self psychologists demonstrated the importance of supporting self-esteem in the classroom. Two self psychologists who have contributed to the thinking of the guidance tradition are Dreikurs (1968) and Ginott (1972). Dreikurs introduced the idea that children misbehave not because they are immoral, but because they adopt mistaken goals of behavior. Rather than punish, teachers need to use strategies that redirect children's mistaken goals. Ginott has contributed much to the language of the guidance tradition. Ginott's position that teachers must show acceptance of the child even while they address unacceptable behavior is at the heart of the guidance approach.

What was the significance of discipline trends in the 1980s?

During the 1980s many school systems placed an emphasis on "back to the basics" and "educational excellence," even at the early primary and preschool levels. To enforce compliance with these practices, schools began using new, *obedience* discipline systems at all levels of education. Proponents argued that such systems as *assertive discipline* permitted "the teacher to teach and the *student to learn*"; critics charged that undesirable side effects often resulted. The atmosphere of the classroom was becoming more negative; children were being ill-prepared to function in a democracy; teachers were being reduced from professionals to technicians. By the end of the 1980s, vigorous debate about the use of obedience-based discipline in the nation's schools was occurring.

What is the state of the guidance tradition today?

Due to the efforts of early childhood and conflict management educators, by the end of the decade arguments for the use of guidance again began to be heard. A landmark NAEYC publication (1987, 1997) focused national attention on the need for education to be "developmentally appropriate"—responsive to the stage and needs of each child. Guidance rather than punishment empowered the active learning advocated by the NAEYC work. Some authors maintained that because of the punitive connotations attributed to *discipline,* the term should be discontinued, or at least used with qualifiers. Authors now generally agree that interactive, developmentally appropriate teaching techniques and guidance go together.

What is the role of parents in the guidance tradition?

Parent-teacher partnerships have been an important part of the guidance tradition. Froebel saw the kindergarten as an extension of family life and encouraged home visits and the involvement of parents. Montessori wrote of the need for collaborative relations between the directress and the parent, with parents welcome to visit the Children's Houses at any time.

Building on the tradition of British and American nursery schools, Head Start and other modern early childhood programs have demonstrated the value of close parent-teacher relations. The "professionalization" of the public schools earlier in the 20th century gave rise to paternalistic attitudes toward parent-teacher relations at this level (Greenberg, 1989). New awareness of the importance of parent-teacher partnerships is serving to change the mind set of many K–12 educators. The view that the child, teacher, and parent are on the same team, working together, is integral to the guidance approach.

FOLLOW-UP ACTIVITIES

Note: In completing follow-up activities, the privacy of all involved is to be respected.

Reflection Activity

The reflection activity encourages students to inter-relate their own thoughts and experiences with specific ideas from the chapter.

Think about a teacher at any level of your education who most embodied guidance in his teaching. What qualities or skills characterize the teacher's approach? What is a main insight you have gained from that teacher who is assisting you in your professional development? How does this insight relate to what the chapter says about guidance and its use in the classroom?

Application Activities

Application activities allow students to interrelate material from the text with real life situations. The *observations* imply access to practicum experiences; the *interviews,* access to parents and teachers. Students may compare or contrast observations and interviews with referenced ideas from the chapter.

1. **Who were the pioneers of the guidance tradition?**
   a. Each of the pioneers advocated teaching practices that empower children to be active, involved learners. Observe a classroom in which such teaching is in practice. What kind of guidance/discipline practices do you see in use?
   b. Interview an early childhood teacher or college professor who has studied the work of Froebel, Montessori, Dewey, or Piaget. What does the person believe to be significant about how the pioneer educator thought about discipline issues?
2. **Who were mid-20th century influences in the guidance tradition?**
   a. An emphasis of the self psychologists is support of the child's self-esteem. Observe an instance in the classroom when an adult supported a child's self-esteem. What did the teacher say and do? How did the child respond?
   b. Interview a teacher who values the ideas of either Dreikurs or Ginott. What is important to the teacher in the psychologist's writings?
3. **What was the significance of discipline trends in the 1980s?**
   a. Observe an instance in a classroom when a teacher intervened to stop a conflict or disruptive situation. Respecting privacy, how did the adult teach or fail to teach more appropriate social skills through the intervention? Did the teacher use guidance or conflict management? Why do you think so?
   b. One issue raised in the debate of the obedience discipline systems of the 1980s is the role of punishment. Interview a teacher about what he considers to be the difference between discipline and punishment. When, if ever, does the teacher believe punishment is justified?
4. **What is the state of the guidance tradition today?**
   a. Developmentally appropriate practice responds to the level of development and the needs of each child. Observe an instance of developmentally appropriate practice in a classroom. What are typical behaviors of the children? How does the teacher handle any problems that may arise?
   b. Interview two teachers at the prekindergarten to third grade level who are familiar with the term *developmentally appropriate practice.* How are the teachers' comments similar? How are the comments different?
5. **What is the role of parents in the guidance tradition?**
   a. Observe an instance of productive parent-teacher relations at work. What seem to be the benefits of the productive relationship for the child in the classroom?
   b. Interview a teacher who has taught for five or more years. Talk with the teacher about how his views have changed/or stayed the same regarding parent-teacher relations.

RECOMMENDED RESOURCES

Carlsson-Paige, N., & Levin, D. E. (1992). Making peace in violent times: A constructivist approach to conflict resolution. *Young Children, 48*(1), 4–13.

Derman-Sparks, L. (1993). Empowering children to create a caring culture in a world of differences. *Childhood Education, 70*(2), 66–71.

Dewey, J. (1969). *The school and society.* Chicago: The University of Chicago Press.

Gage, J., & Workman, S. (1994). Creating family support systems: Head Start and beyond. *Young Children, 50*(1), 74–77.

Gandini, L. (1993). Fundamentals of the Reggio Emilia approach to early childhood education. *Young Children, 49*(1), 4–8.

Gartrell, D. J. (1997, September). Beyond discipline to guidance. *Young Children.*

Kristensen, N., & Billman, J. (1987, April). Supporting parents and young children. *Childhood Education, 63*(3),

Porro, B. (1996). *Talk it out: Conflict resolution in the elementary classroom.* Alexandria, VA: Association for Supervision and Curriculum Development.

REFERENCES

Albert, L. (1995). *A teacher's guide to cooperative discipline.* Circle Pines, MN: American Guidance Service.

Berger, S. K. (1991). *The developing person through childhood and adolescence.* New York: Worth Publishers, Inc.

Bredekamp, S., & Copple. (Eds.) (1997). *Developmentally appropriate practice in early childhood programs* (3rd ed.). Washington, DC: National Association for the Association of Young Children.

Brewer, J. A. (1995). *Introduction to early childhood education: Primary through the primary grades.* Needham Heights, MA: Allyn and Bacon.

Canter, L., & Canter, M. (1976). *Assertive discipline.* Seal Beach, CA: Canter and Associates, Inc.

Canter, L. (1988). Assertive discipline and the search for the perfect classroom. *Young Children, 43*(2). 24.

Canter, L. (1989). Let the educator beware: A response to Curwin and Mendler. In J. W. Noll, *Taking sides: Clashing views on controversial educational issues.* Guilford, CT: The Dushkin Publishing Group, Inc.

Charles, C. M. (1996). *Building classroom discipline.* White Plains, NY: Longman Inc.

Cherry, C. (1983). *Please don't sit on the kids.* Belmont, CA: Pitman Learning.

Clewett, A. S. (1988). Guidance and discipline: Teaching young children appropriate behavior. *Young Children, 43*(4), 26–36.

Combs, A. W. (Ed.). (1962). *Perceiving, behaving, becoming: A new focus for education.* Washington, DC: Association for Supervision and Curriculum Development.

Curwin, R. L., & Mendler, A. N. (1988). *Discipline with dignity.* Alexandria, VA: Association for Supervision and Curriculum Development.

Curwin, R. L., & Mendler, A. N. (1989). Packaged discipline programs: Let the buyer beware. In J. W. Noll, *Taking sides: Clashing views on controversial educational issues.* Guilford, CT: The Dushkin Publishing Group, Inc.

deMause, L. (Ed.). (1974). *The history of childhood.* New York, NY: Peter Bedrick Books.

Dewey, J. (1900/1969). *The school and society.* Chicago: The University of Chicago Press.

Dewey, J. (1944/1966). *Democracy and education.* New York: The Free Press.

Dreikurs, R. (1968). *Psychology in the classroom* (2nd ed.). New York: Harper and Row, Publishers.

Dreikurs, R., Grunwald, B. B., & Pepper, F. C. (1982). *Maintaining sanity in the classroom.* New York: Harper and Row, Publishers.

Elkind, D. (1987). *Miseducation: Preschoolers at risk.* New York: Alfred A. Knopf.

Erikson, E. H. (1963). *Childhood and society.* New York: W. W. Norton and Company, Inc.

Gage, J., & Workman, S. (1994). Creating family support systems: Head Start and beyond. *Young Children, 50*(1), 74–77.

Gandini, L. (1993). Fundamentals of the Reggio Emilia approach to early childhood education. *Young Children, 49*(1), 4–8.

Gartrell, D. J. (1987a). Assertive discipline: Unhealthy for children and other living things. *Young Children, 42*(2), 10–11.

Gartrell, D. J. (1987b). Punishment or Guidance? *Young Children, 42*(3), 56–61.

Gartrell, D. J. (1992). Discipline. In Williams, L. R., Fromberg, D. P. (Eds.). *Encyclopedia of early childhood education.* New York: Garland Publishing, Inc.

Gartrell, D. J. (1995). Misbehavior or mistaken behavior. *Young Children, 50*(5), 27–34.

Gartrell, D. J. (1997, September). Beyond discipline to guidance. *Young Children.*

Ginott, H. (1972). *Teacher and child.* New York: Avon Books.

Greenberg, P. (1988). Avoiding 'me against you' discipline. *Young Children, 43*(1), 24–25.

Greenberg, P. (1989). Parents as partners in young children's development and education: A new American fad? Why does it matter? *Young Children, 44*(4), 61–75.

Greenberg, P. (1992). Ideas that work with young children. How to institute some simple democratic practices pertaining to respect, rights, responsibilities in any classroom. *Young Children, 47*(5) 10–21.

Hamachek, D. E. (1971). *Encounters with the self.* New York: Holt, Rinehart and Winston, Inc.

Hitz, R. (1988). Assertive discipline: A response to Lee Canter. *Young Children, 43*(2), 24.

Keating, B., Pickering, M., Slack, B., & White, J. (1990). *A guide to positive discipline.* Boston: Allyn & Bacon.

Kohn, A. (1993). *Punished by rewards.* Boston: Houghton Mifflin Company.

Kristensen, N., & Billman, J. (1987, April). Supporting parents and young children. *Childhood Education, 63*(3).

Lilley, I. M. (Ed.). (1967). *Friedrich Froebel: A selection from his writings.* London: Cambridge University Press.

Locke, B. (1919, July). Manufacturers indorse [sic] the kindergarten. *Kindergarten Circular No. 4.* Washington, DC: Department of the Interior, Bureau of Education.

Marion, M. (1995). *Guidance of young children.* Columbus, OH: Merrill Publishing Company.

Maslow, A. H. (1962). *Toward a psychology of being.* Princeton, NJ: D. Van Nostrand Company, Inc.

Montessori, M. (1912/1964). *The Montessori method.* New York: Schocken Books.

Osborn, D. K. (1980). *Early childhood education in historical perspective.* Athens, GA: Education Associates.

Piaget, J. (1932/1960). *The moral judgment of the child.* Glencoe, IL: The Free Press.

Prutzman, P. (Ed.). (1988). *The friendly classroom for a small planet.* Philadelphia: New Society Publishers.

Purkey, W. W. (1970). *Self-concept and school achievement.* Englewood Cliffs, NJ: Prentice-Hall, Inc.

Render, G. F., Padilla, J. E. N. M., & Krank, H. M. (1989). Assertive discipline: A critical review and analysis. *Teachers College Record, 90*(4). New York: Teachers College, Columbia University.

Reynolds, E. (1996). *Guiding young children.* Mountain View, CA: Mayfield Publishing Company.

Rogers, C. R. (1961). *On becoming a person.* Boston: Houghton Mifflin, Co.

Shickedanz, J. A., & Shickedanz, D. I. (1981). *Toward understanding children.* Boston: Little, Brown.

Standing, E. M. (1962). *Maria Montessori: Her life and work.* New York: The New American Library, Inc.

Stone, J. G. (1978). *A guide to discipline* (Rev. ed.). Washington, DC: National Association for the Education of Young Children.

Weber, S. H. (1919, December). The Kindergarten as an Americanizer. *Kindergarten Circular No. 5.* Washington, DC: Department of the Interior, Bureau of Education.

Wichert, S. (1989). *Keeping the Peace: Practicing cooperation and conflict resolution with preschoolers. Philadelphia: New Society Publishers.*

2

Mistaken Behavior

GUIDING QUESTIONS

As you read Chapter 2, you will discover answers to the following questions:

- **What is inappropriate about using the term *misbehavior*?**
- **What is the concept of mistaken behavior?**
- **What are relational patterns?**
- **What are the three levels of mistaken behavior?**
- **Can mistaken behavior be intentional?**
- **How does the teacher communicate with parents about mistaken behavior?**

As educators shift the paradigm away from traditional discipline toward guidance, they need to reevaluate widely used terms such as *misbehavior*. As commonly used,

> **Misbehavior** implies willful wrongdoing for which a child must be disciplined (punished). The term invites moral labeling of the child. After all, what kind of children misbehave? Children who are "naughty," "rowdy," "mean," "willful," or "not nice." Although teachers who punish *misbehavior* believe they are "shaming children into being good," the result may be the opposite. Because of limited development and experience, children tend to internalize negative labels, see themselves as they are labeled, and react accordingly" (Gartrell, 1995, p. 28).

When a child has difficulties in a classroom, the teacher who uses guidance has more important tasks then to criticize (and perhaps reinforce) children's supposed character flaws. For one thing, the teacher needs to consider the reasons for the behavior—a basic guidance technique. Was the behavior a result of a mismatch of the child and the curriculum, just a "bad day" for the child, or serious trouble in the child's life outside school (Gartrell, 1995)? Equally important, the teacher needs to decide how she can intervene to teach the child a more acceptable way to solve the problem. By fixating on the child's *misbehavior,* the teacher may have difficulty in carrying out important guidance tasks. The term suggests that the proper course

How to share materials, as these kindergarten children are discovering, takes time to learn.

of action may be retribution against the misbehavior rather than guiding the child to learn a more productive way of behaving.

Teachers who use guidance work to free themselves of value judgments about the child. They do not view children as sometimes "good" and sometimes "bad," or being on balance "good children" or "bad children" (Greenberg, 1988). In the guidance approach, teachers take a more positive view of human nature. They believe that with the assistance of caring adults, children develop healthy self-concepts and grow toward social responsiveness. What, then, explains the *misbehavior* that young children show? Personal and social development are complicated, life-long processes. At the very beginning of living and learning, *children make mistakes.*

In the guidance approach, this understanding about child development is all important. When children begin programs outside of the home, they typically are two months to six years in age. To put these ages in perspective, remember that even "big" seven- and eight-year olds have lived only about one-tenth of the average life span. Six-year-olds have been around for only 72 months. With limited experience and development, young children are in the beginning stages of learning interpersonal skills. In truth, mastering the complex abilities of expressing strong emotions acceptably and getting along with others requires adulthood; some adults never master these skills. Anyone who has worked with young children knows their competence and resiliency as learners. Yet, in these most complex learning activities, children (and adults) make mistakes. A guidance approach requires that the adult regard behavior traditionally thought of as *misbehavior* as *mistaken behavior* (Gartrell, 1995).

This second chapter of the unit provides a psychological foundation for the guidance approach. The chapter develops the concept of **mistaken behavior.** Three levels of mistaken behavior are explained. Teacher responses to each of the levels—basic guidance techniques—are introduced. The chapter concludes by discussing the use of the concept of mistaken behavior when communicating with parents.

THE CONCEPT OF MISTAKEN BEHAVIOR

As children learn skills and concepts, they make mistakes. Under the right circumstances, errors in the cognitive domain are accepted as part of the learning experience. Correction, when given, is responsive to the child's development and experience. It is offered in the form of helpful expansion or direction, and certainly is not given as criticism of the child's character. For example, a three-year-old child says, "I gots itchy feets." A sensitive teacher is likely to show acceptance of the child's expressions, gently model the conventional terms in her response, and offer to help: "You have itchy feet; are your socks making you itch? How about if we take a look?"

Perhaps because of the higher emotional costs, adults have difficulty reacting similarly to children's mistakes in *behavior*. Missing the opportunity to teach a constructive behavioral lesson—one that affirms the child even as it guides to acceptable alternatives—adults often resort to criticism and punishment. The adult may see the intervention as "a lesson the child has to learn," but for the child the result is humiliation. That an alternate, more constructive response could be used may not occur to the adult, unless she becomes aware of the possibility.

Inez and Hector were quarreling over who would use a car on the block road they had built. The teacher went to the children and declared: "You children don't know how to share the car properly, so I will put it away." As the teacher walked off with the car, Inez sat down at a table and looked sad. Hector frowned at the teacher's back, made a fist, and stuck one finger in the air. It was his index finger, but the sentiment was still expressed.

The teacher in this case was punishing the children for mistaken behavior, *not* teaching them how to solve their problem. As suggested by their responses, the likely message for the children was that they are incapable of playing together, solving their own problems, and using school materials. Because young children are actively engaged in self-concept development, such actions that result in perceptions of unworthiness need to be avoided.

In contrast, an adult might have used a guidance approach in the situation. One guidance response is to hold the car and talk with the children to reach a resolution. A variation would be to stop the play and have the children themselves work out a solution (Wichert, 1989). The adult might have said, "Looks like you both want to use the car. This is a problem. How can you solve the problem?" Guidance means teaching children how to solve their problems rather than punishing children for having problems they cannot solve (Gartrell, 1991, 1995).

In candid moments teachers recognize that they sometimes hold children to standards that they themselves do not always meet. Take the matter of "losing one's temper," a not unknown emotional state to most adults.

For a special first grade cooking activity, the teacher planned to have two teacher aids and a parent come in, so the children could work in small groups. The principal reassigned the aides at the last minute, and the parent failed to make it. The teacher did the best she could with the whole class and later improvised when the music specialist went home with the flu. In an after-school meeting with the other first grade staff, the teacher's proposal for more journaling and fewer work sheets was rejected. On the way home for a quick supper before an evening of parent conferences, the teacher got a speeding ticket. When she got home expecting supper to be ready, she discovered that her husband and children had forgotten to fix it. The teacher did not say, "That's OK, dear family; I'm sure you had a hard day too." (What would you say?)

The ability to balance one's own needs with the needs of others is a high-level human ability. Perhaps the one skill that is more difficult is assisting children to learn it. Adults frequently operate from the misconception that children know how to behave and that mistaken behavior is the result of a willful decision to do "wrong." In truth, the decision to act out or defy is made because the child does not yet have the cognitive and emotional resources necessary for more appropriate responses. Children gain these resources over time through modeling and teaching of caring adults.

RELATIONAL PATTERNS: A PARADIGM FOR SOCIAL DEVELOPMENT IN THE CLASSROOM

Building from the work of the developmental and self psychologists, Steven D. Harlow developed a system for understanding children's social development in the classroom. Harlow's paradigm involved three **relational patterns: survival relational pattern, adjustment relational pattern,** and the **encounterer relational pattern** (1975). Although he directed his monograph to special education, Harlow actually provided a perspective about social development that pertains to all learners. Harlow's paradigm

The adult accepts children as worthwhile individuals who, like all of us, sometimes make mistakes.

is helpful in that it also provides a model for understanding mistaken behavior. With Harlow's permission, portions of his monograph are presented:

> As a way of viewing children's functioning in the classroom setting, it might be helpful to examine general relational patterns that individual children disclose. By relational patterns, I mean ways in which children relate to situations, persons and things in the school environment. The patterns I would like to examine are: surviving, adjusting, encountering, all of which differ in their openness to experience, maturity, and their capacity to operate freely.
>
> The most immature and the least open of the relational patterns is that of survival. A child operating at the survival level is concerned with merely getting through time and space without disturbing his established ways of satisfying needs. For whatever reason—perhaps he has learned that his environment is a dangerous and painful place, and cannot by his efforts be mastered—the child wishes to keep things constant and reduce the amount of change in his world. Accordingly, his behavior is extremely stereotyped and rigid. When confronted by a new situation, he will ignore its special demands and treat it as if it were no different than previous situations.
>
> The second relational pattern is that of adjustment. At this level, the child is less preoccupied with predictability and is far more open to others than was true of the survivor. The adjustor's concern is that of learning what is expected of him by others and then producing corresponding behavior. His sensitivity to a reference group's norms and expectations is characteristic of David Riesman's other-directed individual. His reinforcements and rewards come from the response of others to his behavior. . . . New ways of thinking and behaving are first sanctioned by an individual or reference group representing authority, before they are considered by the adjustor. . . .
>
> The relational pattern of greatest maturity (and it should be added that maturity has little to do with chronological age) is that of the encounterer. Many educators and psychologists (among them Jean Piaget, Eric Erikson, and John Holt) have described the individual functioning at this level. In contrast with the adjustor and survivor, the encounterer is less concerned with security and certainty and much more occupied with what Erikson referred to as the inner mechanism that permits the individual "to turn passive into active" and to maintain and regain in this world of contending forces an individual sense of centrality, of wholeness, and of initiative.

In regard to the teacher's understanding of relational patterns, Harlow is clear that the teacher should not label children by the patterns they show. Instead, the teacher should consider how to assist children to progress to a more mature relational pattern. Harlow states:

> The purpose of the paradigm is to help describe and understand a child's functioning in order to encourage him to a higher level of functioning. Rather than a label that indicates to school personnel a condition of some endurance, the typology describes functioning that is amenable to change. Further, the paradigm permits a child to be described in different terminology, as the situation indicates, for example, a child may be a "survivor" in confronting reading activities but an encounterer during free class time (p. 28).

Children at each relational level pose challenges and opportunities for teachers. The child at the survivor level is difficult for teachers to accept because of the nonsocial, at times antisocial, characteristics of the child's behavior. Yet, the trust made possible by a positive adult-child relationship empowers the child to progress to a higher relational pattern (Harlow, 1975).

Children at the adjustor level also can be challenging. Daily, teachers must respond to children, who fearing criticism, show anxiety over the completion of activities. Some children put off starting tasks, or don't start at all. Others ask the teachers or a friend to do it for them—or copy. Even when they have finished, many young children show taxing persistence in pursing the blessings of authority. As the following anecdote shows, teachers of young children must work hard to encourage progress from the adjustor pattern of relations.

After much encouragement by her kindergarten teacher, Emily completes a creative "family day" card for her mother.

Emily:	Did I do it good?
Teacher:	You worked hard, and your mother will love it.
Emily:	But did I do it good?
Teacher:	What's important is that you like it.
Emily:	But is it good?
Teacher:	Emily, I like whatever you make, just because you are you.
Emily:	(Smiles.) Now, I'm gonna do one for my sister.

Some teachers are notorious for preferring the obedience of children at the adjustor level to the independence of children who relate as encounterers. Yet, Harlow's paradigm indicates that children at the encountering level are learning most effectively about themselves and the world (1975). As psychologists ranging from Piaget (1932/1960) and Kamii (1984) to Maslow (1962) and Combs (1962) have written, children need freedom to interact and problem-solve for healthy development to occur. The Harry Chapin song, "Flowers Are Red," illustrates the effect an emphasis on conformity has on a young child. In the song a child wants to paint flowers every color of the rainbow. His kindergarten teacher admonishes that "Flowers are red, young man, and leaves are green." Later in a new school, the teacher asks the boy why his flowers are only red. The child responds with the words he was taught. The challenge to the teacher is to maintain harmony in the classroom at the same time she encourages the *autonomous* behavior of the children at the encountering level.

At any relational level, the cause of mistaken behavior in the young child is insufficient understanding about how to act maturely in the complex situations of life. With the internal need to go forward and to learn, but with limited ability to balance one's own needs with those of others, mistaken behavior will occur. Using Harlow's relational patterns, three levels of mistaken behavior can be derived. Knowledge of the three levels assists the teacher in understanding and working with children when they make mistakes.

Children who learn in ways that are creative and interactive learn best. (Bottom photo courtesy Michael Crowley, Family Service Center, Kootasca Head Start, Grand Rapids, Minnesota)

THREE LEVELS OF MISTAKEN BEHAVIOR

Mistaken behavior is a natural occurrence, the result of attempts by inexperienced, developmentally young children to interact with a complicated, increasingly impersonal world. When mistaken behavior occurs, adults significantly affect what children learn from the experience. Guidance-oriented responses that encourage children to keep trying and to continue learning empower healthy self-concepts and full personal development. On the other hand, punitive responses coerce children to abandon the need to experience fully and to adopt instead defensive behaviors, usually in compliance with the teacher's expectations. Punishment can even create a well of unmet emotional needs and lead to survival level relational patterns; withdrawing from situations, reacting with overt or covert hostility, or showing anxiety (Kohn 1993).

Adults help children toward healthy development if they regard mistaken behavior as an opportunity to teach and to learn, and if they realize that we all, including adults, make mistakes. The interactions of the adult and child together determine the path of the child's behavior in the educational setting, not the child alone.

Over many years of observing young children in classrooms, the author has noted patterns in mistaken behavior that parallel the levels of social relations discussed by Harlow. In fact, by extending Harlow's paradigm, a model for understanding and addressing mistaken behavior emerges, one that treats mistaken behavior as occurring at three different levels (Gartrell, 1995):

1. Experimentation
2. Socially influenced
3. Strong needs

Level One is **experimentation mistaken behavior.** Level One mistaken behavior is the equivalent of Harlow's category of encountering. Experimentation mistaken behavior occurs when the child reacts to one of two motives: curiosity—she acts to see what will happen; or involvement—the child's actions in a situation do not get the results expected (the "experiment" does not work out). In a previous anecdote Hector and Inez argued about a car; this incident illustrates experimentation mistaken behavior, as a result of their total involvement in the situation.

Corresponding to "adjustor" social relations is Level Two mistaken behavior, which is **socially influenced mistaken behavior.** Socially influenced mistaken behavior happens when children are reinforced in an action, sometimes unintentionally, by others important to them. Examples include a child's learning an expletive from someone at home, or being influenced by classmates to call another child a derogatory name. Often, Level Two mistaken behavior occurs when an experimentation mistaken behavior is reinforced by a significant other. Level Two mistaken behavior is a learned behavior (Gartrell, 1995).

The social relations pattern of the *survivor* is close in concept to mistaken behavior at Level Three, **strong needs mistaken behavior.** Level Three is the most serious. Children show Level Three mistaken behavior as a reaction to difficulty and pain in their lives that is beyond their capacity to cope with and understand. Most often, strong needs mistaken behavior occurs because of untreated health conditions, painful life experiences, or a combination of the two. Serious mistaken behavior in the classroom happens because a child is reacting to strong unmet needs, acting out against a perceived hostile and uncaring world.

Common Sources of Motivation

The relationship of Harlow's relational patterns and the levels of mistaken behavior is close. The motivational sources of each are the same. At the level of encountering *and* experimentation mistaken behavior, the motivation is curiosity or involvement. At the level of adjusting *and* socially influenced mistaken behavior, the motivation is the desire to please and identify with others. At the level of the survival *and* strong needs mistaken behavior, the motive is unmet basic needs. When a child at any of the three relational patterns acts in a way that is disruptive to the group or harmful to self or others, the child is showing mistaken behavior at that level. In other words, mistaken behavior is the result of miscommunication at the child's particular level of relational pattern in the situation, as indicated in Table 2.1 below.

Table 2.1
Common Sources of Motivation
Relational Patterns and Levels of Mistaken Behavior

Motivational Source	Relational Pattern	Level of Mistaken Behavior
Desire to explore the environment and engage in relationships and activities	Encounterer	One: Experimentation
Desire to please and identify with significant others	Adjustor	Two: Socially influenced
Inability to cope with problems resulting from health conditions or life experiences	Survivor	Three: Strong needs

In the chapters to follow, the levels of mistaken behavior serve as a reference for understanding children's behavior. The remainder of this chapter further examines each of the three levels of mistaken behavior.

Level One: Experimentation Mistaken Behavior

As children begin to master the social expectations of the classroom, the continuous process of making decisions results in mistaken behavior. In early childhood classrooms, children naturally do things to see what will happen, or because they are totally involved in a situation. For reasons of curiosity and involvement, all children who are responding at Harlow's encountering relational level occasionally will show experimentation mistaken behavior.

(Level One mistaken behavior as a result of involvement)
At lunch in a Head Start classroom, three-year-old Rodney said to the teacher, "Gimme the bread."

With a serious look, the teacher responded, "What are the magic words, Rodney?"

Not hesitating for a moment, Rodney raised his arms, spread his fingers and chanted, "Abra-cadabra!"

Smiling about the response, the teacher passed the bread. She commented, "Those are great magic words, Rodney, but the magic words for the table are 'please' and 'thank you,' OK?" Rodney nodded, took the bread and said, "Thank you, please."

Sometimes there is an element of charm in mistaken behavior at this level, especially in young children. The novelty of children's responses in everyday situations is an elixir of great worth to many an early childhood teacher. The ability to understand that the child is trying to learn through experimental mistaken behavior is the hallmark of the guidance approach at this level. A sense of humor and the avoidance of overreaction are useful guidance techniques.

Some mistaken behaviors, such as the use of unacceptable words, can be shown by the child at any of the three levels. The intensity and frequency of the mistaken behavior tend to identify the level for the teacher. "Swearing" provides a useful illustration of this crossover pattern; an example of using unacceptable words at the experimentation level follows:

(Level One mistaken behavior as a result of curiosity)
A teacher enjoyed having Karen in the kindergarten for her enthusiasm and spontaneity. One day during choice time Karen approached her and said with a grin, "Shit, teacher."

The teacher look at Karen, hid a smile, and responded: "Some words bother people, Karen, and this is one of them. You are learning new words every day, though, and I like that. You just need to use other words in kindergarten."

In the anecdote, no moral issue was made, and the child was not punished for attempting to learn about the limits of acceptability in the classroom. Instead the teacher reinforced the limits in a matter-of-fact way without putting down Karen's efforts at "vocabulary development." Had the teacher made this more of an issue, the word's power would have been reinforced, and Karen might have used it in a Level Two or Level Three situation. This possibility still existed but was reduced by

A sense of humor and the ability to avoid overreaction are useful guidance techniques.

the teacher's response. In line with the guidance approach, the teacher let Karen know that her status as a member of the group was not in question, even while she addressed the mistaken behavior.

Level Two: Socially Influenced Mistaken Behavior

As mentioned, Level Two mistaken behavior is **learned behavior.** At the second level, the child is reacting to the influence of others, repeating behavior that is modeled, taught, or suggested. In accord with Harlow's adjustment relational pattern, at Level Two children are conforming to the authority of persons important in their lives. Typical sources of social influence—intentional or unintentional—that can result in Level Two mistaken behavior include:

- parents or other adult family members;
- siblings or other relatives who are peers;
- friends and neighbors;
- other children in the center or school;
- the teacher or care giver;
- other adults in the center or school.

(Level Two mistaken behavior as a result of family influence)

Every so often Matt's dad got quite upset at home, especially when his handyman efforts went wrong. When dad got upset, he swore. In second grade, when Matt spilled too much glue on his paper one day, he used an expression quite familiar to him, "Damn it to Hell!"

The teacher heard the comment and saw what happened. She quietly told Matt that she didn't blame him for getting upset. The teacher said that next time, he could use other words that don't bother people at school like "ding-dong it" and come to her for help.

Reality suggests that on occasion many adults use language not dissimilar to Matt's dad. Matt's frustration was real and the expletive was understandable, if not appropriate. The teacher understood the situation, knew that Matt had heard the expression outside of class, and took a guidance rather than a punishment approach.

If the teacher had put Matt's name on the board or withheld a privilege, she would have made a simple problem into something possibly more lasting and serious. Of course, additional intervention is needed if Matt continued to use unacceptable language. As Ginott wrote in *Teacher and Child* (1972), firmness without harshness is essential in guidance. The guidance teacher is consistently friendly even IF the situation dictates that she needs to be firm.

The difference in teacher response to Level One and Level Two mistaken behavior is often the degree of firmness. At the experimentation level, children are in the process of learning new behaviors. Teachers need to appreciate the tentative nature of this situation and not overreact. At the socially influenced level, teachers need to recognize that learning has already occurred and that the course of the learning needs to be changed. Children, like all of us, are more able to change if they know they are accepted, their efforts are appreciated, and there are definite expectations about their behavior. Children learn when they are taught what they can do instead and not just what not to do.

Sometimes, teaching to alter socially influenced mistaken behavior consists of reminders about limits and requests for alternate responses—as happened with Matt. Other times, the teacher works at consciousness raising to help children become more sensitive to a child or situation. The following anecdote involves children in a prekindergarten classroom.

(Level Two mistaken behavior as a result of peer influence)

Charlie had just progressed from crutches to a new leg brace. Several children noticed that the brace squeaked. By the end of the day, they were laughing among themselves about "Squeaky leg, Charlie."

The next day the teacher talked with Charlie and at a **class meeting** announced that he had something to show everyone. With a grin, Charlie pulled up his pant leg and announced, "Look, guys, I got a new leg brace. It squeaks some, but it works pretty good." With that he invited the children to come over and look at the brace close-up. He flexed his leg for them and made the brace squeak. The teacher then explained about Charlie's leg brace and how well he could walk with it. The children were impressed; the name-calling stopped.

The following day the teacher was absent. When she returned, the substitute called and reported, "I must tell you what happened yesterday. Just as I walked in the door, three children came up to me and said that Charlie has a new leg brace. They said it squeaks, but he gets around on it "really good."

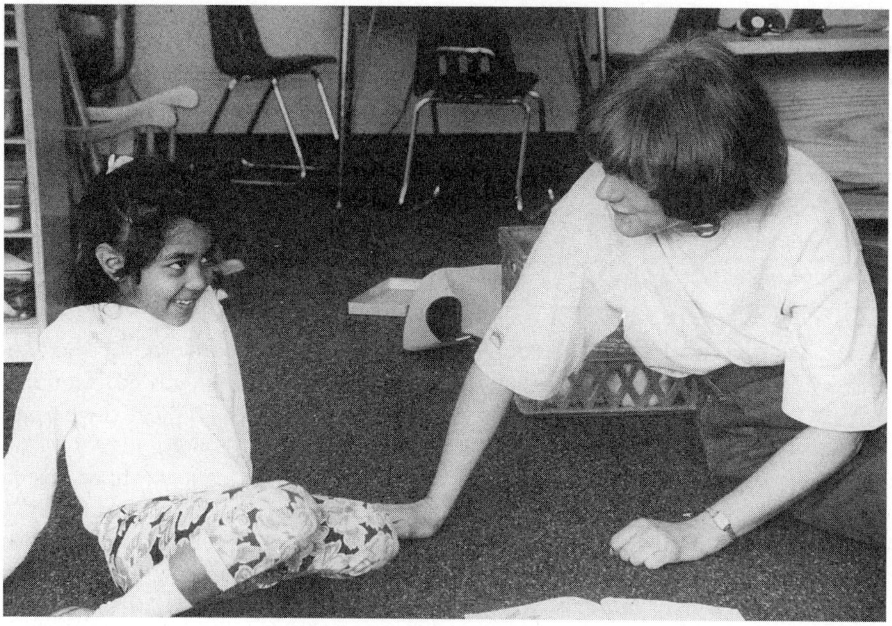

With friendliness and a smile, the teacher still can respond firmly to a mistaken behavior.

The teacher adjusts to the situation, being firm about limits when needed, teaching alternatives, and raising consciousness. Teaching more so than "disciplining" is standard in the guidance approach. Being consistently friendly is the key.

Level Three: Strong Needs Mistaken Behavior

Stone (1973), Warren (1977), Honig (1986), McCracken (1986), Erickson & Pianta (1989), and Slaby et al. (1995) make the fundamental point that serious mistaken behavior is due to trouble in children's lives that is beyond their ability to cope with and understand. At Level One, a child might experiment with a swear word to see what the reaction will be. A child at Level Two will use an expletive learned from others to express a spontaneous feeling (that passes quickly unless a teacher overreacts). At Level Three, reacting from strong needs, a child might let loose a string of expletives over a simple frustration, having completely lost control. The primary sign of the strong needs level is dysfunctional behavior with a definite emotional underlay that tends to be repeated—extreme behaviors repeated over time.

On occasion, any child (or adult) experiences a *Level Three day*. Anxiety, irritability, frustration, inattentiveness, hostility, withdrawal, or fatigue are common Level Three behaviors. Any of these can result from a short-term upset to an individual's physical or emotional health. With young children, Level One situations occasionally generate Level Three reactions—children feel deeply about things. The teacher needs to watch for how quickly the child recovers from the upset and whether such episodes are infrequent or common. When serious mistaken behavior is repeated often or continues for more than a day, the teacher should be alert to the possibility that basic needs of the child are not being met.

Two sources of strong needs mistaken behavior operate independently or together. These sources are *physical discomfort,* due to a health-related problem, and *emotional discomfort,* due to neglect or abuse of a child's needs.

Health Factors and Level Three Behaviors. In their concern for the whole child, early childhood professionals sometimes detect chronic physical conditions such as vision or hearing disabilities, speech impairments, atypical developmental patterns, or perceptual-motor difficulties. Teachers of young children regularly observe acute conditions such as hearing infections, allergy flare-ups, and untreated illnesses. In the last few years, teachers also have become more cognizant of possible neglect and abuse related conditions: hunger, hygiene problems, lack of sleep, pre-natal drug and alcohol involvement, and unexplained injuries. All these conditions, with physical etiologies and emotional ramifications, affect the behavior of children at school. A review process in which mistaken behaviors are evaluated for possible health-related causes is important in all programs serving young children. The process may be as informal as observing and asking the child a question, or as formal as a meeting that involves the parents and a resulting plan of action.

Emotional Factors and Level Three Behaviors. Like adults, young children experience Level Three days now and then. When these days occur frequently and serious mistaken behavior persists, basic emotional needs are not being met. In the eloquent little book, *What About Discipline?* (1973), Stone discussed the connection between mistaken behavior and trouble in the children's life:

> People who persist in thinking of childhood as a time of happy innocence are fooling themselves. Every child's life includes some stress and frustration and it comes out in the child's behavior. Young children are not good at covering up their feelings or at expressing them in words.
>
> While most of these troubles fall under the category of normal stress, there are children whose lives are marked by deep unhappiness. Some children have to endure violence against themselves or other family members or the disruptive effects of drug dependency or mental illness by a family member. Children feel helpless at such times, as they do in the face of divorce, illness, and death.
>
> When people are going through trouble in their personal lives, most show it in other parts of their lives. Adults may be unable to concentrate, for example. They may brood about their problems and not see or hear what is going on around them. They may try to deny their feelings but then get into arguments or fights because they are angry or worried. It is the same with children (pp. 8–11).

level of stress tolerance varies

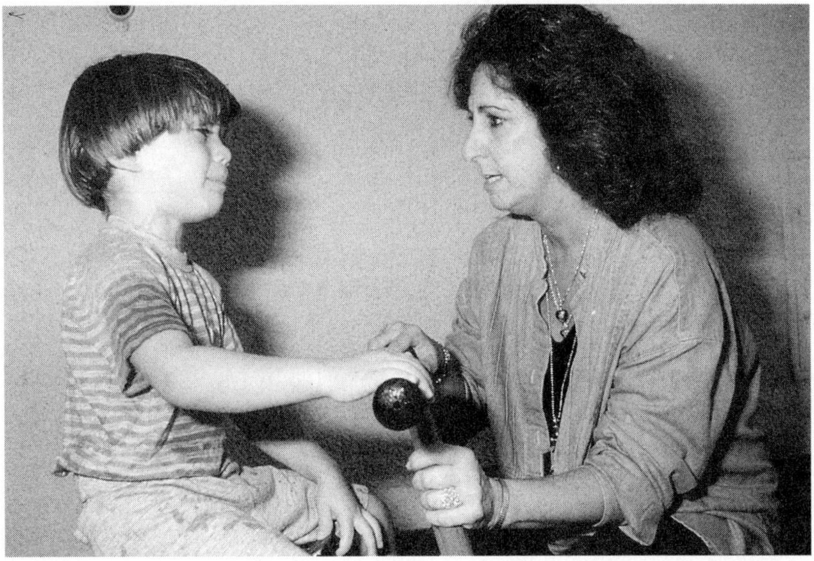

Stress and frustration are a part of life, even for young children.

Stone complements Harlow's discussion of the survival relational pattern. Harlow's words help the teacher to understand dynamics behind serious mistaken behavior in the classroom:

> When problems arise, the survivor unsuccessfully attempts to meet them with generally inappropriate behavior. He may, for example, be prone to lash out destructively or withdraw completely when a problem presents itself. To the observer, it would appear that such behavior is self-defeating—and it is—but it serves the function of preventing the child from involving himself and opening himself to something in his environment that may prove overwhelming. Here, after all, is a child with little confidence in his ability to alter matters by direct action (1975, p. 34).

Responding to Level Three Mistaken Behavior. When a child shows behavior that is disruptive or harmful, teachers need to enforce limits and protect the general need for safety. If mistaken behavior is serious, and especially if it continues over time, however, firm interventions in themselves will be inadequate to improve the situation. The "catch 22" with children behaving at Level Three is that although they need a helping relationship with a teacher the most, they are often the most difficult to work with and accept. A reminder from Warren applies here: The teacher must work to build a helping relationship with each child based on acceptance and respect. Such a relationship is essential if the teacher is to guide the child toward more productive patterns of behavior (1977).

The beginnings of such a relationship include effort by the teacher to understand reasons for the mistaken behavior. Such efforts go beyond the common disclaimer, "She has a rough home life," to learning about the actual circumstances affecting the child.

After five weeks of school, a second grade teacher noted the following pattern in a child's behavior. During the middle of the week, Wendy showed an interest in activities and cooperated easily with fellow students and the teacher. By Friday, however, Wendy was less able to concentrate, avoided contacts with other students, and was irritable in dealings with the teacher. Usually, Wendy was not fully back into the swing of things until Tuesday of the following week.

The teacher contacted the mother who disclosed that she and Wendy's father had separated. Until a divorce was finalized, Wendy was living with her mother during the week and with the father on weekends. Fortunately in this case, the mother expressed confidence that the father was caring appropriately for Wendy. The teacher hypothesized that the separation and the transition from one home to the next were affecting her. The teacher encouraged each parent to help Wendy understand the situation and to assist her during the transitions. For the teacher's part, she became less judgmental about Wendy's behavior and did her best to support Wendy during times of greatest need. Over a few weeks, Wendy began to adjust, and the mistaken behavior decreased.

As illustrated in the anecdote, the teacher seeks to understand what is going on with the child. Full understanding may not occur, but new information almost always is attainable and can help in building relations. Efforts to increase understanding should include discussions with the parent, other staff, and the child. Discarding the myth that the professional teacher works alone, she needs to communicate with other personnel; i.e., through teaming arrangements, staffings, and cross-agency collaborations. The more serious the mistaken behavior, the more the teacher may need to work with others to bring about a positive resolution.

Strong needs mistaken behavior then requires a multistep problem-solving strategy that involves a clear but flexible plan. The plan should include components for: (a) getting more information; (b) building a helping relationship with the child; (c) preventing problem situations; (d) intervening in nonpunitive ways; and (e) teaching the child acceptable behavioral alternatives. When the plan is working, in Harlow's words:

> What occurs then, over time, is that the survivor's need for predetermined constancy is replaced by a new network of dependable relationships, which are based upon his successful actions on, or mastery of, at least a portion of the classroom environment. . . . As the child begins to sense his powers of mastery, a new self-regard emerges. This self-regard enables the child to open himself to endeavors that before would have proven to be defeating (1975, p. 34).

The discussion of Level Three mistaken behavior has been more lengthy than Level One and Two for a particular reason. Children at Level Three pose the most difficulties for teachers. Their situations are the most complex, and responses by the teacher need to be the most comprehensive. (See Chapter 11). Strategies for assisting children who are showing each level of mistaken behavior are provided in the remaining chapters.

MISTAKEN BEHAVIOR AND INTENTIONALITY

Because the concept is new, readers may be tempted to associate mistaken behavior with "accidents" and misbehavior with acts "done on purpose." Mistaken behavior includes both accidents and intentional actions. A pre-schooler on a trike who runs over the toe of another child by accident has shown Level One mistaken behavior. The accident was the result of loss of control or failure to look where one is going. The accident was unintentional but was Level One because it was a mistake that arose from involvement.

A child may run over another's foot for a second reason related to Level One: The trike rider hits the other's foot "accidentally on-purpose" to see what will happen. The lack of development of young children means that they have difficulty understanding how another child would feel under such circumstances. The act was intentional, but was done without full awareness of the consequences, and so is Level One mistaken behavior. The importance of the term *mistaken behavior* is that

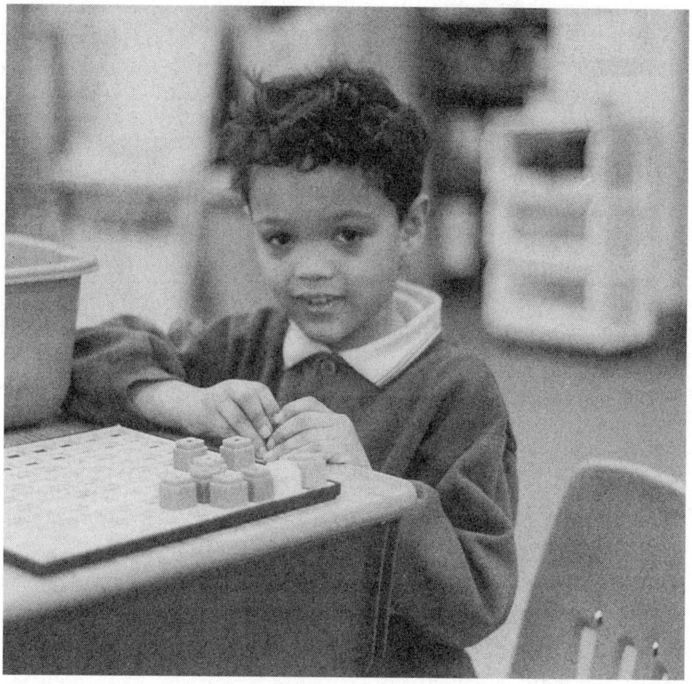

With trust in the environment, the child succeeds at tasks that before would have been self-defeating.

it reminds the adult that the trike rider needs guidance about human feelings and the consequences of actions, not punishment for making a mistake.

Of course, hitting another child's foot might also be a Level Two or Three mistaken behavior. At Level Two, one child follows another on a trike. The second rider sees the first swing close to a bystander and follows suit, but strikes the bystander's foot. At Level Three, a trike rider comes to school with feelings of hostility and acts out against an innocent child. When the teacher hypothesizes that Level Two or Level Three is involved, she reacts with increasing degrees of firmness while retaining the element of friendliness, which is at the heart of guidance. If the situation indicates strong needs mistaken behavior, the teacher follows-up as suggested for Level Three. The follow-up is important because serious mistaken behavior is shown when children are victims of life circumstances that they cannot control. The acting out may have been intentional but the motive was not understood by the child. The mistaken behavior was an unintentional request for assistance, not punishment.

Whatever the level of mistaken behavior, the teacher responds to the immediate situation by using guidance. She first gives attention to the "victim." This action shows support for the child who deserves it; lets the trike rider know the teacher is aware of what happened; and may help the teacher calm down. The teacher then decides whether to use **conflict management** with the children together or a **guidance talk** with the trike rider. This decision is based on the emotional state of each child and on the teacher's idea of who needs to learn what in the situation.

If conflict management is used, the teacher helps each child to understand what happened. The teacher then encourages the child who was hurt to the tell the other child how it made her feel. Then the teacher may ask the children to discuss what would make the other child feel better, and what the trike rider could do next time to make sure the incident does not happen again. A strength of mediation in a situation like this is that it helps to empower the child who was "victimized" and models for both children how to solve problems using words (Wichert, 1989).

If the teacher chooses to use a guidance talk, she builds empathy by pointing out that the trike rider hurt the other child and that the teacher cannot let anyone, including the trike rider, be hurt at school. The teacher discusses with the trike rider how that child could avoid the problem next time. Although the teacher does not force an apology, she asks how the trike rider could help the child who was hurt feel better. The teacher then assists the trike rider to return to positive activity, which often includes helping the child to make amends (Gartrell, 1995). A strength of the guidance talk is that it shows that the teacher cares enough about the trike rider to believe the child can change.

Whether the teacher decides to use conflict management with both children or a guidance talk with one, she avoids the traditional discipline reaction. The teacher does not lecture about how naughty the behavior was or automatically put the trike rider in a time out. The teacher may or may not request the child to give up the trike, depending on the outcome of the guidance exchange. The goal is to help children learn from the mistake, not punish them for making it.

Again, the value of the term *mistaken behavior* is that is has different implications than the conventional term, *misbehavior. Misbehavior* tends to connote a judgment of character that leads to punishment. *Mistaken behavior* precludes character assessment and asks that the other be accepted as a person of worth (by virtue of being alive). The person may need to face consequences, but at the base of those consequences is guidance, so that the possibility of change is maximized.

A premise in the guidance approach is that even "willful acts" that are done "on purpose" still constitute mistaken behavior. A child who deliberately bites or intentionally disobeys has made a mistake. The adult who is able to approach children as worthwhile individuals who make mistakes is in a philosophically strong position to assist with healthy personal and social development.

Visual Summary: Three Levels of Mistaken Behavior

Mistaken behaviors have distinct motivational sources. Behaviors that appear similar can be a result of differing motivations, and so be at different levels. The teacher must observe carefully to infer the motivation and the level of mistaken behavior to respond effectively. Table 2.2 illustrates how sample mistaken behaviors can be at different levels.

In the guidance approach, the teacher responds to children not just on the basis of the discrete behavior shown but on a judgment about the meaning of the behavior for the child. This judgment is a high-level skill that takes practice and sensitivity. The chapters to follow assist the adult in interpreting and responding to mistaken

Table 2.2
Sample Mistaken Behaviors by Level

Incident of Mistaken Behavior	Motivational Source	Level of Mistaken Behavior
Child uses expletive	Wants to see teacher's reaction	One
	Wants to emulate important others	Two
	Expresses deeply felt hostility	Three
Child pushes another off trike	Wants trike; has not learned to ask in words	One
	Follows aggrandizement practices modeled by other children	Two
	Feels need to act out against world by asserting power	Three
Child refuses to join in group activity	Does not understand teacher's expectations	One
	Has developed a habit of not joining in	Two
	Is not feeling well or feels anxiety about participating	Three

behavior in ways that enforce limits and teach alternatives, yet respect children's need for self-esteem.

COMMUNICATING WITH PARENTS ABOUT MISTAKEN BEHAVIOR

As teachers know, parent's views about their children and the subject of discipline vary a great deal: "My kid is basically a good kid who just needs some TLC." "My child is willful and will try to get away with things unless the teacher is strict." In discussing children's behavior with parents, the teacher first seeks to understand how the parent views the child. This step will help in deciding how to communicate in terms the parent can accept. Second, the teacher needs to realize that however they see their children, parents want the best for them.

Parents who have positive views about their children generally accept the concept of mistaken behavior and its three levels. Out of an adult sense of fair play, however, parents neither want their child "to get away with things" nor other children to treat their child unfairly. In explaining behavior in terms of "making a mistake," the teacher needs to emphasize that the child is in a developmental process of learning more acceptable alternatives and that the teacher is providing guidance to help the child do so. With relatively mild mistaken behavior, the teacher might say that she doubts that the behavior will occur again but will continue to watch the situation.

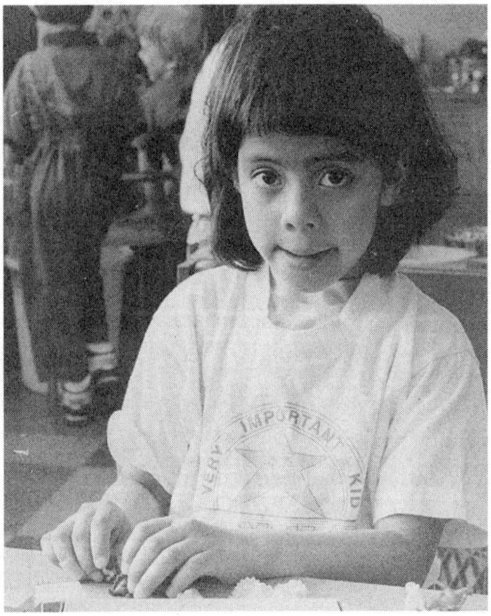

Parents who feel positively about their children generally accept the concept of mistaken behavior.

Especially with more serious behaviors, the teacher must be clear to the parent that children, like all of us, make mistakes. At the same time, the child needs to learn from the mistake, and the role of the teacher is to help. That a hurting or disruptive behavior is "a mistake" does not justify it. Guidance is not necessarily permissive. In the terms of Haim Ginott, "Helpful correction is direction":

> Frank, age five, pinched his friend, Sam. . . . The teacher who witnessed the event said to Frank, "I saw it. People are not for pinching." Frank said, "I am sorry." The teacher replied, "To be sorry is to make an inner decision to behave differently." "O.K.," replied Frank. He went over to Sam to resume his play (1972, p. 129).

Although Frank may not have understood the teacher's exact words, he got the message. The teacher modeled guidance by being firm, not harsh, and by clearly educating Frank about his actions.

The goal in communicating with the parent is to convey a stance of acceptance of the child and of appropriate guidance in relation to the child's behavior. The levels of mistaken behavior provide a helpful vocabulary for the teacher in working toward this goal. If a child is having problems, the teacher also needs to communicate about the effort and progress and achievements the child has made. Parents, like all of us, accept suggestions for improvement more easily when progress is recognized.

At times, parents will be more critical of the child than the teacher. Parents can express skepticism about their children's behaviors and still be nurturing parents. Occasionally, however, a teacher encounters a parent who has overly negative views about the child or unrealistic reactions to the child's mistaken behavior. One important comment needs to be made here. If a teacher believes that difficulties in parent-child communication are posing Level Three problems for the child, then the teacher needs to take a comprehensive problem-solving approach that includes collaboration with others. The teacher works with the family as well as with other professionals to solve difficult problems. Succeeding chapters discuss parent-teacher communication under these circumstances.

SUMMARY

What is inappropriate about using the term *misbehavior?*

The complexity of helping young children learn social skills leads some adults to have the misconception that children know how to behave; they just choose misbehavior. Misbehavior connotes willful wrongdoing for which a child needs to be disciplined (punished). The term focuses on the child, rather than the behavior, for who misbehaves but children who are "rowdy," "willful," "spiteful," or "immature?" In reacting to a misbehaving child, the teacher sometimes tries to shame the child into compliance, but this action may have the long-term opposite effect. Because of a lack of development and experience, the child internalizes the teacher's negative message and may act out even more.

What is the concept of mistaken behavior?

Teachers who use guidance have a positive view about the potential of the child. They see life skills as difficult to learn, and they recognize that children are just at the beginning stages of learning these skills. In the process of learning life skills, children, like all of us, make mistakes. These teachers recognize that the decision to act out or defy is because the child does not yet have the cognitive and emotional resources for more mature responses. The concept of mistaken behavior frees the adult from the emotional baggage of value judgment about the child and allows the adult to focus fully on the problem, its causes, and its solutions. When teachers think of *misbehavior* as *mistaken behavior,* they are in a better position to accept the child as a worthwhile individual and teach the child more acceptable ways to act.

What are relational patterns?

Building from the work of the developmental and self psychologists, Steven D. Harlow has developed a system for understanding social development in the classroom, which he calls *relational patterns.* The three relational patterns Harlow identified are *surviving, adjusting,* and *encountering.* Because of a perception that the environment is a dangerous place, the child at the *survival level* resorts to extreme behaviors and may act out as a means of protection from perceived harm. A child at the *adjustor level* has a primary motive of desiring to please others, especially those in authority. A child at the *encountering level* is less concerned with security and approval and more occupied with exploring new ideas, materials, and experiences.

Children at each level of social relationship pose particular challenges for the teacher. The teacher attempts to build relations and a sense of trust with the survivor to make learning safe. With the child at the adjustor level, the teacher works to lower anxiety levels and nudge toward independence. The teacher must temper a personal need for control and develop a spirit of partnership with a child at the encountering level. In general, the teacher needs to avoid labeling children by relational pattern and to assist children to progress across the differing patterns through the range of classroom experiences they share.

What are the levels of mistaken behavior?

The levels of mistaken behavior correspond to the three relational patterns. Level One is *experimentation mistaken behavior,* which corresponds to the relational pattern of encountering. Children show Level One mistaken behavior through curiosity or involvement. When children do things to see what will happen, they are showing curiosity-related mistaken behavior. When children are involved in ongoing activities and get embroiled in a conflict, they are showing involvement-related mistaken behavior. With Level One mistaken behavior, the teacher avoids overreaction but educates to more appropriate alternatives of behavior.

Level Two is *socially influenced or learned mistaken behavior.* Children show Level Two mistaken behavior when they are influenced toward an inappropriate act by significant others, either peers or adults. The influence can be either intentional or unintentional. With Level Two, the teacher acts in a firm but friendly manner to reinforce a limit, raise consciousness levels, and teach alternative behaviors.

Level Three is *strong needs mistaken behavior.* All serious mistaken behavior is caused by strong unmet needs that the child cannot cope with and understand. The source of the unmet needs might be health conditions that are untreated, emotional suffering from experiences either at home or school, or a combination of the two. To deal with strong needs mistaken behavior, the teacher takes a multistep approach that includes: (a) getting more information, (b) building a helping relationship with the child, (c) preventing problem situations from arising, (d) intervening in nonpunitive ways, and (e) teaching the child behavioral alternatives. Almost always, the teacher collaborates with others—including the child, the parent, and other professionals—to set and implement a guidance plan. The more serious the mistaken behavior, the more the teacher may need to work with others in its solution.

Can mistaken behavior be intentional?

Readers may be tempted to associate mistaken behavior with "accidents" and misbehavior with intentionality. *Mistaken behavior* includes both. Because young children do not yet possess the social awareness of the adult, they do not have the personal resources to act "properly" in all situations—especially when emotions are running high. Young children cannot easily understand behavioral alternatives, others' motivations, or possible consequences. Young children are not bad, they just have not yet learned to act maturely. In both psychological and social terms; children are vulnerable to making mistakes. For these reasons, teachers are better served by using the term *mistaken behavior,* whether intention is inferred or not. By thinking in terms of mistaken behavior, the adult is more able to accept the child as a worthwhile, developing person and to guide, in firm but friendly ways, toward more appropriate behaviors.

How does the teacher communicate with parents about mistaken behavior?

Parents' views about their children and the subject of discipline vary. In communicating with parents, the teacher first seeks to understand how the parent views the child. Parents who see their children positively generally accept the concept of mistaken behavior and its three levels. Whether the teacher uses the term or not, she needs to convey to parents that children, like all of us, make mistakes. When discussing the problems a child is having in the classroom, the teacher needs to convey that the child is trying to get along and already has some strengths. The teacher and parent just need to work together to help the child learn from mistakes that might be made. If a teacher believes that level three mistaken behavior is involved, she collaborates with other professionals as well as the family to develop and implement a constructive plan.

FOLLOW-UP ACTIVITIES

Note: In completing follow-up activities, the privacy of all involved is to be respected.

Reflection Activity

The reflection activity encourages students to interrelate their own thoughts and experiences with specific ideas from the chapter.

Think back to a classroom incident that you witnessed or were a part of when a teacher intervened. Use references from the chapter to determine what level or levels of mistaken behavior were involved. Did the teacher respond as though the incident was misbehavior or mistaken behavior? Why did you reach this conclusion?

Application Activities

Application activities allow students to interrelate material from the text with real life situations. The observations imply access to practicum experiences; the interviews, access to teachers and parents. Students may compare or contrast observations and interviews with referenced ideas from the chapter.

1. **What is inappropriate about using the term *misbehavior?***
   a. Respecting privacy, observe an incident in a classroom where a teacher intervened. Do you think the teacher regarded the situation as misbehavior or mistaken behavior. What difference did the teacher's decision make for the child or children involved? For the teacher?
   b. Respecting privacy, interview a teacher about common problems she sees involving children in the classroom. To what extent does the teacher seem to think misbehavior is involved? Mistaken behavior? Based on the teacher's responses and your reading of the chapter, what do you think are the main priorities of the teacher in leaning toward misbehavior or mistaken behavior?
2. **What is the concept of mistaken behavior?**
   a. Observe a problem situation in a prekindergarten, kindergarten, or primary grade classroom. Analyze the situation using the concept of mistaken behavior. In what ways does the concept apply or not apply to the situation observed?
   b. The concept of mistaken behavior is a new one for many teachers. Talk with a teacher about the concept. What parts of it are they comfortable with; what parts are they not sure about? What more would they like to know about the concept?
3. **What are relational patterns?**
   a. Observe one child who is at two different relational patterns in two differing classroom situations. Which two relational patterns seemed to be operating? Discuss why the situations may have elicited different responses from the child.
   b. Observe children at each of the three relational patterns. In what ways does Harlow's model apply to the children? In what ways does Harlow's model not seem to apply?
4. **What are the three levels of mistaken behavior?**
   a. Observe an example of Level One, experimentation mistaken behavior. What did you observe that makes you think the mistaken behavior is at this level? In what ways does recognizing this level of mistaken behavior help you to understand the child?

b. Observe an example of Level Two, socially influenced mistaken behavior. What did you observe that makes you think the mistaken behavior is at this level? In what ways does recognizing this level of mistaken behavior help you to understand the child?
c. Observe an example of Level Three, strong needs mistaken behavior. What did you observe that makes you think the mistaken behavior is at this level? In what ways does recognizing this level of mistaken behavior help you to understand the child?

5. **Can mistaken behavior be intentional?**
a. Observe an act of harm or disruption by a child that you believe to be intentional. Try to explain the behavior using the concept of mistaken behavior. In what ways does the concept apply? In what ways does it not apply?
b. Interview a teacher about the approach she takes when intervening in a problem situation. In what ways is the approach different if the teacher believes a child caused the problem by accident or on purpose? In what ways is the approach the same?

6. **How does the teacher communicate with parents about mistaken behavior?**
a. Talk with a teacher about the approach she uses when talking with a parent about a problem the child is having in the classroom. What is important for the teacher to convey to the parent? How does the teacher's approach relate to the concept of mistaken behavior?
b. Talk with a parent about the approach she would like a teacher to use if the parent's child were having a problem in the classroom. How do the parent's comments relate to the concept of mistaken behavior?

RECOMMENDED RESOURCES

Erickson, M. F., & Pianta, R. C. (1989). New lunchbox, old feelings: What kids bring to school. *Early Education and Development, 1*(1), 35–49.

Gartrell, D. J. (1995). Misbehavior or mistaken behavior? *Young Children, 50*(5), 27–34.

Parry, A. (1993). Children surviving in a violent world—Choosing nonviolence. *Young Children, 48*(6), 13–15.

Slaby, R. G., Roedell, W. C., Arezzo, D., & Hendrix, K. (1995). *Early violence prevention*. Washington, DC: National Association for the Education of Young Children.

Studer, J. R. (1993). Listen so that parents will speak. *Childhood Education, 70*(2), 74–76.

Weber-Schwartz, N. (1987). Patience or understanding? *Young Children, 42*(3), 52–54.

Zatorski, J. (1995). I am a mirror, I am a window, for a child who needs me. *Young Children, 48*(6), 18–19.

REFERENCES

Combs, A. W. (1962). A perceptual view of the adequate personality. In A. W. Combs (Ed.). *Perceiving, behaving, becoming: A new focus for education*. Washington, DC: Association for Supervision and Curriculum Development.

Erickson, M. F., & Pianta, R. C. (1989). New lunchbox, old feelings: What kids bring to school. *Early Education and Development, 1*(1), 35–49.

Gartrell, D. J. (1991). *Developmentally appropriate guidance of young children*. (Rev. ed.). St. Paul, MN: Minnesota Association for the Education of Young Children.

Gartrell, D. J. (1995). Misbehavior or mistaken behavior? *Young Children, 50*(5), 27–34.

Ginott, H. G. (1972). *Teacher and child*. New York: Avon Books.

Greenberg, P. (1988). Avoiding 'me against you' discipline. *Young Children, 43*(1), 24–31.

Harlow, S. D. (1975). *Special education: The meeting of differences*. Grand Forks, ND: University of North Dakota.

Honig, A. S. (1986). Research in review. Stress and coping in children. In J. B. McCracken (Ed). (1986). *Reducing stress in young children's lives*. Washington, DC: National Association for the Education of Young Children.

Kamii, C. (1984, February). Autonomy: The aim of education envisioned by Piaget. *Phi Delta Kappan*, 410–415.

Kohn, A. (1993). *Punished by rewards*. Boston: Houghton Mifflin Company.

McCracken, J. B. (Ed). (1986). *Reducing stress in young children's lives*. Washington, DC: National Association for the Education of Young Children.

Maslow, A. H. (1962). Some basic propositions of a growth and self-actualization psychology. In A. W. Combs (Ed.). *Perceiving, behaving, becoming: A new focus for education*. Washington, DC: Association for Supervision and Curriculum Development.

Piaget, J. (1932/1960). *The moral judgment of the child*. Glencoe, IL: The Free Press.

Slaby, R. G., Roedell, W. C., Arezzo, D., & Hendrix, K. (1995). *Early violence prevention*. Washington, DC: National Association for the Education of Young Children.

Stone, J. G. (1973). *What about discipline?* Cambridge, MA: Education Development Center.

Warren, R. (1977). *Caring: Supporting children's growth*. Washington, DC: National Association for the Education of Young Children.

Wichert, S. (1989). *Keeping the peace: Practicing cooperation and conflict resolution with preschoolers*. Philadelphia, PA: New Society Publishers.

3
Guidance: The Bottom Line

GUIDING QUESTIONS

As you read Chapter 3, you will discover answers to the following questions:

- **How are positive teacher-child relations the basis of the guidance approach?**
- **How does guidance reduce the need for mistaken behavior?**
- **What does "guidance is solution-oriented" mean?**
- **Why is teamwork with staff and other professionals part of guidance?**
- **How are parent-teacher partnerships important in the guidance approach?**

As discussed in Chapter 1, guidance has a strong tradition in progressive educational thought. Infused by the work of the developmental and self psychologists, the approach builds upon the ideas of Ginott, Dreikurs, and others who articulated discipline models based on mutual respect. Whatever title we give it, guidance has a look and a feel that make it unmistakable. This chapter continues the theme of Unit One by introducing five principles of the guidance approach. If these principles are present in a classroom, then the reader may be assured that guidance is being practiced. The principles are that guidance:

1. depends on positive teacher-child relations;
2. reduces the need for mistaken behavior;
3. takes a solution-orientation;
4. means teamwork with staff and other professionals;
5. involves parent-teacher partnerships.

Each principle implies definite teaching practices which together constitute the guidance approach.

GUIDANCE DEPENDS ON POSITIVE TEACHER-CHILD RELATIONS

In *Caring* (1977), Warren perceptively comments that teachers cannot feel love for each child and need not feel guilty when they realize this. Warren states, however, that the teacher does have an obligation to build positive relationships with all children and to help them feel a sense of belonging with the group. Building relations with persons we don't feel comfortable around is hard for all human beings. The task may be especially difficult when children show Level Three mistaken behaviors, which can be extreme and violent. Still, as Weber-Schwartz points out in her important article "Patience or Understanding," seeking to understand a child is an important step in increasing the level of acceptance (1987). Productive human relations is an essential life goal in a democratic society and an important professional goal for the teacher (Read, Gardner, & Mahler, 1993).

The early childhood teacher builds positive relations with children based on the role that he fills. The role is different from that of the parent whose relationship with the child is highly personal and subjective (Katz, 1980). The unique task of the early childhood teacher is to facilitate the transition of the child from the intense, private relationship with the parent to the more public and collectively driven relationship with the teacher (Daniel, 1993; Edson, 1994).

In early childhood education terms like *removed* and *impersonal* inadequately describe the teacher-child relationship. Adjustment to school is easier for children who feel positively about themselves in the school situation (Erickson & Pianta, 1989). The essential ingredient for this disposition is personal affirmation by the teacher, **unconditional positive regard** for the person of the child.

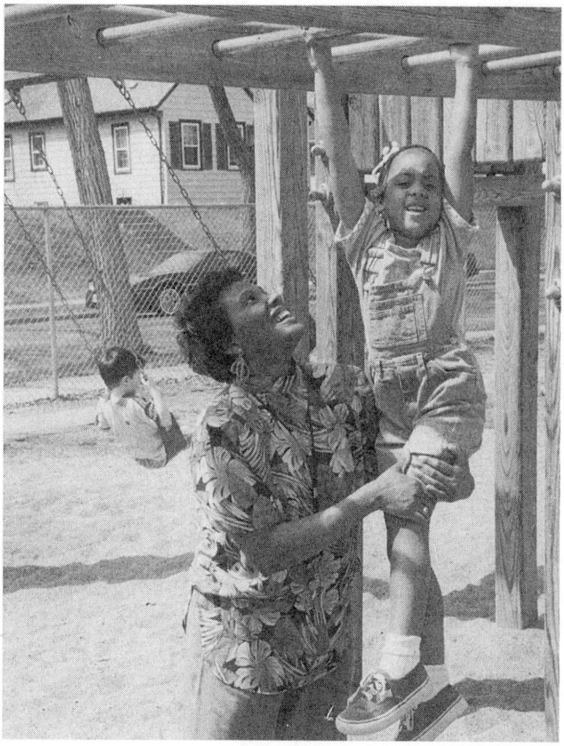

Productive human relations is an essential goal for the teacher.

Unconditional Positive Regard

The premise that discipline techniques should communicate respect for the child (Curwin & Mendler, 1988) is a critical element in guidance. Central to the approach is unconditional positive regard. Unconditional positive regard means full acceptance of the child as a developing human being despite mistaken behaviors that the child may show. While the teacher addresses the mistaken behavior, firmly if necessary, he simultaneously supports the intrinsic worth of the child as a member *in good standing* of the group.

The teacher comfortable with unconditional positive regard creates a spirit in the classroom where all children feel welcome and that they belong. This means that he practices **liberation teaching**, the acceptance, support, and empowerment of children who might be singled out negatively for physical, cultural, or behavioral reasons. He teaches that differing human qualities and circumstances are to be respected and learned from.

In the language of the conflict resolution movement, the teacher works to create a **peaceable classroom** (Kreidler, 1984), in which mutual respect and positive communication skills flourish (Girard & Koch, 1996). In the guidance tradition, the term **encouraging classroom** applies. In the encouraging classroom, the teacher has a positive expectation of productive, caring behavior from the class and shows active leadership to empower this behavior. A key technique in creating a classroom that is peaceable and encouraging is the rejection of punishment as a method of behavior control.

The Problem with Discipline

In the use of conventional discipline, teachers tend to blur the distinction between nonpunitive and punitive interventions. Children who *misbehave* have their names written on the board, are put into time out, given detention, deprived of class rewards, or publicly embarrassed in other ways. Arguments for the use of punishment seem to be two. First, the teacher sends the message to the child that unless he behaves "properly," he will be ostracized from the group. Second, the teacher is letting the other children know that unless they behave, they too will be ostracized.

Teachers who use guidance reject the implicit reliance on punishment inherent in discipline. The problem they see with the *first argument* is that although the teacher believes that he is shaming the child into "being good," the result may be the opposite due to the self-fulfilling prophecy (Ginott, 1972). "Because of limited development and experience, children tend to internalize negative labels, see themselves as they are labeled, and react accordingly" (Gartrell, 1995).

> Early in the kindergarten year, Jamal got upset with another child and punched her in the stomach. The teacher became furious and marched Jamal to the time-out chair. Later in the day the principal gave him a "stern lecture." Two days later, Jamal got into another argument and hit again. As the teacher came toward him, Jamal walked to the time-out chair by himself and said, "I know. I'm going 'cause I'm no good." The teacher knelt beside him and explained that he did not upset her but that his behavior did. Afterwards, she worked to improve their relationship.

Teachers who use guidance also disagree with the *second argument.* What is the emotional climate of the classroom where children are repeatedly reminded of the consequences of misbehavior? Some teachers would say an orderly atmosphere. However, for a teacher who values guidance, the atmosphere is *an unpleasant one.* Tension arises among the many children who do not want to be ostracized. Sometimes the tension is so intense that the ordinary risks involved with learning become difficult challenges. Children grow afraid to try because they fear that their behaviors will be viewed negatively (Kohn, 1993).

On the other hand, for those children already stigmatized as *trouble-makers,* the threat of ostracism may lose its power. These children not only come to see themselves negatively, but they may grow to care little about themselves in the school situation.

A first-year teacher used a bit of guile to appeal to the pride of a group of very active boys in her third grade class. By December, she had them functioning fairly well in the group and working fairly hard.

In January, the principal gave a staff training in a new discipline system he expected the whole school to use. Names were to be written on the board for *bad behavior*, and children were to be given disciplinary referral slips for repeat offenses. A roller skating party was to be held at the end of the winter term. Children with three disciplinary referral slips were to be excluded.

The teacher felt obligated to use the system and found she was writing the names of the boys on the board quite a bit. A few days before the class party, a popular member of the "rambunctious group" got his third referral slip. By the day of the party, the boys' friends also had gotten three slips; almost, it seemed to the teacher, on purpose. During the spring term, the teacher went back to her previous approach and worked hard to regain positive relations with the boys. She felt she almost got back to that point by the end of the year, but not quite.

Building Positive Teacher-Child Relations

Positive teacher-child relations depend upon acceptance of each child as a welcome member of the group. A sense of unconditional positive regard is established when the teacher accepts and supports each child, despite the mistaken behaviors that the child may show. The teacher rejects conventional discipline. The teacher uses an approach to relations with the individual and the group that, instead of instilling fear and resentment, builds the mutual respect of the encouraging classroom—a sense of community within the class. Central to building positive relations through the guidance approach are the avoidance of embarrassment and the replacement of praise with private and public encouragement.

Avoiding Embarrassment. A common practice in conventional discipline is the use of embarrassment, making an example of a child as a means of controlling the group. Many adults can recall being embarrassed by teachers, even if those incidents occurred years and years before (Gartrell, 1997). When teachers use embarrassment to control behavior, they may think they are reacting to a situation of the moment, but the injury to self-esteem may last a lifetime.

To prevent the effects of embarrassment, the teacher seeks alternatives to singling out children. A simple premise applies to the classroom where unconditional positive regard is practiced. All children are accepted as welcome members of the class,

– not rewards or praise but encouragement
– build a relationship UPR

no matter what mistaken behavior they may show, simply because they are in the class. A child who shows chronic mistaken behavior is helped to learn more acceptable responses, firmly if needed, but as privately as possible. The child is helped to learn life skills, not under the threat that otherwise he will be excluded from the group but with the understanding that the help is there because the child is a member of the group.

> A teacher was attempting to begin a large group activity with a class of four-year-olds. She *did not say:* "Mark and Clarice, we are all waiting for you."
>
> She *did say:* "We are almost ready to start, I like the way you are coming to the circle so quickly." As she enthusiastically began the activity, Mark and Clarice hurried to join the group.

Such generalized comments, which recognize progress as well as accomplishment, are not as direct as personal references, but with practice they work. With individual preschoolers, the strategic placement of adults prior to large groups is also an effective strategy. During the activity, if more than a few children show inattentiveness, a change is needed, often by a new activity that allows for increased involvement. The old notion that the teacher stays with the lesson plan no matter what has no place in early childhood practice. An encouraging classroom atmosphere is preserved by the teacher who is flexible and knows when to go on to something new.

With primary grade and older children, Jones (1993) advocates the intentional use of body language. Jones' preventive strategy is to establish contact with students through movement around the classroom, quick individual help, smiles, nods and other friendly gestures. If intervention is needed, a first level consists of a glance and a glance with a hand gesture. Rather than chastising a child on the other side of the room, the teacher continues teaching while making his way toward the child. Usually establishing proximity restores attention. If necessary, the teacher whispers a few words, perhaps requesting a private conference later. Through body language, the grade school child is apt to get the message without experiencing humiliation (Jones, 1993).

Beyond Praise. A challenging idea to many teachers is that praise as well as criticism can work against positive teacher-child relations (Hitz & Driscoll, 1988; Kohn, 1993). When a teacher praises a child, the child becomes the institutionalized winner in the situation, and all others become the losers. Resentment and hurt are felt by many of those not recognized, and the child "positively" singled out is apt to feel *mixed* emotions—pleasure *and* embarrassment (Hitz & Driscoll, 1988; Kohn, 1993). The use of praise to set a "positive example," remains a common teaching practice. Teachers fail to see that such praise is meant only secondarily for the recipient; the real motive is control of the class by building dependency on the teacher.

An indication of professional development is when teachers step back and review how they use praise. Often, they can praise less and teach more effectively when they look beyond children's behavior to possible changes in the daily program.

> A group of five- and six-year-olds attended a child care center on alternative days when they were not at school. The center policy was a nap each day, even though the children did not rest at kindergarten. The teachers had a difficult time keeping the children quiet during the nap. One incentive they used was to praise the "best rester" each day and have that child lead the line. On this day the teacher chose Carrie. From the others, a chorous of complaints were heard:
>
> Jeremy: "I was sleepin' too."
> Neil: "She always gets picked 'cause she sleeps!"
> Carole: "I didn't say nothin' during rest, and I never get to be first."
> Darrell: "Who wants to lead the line anyway?"
> Carrie: "It's OK, Teacher, somebody else can do it."
>
> After a staff meeting to discuss the situation, the teachers decided to replace nap with "quiet time." The group stayed on their cots, but each day a story was read followed by a "super silent reading time." The children liked the new guidelines and either looked at books or slept. After rest, a random system for lining up—"everyone wearing blue"—was introduced. The teachers found that the program change was a big improvement.

Recognition of achievement and progress, like criticism, should be given carefully. Unconditional positive regard means that the teacher avoids holding a child up for comparison, *either by praise or criticism* (Kohn, 1993).

The Use of Encouragement. The notion that "all praise is good" has been taken for granted in childhood education (Kohn, 1993). Hitz and Driscoll argue persuasively that what young children need is not praise but **encouragement** (1988). As discussed, praise focuses on achievements, tends to single out individuals, and builds dependence on the teacher. Praise is often given not so much to recognize individuals as to manipulate the group (Kohn, 1993). In contrast, carefully given encouragement recognizes effort, usually does not single out, and affirms self-esteem (Hitz & Driscoll, 1988; Kohn, 1993). Encouragement can be private or public.

Private encouragement is honestly meant for the child being recognized. Control of the group is not a motive. Individual recognition of effort and progress means a great deal to the child; he knows that a remark made in private is meant only for him. Private encouragement typically is given in one-to-one situations; before other children have arrived in the room, for instance, or during individual activities when other children will not notice. Contrast the likely meaning of these two remarks for Chenille, a first grader:

Praise in front of class: "Chenille is such a good listener today. She gets to help with the snack."

or

Private encouragement as children get ready for lunch: "You were really listening today, Chenille; thank you for your cooperation."

Public encouragement takes two forms. The first is group-focused recognition that supports the efforts of the whole class and not just selected individuals. As distinct from praise of the individual, group-focused recognition builds group spirit and positive relations. Notice the likely effects of these contrasting sets of comments:

Praise: "Everyone needs to be sitting like a pretzel, just like Chad and Leslie."

or

Public encouragement: "You are all sitting just like a plate of curled up pretzels and are almost ready for the story."

Praise: "Veda and Charlene were the best workers today. They get to choose their free time activity first."

or

Public encouragement: "Everyone has been working so hard today that I think we all deserve a little extra free time."

The second form of public encouragement recognizes individuals. On occasion a teacher may have a good reason for bringing class attention to an individual child; for instance, a child who has struggled against a problem or disability with which the class is familiar. In electing to use public recognition, the teacher needs to decide whether the comments are meant for the child's benefit or for "crowd control." He needs to think about what the recognition will mean to the child *and* to the other children. The goal should be to affirm the child's self-worth, to nurture feelings of empathy in the group, to maintain positive relations with each member of the group, and therefore with the group itself.

A contention of the guidance approach is that **conditional acceptance** and the criticism and praise that drive it gives rise to feelings of failure and low self-esteem. (Honig & Wittmer, 1996). Most early childhood teachers agree that the young child needs to feel accepted by the group to participate in activities successfully (Bredekamp, 1997). Unconditional positive regard is sound preventive practice. In the encouraging classroom where it is found, children try hard to learn and get along because they know that they may make mistakes, but they will not fail.

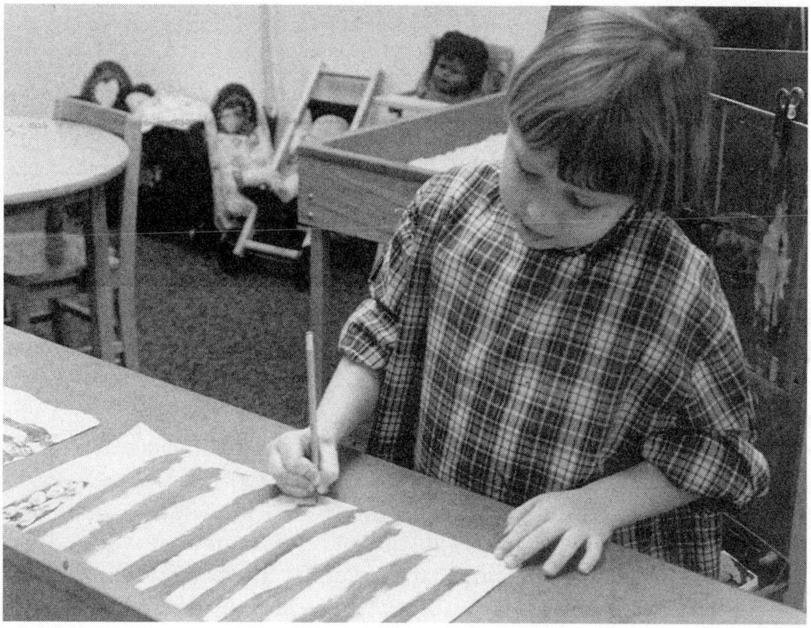

Encouragement recognizes effort, often is private, and affirms self-esteem.

Ginott's Cardinal Principle

Unconditional positive regard is a venerable idea that was used in the nursery school movement of the 1920s considerably before Rogers coined the term (Read, Gardner, & Mahler, 1993). In 1972, Ginott gave new articulation to the idea with his "Cardinal Principle." Since relationships grow from teachers' communication skills, then effective teacher-child communication is at the heart of the guidance approach. Ginott phrased his principle this way:

> At their best, teachers address themselves to the child's situation. At their worst, they judge his character and personality. This, in essence, is the difference between effective and ineffective communication (1972, p. 70).

This principle is also the difference between guidance and punishment.

> Cheryl spilled her juice for the second time in a week. The teacher *did not say,* "Klutzy Cheryl, you did it again. When are you going to learn to not be messy?"
>
> The teacher *did say,* "It's OK, Cheryl, we all spill, even teachers. The sponge is in the bucket. If you need help, let me know."

Labeling. The teacher above recognized that "labeling is disabling," and avoided what Ginott calls "teaching at its worst" (Ginott, 1972). Labeling children, either intentionally or unintentionally, has two broad negative effects. First, as the **self-fulfilling prophecy** suggests, children learn to see themselves in the way they are labelled. The label is incorporated into the child's self-concept and may influence future behavior. Without fortunate counter experiences that tell the child, "I'm not like that," the child's views and feelings about self may be permanently affected.

Second, the label causes adults to focus on the particular behavior they have come to expect. They fail to see other important patterns and qualities in the child. By labeling, adults limit their ability to work productively with children. Every child is greater than the sample of behavior that stands out to the teacher. So much development has yet to occur that the teacher must avoid constricting that development by labeling (Erickson & Pianta, 1989). The ability to value the child as a still developing person allows for teaching responses that the author terms *liberating*.

A key understanding about labeling is that it occurs even when the adult does not specifically "call names." A teacher scolds a child by saying that what he did was "not nice." As a result of "developmental immaturity and limited experience," the child internalizes the message as "I'm not nice" (Erickson & Pianta, 1989). As Ginott suggests the challenge is to convey to children that although the teacher is upset with what happened, he still accepts them as individuals of worth and welcome members of the group (Ginott, 1972). In other words, **teachers must select words carefully when they choose to intervene.** Assess for yourself which intervention is more supportive of the child's developing self:

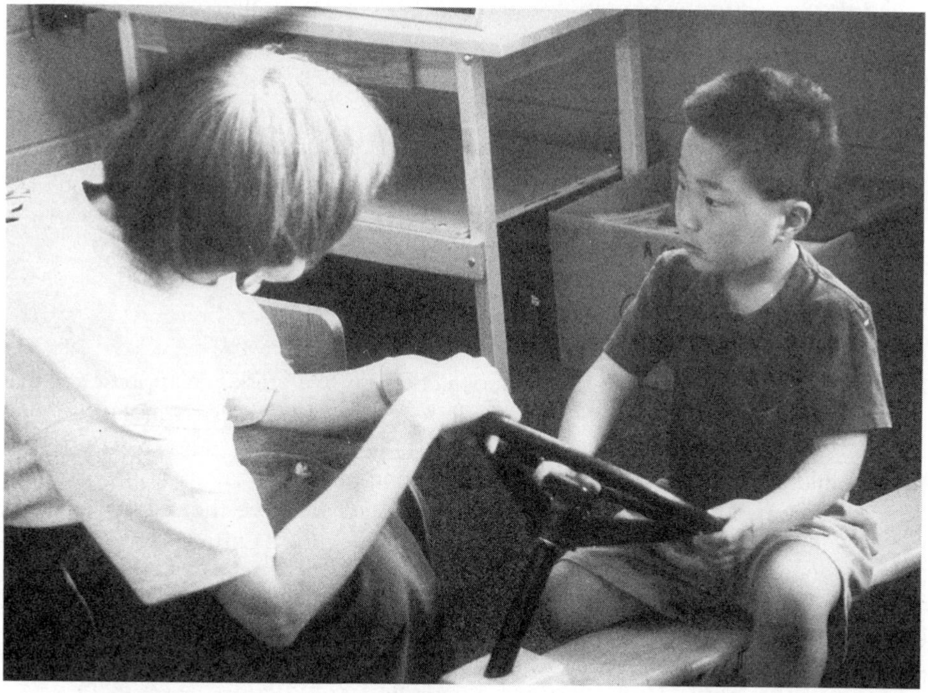

When teachers intervene, they must select their words with care.

"Kyle, you are being rowdy." "If you don't work more quietly, I will move you."	"The talking is too loud. You choose, Kyle; work quietly or find a different seat."
"Zach, don't you be lazy. You used the blocks. If you don't put them away, you won't go outside."	"Zach, all who used the blocks need to put them back. As soon as they're away, we can go out."
"Class, you are being antsy again. Story time is now over; go and take your seats."	"OK, everybody, we need a break. Let's stand up and stretch. When the music starts, let's all 'get the wiggles out.' "

After a few weeks of Head Start, a three-year-old named Jimmy began to show a strange behavior when he arrived in the morning: He began to kick the teacher in the leg! Sue, the teacher, tried an assortment of techniques none of which worked, but steadfastly refused to brand Jimmy with character references. Finally, she tried a new approach. When Jimmy first walked in the door, the teacher approached him quickly, gave him a hug and told him how happy she was to see him. After a few days of this new welcome, Jimmy would arrive, give the teacher a wide berth and say, "Hi, Teacher."

Four years later, Sue received a Christmas card from Jimmy and his mother. Written on the card were these words: "Dear Teacher, I'm havin' a nice Christmas. I hope you are. I still remember you. Do you remember me?"

Firmness Not Harshness. An erroneous criticism of a guidance approach is that it is permissive, sacrificing limits to maintain relations. In fact, positive relations with children depend on the reliability of limits, responsibly set and enforced (Hendrick, 1996). Children have the right to programming and practices that are appropriate for their development and personal backgrounds. Teachers have the responsibility to use guidelines that enable productive child activity. Ginott's Cardinal Principle illustrates that how, and not whether, teachers enforce limits is the issue.

Individual teachers have their own levels of tolerance and behavioral expectations. Such limits are the teacher's to decide. A guidance approach argues that when the teacher intervenes, he does so with appropriate firmness for the situation but without the punishing effects of being harsh. Nonpunitive intervention takes experience and understanding. The Cardinal Principle gives direction to intervention that is firm but friendly, maintains limits, but still supports the self-concept of the child.

> The teacher who uses guidance is not permissive; she does not let children struggle vis-a-vis boundaries that may not be there. Instead he provides guidance and leadership so that children can interact successfully within the reasonable boundaries of the classroom community (Gartrell, 1995, p. 27).

GUIDANCE REDUCES THE NEED FOR MISTAKEN BEHAVIOR

Because of the intrinsic dynamic within their brains and bodies, young children normally come to school ready to learn and grow. When children have trouble in the school environment, two factors tend to be involved: (1) the challenges of childhood and (2) the match between the child and the program.

The Challenges of Childhood

The first factor has to do with the challenges of childhood. All young children bring insecurities—the fear of abandonment, the fear of failure—into the early childhood classroom. These anxieties, combined with only a beginning understanding of social expectations, mean that young children make mistakes (Greenberg, 1988). Many such mistakes are the product of every day life in the classroom—not wanting to share the playdough, quarreling over a pencil—these the teacher monitors but may not prevent. Through learning to solve problems and resolve conflicts in a climate of positive regard, the child gains life-long personal and social skills (Wittmer & Honig, 1994).

The teacher does not work to prevent all problems, but neither does he manufacture additional problems. The caring teacher may pose *challenges,* but only if he believes the child has a good chance to succeed in the face of the challenges. His role is to assist children in overcoming the anxieties they feel, and come to understand social expectations (Erickson & Pianta, 1989). Anxiety levels of the children and the potential for harm are two determinants in the teacher's decision about whether and when to intervene.

A knowledge of the levels of mistaken behavior helps with guidance decisions. For example at Level One, experimentation, children are likely to argue over materials. The teacher may avoid a needless problem by providing an expanded choice of materials. Or, the teacher may help to resolve the dispute by encouraging the child to negotiate a compromise. If necessary, he redirects a child to another material.

At Level Two, social influence, a child may repeat a name used by others such as the timeless, "poopy butt." In this situation the teacher privately reinforces a guideline about name calling and teaches "nonhurting" words to use. A "class meeting" may also be called, even at the preschool level, to discuss (in terms that do not single out) the need to appreciate each other (Greenberg, 1992).

A child who frequently becomes upset over small frustrations is showing Level Three, strong needs mistaken behavior. As discussed in Chapter Two, children who show serious mistaken behavior have strong needs that they are unable to cope with on their own. The difficulties may be physical—health conditions and disabilities—and/or emotional, the effect of negative experiences and unhealthy attachments.

The teacher uses the multistep approach necessary with Level Three: reinforces limits nonpunitively, seeks more information about the child, builds a collaborative intervention strategy, and develops the relationship. The relationship helps the child develop trust in the school environment. The strategy assists the child to avoid problem situations and to express strong feelings in acceptable ways.

The job of the early childhood teacher is to be familiar with the kinds of mistakes children are likely to make, just because they are children. By preventing some problems and assisting children to resolve others, the teacher removes obstacles to the child's intrinsic construction of meaning based on successful experience (Carlsson-Paige & Levin, 1992). The discussion of children's nature and its relation to mistaken behavior is continued in Chapter 4.

The Match of the Child and the Program

A second factor in mistaken behavior lies in children's reactions to teaching practices that are not **developmentally inappropriate.** A primary cause of inappropriate practice in early childhood education is an over-reliance on teacher-direction. Pressures for a teacher-directed academic program have always existed in schools. In the last 25 years or so, these pressures have come to affect even kindergartens and preschools (Elkind, 1989; Greenberg, 1992). Willis (1993) cites several pressure points for this trend. First is the nationalistic urge to catch up with other nations perceived to have their students ahead in the "learning race"—in 1958, the Soviet Union with the launching of the first satellite, Sputnik, and now the Japanese. Second is the erroneous belief that one can teach children anything at any age. A third source of this pressure is the notion that because more children are attending preschools and watching educational television, they are ready earlier for academically oriented instruction. A fourth is the desire of some parents to have their children get an early academic advantage.

One result of these pressures is the academic preschool written about by Elkind (1989) and Greenberg (1992). In the academic preschool, teachers use a variety of reinforcements to teach the basics with little regard for individual development characteristics. Another more pervasive effect is the *escalated* or *pushed-down curriculum* in which teachers think they must accelerate instruction to prepare children for the next level of education (Willis, 1993). In general, this trend has resulted in practices that are inappropriate for young children who are not developmentally ready for conceptually oriented seat work until well into the primary years. A typical complaint as a result of this emphasis is that many, often boys with summer birthdays, are not ready for kindergarten. They show such behaviors as difficulty in attending, short attention spans, perceptual/motor difficulties, and low frustration levels (Charlesworth, 1989).

With the trend toward earlier academics, schools have urged families to start young five-year-olds a year later than usual, so they can receive "the gift of time." As well, special classes have become popular for the immature kindergarten child, sometimes called *developmental* or *junior kindergartens.* Charlesworth (1989) argues that these stopgap measures have not proven effective and support essentially erroneous pedagogical conclusions about the characteristics of young learners. Works ranging from Elkind (1989) to Bredekamp (1997) argue that programs need

A factor in reducing mistaken behavior is the relevance of the educational program to the child.

to be developmentally appropriate for all children not just for those who can sit still through formal academic programming.

Growing understanding about the importance of development in education is having an effect on how teachers interpret discipline issues. Behaviors that teachers previously regarded as immature and disruptive are now seen as an indication that programming is not appropriate for the development and learning style of a child. This new awareness shifts the responsibility for **"institution-caused"** mistaken behavior from the child to teachers and administrators.

A basic factor in reducing the need for mistaken behavior, then, is the relevance of the educational program to the child. To further healthy development, the teacher uses programming that has meaning for children and at which they can succeed. In this effort, developmental characteristics must be accommodated by appropriate curriculum and methods. Family backgrounds must be affirmed by culturally responsive teaching practices. As a professional, the teacher works with colleagues to improve the acceptance of these ideas in the center or school (Bredekamp, 1997).

Within the classroom, the teacher designs and implements programming in line with accepted guidelines for appropriate and responsive practice. He monitors, and on occasion more formally assesses, the match between the needs and backgrounds of the children and the educational program. Deviations from expectations mean that revision may be necessary to improve the match (Hendrick, 1996). Modification of the program to improve learner-engagement is at the heart of reducing much mistaken behavior (Bredekamp, 1997). The anecdotes that follow illustrate how two teachers fine tuned music activities to respond more appropriately to the developmental and cultural needs of their children.

(Improving the developmental match with rhythm instruments) A kindergarten teacher was working for the first time with rhythm instruments. He held up the various instruments—tambourine, triangle, rhythm sticks, bells, blocks—and asked who wanted to use each. Many hands shot up for the "exotic" instruments; not many for the rhythm sticks. He observed that some children were crestfallen when they didn't get the choices they wanted, and others pressured those near them to trade.

After several minutes of stock market maneuvers, the teacher got the activity explained: He would start the cassette tape, call out the name of an instrument, and just that group would play. Unexpectedly, the children made rhythms at will, without much sense of either the beat or the instrument group called. The teacher saw that some adjustments were needed.

For the next two weeks during choice time, the music center materials included a set of each rhythm instrument. The children used the instruments each day while they listened to music on their headphones. After the two weeks of exploration, the teacher resumed the large group rhythm activity but with an expanded supply of instruments borrowed from another classroom. The rhythm band quickly improved its skills.

(Improving cultural responsiveness with rhythm sticks) A teacher had been working with preschoolers using rhythm sticks for a few weeks when two Native American (Ojibwe) children joined the program. The teacher told D.J. and Cheyenne that they could participate with the group or sit and watch. The two boys watched, then noticed two extra sticks on a chair behind the teacher. They each picked up a stick, cupped one ear, and began drumming the sticks on the chair to the music. The teacher became upset, took the sticks, and told them to sit quietly for the rest of the activity.

Afterwards, a teacher aide who was also Ojibwe explained that the children were using the sticks as their older relatives did, to "beat the drum and sing like at a pow-wow." Embarrassed, the teacher asked the aide's help to organize a pow-wow for the preschool, which included two boys' relatives as singers. D.J. and Cheyenne were proud to sit with the singers and dance with the rest of the class.

The teacher reduces the need for mistaken behavior by using practices that are developmentally appropriate and culturally responsive (Bredekamp, 1997).

GUIDANCE TAKES A SOLUTION-ORIENTATION

Referring to child-rearing practices of the past, Berger states:

> Except for a few dissenters . . . most people were much more interested in disciplining children to keep them from becoming sinners or degenerates than in nurturing them so that they would preserve their natural curiosity and enthusiasm (1989).

Only in the twentieth century has empathy for the condition of childhood become a broad-based social value (deMause, 1974; Osborn, 1980). The understanding that children show mistaken behavior out of developmental immaturity and unmet basic needs is a distressingly recent occurrence.

A guidance view of discipline holds that children should not be punished for having problems, but they should be assisted in developing the life skills necessary to solve their problems (Gartrell, 1995; Honig & Wittmer, 1996). Rather than reinforce the labeling of children as good or bad, model students or rowdy, guidance is about helping all children to get along, solve problems, and express strong feelings in acceptable ways.

Even young children are put into situations where they must make moral decisions. This ability cannot be built through punitive discipline. Only a guidance approach empowers children to build the self-control *and* self-acceptance necessary to say yes or no "because it is the right thing to do" (Gartrell, 1997; Wittmer, & Honig, 1994). Rather than moralistic in tone, guidance is interactive. Guidance requires positive leadership. It requires teachers to make firm decisions. The decisions need to model ethical considerations, however, and be based not on an infallible sense of authority but on an understanding of young children and their needs. The NAEYC *Code of Ethics* (1989) provides invaluable guidance in the use of the teacher's authority. (See Appendix A.)

Conflict Management

In the guidance approach, the adult teaches techniques for *conflict management* as an ongoing part of the education program. Conflict management skills are critical in a democracy, but the widespread notion that children are incapable of solving their disputes peaceably is only now beginning to change. In 1984, Kreidler's landmark work, *Creative Conflict Resolution: More than 200 Activities for Keeping Peace in the Classroom,* provided a practical guide for a caring community in which children learn the skills of responding to conflict creatively. His text has been followed by many including in the early childhood field writings by Wichert (1989), Carlsson-Paige & Levin (1992), Levin (1994), and Slaby, Roedell, Arezzo, and Hendrix (the NAEYC publication, *Early Violence Prevention,* 1995). These writings demonstrate how even preschool children can be empowered to peaceably resolve disputes.

Although not the most recent work, Wichert's *Keeping the Peace: Practicing Cooperation and Conflict Resolution with Preschoolers* provides a usable construct for teaching young children to mediate their own problems. In Wichert's schema, children operate at one of three skill levels to resolve classroom difficulties. At *high adult intervention,* the teacher actively assists children to calm children, focus on the problem, and move toward resolution (Wichert, 1989). In *minimal adult intervention,* "children define the problem using their own language and the adult merely clarifies when needed" (Wichert, 1989, p. 56). At the level of *negotiation children take charge,* removing themselves from the situation to discuss and solve the problem (Wichert, 1989).

A preschool in northern Minnesota set up *talk-and-listen chairs* for the resolution of conflicts. At the beginning of the year when two four-year-olds were having an argument, a teacher would accompany them to the chairs. She would mediate while the children took turns talking, exchanging chairs, and listening until the difference was resolved. By spring, the use of the chairs was routine, and the children went to them on their own. Views differ on the practice of having children leave the place of activity to resolve difficulties in a formal fashion. The prospect of using the chairs is often an incentive toward resolution in itself. Talk-and-listen chairs provide an example of a conflict management technique and illustrate the direction of Wichert's strategy—from high adult intervention to children taking charge.

The Teacher as Democratic Leader

If conflict management is to be used successfully, then adults must be sure about their role in the classroom. In distinguishing the democratic classroom from the autocratic, Dreikurs characterized the teacher as a leader winning cooperation in the one and a boss demanding cooperation in the other. In the autocratic classroom, the teacher takes sole responsibility for transactions and takes the position, "I decide,

Frequently, the teacher waits to see whether children can resolve a difficulty on their own.

you obey." In contrast, the teacher in the democratic classroom is more like a manager or coach who shares responsibility with the team (Dreikurs, 1972).

Student teachers sometimes find difficulty in assuming the leadership that is required in the teacher's role. Out of concern for children's feelings, they confuse leadership with dictatorship (Hendrick, 1996). A teacher can be a friend to children, but the relationship must be that of an adult friend to a child. Even democracies need strong leaders.

In the democratic classroom, the teacher creates a climate of mutual respect. Children reciprocate this feeling when they are empowered to make choices on their own and decisions with others (Hendrick, 1996; Wittmer & Honig, 1994). This is but one reason that play, or self-selected work time, is important in the daily schedule. Play not only gives children the freedom to make mistakes and experience disagreements but also the opportunity to resolve these difficulties as well. The teacher knows he is using conflict management well when children spontaneously use the communication skills on their own.

Crisis Intervention

Young children are just beginning to understand the complexities of social situations, and they feel emotions strongly. Even under the best of circumstances they will not always resolve problems with words. On occasion they need to be rescued from their own behavior. The test of guidance is when the adult must physically intervene to prevent harm. Although early intervention to head off a crisis is preferable, it is not always possible (Hendrick, 1996). When communication has broken down and physical or psychological harm is possible, the teacher must act.

In guidance, physical intervention is limited to *passive restraint* and brief periods of supervised removal; these are methods of last resort when a danger of harm or serious disruption exists. If a time-out chair or other crisis intervention practices are used *often,* teachers need to review their approach because (a) the techniques are not working, and (b) the atmosphere may be becoming more punitive than is desired (Clewett, 1988). When the teacher does restrain or remove a child, after feelings have cooled he explains why the behavior compelled the intervention and how the child might respond differently next time. The teacher then assists the child to make restitution and reenter the group. A point of distinction in a guidance approach is that after intervention the teacher works for **reconciliation** and helps the child to regain self-esteem (Gartrell, 1997).

Learning While Teaching

In 1977, Kounin wrote about "withitness" to describe a teacher's ability to identify those key situations in the classroom that need to be addressed. Discussed in Charles (1996), the term has become a staple in the literature of classroom management. From this classroom research, Kounin concluded that effective teachers—the ones with "eyes in the back of their heads"—have withitness; ineffective teachers do not (Kounin, 1977).

Withitness, like other teaching skills, takes time to master, and even experienced teachers can be fooled. When teachers recognize that becoming fully informed is the goal but that they must often act on less than complete information, then withitness is put in its proper perspective. When teachers miscalculate a situation, then a sensible practice is to recognize both their fallibility and their potential to learn, and go on from there (Hendrick, 1996). In current terminology, teachers who have the ability to learn from their mistakes are proactive rather than reactive, professionals rather than technicians (Duff, Brown, & Van Scoy, 1995).

A circus was set up in a large room of a day care center. Different activities were occurring in various parts of the room, including a very popular cotton candy concession. Brian, age five, was standing in line when he was pushed from in front. He accidentally bumped against a three-year-old who fell down and was hurt. A teacher arrived on the scene, looked over the situation, and told Brian to go to the end of the line for pushing. A few minutes later the teacher noticed that Brian was crying. A student teacher who had seen the incident explained what had happened. The teacher helped Brian get his place back in line, happily the next one to receive a wand of cotton candy.

Teachers often have difficulty knowing exactly what happened in a situation and how to intervene. These skills take continuing practice. An important guideline is that anytime a teacher can act more like a mediator in a courtroom and less like a police officer on the street, he is working to understand the situation. Quick judgments sometimes are necessary, but a more positive resolution may come about if the teacher delays action to gather information and collect his thoughts (Hendrick, 1996).

> In a Minneapolis kindergarten, Shad, a child who rarely initiated conversations, was using a truck during a choice time. The teacher did not see exactly what happened but heard Shad crying and saw Sharon pushing the truck to another part of the room. The teacher was tempted to confront Sharon, who was looking over her shoulder, but went first to Shad and quietly talked with him. When the teacher got up and walked to where Sharon was, the five-year-old did not argue that she had the truck first. Instead Sharon said, "I didn't mean to." This response allowed the teacher to assist Sharon to make amends.

A task of the professional teacher is to develop techniques for anticipating situations that may require intervention. Another important task is to be as familiar as possible with the child in the situation. A teacher cannot always learn what is bothering a child, but the attempt to learn is likely to yield positive results. First, the teacher gains new information that may increase understanding about the child. Second, the *effort* to gain new information tends to improve the teacher-child relationship. From a modification in relations, the child may come to see school in a different light.

Accepting Our Humanness

Teachers need to monitor their own feelings to retain consistency in their communications with children (Hendrick, 1996). They watch out for their own Level Three days.

> After a night of little sleep, due to teething by an infant and a spouse out of town, a teacher (who also happened to have a sinus headache) modified plans about the intensity of activities. This became a day for more reliance on coworkers, soft-pedaling of expectations for the group, and increased use of educational videos and self-defining activities. The day proved long but not as long as it might have been. The spouse returned that evening, and the infant felt better.

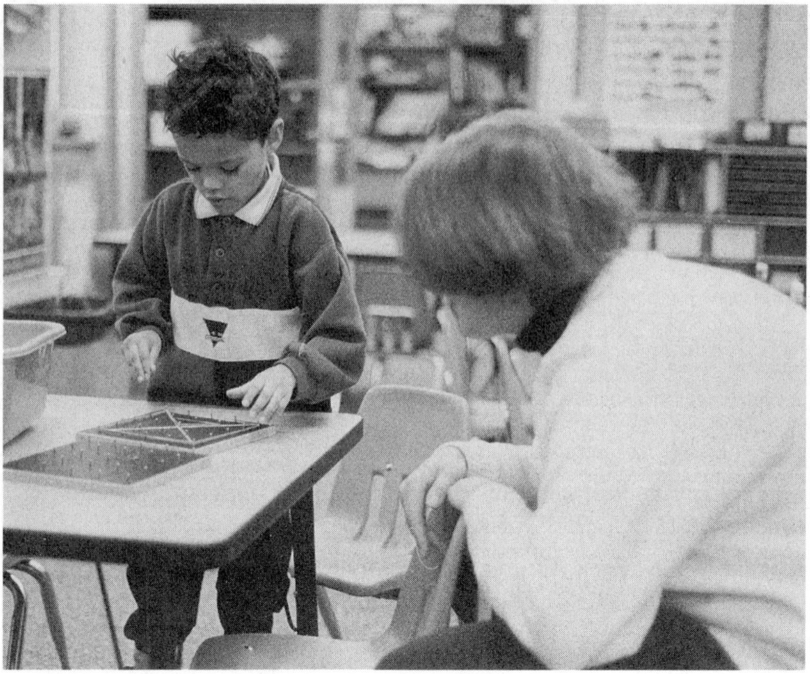

The teacher gains new information that assists in understanding behavior and building relations.

Often when teachers are affected by personal circumstances, they let the class know. In a caring classroom even three-year-olds will make an effort to "help teacher feel better." (Teachers report, however, that this practice loses its effectiveness if used on a daily basis.) Teachers who keep a list of strategies and activities to help them through physically or emotionally rough days have shown understanding about their importance in the lives of young children.

Despite the best of intentions and because they are human, teachers too make mistakes. They may misinterpret situations, overreact to a child, be punitive toward a group, or be unprofessional to an adult. Use of a guidance approach does not presume teaching perfection. Mastering the problem-solving orientation is a long process. In guidance, a teacher has a right to make mistakes, but what is important is that he learns from them. The professional teacher learns even while teaching.

GUIDANCE MEANS TEAMWORK WITH OTHER ADULTS

A myth that still afflicts education is that the teacher handles all situations alone. Perhaps the myth goes back to the one room schools of rural America's past and the expectations upon the teachers who taught in them. Many adults wanted no part of the teachers' job, which was seen as making unruly, undisciplined youth sit obediently and master the three Rs. Depending on their demeanor and perceived success, teachers were revered as saintly, like the first Montessori directresses in the tenements of Rome; respected for their iron discipline, like the school masters of British boarding schools; or made the butt of jokes, like the fabled Ichabod Crane. In any case, the adult community expected teachers to sink or swim on their own with minimal support from administrators, other teachers, or parents.

A remnant of the myth of the self-sufficient teacher still can be seen in relation to the first year of teaching. Some administrators remain oriented more to performance reviews than mentoring relationships. Happily, this trend is beginning to change. Early childhood educators are among those who have pointed out the need for new teachers to be eased into the profession by working with mentors. A new consciousness about the importance of family and community involvement for educational success is further indication that the myth of teacher as "supermarm" may be coming to an end.

Team Teaching

There is **team-teaching** and then there is the **teaching team.** The two concepts are different. **Team-teaching** is the practice, mainly at the K-12 level, of having two similarly licensed teachers working together with the same group of children. Thornton (1990) provides a useful account of the problems and promise when two teachers work together. For Thornton, mutual trust is a prime ingredient and this quality takes hard work, communication, and time.

When the relationship is established, the benefits are many. Cooperative planning, implementation, and evaluation of the program take pressure off each individual. Through teamwork, developmentally appropriate, active learning experiences are easier to initiate. The choice of two personalities with whom to relate can be empowering both for the children and for their parents (Thornton, 1990). By virtue of their differing personalities, two teachers can respond more effectively to the wide array of learning and behavioral styles represented in any group of young children. When team-teaching is working, each member has a built-in support system.

The Teaching Team

The technical name for the teaching team is differentiated staffing, or the use of adults with differing credentials and experience bases to serve the same group of children. The traditional teaching team format is the teacher and the paraprofessional ("para" or "aide"). In actuality, classroom volunteers as well as staff can comprise the team. In modern educational settings, a teacher may work with volunteers, paraprofessionals, Title I teachers, special education teachers, and other specialists, all in the same class—a comprehensive staffing arrangement to be sure.

When a para and teacher work together as a team, the teacher provides supervision for the learning environment, but the para works with small groups, individual children, and on occasion with the full group. In other words the para also teaches. Conversely, if the situation warrants, the teacher may wipe up a spill or help a child change clothes (Read, Gardner, & Mahler, 1993).

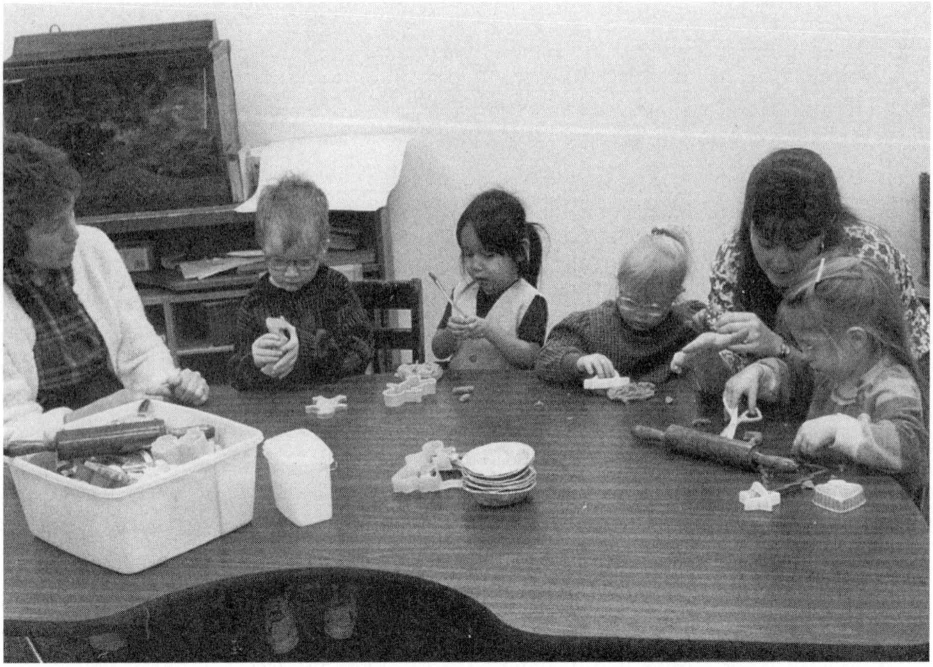

When the teaching team concept is used, children and adults benefit.

In classrooms where a strict separation of professional and paraprofessional roles is maintained, the general assumption is that only the teacher does the teaching. Despite appearances, this view is incorrect. In reality, all adults in a classroom serve as models for young children, and so all are teachers. The adult who accepts this premise accepts the concept of the teaching team.

The advantages of the teaching team are similar to those of team-teaching, but the teaching team goes further in its model of democracy. When children see adults in differing social roles converse and work together, they learn that social and cultural differences need not be threatening. The teacher-parent relationship is the most direct example and offers the most benefit to the child. Nonetheless, when a teacher and aide work together amicably, the child's expanding social world becomes that much more reliable and friendly. The children are likely to follow the lead of the teacher and feel respect for all the adults in the classroom.

When the efforts of the aide are appreciated, he feels affirmed. Negative feelings that result from being "stigmatized" (disqualified from full membership in the group) do not arise. Disagreements do not become conflicts but get resolved. Like children, assistants who feel accepted participate fully (Read, Gardner, & Mahler, 1993).

Of course, not all paras are prepared to function as "associate teachers" on the team. Using the criteria of state regulations, program policy, and personal readiness, the teacher, as team leader, determines how much responsibility other team members are to be given. Unpressured discussion about roles, along with ongoing communication about duties, are important to make teaming work.

Over the last 25 years, a variety of terms have been used to describe teaching team members. The terms usually reflect the educational programs completed by the member and the roles defined by the program or district. Such terms as *volunteer, paraprofessional, teacher-aide, teacher assistant, associate teacher, Child Development Associate, teacher, lead teacher, center supervisor,* and *early childhood educator* illustrate the complexity of the mix of roles. In 1994, the National Association for the Education of Young Children (NAEYC) issued a position statement titled, "A Conceptual Framework for Early Childhood Professional Development," which is helping to clarify the role definitions for both programs and educational institutions. The point of the teaching team is that it is comprised of adults from various roles and backgrounds working together, with mutually respectful communication and trust. The positive atmosphere in such classrooms radiates to the children.

The Teaching Team in the Primary Grades. On the surface, the teaching team concept seems to have less relevance to K-3 classrooms. In most schools the system is set: one teacher, twenty to thirty-five children. When an aide or para is present, it is usually for a small part of the day. The aide likely has "para-professional" duties specified in the "master contract."

Primary grade teachers who wish to incorporate a team concept into their classrooms sometimes have limited options, but it is happening. The growing practice of **inclusion,** or broad-scale integration of children with disabilities in the "regular" classroom, is advancing the teaching team concept. Some teachers recruit parents, college students, or senior citizens to come into classrooms on a regular basis. These volunteers read to children, supervise learning situations, work with small groups, or otherwise lend their experience. In a growing number of schools, students from the upper grades assist in prekindergarten, kindergarten, and primary classrooms. Where such efforts are organized and supervised, programs run smoothly, and both older and younger children benefit.

Teacher as Team Leader. With the use of a teaching team, the teacher's role changes. He no longer undertakes all teaching transactions. Instead, he manages an active learning laboratory, teaching and modeling continuously, but also supervising others who are helping. Informally, the new role approaches that of the "early childhood educator" written about by Almy in 1975. It is an uncomfortable role for many new teachers just entering the profession and for others, steeped in the traditional notion of what a teacher does.

We are still learning about the teacher's role in the differentiated staffing situation, and about the effects of the teaching team for the classroom and children's behavior. In some ways the role poses additional new tasks for teachers. In others it offers new freedoms and possibilities—in particular the ability to reach children who in the old system might have passed through unaided. Here is the connection with guidance discipline. With more adults in the classroom on a regular basis, the chances for positive relations with adults increases, and the need for mistaken behavior diminishes.

Working with Other Professionals. Besides team members in the classroom, the teacher communicates with other professionals: administrators and specialists in the

The growing practice of inclusion is advancing the teaching team concept.

program or school; specialists from other agencies. As Kagan and Rivera point out (1991), the "buzzword" for such communication is **collaboration.** The word is a useful one if it has the meaning the authors intend:

> We have defined collaborations as those efforts that unite and empower individuals and organizations to accomplish collectively what they could not accomplish independently (Kagan & Rivera, 1991, p. 52).

In early childhood settings, collaborations typically revolve around two criteria: (a) specifics of the program itself—resources, scheduling, content, methods; and (b) matters pertaining to the children in the class. When children show serious mistaken behavior, collaboration is often required. Information exchanges within the school or center, professionally done, assist the teacher to better understand the child and the situation. As Hendrick points out, however, discussions involving formal diagnosis or possible referral should not be effected between professionals by themselves (1996). Professional ethics, and often statute and policy, warrant the involvement of parents. (See NAEYC Code of Ethics, Appendix A.)

When parents, the teacher, and other professionals meet for a possible referral or special services, the teacher assists the collaboration by remaining sensitive to the discomfort that many parents feel in the presence of professionals. Such collaborations are strengthened when representatives of all concerned programs participate, such as day care staff with the kindergarten teacher, or Head Start personnel with early childhood special education teachers. The promise of collaboration is that the process allows for a comprehensive and unified plan that can assist a troubled child. The use of the teaching team makes many of the ideas in this book work more easily for the guidance teacher.

Head Start
"Oh, yes, Joanie's parents—I recognized you from her drawings!"
Ray Morin

Joanie's Parents (Courtesy of Mrs. Ray Morin)

GUIDANCE MEANS PARTNERSHIPS WITH PARENTS

In a rural community in Minnesota, a principal informed a long time third grade teacher that she was assigned to a first grade class the next fall. The teacher requested that she be allowed to invite parents into the class to help with activities. The principal reluctantly agreed but told the teacher the idea would never work.

By the end of mid-October, the teacher had seventy-five percent of the parents, including many working parents, coming into class on a regular basis. By December, the teacher reported that every parent had been into the classroom at least once. The principal responded warmly. She said she was sold on the idea the day a substitute had taught in the first grade and offered this reaction: Between the parents and the children, the classroom ran itself.

In a commentary in the NAEYC journal, *Young Children,* Greenberg discusses roadblocks to effective parent-teacher relations, including the issues of gender bias, racism, and classism (1989). Greenberg develops the argument that as the century progressed, schools grew more "professional," and parents became less welcome in them—especially parents from cultural and income backgrounds different than school personnel. Moreover, the administrative structure of schools became male-dominated, making communication difficult for single parents, most of whom are women, and for the women teachers of young children (1989). Greenberg defines the resulting problem this way:

> If, when they were children, parents had a great many frustrations and failure experiences in school, they may not like schools very much. This feeling can be contagious to their children. It can be true in any family. It seems to be particularly true of low-income minority families, though of course it's by no means always so. In this case, many children feel they have to choose to spurn the family and throw themselves into succeeding at school, or to spurn school success to win family approval. This is a tough spot to put a young child in! Children who have to buck school to avoid disapproval at home are often big-time discipline problems.

In further response to this issue, Greenberg concludes:

> Conversely, children whose parents expect them to cooperate and to do their best at school, and who are proud when they do, tend to have better self-discipline. [The children] are striving to achieve family approval; to do this they must earn the teacher's approval. Encouraging a high degree of family enthusiasm for their children's public schools and child care centers is one of the best ways in which teachers can . . . build children's self-esteem and reduce discipline problems. . . . (pp. 61–62).

For the reasons mentioned by Greenberg, partnerships with parents are integral to a teacher's use of guidance. Building such relations requires teachers to put aside biases and focus on what they and parents have in common, the well-being of the child (Brand, 1996; Kasting, 1994; see recommended resources). Exceptional teachers always have gone out of their way to make parents feel welcome and esteemed. Authorities in the field make the point that the responsibility to reach even hard-to-reach parents lies with the teacher (Galinsky, 1988; Greenberg, 1989; Gestwicki, 1992).

Whatever the existing practices of a school or center toward collaboration with parents, the teacher does well to note two generally accepted ideas in early childhood about parents:

- There is no more important profession for which there is so little preparation as being a parent.
- Parents are the primary educators of their children; teachers only help.

Writers such as Brand (1996) and Kasting (1994) are now answering Greenberg's call for prospective teachers to have more preparation in working with parents and for administrators to give more attention to parent-teacher relations. The child is an extension of the family unit. The teacher who knows and works with the family will be more successful in guiding the development of the child.

Awareness of the importance of parent involvement in their children's education is growing in the society. Despite busy schedules, many parents are willing to become involved. They need invitations, choices regarding their involvement, and support from the teacher. With increased parent participation, children learn they are supported at home and at school. The need for mistaken behavior then becomes less.

SUMMARY

How are positive teacher-child relations the basis of the guidance approach?

As a professional, the teacher works to accept each child as a welcome member of the group. This *unconditional positive regard* does not mean that the teacher is permissive, but that he separates the mistaken behaviors a child may show from the personality of the child—addressing the behaviors while affirming personal worth. The teacher avoids singling children out either for criticism or praise. He offers private, individual encouragement, or encouragement that is public but group-focused. To maintain positive relations, the teacher practices the *Cardinal Principle,* avoids labels, is firm but friendly, and practices liberation teaching. Children who feel accepted as individuals and members of the group have less need for mistaken behavior. The teacher works to include all children as class members "in good standing." This is the essence of the encouraging classroom.

How does guidance reduce the need for mistaken behavior?

The teacher recognizes that when children have trouble in the school environment, two factors tend to be involved. First are the challenges of childhood. The teacher accepts the fact that young children come to school eager to learn, but in the process of learning they make mistakes. The teacher assists children to learn from mistakes more effectively when he understands the three levels of mistaken behavior.

A second factor lies in children's reactions when teaching practices are not developmentally appropriate. The teacher improves the match by using developmentally appropriate and culturally responsive teaching practices. When their motivations, needs, and family backgrounds become the driving force for the educational program, children do not become passive, bored, or frustrated; they become active, involved, and successful.

What does "guidance is solution-oriented" mean?

The teacher creates an environment in which problems can be resolved. He does so by teaching and modeling conflict-management skills. He does so as well by modeling democratic leadership skills. The teacher is a friend to children, but he is an adult friend to a child. He intervenes nonpunitively, using removal and passive restraint only as methods of last resort when communication has broken down and harm is a possibility. After direct intervention, the teacher assists the child in reconciling with the group and salvages the child's self-esteem.

The teacher learns even while teaching. He practices such skills as withitness but recognizes that teachers usually do not know all that has happened in a situation. The teacher improves chances for problem resolution to the extent that he can act more as a mediator and less as a police officer. Not every situation will be successfully resolved, of course, and teachers will at times show human frailties. Being models to children, teachers as professionals must recognize their mistakes and learn from them.

Why is teamwork with staff and other professionals part of guidance?

Children benefit from positive relations with all adults who may be in the classroom. Effective communication among adults allows for comprehensive strategies for working with mistaken behavior. For these two reasons, the myth that the teacher handles all situations alone needs to end. In the guidance approach, the teacher moves toward a teaching team model in the classroom and involves fellow staff and volunteers of diverse backgrounds to provide responsive programming. Children gain a sense of reliability in their expanding social worlds when they see adults of different backgrounds working together amicably. They gain in esteem and understanding from increased individual attention.

The teacher collaborates with other professionals: administrators and specialists in the center or school as well as specialists in other agencies. When such collaboration involves diagnosis of children's behavior or possible referral, the teacher involves parents as partners in the collaborative process. Through collaboration, adults can accomplish together what they might not be able to do alone.

How are parent-teacher partnerships important in the guidance approach?

The teacher recognizes that being a parent is a difficult job and that many parents, for personal and cultural reasons, feel discomfort in communicating with educators. The teacher's job is to initiate relations even with hard-to-reach parents. Although busy, many parents respond positively to invitations to become involved in their children's education. The need for mistaken behavior diminishes when parents and teachers work together.

FOLLOW-UP ACTIVITIES

Note: In completing follow-up activities, the privacy of all involved is to be respected.

Reflection Activity

The reflection activity encourages students to interrelate their own thoughts and experiences with specific ideas from the chapter.

Identify the guidance principle (listed at the beginning of the chapter) that is the most important to you in your professional development. Relate the principle to an experience of yours as a student either before entering your teacher preparation program or since. Why is this experience important to you?

Application Activities

Application activities allow students to interrelate material from the text with real life situations. The observations imply access to practicum experiences; the interviews, access to teachers or parents. Students may compare or contrast observations and interviews with referenced ideas from the chapter.

1. **How are positive teacher-child relations the basis of the guidance approach?**
   a. Observe an instance in which a teacher affirmed positive regard for a child. What did the teacher say and do? What did the child say and do? How do you think the child's behavior might be influenced by such an exchange?
   b. Talk with a teacher about a sensitive topic: Explain that your textbook says that teachers do not always have natural positive feelings towards every child. Ask the teacher how he builds relationships with children who are "more difficult to like or understand."
2. **How does guidance reduce the need for mistaken behavior?**
   a. Observe an instance when a teacher acted to "head off" or resolve a problem in a firm but friendly manner. Think about what level of mistaken behavior was at work. Reflect about how the teacher showed understanding of the child or children involved.
   b. Observe an activity that seemed a "good match" between the levels of development of the children and what the activity asked the children to do. Discuss the amount of productive behavior and/or mistaken behavior you observed in the activity.
   c. Ask a teacher to discuss a change he has made to the curriculum or schedule to improve the match between the needs of the children and

the expectations of the program. How did the change make the day "go better" for the children, and for the teacher?

3. **What does "guidance is solution-oriented" mean?**
   a. Observe an instance when a teacher assisted children to resolve a problem. What did the teacher say and do? How did the children react? What do you think they learned from the experience?
   b. Ask a teacher to recall an instance when he assisted children to resolve a behavior problem. Ask the teacher his feelings about the experience. What would the teacher do differently or the same if a similar situation were to arise again?
4. **Why is teamwork with staff and other professionals part of guidance?**
   a. Observe a productive teaching team in operation. Note the kinds of communication that occur between the team members, verbal and nonverbal. What seems to characterize the communication you have observed?
   b. Interview a lead teacher and/or another member of a teaching team. Ask what is important to each in maintaining positive relations between the adults and a positive atmosphere in the classroom.
5. **How are parent-teacher partnerships important in the guidance approach?**
   a. Observe a classroom in which parents are participating as volunteers. What actions on the part of the teacher(s) seem to help the parents feel welcome. How are the parents participating?
   b. Interview a parent who is actively involved in a program. Ask how the parent's involvement has affected the parent and the child.

RECOMMENDED RESOURCES

Brand, S. (1996). Making parent involvement a reality: Helping teachers develop partnerships with parents. *Young Children, 51*(2), 76–81.

Carlsson-Paige, N., & Levin, D. E. (1992). Making peace in violent times: A constructivist approach to conflict resolution. *Young Children, 48*(1), 4–13.

Kasting, A. (1994). Respect, responsibility, and reciprocity: The 3Rs of parent involvement. *Childhood Education, 70*(3), 146–150.

Kosnik, C. (1993). Everyone is a V.I.P. in this class. *Young Children, 49*(1), 32–37.

National Association for the Education of Young Children (1989). *The National Association for the Education of Young Children code of ethical conduct.* Washington, DC: Author. (Included as Appendix A.)

Thornton, J. R. (1990). Team teaching: A relationship based on trust and communication. *Young Children, 45*(5), 40–42.

Weber-Schwartz, N. (1987). Patience or understanding. *Young Children, 42*(3), 52–54.

Wittmer, D. S., & Honig, A. S. (1994). Encouraging positive social development in young children. *Young Children, 49*(5), 4–12.

REFERENCES

Almy, M. (1975). *The early childhood educator at work.* New York: McGraw Hill Book Company.

Berger, S. K. (1986). *The developing person through childhood and adolescence.* New York: Worth Publishers, Inc.

Brand, S. (1996). Making parent involvement a reality: Helping teachers develop partnerships with parents. *Young Children, 51*(2), 76–81.

Bredekamp, S. (1997). *Developmentally appropriate practice in early childhood programs* (3rd ed.). Washington, DC: National Association for the Education of Young Children.

Carlsson-Paige, N., & Levin, D. E. (1992). Making peace in violent times: A constructivist approach to conflict resolution. *Young Children, 48*(1), 4–13.

Charles, C. M. (1996). *Building classroom discipline.* White Plains, NY: Longman, Inc.

Charlesworth, R. (1989). 'Behind' before they start? Deciding how to deal with the risk of kindergarten 'failure'. *Young Children, 44*(3), 5–13.

Clewett, A. S. (1988). Guidance and discipline: Teaching young children appropriate behavior. *Young Children, 43*(4), 26–31.

Curwin, R. L., & Mendler, A. N. (1988). *Discipline with dignity.* Alexandria, VA: Association for Supervision and Curriculum Development.

Daniel, J. E. (1993). Infants to toddlers: Qualities of effective transitions. *Young Children, 48*(6), 16–21.

de Mause, L., ed. (1974). *The history of childhood.* New York: Peter Bedrick Books.

Dreikurs, R. (1972). *Discipline without tears.* New York: Hawthorn Press Books, Inc., Publishers.

Duff, R. E., Brown, M. H., & Van Scoy, I. J. (1995). Reflection and self-evaluation: Keys to professional development. *Young Children, 50*(4), 81–88.

Edson, A. (1994). Crossing the great divide: The nursery school child goes to kindergarten. *Young Children, 49*(5), 69–75.

Elkind, D. (1987). *Miseducation: Children at risk.* New York: Alfred A. Knopf.

Erickson, M. F., & Pianta, R. C. (1989). New lunch box, old feelings: What kids bring to school. *Early Education and Development, 1*(1), 35–49.

Galinsky, E. (1988). Parents and teacher-caregivers: Sources of tension, sources of support. *Young Children, 43*(4), 4–12.

Gartrell, D. J. (1995). Misbehavior or mistaken behavior? *Young Children, 50*(5), 27–34.

Gartrell, D. J. (1997, September). Beyond discipline to guidance. *Young Children.*

Gestwicki, C. (1992). *Home, school, and community relations.* Albany, NY: Delmar Publishers.

Ginott, H. G. (1972). *Teacher and child.* New York: Avon Books.

Girard, K., & Koch, S. J. (1996). *Conflict resolution in the schools: A manual for educators.* San Francisco: Jossey-Bass Publishers.

Greenberg, P. (1989). Parents as partners in young children's development and education: A new American fad? Why does it matter? *Young Children, 44*(4), 61–75.

Greenberg, P. (1988). Avoiding 'Me against you' discipline. *Young Children, 43*(1), 24–31.

Greenberg, P. (1992). Why not academic preschool? Part 2. Autocracy or democracy in the classroom. *Young Children, 47*(3), 54–64.

Hendrick, J. (1996). *Whole child.* Columbus, OH: Merrill/McMillan.

Hitz, R., & Driscoll, A. (1988). Praise or encouragement? *Young Children, 47*(3), 6–13.

Honig, A. S., & Wittmer, D. S. (1996). Helping children become more pro social: Ideas for classrooms, families, schools, and communities, Part 2. *Young Children, 51*(2), 62–70.

Jones, F. H. (1993). *Instructor's guide: Positive classroom discipline.* Santa Cruz, CA: Fredric H. Jones & Associates.

Kagan, S. L., & Rivera, A. M. (1991). Collaboration in early care and education: What can and should we expect? *Young Children, 46*(1), 51–56.

Kasting, A. (1994). Respect, responsibility, and reciprocity: The 3Rs of parent involvement. *Childhood Education, 70*(3), 146–150.

Katz, L. G. (1980). Mothering and teaching—Some significant distinctions. L. G. Katz (Ed.). *Current Topics in Early Childhood Education.* Norwood, NJ: Ablex Publishing Corp.

Kohn, A. (1993). *Punished by rewards.* New York: Houghton Mifflin.

Kounin, J. (1977). *Discipline and group management in classrooms.* New York: Holt, Rinehart and Winston.

Kreidler, W. J. (1984). *Creative conflict resolution: More than 200 activities for keeping peace in the classroom.* Glencoe, IL: Scott, Foresman.

Levin, D. E. (1994). *Teaching children in violent times: Building a peaceable classroom.* Cambridge, MA: Educators for Social Responsibility.

National Association for the Education of Young Children (1989). *The National Association for the Education of Young Children code of ethical conduct.* Washington, DC: Author.

Osborn, D. K., & Osborn, J. D. (1989). *Discipline and classroom management.* Athens, GA: Daye Press, Inc.

Read, K. H., Gardner, P., & Mahler, B. C. (1993). *Early childhood programs: Human relationships and learning.* Fort Worth, TX: Harcourt Brace Jovanovitch College Publishers.

Slaby, R. G., Roedell, W. C., Arezzo, D., & Hendrix, K. (1995). *Early violence prevention: Tools for teachers of young children.* Washington, DC: National Association for the Education of Young Children.

Thornton, J. R. (1990). Team teaching: A relationship based on trust and communication. *Young Children, 45*(5), 40–42.

Warren, R. (1977). *Caring.* Washington, DC: National Association for the Education of Young Children.

Weber-Schwartz, N. (1987). Patience or understanding. *Young Children, 42*(3), 52–54.

Wichert, S. (1989). *Keeping the peace: Practicing cooperation and conflict resolution with preschoolers.* Santa Cruz, CA: New Society Publishers.

Willis, S. (1993, November). Teaching young children: Educators seek 'developmental appropriateness'. *Curriculum Update,* 1–8.

Wittmer, D. S., & Honig, A. S. (1994). Encouraging positive social development in young children. *Young Children, 49*(5), 4–12.

Unit Two

Building the Encouraging Classroom

CHAPTER SUMMARY

4 Creating a Climate for the Encouraging Classroom

Chapter 4 examines considerations in creating a climate for the encouraging classroom: (a) The teacher is a professional, not a technician; (b) a learning dynamic is intrinsic to the child; (c) developmentally appropriate practice defines the nature of teacher-child relations; (d) liberation teaching is a part of the encouraging classroom; (e) the teacher creates a climate for partnerships with parents.

5 Organizing the Encouraging Classroom

Chapter 5 discusses organizing the encouraging classroom through the use of learning centers, thematic instruction, and classroom routines. The discussion includes the role of learning centers at the preprimary and primary levels; learning centers and theme-based instruction; a teacher's perspective on the use of routines; and encouraging parents to be classroom volunteers.

6 Managing the Encouraging Classroom

Chapter 6 explores management of the encouraging classroom to reduce the need for mistaken behavior. Topics include setting up the daily program, mixing active and quiet times, the place of large groups, managing transitions, and working with parents and other volunteers in the classroom.

7 Leadership Communication with the Group

Chapter 7 addresses the use of leadership communication with the group, including establishing leadership at the beginning of the school year; implementing guidelines instead of rules; providing encouragement; discussing inclusively, using the class meeting; and communicating with parents to maintain partnerships.

8 Leadership Communication with the Individual

Chapter 8 explores leadership communication with the individual to reduce and prevent mistaken behavior. In the encouraging classroom, the teacher uses leadership to support the individual by listening to life experiences; by using contact talk, the compliment sandwich, humor, and touch with precaution; and by using leadership communication in the parent-teacher conference.

4

Creating a Climate for the Encouraging Classroom

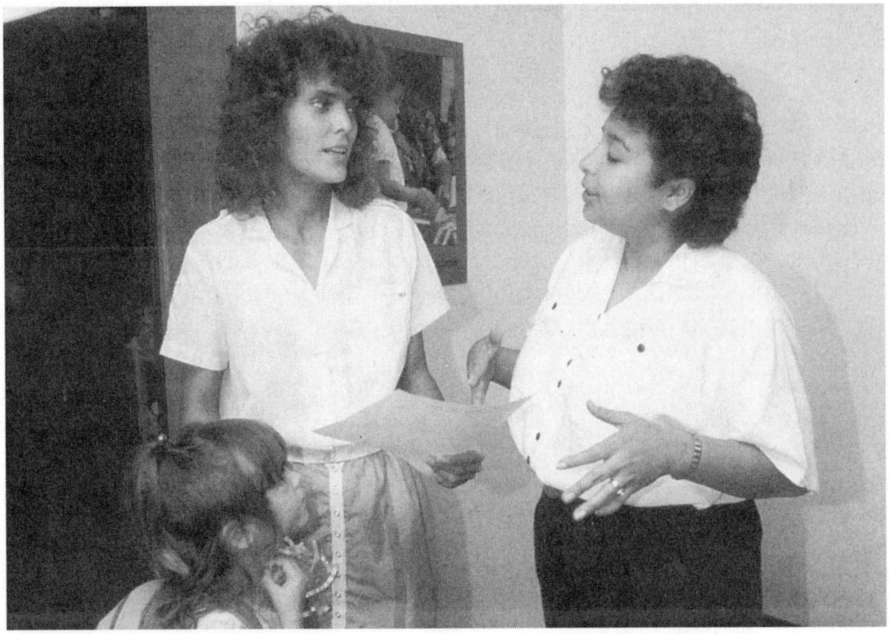

GUIDING QUESTIONS

As you read Chapter 4, you will discover answers to the following questions:

- **What are the differences between a teacher who is a professional and a teacher who is a technician?**
- **What should teachers know about the learning dynamic that is intrinsic to young learners?**
- **How does the use of developmentally appropriate practice improve teacher-child relations?**
- **Why is liberation teaching fundamental to the encouraging classroom?**
- **How does the teacher create a climate for partnerships with parents?**

Teachers in earlier times seemed to have "magic answers" to problems in the classroom. Children were more obedient, and the teacher's rule was absolute. Yet, the nature of the remedies of yesteryear—the hickory stick, the dunce cap, a statement written 500 times—made school a place that many children feared or even despised.

Now teachers recognize that they don't have magic answers. Human motivations, relationships, and behaviors are complex, especially when young children are concerned. All intervention methods with children have consequences that last beyond the act of intervention (Gartrell, 1995). Before the modern era in education, the consequence of strict teaching and punitive discipline was that most children dropped out of school, many taking negative attitudes toward education with them. Today, schools are accountable for all students. Educators can no longer allow children "at risk for failure" to fall through the cracks as actual, or psychological dropouts.

Societal pressure that all children be educated successfully puts educators in a serious dilemma. The many challenges to traditional family structure, more interactive parenting styles, and the revolution in electronic information accessible to the young contribute to a culture that has made conventional, obedience-driven classroom discipline obsolete. Students come to school no longer expecting to be "seen and not heard." Teachers no longer can regard effective discipline as merely the decisive reaction at the precipitous moment. Guidance is replacing discipline in the classroom because it is more in tune with current cultural practices in the raising and educating of the young (Gartrell, 1997).

The approach to working effectively with today's students needs to be guiding rather than prescriptive, proactive rather than reactive, comprehensive rather that one dimensional. An education program that reduces the need for mistaken behavior; intervention techniques that guide rather than punish; and partnerships among adults, and especially with parents, are all components of an effective guidance program. For guidance to be fully practiced, a particular classroom climate needs to exist. This first chapter in Unit Two presents five considerations that, when addressed, create the climate for the encouraging classroom. The five considerations are:

- The teacher is a professional, not a technician
- Teachers need to support the learning dynamic that is intrinsic to young children
- The use of developmentally appropriate practice (DAP) improves teacher-child relations
- Liberation teaching is fundamental to the encouraging classroom
- The teacher creates a climate for partnerships with parents

The teacher who accepts these considerations and incorporates them into teaching practices moves comfortably into guidance as the mode of relations with children. The education program becomes one in which many common mistaken behaviors become unnecessary; children learn from the mistakes they do make; and the serious problems that some children face become more manageable.

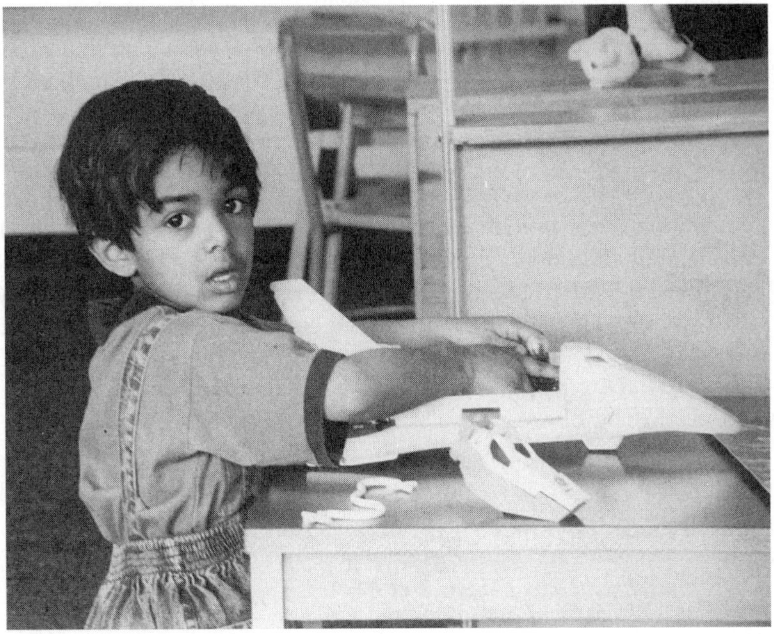

Human motivations, relationships, and behaviors are complex, especially when young children are concerned.

A PROFESSIONAL, NOT A TECHNICIAN

In discussing discipline trends of the 1980s, Chapter 1 took the position that discipline based on obedience is *reductionistic* both of the child and the teacher. When using *obedience-based discipline,* teachers are reduced to the status of technicians, trained to follow a specific set of rules in predetermined inflexible ways. The guidance approach asks that the teacher be a *professional.* How the teacher responds to situations in the classroom defines the difference between the teacher as technician and as professional. **The professional teacher:**

1. *Uses diagnostic skills to assess the situation.* The technician tends to determine only whether a rule has been violated or not. The professional recognizes that each situation is different and attempts to understand at a deeper level what actually is occurring.
2. *Makes judgments—actually hypotheses—about the situation and takes action based on the hypotheses.* The technician responds in an inflexible manner—X behavior happened, therefore punishment Y is called for. The professional uses a problem-solving approach. She works to resolve the conflict and to teach the child alternative behavioral patterns. (In other words, the technician punishes the child for having the problem; the professional teaches the child to solve the problem)

3. *Makes the effort to learn from the experience.* On a daily basis, the teacher makes quick assessments and takes quick actions. Even experienced teachers find that interventions do not always work out as intended. Professionalism means that even though the teacher does not always make the right decision, she endeavors to learn from the experience to improve the quality of relations with an individual child and the class.

Guidance supports the potential of the child to learn as well as the teacher. Although guidance provides no magic answers for teacher-technicians, it offers ideas to think about, try, and learn from—opportunities for teachers to feel better about who they are and how they are with children. Guidance offers the promise of professional growth, which is difficult for teachers locked into the technician role. Teachers who are professionals want to empower the learning and healthy development of young children, and themselves.

THE LEARNING DYNAMIC

Awareness of an unfolding human potential goes back at least to Socrates. Froebel, Montessori, and Dewey all wrote about the need to respect the dynamic of development within the child. Two mid 20th century psychologists, Jean Piaget and Erik Erikson, have added greatly to our understanding about development and its importance in teaching and learning. To bring the major contributions of Piaget and Erikson up-to-date, the interpretations of a "second generation" of developmental psychologists have been brought to the discussion of these two great authorities.*

Piaget and Developmental Stages

Jean Piaget's clinical studies with his own and other children brought developmental theory into the forefront of 20th Century psychology. Piaget discovered that in the process of growing and learning each person passes through "a biologically determined sequence of stages" (Charlesworth, 1996). Piaget identified four major stages of development. The common age span of each is included, although individual children may take more or less time to pass through the first three stages.

- Sensori-motor (birth to two)
- Preoperations (two to seven)
- Concrete operations (seven to eleven)
- Formal operations (eleven through adulthood)

* Current research on brain development is adding daily to our understanding of the etiology of human behavior. Future editions of texts like this will increasingly include material on the neuro-psychology of child development. The author believes that the contributions of psychologists like Piaget and Erikson will be supported by these exciting new discoveries.

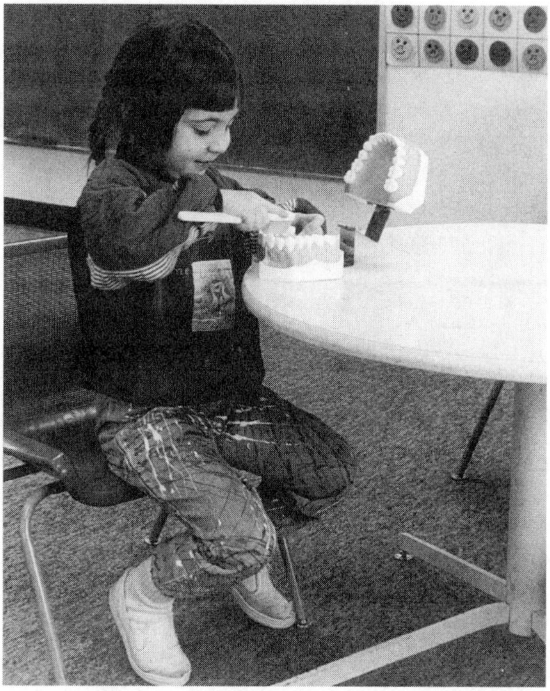

The child constructs knowledge through interacting with the environment.

In Piaget's view, the way a child responds to a situation is linked to her stage of development. Although a child's mode of thinking is limited by the psychological characteristics of the developmental stage, the process of learning is always active. The child constructs knowledge (derives meaning) through interacting with the environment. As each new stage is reached, the old ways of thinking are not lost but are integrated into the new ways (Charlesworth, 1996).

Charlesworth's interpretation of Piaget is helpful in understanding about the development of thought. Cognitive development begins during the sensori-motor stage as the infant forms schemata, or sensory impressions, of what she perceives. By the beginning of the preoperational stage, the toddler is linking similar schemata into preconcepts (Charlesworth, 1996).

Preconcepts represent the start of symbolic thought and often contain *over generalizations,* calling all four-legged animals "kiki" (for kitty), and *over specializations,* expressing shock at seeing a teacher in an unexpected setting like a store (Charlesworth, 1996). Gradually, during the preoperational stage, the child forms new preconcepts and refines existing concepts to accommodate the outside world.

Until concrete operations develop (between six and eight years), the child's perception process is limited by a tendency to focus on the outstanding elements of what is perceived. The young child does not yet have the ability to comprehend the complexities of situations. Within the limits of perceptual ability, however, the child notices and processes information with great efficiency. From the "Piagetian perspective," the role of the teacher is not to correct beginning concepts but to act "as a guide and supply the necessary opportunities [for the child] to interact with objects and people" (Charlesworth, 1996, p. 252) and so construct knowledge for herself.

In a midwestern American Indian community, a Head Start class returned early from a trip to the beach on a very windy day. They were discussing why they had to leave early when the teacher asked, "What makes the wind blow anyway?"

A four-old named Virgil exclaimed, "Don't you know, teacher? The trees push the air."

Realizing that he could not explain to anyone what makes the wind blow, the teacher commented, "You are really thinking, Virgil; how do you know that?"

Amused at the teacher's obvious lack of knowledge, Virgil explained, "Cause the leaves is fans, of course."

Undoubtedly Virgil's understanding of what makes the wind blow has changed since that experience. But to this day the teacher—who happens to be the author—remains impressed with Virgil's preoperational stage of thinking.

As this anecdote illustrates, through experiences with peers, adults, and physical things, the learner perceives new, often conflicting information. The child learns by mentally processing this information and constructing knowledge from it. The need to reach **equilibrium,** harmony between perceptions and understanding, out of **disequilibrium,** dissonance between perceptions and understanding is intrinsic. Piaget believed that the disequilibrium felt by the child is a primary source of the intrinsic motivation to learn (Charlesworth, 1996).

Jinada and Lorenzo were playing house. Jinada commented, "I'm the momma so I'll get breakfast."

Lorenzo retorted, "Poppas get breakfast, so I will get breakfast." A heated exchange followed.

Having heard the argument, the teacher intervened: "Jinada, you have a momma in your house and she makes breakfast. Lorenzo, you have a poppa in your house, and your poppa makes breakfast. Since you two are a momma and a poppa in the same house, maybe you can make the breakfast together."

Jinada said "Yeah, and I will make the toast and the cereal."

Lorenzo added, "I will put them dishes and spoons on the table." The two children proceeded to "make" and "eat" breakfast. Afterward, the teacher was amused to hear Jinada say, "But we got to go to work so we'll clean up later." Lorenzo says, "Yeah," and the two went off to work.

The motivation to do a puzzle lies in the need to create equilibrium through putting the pieces in place from the disequilibrium of the missing pieces.

Developmental Egocentrism. In Piaget's developmental theory, a key idea is that young children show what the present author terms **developmental egocentrism.** Piaget believed that young children show egocentrism as a result of their limited development. Due to their still developing cognitive abilities, young children understand events from their own perspectives and have difficulty accommodating the viewpoints of others. Critics of Piaget's interpretation of egocentrism cite evidence that children in the pre-operational stage are capable of "pro-social" acts. This capability is, of course, true, but it represents a misinterpretation of the meaning of egocentrism in the young child. Rather than implying that the child is capable only of selfish behaviors, egocentrism in the developmental sense refers to the inability of young children to understand the complexity of social factors at work in any situation.

Take the situation of a preschooler who becomes terrified when a grasshopper lands on his shoulder. A second young child hears his screams, brushes the grasshopper off, and pats him on the back. The second child likely did not respond from high level empathetic analysis but from the discomfort she felt at the first child's distress. (She happened to notice the main elements of the situation which were the first child's screams and "the big grasshopper.") The second child was indeed pro-social, but from reasoning that was developmentally egocentric unlike an adult's. However, adult acknowledgment that the second child might receive for being helpful is just the kind of reinforcement from significant others that can make social responsiveness a more conscious part of a child's behavior as she develops. (DeVries & Zan, 1996). The two authors state the matter this way (1996):

> Young children often appear selfish when, for example, they grab objects from others and demand to be first in line or first in a game. This behavior often happens because young children have difficulty understanding others' points of view. Such selfishness in young children is not the same as selfishness in older children and adults (p. 266).

Before children grow into concrete operations, their social understanding is limited. They see the world from their own perspectives—often blaming themselves or becoming upset when they don't understand the full set of social dynamics. Understanding developmental egocentrism, the role of the teacher is to adapt the curriculum so that young children can engage in meaningful social experiences. Building the encouraging classroom in which such experiences are possible takes hard work (Honig & Wittmer, 1996) and high level understanding (Charlesworth, 1996). Piaget knew then what researchers are reaffirming today: that healthy social, moral, and cognitive development will result (Piaget, 1932/1960).

Two student teachers organized a game of musical chairs with twelve preschoolers. To their amazement, the first child "put out" began to cry, the second moped, and the third swept a book off a shelf. The two noticed that as the remaining children left the game, none looked happy. The last child out complained that the winner pushed and "It's not fair."

After discussion with their supervisor, the student teachers realized that the children were unable to comprehend the rules of the game. The children probably thought they were being punished by being put out and felt hurt, frustrated, and guilty.

Not to give up, the student teachers organized the game on another day, but with different rules. The children helped to tape their names to chairs. They were then asked to suggest the names of animals and came up with "chickens," "dolphins," and "elephants." When the music stopped, the children proceeded to their chairs, moving like the animal selected. The game continued for 40 minutes, all of the children participated, and all—including the student teachers—had a good time.

Autonomy. In Piaget's perspective, the challenge of development is for children to build understanding about the perspectives of others and the capacity for intelligent decision making. Piaget referred to the individual's ability to make intelligent, ethical decisions as *autonomy.* For educators who take a Piagetian perspective, *intellectual* and *moral autonomy* are the most important goals of education (Kamii, 1984). *Autonomy* means being governed by oneself—as opposed to *heteronomy,* or being governed by others. Writing about moral autonomy, Kamii, a leading authority on the concept, states:

> Autonomy enables children to make decisions for themselves. But autonomy is not synonymous with complete freedom. . . . There can be no morality when one consider's only one's own point of view. If one takes the other people's views into account, one is not free to tell lies, to break promises, to behave inconsiderately (1984, p. 411).

Progress toward autonomy happens through adult guidance.

Early childhood education provides the first institutional experience for children in relation to issues of autonomy. Yet, young children's limited social experience and developmental egocentrism make instruction for autonomy an exasperating part of preschool-primary instruction. Charlesworth phrases the teacher's dilemma concisely:

> How often the adult says of the young child, "I know he knows better!" And the adult is right; the child does "know better," but is not yet able to reason and act consistently with his knowledge. It is not until the child is close to six that be begins to develop standards, to generalize, and to internalize sanctions so that he acts morally not just to avoid punishment but because he *should* act that way (Charlesworth, 1996).

Clearly, given Piaget's discoveries about the course of development, mastering autonomy progresses throughout childhood and into adulthood. Teachers who recognize the young child's limited ability to conceptualize about moral decisions understand the importance of an approach that teaches rather than punishes and allows the child to develop in healthy ways.

At all levels of education, Piaget regarded authoritarian adult roles as unhelpful in the process of empowering autonomy (Piaget, 1932/1960). Interpreting right and wrong for children through the use of rewards and punishments reinforces *heteronomy* (Kamii, 1984, p. 410). In agreement with Piaget, Charlesworth comments that:

> A just community is a developmentally designed school democracy that stimulates moral and social advancement. Some of the approaches used are:
>
> - encouraging student generated rule-making;
> - providing support structures (such as clear rules, a system for taking turns, etc.);

- promoting group decision-making;
- using spontaneous interpersonal conflicts as the basis of discussion [conflict management];
- fostering a moral community;
- developing caring relations;
- promoting cooperative learning (1996)

For developmental psychologists, knowledge is not fixed and finite, to be transferred by teachers to the minds of passive students. Learning in both the intellectual and moral spheres is a *constructive process,* that is the learner constructs meaning from interactions with peers, adults, and materials. From this perspective, social experience is fundamental to the educational process. Through interactions with adults and peers, the individual constructs, alters, and integrates mental concepts and, in turn, contributes to the thinking of others. Democracy within the classroom becomes the vehicle of society to further individual development and to replenish itself. A legacy of Piaget—like that of John Dewey—is the interrelation of the development of the child and the functioning of the society, with the common reference point being the interactive classroom, our growing understanding of human development, and of the role of guidance.

Erikson: Initiative and Industry

The psychologist, Erik Erikson, framed the nature of the intrinsic dynamic of development in his much quoted theory, "Eight Critical Ages" (1963). The third critical age, *initiative versus guilt,* identifies the drive in young children to explore, to try, and to discover. Healthy development during this period depends on responsiveness of the adult to these needs. The teacher structures the environment and provides guidance

The development of both a sense of initiative and belonging during early childhood indicates the importance of this period.

so that children can experience fully while learning nonpunitvely about the limits of acceptable behavior. The saying, "The process is more important than the product," applies to this period, as children learn primarily from the doing and the gratification of *self-defined* results.

In *Miseducation: Preschoolers at Risk,* David Elkind (1987) discusses factors in schooling that affect young children's development. Elkind interprets the third critical age by referring to it as "initiative and belonging versus guilt and alienation." Elkind explains:

> Erik Erikson describes this period as one that determines whether the child's sense of **initiative** will be strengthened to an extent greater than the sense of guilt. And because the child is now interacting with peers, this period is also critical in the determination of whether the child's sense of "**belonging**" will be greater than the sense of alienation. (1987, p. 115).

Elkind's inclusion of "belonging versus alienation" in the early childhood period is insightful. Studying the transition from preschool to kindergarten made by a sample of fifty-eight children, Ladd and Price (1987) found that preschoolers who had high levels of positive social relations were liked by their kindergarten peers. A contributing factor to peer acceptance, and fewer anxieties around the transition, was the presence of friends made previously in the preschool setting.

In a second study,

> Ladd (1989) found that the number of new friendships children formed in the first two months of the school year predicted higher levels of social and academic competence, fewer absences from school, fewer visits to the nurse, and less behavioral disruptiveness (Bukatko & Daehler, 1992, p. 669).

The value of friendships and the ability to make friends clearly are important skills, so important that they appear to be predictive of school success. Given these findings, the teacher who assists a prekindergarten to primary grade child with limited social skills to make friends contributes in a lasting way to the child's future.

During early childhood, children, hopefully, have been immersed in *initiative* experiences with the social and physical world. Because of these early experiences, by the time they reach the next critical period, children are ready for more sophisticated social interactions and learning activities. Erikson's fourth critical period, *industry versus inferiority,* occurs mainly during the primary grade years. A characteristic of children during this time is that they are greatly affected by the judgments of significant others. They are acutely aware of the possibility of failure, and sensitivity in teacher feedback is critical.

The teacher who stresses evaluative comparisons and relies on competition creates social ranking in the class, with the implicit labeling of some students as "winners" and others as "losers." Of the second group, Honig and Wittmer comment:

> Competitive classrooms result in some children becoming tense, fearing failure, and becoming less motivated to persist at challenging events (1996, p. 63).

The seriousness of such an occurrence, of course, is that children so labeled may well be hampered by the label in future learning endeavors (Kohn, 1993). In relation to Erikson's critical period the **conditional acceptance** of children, based on

As children approach middle childhood, they are greatly affected by the judgments of others.

their performance and obedience, is a significant contributor to feelings of inadequacy in primary grade children.

Many teachers believe that classrooms predominantly cooperative in nature fail to teach children about the realities of life. A common view is that schools need to prepare children for "the competition of life" by "toughening them to it." To the contrary, public chastisement and evaluative comparisons are argued by Kohn (1993) to correlate with lower feelings of competence; i.e., inferiority. Teaching practices that lead to feelings of inferiority and low self-esteem include:

- Relying on clearly defined ability groups—the Bluebirds, the Robins, and the Turkey Vultures. (As Bukatko and Daehler [1992] point out, the practice persists.)
- Using peer tutoring, as opposed to cooperative learning, having a clearly defined tutor (the "smart kid") and "tutee" (the "dummy").
- Establishing teacher-domination of classroom transactions with children cast in passive and reactive roles.
- Ignoring children who show higher or lower levels of academic achievement.
- Showing indifference toward children who are unpopular with peers or who are from "nonmainstream" backgrounds.
- Giving undue attention to incorrect responses in written and oral exercises.

- Stressing "power tests" and other comparative evaluation procedures.
- Reacting punitively toward random mistaken behavior within the group.
- Using punishments repeatedly such as time outs, in-school detentions, or exclusion from special events with some children.
- Distancing or reacting in other discriminatory ways toward the parents of some children.

In contrast, a corresponding list of teaching practices that promote industry in children includes:

- Multidimensional grouping arrangements—informal interest groups, cooperative learning groups, heterogeneous study groups, social style matched groups, collaborative peer pairings.
- A variety of means for achieving success available for children.
- Promotion of autonomy through opportunities to make decisions and contribute to the group.
- Cross-age tutoring, using a diverse population of older students.
- Inclusion of other adults in the classroom to maximize personal attention.
- Advocacy and support for unpopular and nonmainstream children.
- Specific, nonembarrassing teacher feedback.
- Low-key, supportive evaluation of children's work.
- Firm and friendly guidance orientation to mistaken behavior.
- Integration of conflict management skills and attitudes in the daily program.
- Collaborative, problem-solving orientation to serious mistaken behavior.
- Involvement opportunities for parents of all chidden.

As they enter middle childhood, teaching at its best nudges children toward a sense of industry—confidence in their ability to achieve successfully. Clearly, the principles of guidance are congruent with teaching practices that promote industry as children proceed through the primary grades.

Adults who have seen the curiosity, openness, and perseverance of young children recognize that a learning dynamic is intrinsic to the human species. For many educators, the children of the schools of Reggio Emilia have renewed our awareness of this dynamic (See Recommended Resources). As the writings of Jean Piaget and Erik Erikson indicate, teachers can severely limit or fundamentally empower that potential. Teachers who seek to create an encouraging classroom recognize that teaching is about helping children to make the most of personal potential, regardless of labels the child might have received in the past due to birth order, cultural heritage, family circumstance, or personal reputation.

DEVELOPMENTALLY APPROPRIATE PRACTICE AND TEACHER-CHILD RELATIONS

Educators often hear from their fellow teachers that their children's ability to learn is limited by their short attention spans. A knowing teacher replies that the activity determines the attention span—as a puzzle done several times in a row, extra time taken to write in a journal, or a "never ending" push on a swing will attest. If allowed the initiative of engagement on her own terms, a concentrating young child is a most effective learner. When the curriculum is developmentally appropriate, the child's attention span frequently is longer than the adult's.

The important NAEYC publication, *Devlopmentally Appropriate Practice in Early Childhood Programs* (1997), has contributed developmentally appropriate practice to describe what many teachers have always done. Thanks to this document, and the many works it has spawned, **DAP** has gained wide acceptance in the prekindergarten field and is taking hold in an increasing number of kindergarten and primary grade classrooms (Gronlund, 1995).

From the guidance perspective, the increased use of DAP is vital. Although the human relations skills of exceptional teachers may permit them to use guidance techniques regardless of curricular expectations, most find it easier to use guidance when the curriculum is responsive to the developmental levels and cultural backgrounds of young children.

Common inappropriate practices such as prolonged periods of sitting and listening, prescribed activities done to exacting standards, critical evaluation of children's work, and teacher-communication that stigmatizes invite mistaken behavior. As discussed in the previous chapter, *curriculum-driven mistaken behavior* is a primary cause of "the classroom as battle ground" (Willis, 1993).

Within the classroom, a professional teacher works to maximize children's engagement in the learning process. Such engagement methods as daily child-chosen

Informal pairings of "neighbors" for projects is one example of multidimensional grouping.

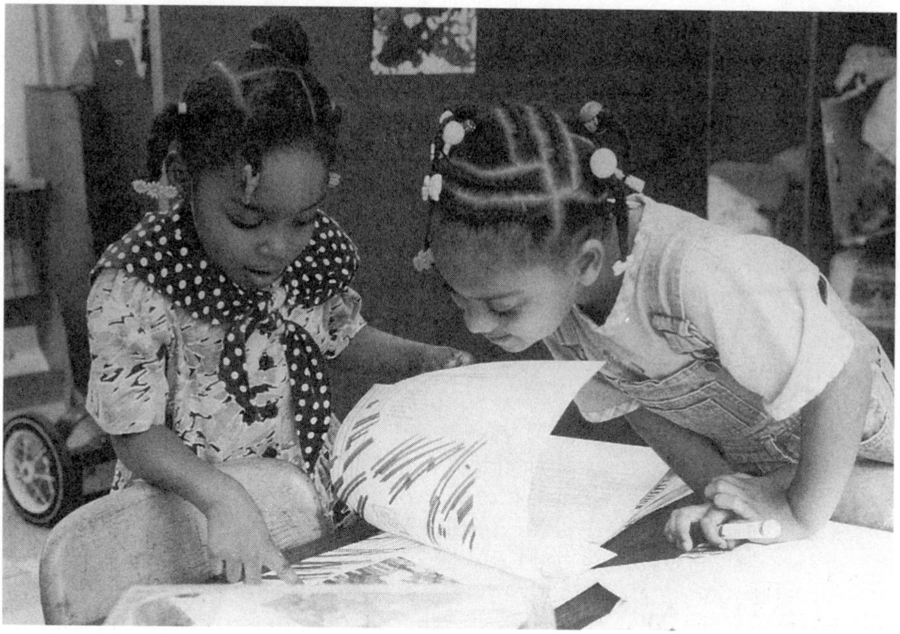

The presence of an intrinsic dynamic for learning is a given in the guidance approach.

activities, creative art and journals (even before they can write conventional script or spell), manipulatives-based math, diverse small group experiences, and active, concise large group sessions allow children to find meaning and success in learning experiences (Brewer, 1996). Utilizing such practices, Table 4.1 illustrates how DAP can reduce mistaken behaviors.

Table 4.1
Increasing Appropriate Practice to Reduce Mistaken Behavior

Moving from Inappropriate Practice	To Appropriate Practice	Reduces Mistaken Behavior
Prolonged sitting and listening	Active, concise large groups	Restlessness, bothering neighbors, confrontation with adults
Prescribed activities done to exacting standards	Child-choice, creative, "no one right answer" activities	Acting out of feelings of failure, frustration inferiority, boredom
Critical evaluation of children's work	Supportive evaluation of children's work	Mix of reactions to lowering of self-esteem
Ostracism of some children due to mistaken behavior	Acceptance of all children as group members	Acting out of feelings of rejection

DAP in the Primary Grades

In many elementary schools, support is growing for teachers to use DAP to *supplement and modify* the traditional academic program. Such practices as integrated curriculum, outcomes-driven education, cooperative learning groups, teaching teams, and authentic assessment allow teachers to be fully professional and classroom practices to become developmentally appropriate (Bredekamp, 1991). In many schools, however, these changes have taken courage and ingenuity on the part of individual teachers.

> (Kindergarten). Despite a kindergarten teacher's statements that it was not developmentally appropriate, a principal decided that a worksheet-based arithmetic system had to be used. Being tenured and known as an individual, the teacher decided she would use the worksheets but in her own way. On the last Friday of each month, the class had a worksheet party. The teacher made plenty of popcorn, and everyone did worksheets. Having used manipulatives to teach the targeted math concepts during the month, the teacher reported that the children "whipped through the sheets, had fun doing them and took lots of papers home."

> (First Grade). A first grade teacher felt compelled to use the basal series adopted by the school district but found that the reading program did not reinforce the children's excitement about learning to read. He supplemented the reading program with "super silent reading" times when he and the children read self-selected books. He introduced "just journaling and jotting" times, when he and the children recorded their own thoughts and feelings in journals. When the teacher discovered children reading and journaling *other* parts of the day, he concluded he now had an *emergent literacy program* that met his expectations.

Like the teachers in the anecdotes, for years individual teachers have been "psychologizing" the curriculum, as Dewey termed it (1900/1969). Many teachers have had to do so quietly, behind closed doors. Some—usually after receiving tenure—have done their own thing openly and endured the label from colleagues of being that "offbeat one at the end of the hall." As one teacher, known for being creative, commented, "I do as little of what I have to do and as much of what I want to do to stay out of serious trouble." It is to be hoped that times are beginning to change.

Working Together for Change

Often, a committee can make a curriculum modification request seem more studied and objective than an individual teacher. For this reason, two or more teachers who attend a workshop or conference together may be successful in introducing developmentally appropriate practices into a school. When all teachers at a grade level, for instance, feel strongly about the need to modify practice, they may succeed by working together.

Tact, civility, and communication—starting with the modifications that are most feasible—are the watchwords. As textbook salespersons and inspirational speakers have long known, educators tend to be receptive to changes that are linked to the latest trends. Movement toward DAP is sometimes easier when it is linked with other buzzwords: *emergent literacy, computer literacy, manipulatives-based math, outcomes-driven education, graduation standards, performance assessment, integrated curriculum, theme-based instruction, inclusive education,* and/or *brain development.*

A noteworthy anecdote about riding the buzzword bandwagon is two first grade teachers who are alleged to have gotten play into their programs by calling it a "self-selected, self-directed autonomous learning period." In many locations, the term *developmentally appropriate practice* in itself is fueling elementary school reform.

Role of the Principal

The stereotype of the elementary principal is of the middle-aged patriarch, the male secondary teacher who eventually got his administrator's license. A problem some teachers have experienced is that such principals neither have taught at the primary level nor seem to care about the needs of young children. As Greenberg has pointed out, sexism in the school sometimes confounds the communication process (1989).

Contrary to this image, many administrators are open to improvements in programming; they see becoming educated about early childhood education a part of their jobs. They ask only for a clearly spelled out rationale that the projected program will be cost effective and results-oriented (Goffin & Stegelin, 1992).

As we enter a new century and a new generation of principals comes to the fore, an increase in administrators with backgrounds in early childhood education can be expected. Nonetheless, knowing the principal well as teachers work to introduce DAP into the school makes sense. In some situations, she will be the teacher's best ally (Goffin & Stegelin, 1992; Burchfield, 1996). In others, the teacher without tenure should work closely with, but stay in the shadow of, teachers who do.

To modify practice in a school or district, teachers need to plan carefully and organize well. Inviting educators from other areas who are using interesting ideas is a useful technique. The DAP book and *Changing Kindergartens* (Goffin & Stegelin, 1992), both published by NAEYC, and articles such as Gronlund's (1995) and Burchfield's (1996) provide useful information for moving ahead.

Two kindergarten teachers in an urban school became tired of worksheets and drills used to teach phonics and counting skills. They heard from a teacher at another school about alternate approaches using emergent literacy techniques and a manipulatives-based math program. The two teachers began attending workshops, collecting sample materials, and talking with primary grade teachers. The teachers got the principal to agree that the new methods were more responsive to the developmental levels of kindergarten children. With the principal's support, the two teachers convinced the third kindergarten teacher to adopt a manipulatives-based math program to replace the use of worksheets. They currently are negotiating to use a new approach to beginning reading/writing, more child-active and less dependent on a preprimer phonics system. The first grade teachers are taking notice of what is going on in the kindergarten. The kindergarten teachers plan to involve them further.

School Anxiety

If a child wants to go to school when ill, something is right; if a child does not want to go when well, something is wrong. Young children who are unhappy at school cannot easily work through anxieties with words (McCracken, 1986). In some children, **school anxiety** shows in direct mistaken behavior—inattentiveness, frequent frustration, and/or irritability. In others, anxiety manifests in physical conditions situationally caused. Symptoms range from a twice-a-year stomach ache to actual ulcers, from occasional headaches to persistent allergies, from sporadic nervousness to high blood pressure and depressive reactions (Cherry, 1981).

School anxiety can result from specific situations such as the morning bus ride or the afternoon power test. Also, the cause can be more pervasive—a general feeling of being:

- disliked by the teacher;
- alienated from other children;
- dislocated from the education program.

School anxiety is a major cause of Level Three mistaken behavior in children—strong unmet physical and/or emotional needs that children act out.

Educators sometimes miss school anxiety as a cause of serious mistaken behavior. With the plethora of problems besetting modern families, teachers tend to look first to the home situation. Previously, serious mistaken behavior and consequent punishment were rationalized by the labeling of a "bad child." More recently, educators attribute "a bad home life" to children who act out—and seek to provide the controls not provided at home.

Much Level Three mistaken behavior *is* caused by situations outside the school. However, teaching practice that fails to accommodate developmental levels and individual circumstances is a primary cause of mistaken behavior in many situations and a contributing factor in others. The use of DAP allows the teacher to interact

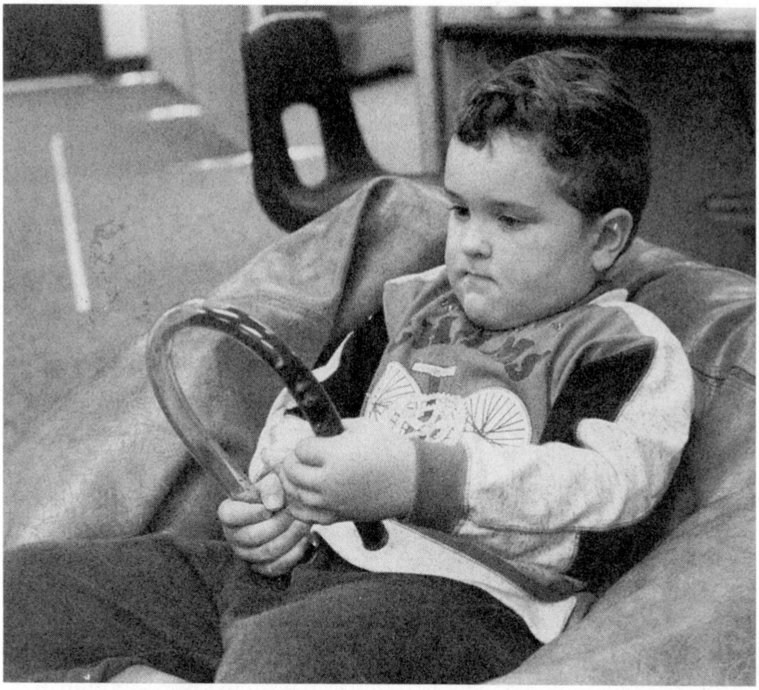

Young children cannot easily work through anxieties with words.

with the child as an individual and empowers children to succeed (Gronlund, 1995). DAP reduces the occurrence of school anxiety and is fundamental to the encouraging classroom.

LIBERATION TEACHING AND THE ENCOURAGING CLASSROOM

Many teachers over the years have stated that their greatest challenge is working with the few children in a class who are difficult to like—or in the words of one frustrated first grade teacher, who are "a pain in the butt." In any classroom, some children will be challenging to the teacher, who may have difficulty coping with, relating to, and understanding them. Although sometimes difficult, a necessary consideration for the encouraging classroom is that the teacher needs to figure out a way to accept every child in the class as a person of worth.

Children come into early childhood classrooms vulnerable in many ways. Many come from nontraditional family situations or from cultural groups different than the teacher's own. Other children may have "established disabilities" such as hearing loss or speech delay, less traditional disabilities such as fetal alcohol syndrome, or less easily diagnosed conditions such as pervasive allergies. Children may have unusual facial appearances, may be short or tall, or may be under- or overweight. Children may have unique learning styles, experience backgrounds, or developmental characteristics.

liberation teaching.
rise from strength
weakness to + growth

114 Unit Two Building the Encouraging Classroom

They may possess a high need for attention or a strong need to act out or to be independent. Young children come into classrooms with a range of behavioral styles, social attributes, cultural backgrounds, physical characteristics, learning capabilities, and levels of self-esteem, any of which can impede or enhance a child's progress in the class.

The teacher responds to each child, given the mix of qualities that comprise that child's developing personality. As the most significant adult outside the family, the teacher has great influence. Responses that aggravate a child's need for security and acceptance and that deny growth are stigmatizing. In Goffman's terms (1963), receiving a **stigma** disqualifies an individual from full participation in the group and so greatly diminishes self-esteem. Children come to school at risk for stigma in many ways. Teacher responses that affirm the child's sense of belonging, worth, and competence empower the child toward growth. Teachers who do so liberate children from vulnerability for stigma. These adults practice **liberation teaching.**

Liberation teaching has its roots in the social psychology of Goffman (1963), the social commentary of such authors as Gottlieb (1973) and Boyer (1991), and the practices of countless caring teachers over the years. The term *liberation* is borrowed from such disparate sources as Catholic theology and the writings of Faber Mazlich (1974).

The self psychologist, Maslow, has particularly contributed to the construct with his discussion of the dual human needs for safety and growth (1962). Within every learner there are two sets of needs, one for safety and one for growth. Of the two needs, the need for safety—security, belonging, identification, love relationships, respect—is the stronger. To the extent the child feels safety needs are unmet, she becomes preoccupied with meeting these needs and is likely to show mistaken behavior.

On the other hand, as safety needs are met, the child is empowered to address the need for growth through such qualities as openness, curiosity, creativity, problem-solving ability, responsiveness, and self-actualization (Maslow, 1962). In Maslow's terms, Liberation teaching is the ability to assist the child to meet safety needs and to nudge the child toward growth.

Other psychologists also have contributed to the liberation concept. In Piaget's work *liberation teaching* is assisting the child to move toward autonomy (Piaget, 1932/1960). In Erikson's modified construct, liberation teaching is empowering the child to grow from shame, doubt, and inferiority to initiative, intimacy, and industry (Elkind, 1989). For Harlow, cited in Chapter 2, liberation teaching is helping the child to rise from the social relations of survival and adjustment to encountering.

An enduring notion of the "real" teacher, sometimes attributed to Socrates, holds that she does not cram students' minds with facts but kindles enthusiasm in students by the knowledge of what they can become. Such descriptions clearly are not new. Why, then, use the term *liberation* when what is being described is plain old "good teaching"? The answer lies in the power of the teacher to affect the present and the future of the child. As the teacher makes the effort to "figure out" that hard-to-like child, to develop a helping relationship with the child, to assist the child in conquering mistaken behaviors, and fitting in as a member of the class, that teacher deserves to know that she is engaged in a special process. In the practice of liberation teaching, the teacher has shown not just that to the child, but perhaps the family and to the other children, that this classroom is an encouraging place.

A CLIMATE FOR PARTNERSHIP WITH PARENTS

> A young child's anxiety in a new school experience may be lessened if there is not an abrupt division between home and school. Children thrive when they feel a continuity between parents and teachers that can be present only when adults have reached out in an effort to understand and respect each other. Just as a teacher's first task in relating to young children is to build a sense of trust and mutual respect, the same task is important in working with parents (Gestwicki, 1992, p. 103).

In addition to the traditional "spring roundup," teachers use a variety of spring and summer activities to acquaint both children and parents with the new year of school. Examples of these activities include: a Head Start program that coordinates spring bus runs for children and parents to kindergarten classrooms the children will be attending the next September; transition journals that provide a three-way dialog between the child and family, the preschool teacher, and the kindergarten teacher; and summer kindergarten readiness classes held in the classrooms children will attend in September. Still, in the days immediately preceding the beginning of school, teachers accelerate efforts at communicating with families. Several veteran kindergarten teachers from Minnesota have unique and effective approaches for building partnerships with parents during this period. The following case study is a composite of the practices of a few of these teachers, combined into the approach of one teacher, Juanita.

Before School Begins

Juanita views both the children and parents as her "customers." Her intent is to build "happy customers." Part of her approach is to reach the parents through the children. Another part is to reach the children through the parents. An axiom that she works with is "if the children are happy, the parents will be too." Juanita knows that parents who themselves had unhappy school experiences will be more likely to accept a teacher if they know that she cares about their kids. Juanita puts this idea to work even before the first day.

About two weeks before school, Juanita sends letters to both the child and the family. To the child she says how happy she is that the child is in her class and how many fun things they will do at school. The teacher encloses an animal sticker and tells each child to watch for that animal when they get to school. The animal emblem is prominently displayed by the classroom door, and Juanita wears a cutout of the emblem during the first week. (See letters in Appendix B.)

In the letter to the family, Juanita says the same things but goes on to invite them to either of two orientation meetings (one late afternoon, the other at night) to be held during the second week of school. In addition, with permission of the principal, she offers each family the option of a home visit, "as a good way for you, your child, and I to get to know each other." She comments in the letter that not all parents are comfortable with a home visit, which is fine. She can make a visit later in the year, if they would like, and she will be telephoning each family a day or two before start-up to discuss any questions they might have. (See Recommended Resources.) Juanita intentionally sends the letter "To the Family of" so that if a parent is a nonreader, someone else in the family may read the letter to the parent.

After Start-Up

On the evening of the first day of school, Juanita telephones to make sure that children have returned home safely, to let the parents know how the child has adjusted, and to ask about any problems that may have occurred. Juanita has said that although she would rather be doing other things after the first day, like going to bed early, she regards these telephone calls as the best investment she makes all year in her relations with parents. For parents without listed telephone numbers, she makes a personal contact right away using notes or informal visits.

On the first day of school, Juanita always has a parent volunteer from the year before to help with separation problems. Juanita greets each child with a name tag as they arrive. Two classes of children attend on A days and B days. At the request of Juanita and the other kindergarten teachers, the district allows half of each class to come in on separate days during the first week. This arrangement means that instead of 24 children attending on the two first days, twelve children attend on each of four days. Parents are always welcome in Juanita's class (and are put to use), although

The results of liberation teaching often speak for themselves.

during the first two weeks or so, they are encouraged to let the children make the adjustment to school on their own, to the extent possible.

In the first days, Juanita allows a lot of exploration time, but she also gets the children used to numerous routines right away. She comments, "A lot of problems never happen if the children know and are comfortable with the routines." Juanita and the volunteer make sure that all children get on the correct buses at the end of the day. Before leaving the classroom, they have a "class meeting" to discuss how happy Juanita will be to see them the next time they come to school. Juanita gives an individual goodby to each child as they leave, a practice she continues all year. After completing kindergarten, she sends each child a letter saying how much she enjoyed having her in her class and wishing her the very best when she begins first grade next fall.

Juanita holds two orientation meetings (which she calls "Greeting Meetings"), and families can attend either one. She gets high school students who had her as a teacher to care for children who come with the parents to the greeting meetings. At the meetings, Juanita answers questions they might have and talks about the education program. To assist in the discussion, she provides each parent with a brochure entitled, "The Education Program in Our Class." (See the sample brochure in Appendix C.) The brochure discusses such matters as the role of play in the program, why manipulatives are used in math, why the art is creative, why a guidance approach is used, and the importance of parent involvement.

Juanita also asks the parents to fill out a brief survey. The one-page survey includes items about their and their child's interests, the child's family background, the

Parents are always welcome in Juanita's class and contribute in many ways. Courtesy, *The Bemidji Pioneer*.

kinds of activities the parents can help with during the year, and other information "that would help me to understand and work with your child." Completing the survey is optional but almost all parents fill it out. The responses provide useful information to discuss at the first conference later in the year. (See Appendix B.)

The teacher attributes the high level of attendance at the orientation meetings to the telephone calls, letters and home visits at the beginning of the school year. She says the first week is exhausting, but the investment is worth it. "That telephone call the first night of school really wins them over. I remember how I felt the first time my child left for kindergarten. I still get tears when I think about it."

Juanita tries hard to communicate with each parent and has even held a conference at a cocktail lounge, where a single parent worked afternoons and evenings. Juanita does have strong feelings about parents who she believes could be doing more for their children. She attempts to be friendly with these parents, nonetheless. She knows that some parents did not receive appropriate nurturing as kids and never had a chance to grow up themselves. She realizes that getting a parent involved may make a difference in that child's life. She knows because she has seen some parents get involved and grow, and as a result their children's attitudes and behaviors change.

> It is not realistic to expect teachers to like all parents. However, it is essential and possible for teachers to respect all parents for their caring and efforts. In most cases, parents do care. This belief is the basis for all teacher interaction (Gestwicki, 1992, pp. 103–104).

Juanita practices Gestwicki's words.

SUMMARY

What are the differences between a teacher who is a professional and a teacher who is a technician?

Professionals use informed judgment formulated through continuing education and experience. They recognize that each child and each situation is unique. They adjust teaching practice on the basis of experience to improve the social and educational climate of the class. The need for mistaken behavior is reduced as a result, and they feel better about themselves as teachers. Professionals learn even as they teach. Technicians view teaching as the effective implementation of preset curriculum and behavioral management systems. They tend to react in rigid ways, determined by school traditions and administrative expectations.

What should teachers know about the learning dynamic that is intrinsic to young learners?

The writings of Piaget document that children adjust their thinking to better accommodate experience and respond as a function of the stage of development they are in. For teaching to be effective, it must be matched to the child's developmental level and active learning nature. Autonomy, or principled and intelligent decision-making is, for Piaget, the goal of education.

Erikson theorized eight critical periods that all humans go through. In the period of initiative versus guilt, preschoolers need support for exploration and creative activity through which they can define success for themselves. Elkind suggests that this age also includes the challenge of belonging versus alienation, a crucial awareness for teachers working with children during their first years outside the home. During the primary years, the critical issue is industry versus inferiority. The teacher's task during this time is to ensure that each learner is building feelings of industry through the successful learning transactions of the encouraging classroom.

How does the use of developmentally appropriate practice improve teacher-child relations?

Within the classroom, the teacher moves toward developmentally appropriate curriculum by offering choices in learning activities; evaluating supportively; keeping large group activities active, enjoyable, and concise; and personalizing the curriculum. The use of developmentally appropriate practice is widely accepted in preschool education. Working with colleagues, teachers are making progress in increasing the use of developmentally appropriate practice at the kindergarten and primary grade levels. Practice that is responsive to the developmental level and individual circumstances of the child reduces the occurrence of mistaken behavior.

Why is liberation teaching fundamental to the encouraging classroom?

The various physical, social, cultural, cognitive, and behavioral circumstances of children put them at risk for stigma in the classroom. A problem many teachers face is how to work with those children they find difficult to accept. To the extent that the teacher figures out how to assist children at risk for stigma to meet the need for safety and to move toward growth, she is practicing liberation teaching. Liberation teaching is a necessary condition for the creation of the encouraging classroom.

How does the teacher create a climate for partnerships with parents?

Before and during the first days of school, the teacher does much to create a climate for partnerships with parents through the use of notes, telephone calls, home visits, and greeting meetings. Initiating partnerships eases the transition of the child from home to school. If parents know the teacher is working to build positive relations with both the child and themselves, they are more likely to become positively involved. Teachers cannot expect to like every parent, but by remaining friendly and accessible, parents may respond. Parent involvement in the education program can make a life-long difference to the child and the family.

FOLLOW-UP ACTIVITIES

Note: In completing follow-up activities, the privacy of all involved is to be respected.

Reflection Activity

The reflection activity encourages students to interrelate their own thoughts and experiences with specific ideas from the chapter.

Identify a consideration for creating an encouraging classroom (listed at the beginning of the chapter) that is the most important to you in your professional development. Relate the consideration you have chosen to an experience of yours as a student either before entering your teacher preparation program or since. Why is this consideration important to you?

Application Activities

Application activities allow students to interrelate material from the text with real life situations. The observations imply access to practicum experiences; the interviews, access to teachers or parents. Students may compare or contrast observations and interviews with referenced ideas from the chapter.

1. **What are the differences between a teacher who is a professional and a teacher who is a technician?**
   a. Observe a teacher you regard as a professional as she responds to situations in the classroom. Note an incident that you believe was handled effectively. Talk with the teacher about her responses.
   b. Interview a teacher you believe to be a professional. Discuss decisions the teacher has made about the program that might be construed as difficult, innovative, or even controversial. Ask about the teacher's reasons for the decisions.
2. **What should teachers know about the learning dynamic that is intrinsic to young learners?**
   a. Observe a young child for behaviors that reflect or contradict an idea of a developmental psychologist about the learning dynamic intrinsic to young children. Discuss the relationship you found.
   b. Select a characteristic of young children as learners from this section of the chapter. Interview a teacher about how she accommodates this characteristic while teaching.
3. **How does the use of developmentally appropriate practice improve teacher-child relations?**
   a. Observe the interactions between a teacher and child in an activity that you believe is developmentally appropriate. Decide why the activity is developmentally appropriate. Determine what you believe to be significant about how the teacher and child communicated.
   b. Interview a teacher who uses developmentally appropriate practice. Ask about adjustments to programming the teacher has made in the last week or two to accommodate the developmental characteristics of individuals or the group of young children.
4. **Why is liberation teaching fundamental to the encouraging classroom?**
   a. Observe an example of liberation teaching. Focusing on the responses of the teacher and the child in the situation, decide why you believe liberation teaching was at work.

b. Ask a teacher to share an experience when she was successful in helping a child who was at risk for stigma. Inquire about how the child was helped and how the teacher felt about the experience.

5. **How does the teacher create a climate for partnerships with parents?**
   a. Interview a teacher about the steps she takes at the beginning of the year to build partnerships.
   b. Interview a parent about what is important for a teacher to do at the beginning of the year to create a climate for partnerships with parents.

RECOMMENDED RESOURCES

Abramson, S., Robinson, R., & Anenman, K. (1995). Project work with diverse students: Adapting curriculum based on the Reggio Emilia Approach. *Childhood Education, 71*(4), 197–202.

Burchfield, D. W. (1996). Teaching *all* children: Four developmentally appropriate curricular and instructional strategies in primary-grade classrooms. *Young Children, 52*(1), 4–10.

Cartwright, S. (1993). Cooperative learning can occur in any kind of program. *Young Children, 48*(2), 12–14.

DeVries, R., & Zan, B. (1996). Assessing interpersonal understanding in the classroom context. *Childhood Education, 72*(5), 268.

Goffin, S. G., & Stegelin, D. A. (Eds.). (1992). *Changing kindergarten*. Washington, DC: National Association for the Education of Young Children.

Gronlund, G. (1995). Bringing the DAP message to kindergarten and primary teachers. *Young Children, 50*(5), 4–13.

Kamii, C. (1984). Autonomy: The aim of education envisioned by Piaget. *Phi Delta Kappan, 65*(6), 410–415.

Rockwell, R. E., Andre, L. C., & Hawley, M. K. (1996). *Parents and teachers as partners: Issues and challenges*. [Chapter 7, especially recommended.]. Fort Worth, TX: Harcourt Brace College Publishers.

Stipek, D., Rosenblatt, L., & DiRocco, L. (1994). Making parents your allies. *Young Children, 49*(3), 4–9.

REFERENCES

Berger, S. K. (1986). *The developing person through childhood and adolescence*. New York: Worth Publishers, Inc.

Boyer, E. L. (1992). *Ready to learn: A mandate for the nation*. Princeton, NJ: The Carnegie Foundation for the Advancement of Teaching.

Bredekamp, S. (1991). The outcomes driven developmental model and developmentally appropriate early childhood education: The Problem of the match. *Quality Driven Education, 1*(5), 44–52.

Bredekamp, S. (Ed.). (1997). *Developmentally appropriate practice in early childhood programs.* (3rd ed). Washington, DC: National Association for the Association of Young Children.

Brewer, J. A. (1996). *Introduction to early childhood education: Primary through the primary grades.* Needham Heights, MA: Allyn and Bacon.

Bukatko, D., & Daehler, M. W. (1992). *Child development: A topical approach.* Boston, MA: Houghton, Mifflin Company.

Burchfield, D. W. (1996). Teaching *all* children: Four developmentally appropriate curricular and instructional strategies in primary-grade classrooms. *Young Children, 52*(1), 4–10.

Charlesworth, R. (1996). *Understanding child development.* Albany, NY: Delmar Publishers.

Cherry, C. (1981). *Think of something quiet.* Belmont, CA: David S. Lake Publishers.

DeVries, R., & Zan, B. (1996). Assessing interpersonal understanding in the classroom context. *Childhood Education, 72*(5), 268.

Dewey, J. (1900/1969). *The child and curriculum.* Chicago: The University of Chicago Press.

Elkind, D. (1987). *Miseducation: Preschoolers at risk.* New York: Alfred A. Knopf.

Erikson, E. H. (1963) *Childhood and society.* New York: W. W. Norton and Company, Inc.

Faber, A., & Mazlish, E. (1974). *Liberated parents liberated children.* New York: Avon Books.

Gantrell, D. J. (1995). Misbehavior or mistaken behavior? *Young Children, 50*(5), 27–34.

Gestwicki, C. (1992). *Home, school, and community relations.* Albany, NY: Delmar Publishers.

Goffin, S. G., & Stegelin, D. A. (Eds.). (1992). *Changing kindergarten.* Washington, DC: National Association for the Education of Young Children.

Goffman, E. (1963). *Stigma.* Englewood Cliffs, NJ: Prentice Hall, Inc.

Gottlieb, D. (Ed.). (1973). *Children's liberation.* Englewood Cliffs, NJ: Prentice-Hall, Inc.

Greenberg, P. (1989). Parents as partners in young children's development and education: A new American fad? Why does it matter? *Young Children, 44*(4), 61–75.

Gronlund, G. (1995). Bringing the DAP message to kindergarten and primary teachers. *Young Children, 50*(5), 4–13.

Honig, A. S., & Wittmer, D. S. (1996). Helping children become more prosocial: Ideas for classrooms, families, schools, and communities, Part 2. *Young Children, 51*(2), 62–70.

Kamii, C. (1984). Autonomy: The aim of education envisioned by Piaget. *Phi Delta Kappan, 65*(6), 410–415.

Kohn, A. (1993). *Punished by rewards.* Boston, MA: Houghton Mifflin Company.

Ladd, G. W. (1989, April). Children's friendships in the classroom: Precursors of early school adaptation. Paper presented at the biennial meeting of the Society for Research in Child Development, Kansas City, MO.

Ladd, G. W., & Price, J. M. (1987). Predicting children's social and school adjustment following the transition from preschool to kindergarten. *Child Development, 58,* 986–992.

Maslow, A. H. (1962). *Toward a psychology of being*. Princeton, NJ: Van Nostrand Company, Inc.

McCracken, J. B. (1986). *Reducing stress in young children's lives.* Washington, DC: National Association for the Education of Young Children.

Piaget, J. (1932/1960). *The moral judgment of the child.* Glencoe, IL: The Free Press.

Rosenholtz, S. J., and Simpson, C. (1984). The formation of ability conceptions: Developmental trend of social construction? *Review of Educational Research, 54,* 31–63.

Willis, S. (1993, November). Teaching young children: Educators seek 'developmental appropriateness'. *Curriculum Update,* 1–8.

5

Organizing the Encouraging Classroom

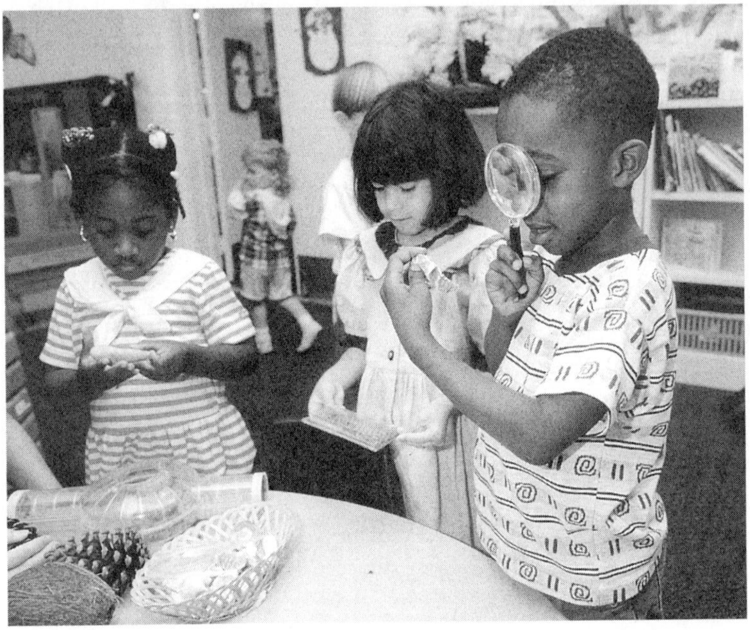

GUIDING QUESTIONS

As you read Chapter 5, you will discover answers to the following questions:

- **What is the role of learning centers in the preprimary classroom?**
- **What is the role of learning centers at the primary level?**
- **How does theme-based instruction facilitate learning in the encouraging classroom?**
- **What is the place of routines in the encouraging classroom?**
- **How does the teacher encourage parents to be classroom volunteers?**

During the 1970s a movement called *open education* took hold in many school districts. Much of the enthusiasm for open education was due to the view espoused by psychologists and educators that children are active, purposeful learners. Despite immediate, widespread popularity, within a decade much of the enthusiasm for open education faded. A main reason for the decline was the way in which open education was implemented. Too much faith was put in the learner to not only be active in the learning process, but to *direct* that process. Many educators believed that given materials and a nurturing atmosphere, children could develop and sustain individual education programs. Adults caught up in the movement became relatively passive in the teaching role, so as not to interfere with the "natural course of learning" of their students. The teacher's role in planning, direct instruction, management, and assessment grew secondary to being a *passive facilitator*.

In early childhood education, knowledge of the learning dynamic in children is a part of the field's tradition and not a short-lived fad. For this reason, and perhaps because of the young age of learners served, early childhood teachers have understood the balance of freedom and guidance children need to learn successfully. They recognize that the role of the teacher is a comprehensive one, which involves planning, managing, guiding, and assessing and not just allowing children "to be free to learn" (Bredekamp & Rosegrant, 1992). Rejecting the idea that any teacher input is interference, early childhood teachers recognize that they are active team leaders upon whom the success of the program rests.

By accepting the planning and managing parts of the role, the teacher can do much to build an encouraging classroom and reduce mistaken behavior. Chapter 5 explores the role of the teacher in the organization of the physical environment, the curriculum, and the classroom routines. A guiding role in the organization of the classroom and the educational program is given to developmentally appropriate practice (DAP). The National Association for the Education of Young Children (NAEYC) policy document (Bredekamp, 1997) provides direction to programs for children that meet their needs, reduce mistaken behavior, and build the encouraging classroom.

LEARNING CENTERS ORGANIZE THE PREPRIMARY CLASSROOM

Organization of the classroom is an important element in the prevention of mistaken behavior. Clearly identified **learning centers*** are beneficial in classrooms throughout the age range. Learning centers are distinct areas within the room that provide a variety of related materials for children's use (Beaty, 1996).

Besides accommodating the active learning style of the young child, centers break the mold of teacher-directed, large group instruction on which some early childhood teachers still rely. Objections to the traditional mode of instruction is that it imposes passivity and conformity on children, restricts the use of critical thinking skills, quickly

* Other commonly used terms are *learning stations, interest centers* and *learning areas,* each with its own particular connotations. The term *learning center* is used in this text.

surpasses children's attention spans, and leads to mistaken behavior (Bredekamp, 1997; Brewer, 1995).

Teachers inexperienced with centers sometimes fear that their use in the classroom will result in chaos. The anxiety around loss of control may be why some early childhood teachers have centers set up but use them only sparingly. In actuality, even three-year-olds use learning centers productively. Centers in the classroom permit what one teacher calls *play with a purpose*. Children aged three to eight are adept at this mode of learning and benefit from being able to select activities of relevance to them. If enough choices are present, center times tend to be busy, positive, and educational (Beaty, 1996; Brewer, 1995).

In **preprimary** classrooms, traditional centers include art, music, dramatic play/housekeeping, reading, blocks, science, sensory table (sand, water, etc.), active play, table activities, and in some classrooms, carpentry (Gordon & Browne, 1989). Modern variations include centers designated for technology, cooking, writing, social/cultural awareness, and dual dramatic play—permanent (housekeeping) and theme-related (Beaty, 1996).

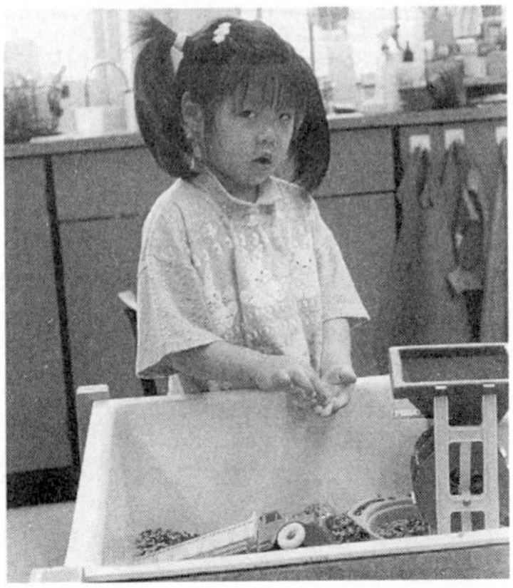

Even three-year-olds use learning centers productively.

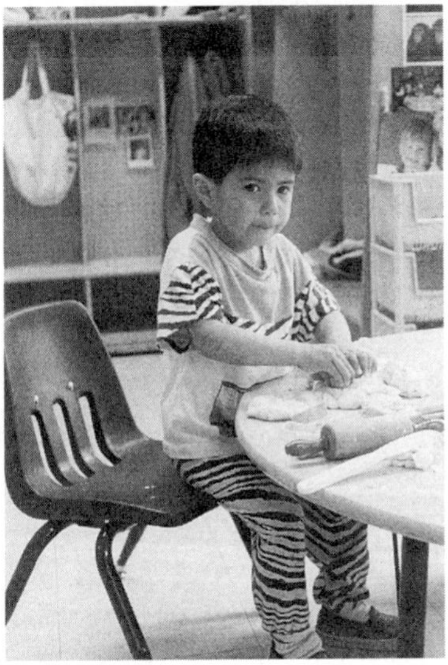

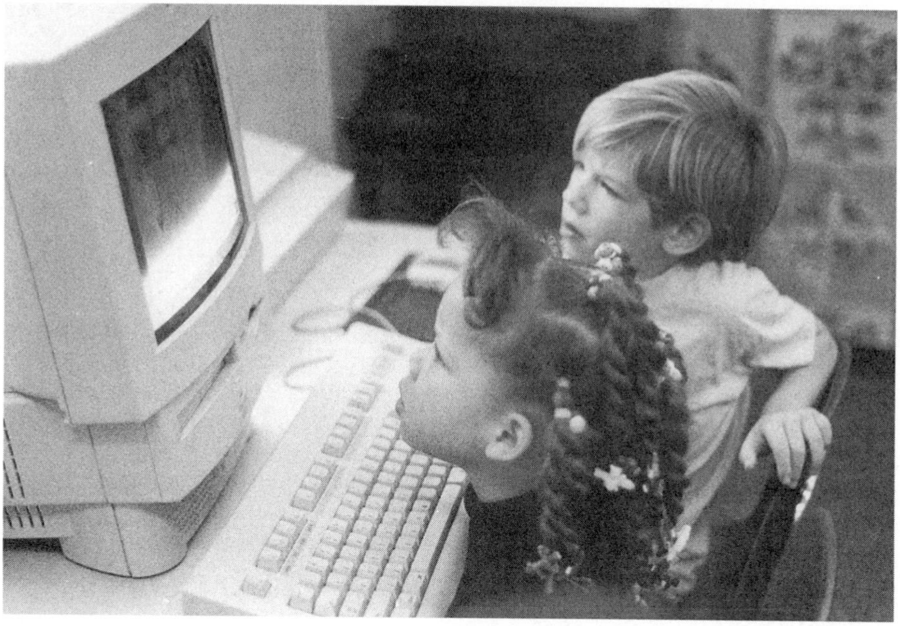

Computer or technology centers are among the newer types of centers found in early childhood classrooms.

When teachers plan the layout of learning centers, they often use traffic flow patterns and noise factors as organizational criteria. A block center, with play spread out on the floor for instance, should not obstruct flow to a restroom, doorway, or cubbies. Due to similar noise levels, a carpentry center might be placed close to an active play area. Science, reading, and table activities, as more quiet centers, might be grouped together (Brewer, 1995). Planning the layout of learning centers in classrooms that almost always pose space and materials limitations is an important, ongoing task of the early childhood teacher.

Carpentry and Active Play

For reasons of noise level and safety, teachers sometimes are reluctant to include carpentry and active play centers in a classroom. In the words of an amazed parent upon her first visit to a classroom, young children are "active critters." They need to be able to move to learn (Bredekamp, 1997). If for no other reason, carpentry is valuable because it is the only opportunity for some children to hammer and saw until middle school. Girls as well as boys enjoy the use of real tools. Ten ounce household hammers, sturdy nails, pine scraps, perhaps a back saw, and safety glasses are all the materials that are needed. An adult should be present to limit the number of children and monitor for safety. With monitoring, accidents at this center are less likely than one might expect—no more than in other kinds of active play.

A kindergarten teacher persuaded a reluctant principal to let her include a carpentry center in the classroom two afternoons a week. Worried about accidents, the principal visited to view the center for himself. The principal arrived just in time to see Anita hit herself on the thumb with a hammer. Anita was about to cry. She noticed though that if she left the table to go to an adult, another child would take her place. With her thumb in her mouth and a tear on her cheek, Anita continued to pound in the nail.

The aide supervising the table and the principal exchanged smiles. The principal returned to the classroom occasionally to visit the carpentry center, but out of interest, not concern.

Like carpentry, an active play center encourages perceptual-motor development. Active play areas are especially important for classrooms in colder climates, where getting bundled and unbundled can take longer than the time spent outside. While active play is vital on a daily basis, some teachers close down active play areas at certain times—circle time, snack, and rest. Even in preschools, children quickly comprehend "open" and "closed" signs.

Typically, active play centers feature a multi-use climber which can be taken down if necessary and a rocker. A separate room is advantageous because the space is often used to supplement the climber with hoppity-hops, balance beams, trikes, and balls. Even in a classroom with limited space, however, teachers can create an effective active play center:

A Head Start program purchased a low mini-exercise trampoline for about thirty dollars. The teacher oriented the preschoolers in its use: only one child at a time; they could only jump so high unless an adult held their hands; they could strap jogger weights to their ankles if they wanted. The trampoline was available during every choice time all year. After a supervised training period, children used it on their own. Several children bounced on the trampoline each day, but wait-times were brief. Few reminders were needed about its use. No injuries occurred. The mini-tramp proved especially helpful for a few very active children in the class. The trampoline became an accepted part of the classroom and was more quiet than the teacher had expected.

Independent Activity at the Preprimary Level

Teachers have various names for the times children spend at centers: free play, play time, choice time, work time, or center time. At the preprimary level, two characteristics of center times mark appropriate practice. First, ample time must be allowed, at least forty-five minutes—once during a half-day program, twice during a full-day

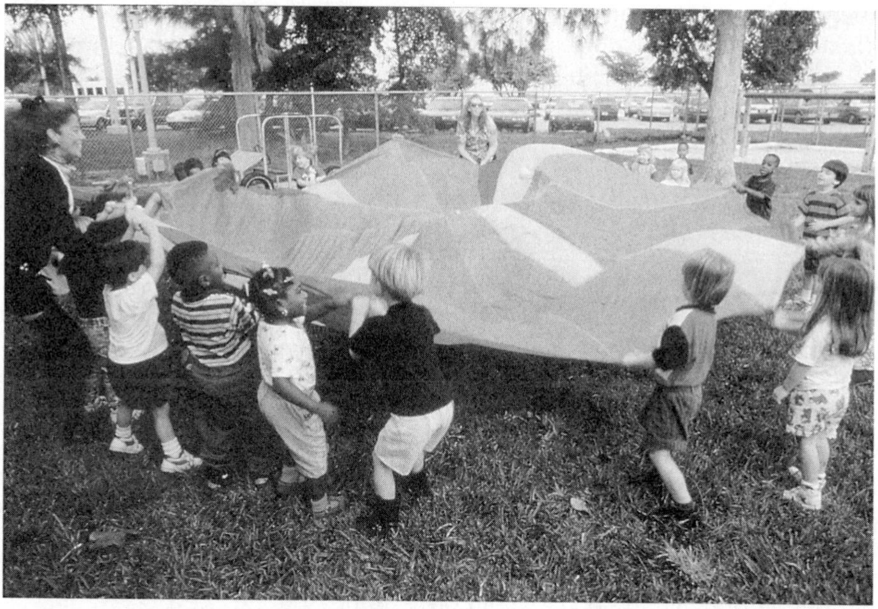

Active play encourages perceptual-motor development.

program. Shorter periods prevent children from becoming fully involved (Rogers & Sawyers, 1988). Unfortunately, some teachers use brief play times as *buffer activities* (in between others), a practice that shows misunderstanding of the importance of the center experience (Beaty, 1996; Brewer, 1995).

Second, preprimary children need choice both in the centers they select and the activities they do. The High/Scope Model has made famous the "plan, do, and review" sequence, designed to increase intentionality and reflection through the learning experience (Hohmann, Banet, & Weikart, 1995). In small groups, children plan what they would like to do during "work time," with the adult and/or child "noting" the choices on paper. Children then "do" independent work times of about an hour, perhaps staying with their choices, perhaps not. Following work time, often during snack, children share what they did, with samples of work encouraged.

Plan, do, and review is just one part of the High/Scope Model. By its implementation of Piagetian thought and a solid research base, High/Scope has done much to legitimize the lasting benefits of child-initiated activity in early childhood (Schweinhart, Barnes, & Weikart, 1993).

A traditional center arrangement, used in some kindergarten classrooms, is for more quiet centers to be open in the morning "when children are fresh" and all centers—including carpentry, music, active play, blocks—during afternoon choice times. This arrangement fails to recognize the active nature of learning for the young child, but it does allow children self-selection among the open centers.

At the preprimary level, the rotation of groups through centers is not developmentally appropriate. The practice deprives children of the developmental benefits of self-selection and self-direction in learning activities. As Montessori discovered at the beginning of the century, no one knows their level of learning better than the children themselves. For Montessori, the right of child-choice extends through the elementary years, a view still outside of the mainstream in American education.

CENTERS AT THE PRIMARY LEVEL

The use of learning centers in elementary schools remains a progressive idea (Brewer, 1995). After kindergarten, centers included in primary classrooms tend to be few and informally designed. Reading centers are fixtures, but less common are music, art, and writing centers. More classrooms do have a computer or two, but well-stocked computer or technology centers are a clear need that is just beginning to be met. As more classrooms get on the Internet, the demand by educators for technology will continue to grow. Although many classrooms do have informal science areas, centers that encourage three-dimensional activity—blocks and other building materials, dramatic play, carpentry, a variety of manipulatives, abundant "sciencing" materials—are too seldom seen.

Earlier in the century, Dewey, Montessori, and Piaget debunked the philosophical separation of mind and body within our schools. Yet, the view of learning as a passive, teacher-controlled process, with discipline used to enforce this view, persists. Educators appear to be telling children that upon entering elementary school, they must foresake their bodies for long periods of the day and use only their minds.

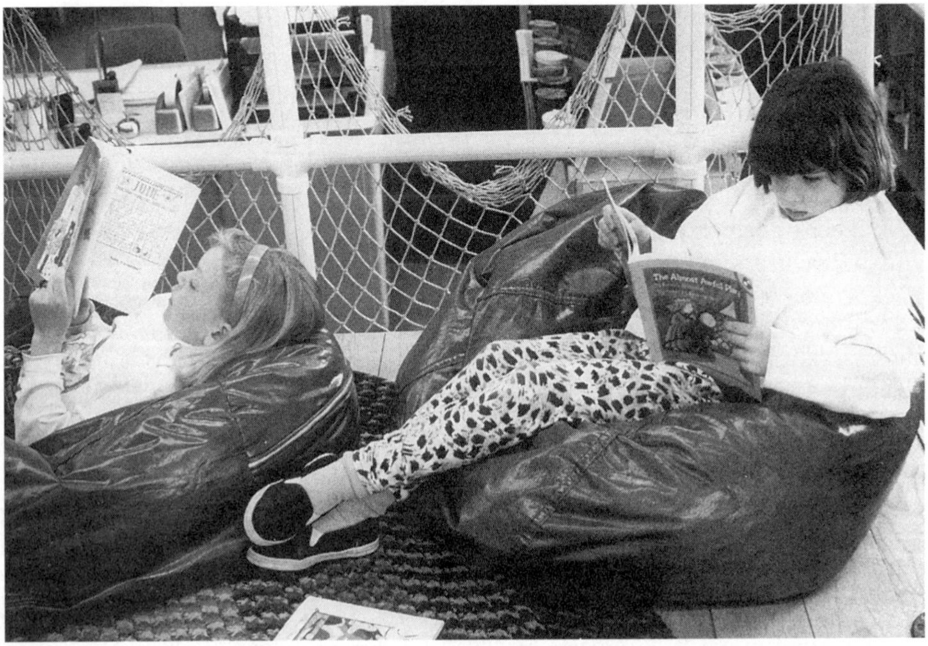

The center most commonly found in primary classrooms is the reading center.

With such an emphasis, educators abandon the natural and essential integration of movement and thought that are so important for healthy development (Wade, 1992; Williams & Kamii, 1986). The fact that classrooms are overcrowded and resources barely adequate may partially explain, but does not justify, this practice.

In an interview with Marilyn Hughes, an elementary teacher with years of K-third teaching experience from Aspen, Colorado, Willis (1993) indicates the "active learning" that occurs at learning centers:

> Learning centers "allow for the broadest range of interactions," says Hughes. Her own classroom featured 20 hands-on learning centers, which were run on student contracts. Some of the centers were set up for independent work; others, for pairs or small groups. Students could respond to the centers in a variety of ways: linguistic, visual, or kinesthetic. Hughes taught her pupils how to move independently through the centers, giving them a chance to pace themselves. The centers placed "hundreds of materials within the reach of the children" (1993, p. 90).

Independent Activity at the Primary Level

The values of self-directing/open-ended activity (**play**) for primary grade children are effectively discussed by Bredekamp (1997) and Perlmutter (1995). Daily child-choice manipulative activity is arguably necessary for children through the primary years (Brewer, 1995; Willis, 1993), though teachers feel hard pressed to find this time in their schedules. Certainly, the integrative values of play present a strong argument for this activity (Rogers & Sawyers, 1988). An expression among progressive educators is "Through play children learn what cannot be taught."

The thought, interaction, and expression that occur during self-directing/open-ended activity improves the satisfaction level of children in the primary classroom. Free for a time from external standards of evaluation, children can experience the gratification of learning for its own sake. With happier children, mistaken behavior decreases. For the professional teacher, the regular open-ended use of learning centers should outweigh any criticism that self-directed center activity is time spent "off task." Justification for the rationale of self-directing/open-ended activity at centers is perhaps the price of teaching progressively as schools enter the 21st century.

Learning Centers and Integrated Curriculum

Bredekamp (1997), Brewer (1995), and Diffily (1996) argue that DAP means shifting away from the study of isolated academic subjects during defined periods and toward the study of **integrated curriculum** in time blocks. Initiated by Dewey in laboratory schools at the beginning of the century, integrated curriculum (often called the *project method*) has been a part of progressive education, including the nursery school movement, ever since (Diffily, 1996). Still, the changeover has yet to occur in most elementary schools, as Brewer (1995) points out:

> The most common approach to curriculum organization in schools in the United States, however, continues to be a subject-matter organization in which learning is segmented

Nonstructured art illustrates the self-direction/open-ended use of learning centers.

A stringing demonstration preceded the work of these six-year-olds in a teacher-instructed/exploratory activity.

The narration with cue to turn the page makes this cassette story a self-directing/self-correcting activity at the reading center.

> into math or science or language arts. You probably remember that in elementary school you had reading first thing in the morning, math right before lunch, and science in the afternoon (p. 112).

Brewer states that in contrast to this fragmentation of the curriculum, a child's learning outside the school is whole and built around personally relevant experiences. She argues that integrating subject matter, as around themes, enables the child to find meaning in learning: "He recognizes that this information is personally useful, not something learned to please an adult, which has no other utility for him" (p. 112).

Myers & Maurer (1987) have proposed a model for learning centers that includes their use in structured instruction as well as play times. The model of Myers & Maurer lends itself to the integrated curriculum. Although these authors directed their approach to the kindergarten, the model applies equally well to the primary grades. The authors assign three different functions to centers depending on instructional intent. The three functions are:

- Self-directing/open-ended
  At each learning center, children select and use materials according to their own interests and abilities.
- Teacher-instructed/exploratory
  The teacher motivates and models exploration of materials at the center according to a preset theme or concept. Children then investigate materials on their own.
- Self-directing/self-correcting
  Children use materials at the center that "have obvious and prescribed uses; the material tells the learner whether a given action is correct or incorrect" (1987, p. 24), i.e., puzzles; object-to-numeral correspondence materials.

The promise of Myers' & Maurer's model (1987) is that it enables the use of centers in a wide variety of primary grade activities. Foremost, in terms of integrated curriculum, the model lends itself to the thematic approach. Themes represent a practical application of integrated curriculum—done perhaps in afternoon time blocks. In the thematic approach, a topic of interest to the children is selected. A variety of activities, some large group, but many involving the use of centers, are undertaken by the children. The children share the results of their discoveries, and the teacher guides and monitors children's progress (Abramson, Robinson, & Anenman, 1995; Walmsley, Camp, & Walmsley, 1992).

THEME-BASED INSTRUCTION IN A SECOND GRADE: A CASE STUDY

The following case study illustrates the uses of learning centers suggested by Myers & Maurer (1987) in elementary school theme-based instruction. The teacher, Mrs. Ryan, is a composite of a few different Minnesota primary grade teachers. Note that the case study involves a second grade class. In younger years, developmentally appropriate practice calls for teachers to be less prescriptive in their use of learning centers. For instance, children would be introduced to the centers and given their choice of which center activity to choose.

Mornings in Mrs. Ryan's second grade class were reserved for specific skill development in the traditional subject areas. Afternoons, however, were spent in **thematic instruction** using an integrated curriculum approach. Mrs. Ryan used the technique of **webbing** to conceptualize and organize themes (Workman & Anziano, 1993). On this day, she and the class decided on a large topic, rather than the more usual specific concept, to plan the theme. The topic, signs of spring, grew from the children's frequent observations of the recent warm weather, flowers, and rain ("finally, 'stead of snow") that arrived in Minnesota (this year by the end of April). They decided to start with "a scientific field trip," a walk around the block to observe and collect specimens that showed spring had arrived. The first web was of activities related to signs of spring the children would do in small groups at different learning centers; Mrs. Ryan called this the "content web" and developed it with the children's input. The second web was of learner outcomes for the children at the different centers. The outcomes came from the school district's list for the second grade (Workman & Anziano, 1993). Mrs. Ryan developed the second web herself.

Mrs. Ryan waited until the end of the first week's activities to generate a third web, a "continued content" web, with the children. This web was the fun part of the theme for her, as the children and she together generated topics and activities to continue their study of the theme. (They would continue with the "signs of spring" as long as their mutual interest held out.) Later, she would construct a second learner outcomes web to correspond to the "continued content web" generated by the group. To illustrate how Mrs. Ryan implemented the theme—using small group teams, active learning, and learning centers—the first week's events are chronicled as follows:

Mrs. Ryan divided the class into four teams. (She established new teams for each theme.) The teams named themselves for animals that returned from migration or awoke from hibernation in the springtime: the bears, the hummingbirds, the bugs, and the skunks.

On Monday two parents, a college intern, and Mrs. Ryan took the four teams outside to tour the area around the school looking for signs of spring. They collected samples of everything from insects to new grass to litter. (One parent drew the line at "dog poop.") Each team recorded its observations.

Upon returning, the teams went to four different centers in the classroom. Each team cataloged their collections and pooled their observations. (Use of centers: teacher-instructed/exploratory). Each team reported its findings to the rest of the class.

On Tuesday, the teacher oriented the class to the theme activities for the rest of the week. The four teams would rotate to a new center each day, with large group sharing at the end. Mrs. Ryan and the class decided to assign the teams alphabetically to centers for Tuesday. She made a chart to show the rotation pattern for the rest of the week. The bears started at center one; the bugs at center two; the hummingbirds at center three; and the skunks at center four.

Center one was a self-directed/self-correcting activity in the science center. The children sorted the entire collection of specimens into boxes labeled "plant things," "animal things," "natural things," and "people-made things." A list of sample items was attached to each box. They counted the items in each category. They decided which set of specimens had the "most" and the "least."

Center two was a teacher-directed/exploratory activity in the reading center. The children studied a large collection of books about spring, including reports made by previous classes. They noted favorite parts of the books and shared them. Although she monitored all of the goings-on, Mrs. Ryan worked primarily with this group.

Center three was a second teacher-directed/exploratory activity in the writing center. Each adult volunteer returned to class on the day his team was at this center. With the adult's help, the children made their own dictionary of words for specimens and other signs of spring; i.e., leaves, litter. They then wrote their chapter of the class report on the topic.

Center four was a self-directing/open-ended activity in the art center. Children made story-pictures of things they have done or would like to do outdoors in the spring. They shared the story-pictures with the others in the team. Later, Mrs. Ryan and a few volunteers displayed each story-picture on the class-made bulletin board—the only kind of bulletin board she has in the room.

Mrs. Ryan looks at the afternoon theme time as an opportunity to use integrated curriculum. Throughout the month she manages to include content in the following subject areas: science, social studies, math, language arts, visual art, health, creative drama, music and physical education. She was able to get permission for the afternoon time blocks for Theme Time by documenting for the principal how she covers outcomes in all eight subject areas. Her preference would be for the children to have

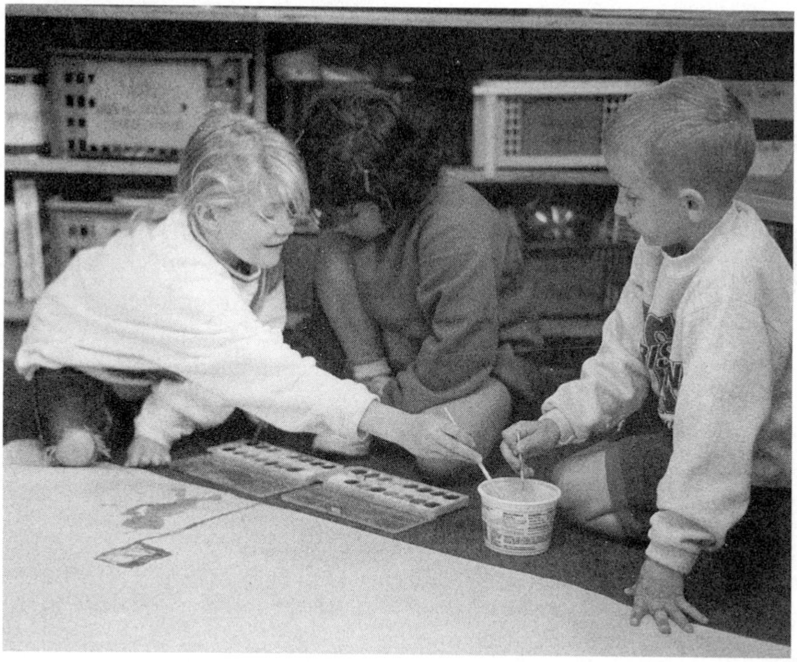

Teacher-directed exploratory activity at an art center is often used in theme-based instruction.

more freedom in selecting center activities (and not to rotate through) but, for this year anyway, the principal was adamant on this point. Mrs. Ryan has found Theme Time to be such an effective instructional vehicle that twice a week she can allow self-directing/open-ended activity at centers for a half hour at the end of the day.

Besides organization and management of the theme, Mrs. Ryan uses **performance assessment** with each child in relation to the school district's learner outcomes. She does so with a variety of **authentic assessment** tools including recorded observations, checklists, and examination of the children's written work kept in portfolios. She states that using the thematic approach "takes real work." However, she sees little mistaken behavior during the time block, "because the children are so busy." She mentioned that when she got volunteers involved the second year to assist with small group activities, "It really helped." Mrs. Ryan believes the children learn so much when they are involved with the themes that the effort is worthwhile.

ROUTINES IN THE ENCOURAGING CLASSROOM: A TEACHERS PERSPECTIVE

Familiarity with the classroom and full use of its many resources help children to become confident, productive learners. Pat Sanford, an experienced kindergarten and primary teacher, offers these thoughts about effective use of the classroom.

Pat says that the secret to classroom management lies in getting children used to routines. For example, she shows them how to store their boots, under their coats with the heels to the wall. This way, the boots won't get knocked over and mixed up with someone else's. Mittens go inside one sleeve. Then children will always know where they are. She makes sure they know where the restroom is (early on the first day) and how to use it.

Materials go back in boxes and on shelves just where they were. Clearly marked labels with pictures and words help the children decide this. Books are to be read and valued; they go back in the bookcase right-side up, facing out. She dislikes the word, "cubby," so each child has a storage bin and knows how to keep papers and belongings there. The children understand that messes during activities are perfectly OK. They also know that cleaning up afterwards is not an optional chore; it is a part of kindergarten life. After commenting about her management style, Pat adds, "Now, if my home only looked like my classroom. . . . "

As a professional, Pat does some things differently than other teachers. Most teachers designate coat hooks and seat locations for children, using printed names to mark the right spots. In Pat's room the children hang their coats and sit at tables wherever they wish:

> Adults like to sit wherever they want; kids should be able to also. Like adults, kids settle in next to someone they're comfortable by. Usually, this is not a problem. If it looks like it might be, I just talk with them privately.

Pat believes that not "institutionalizing" individual space encourages a more comfortable atmosphere. The same goes for the name the children use with their teacher.

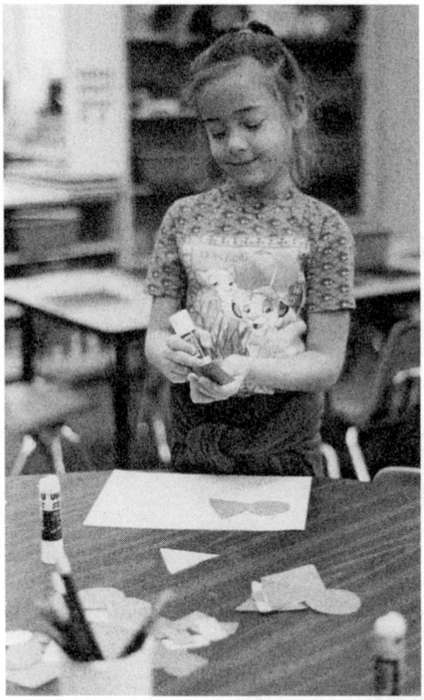

The gains possible through self-directing/open-ended activity help children feel positively about themselves in the classroom situation.

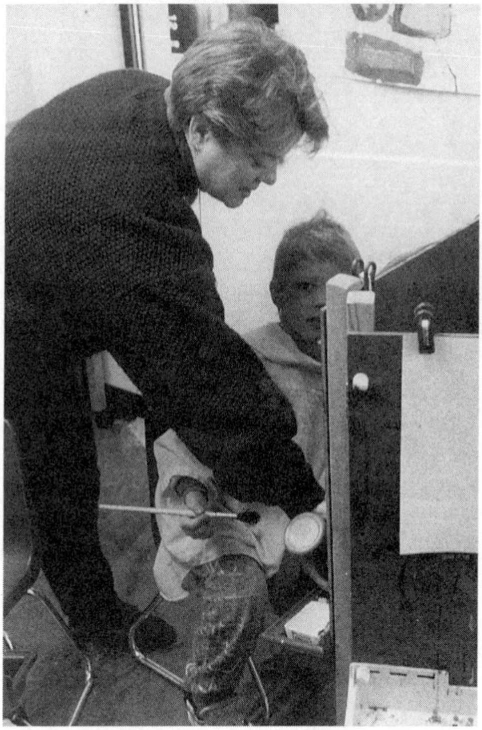

Helping children know that asking for assistance is all right is a part of Pat's approach to teaching routines.

She makes it clear to the children that she does not want to be called "Teacher" ("Because I am a person"). Some call her "Mrs. Sanford," but most call her, "Pat."

Although she believes that helping children get used to routines is important to future school success, she brings a sense of humor to her managerial style. For Pat, the mixture of elementary school rituals and early childhood innocence often brings a smile:

> One day I was supervising a student teacher in Pat's classroom. With a grin, Pat sent me over to stand by a boy for the Pledge of Allegiance. With a hand on his heart he said loudly and with total confidence, "I pledge Norwegians to the flag. . . . "

Finally, Pat is definite about her role as a teacher. "My job is not to prepare children for first grade. My job is to help them have the best kindergarten experience it is possible for them to have." Pat attributes the absence of discipline problems in her classroom to helping the children get used to kindergarten routines, "but in a way respectful to each child."

Whether readers agree with all of her ideas about managing the classroom, Pat offers some thoughtful suggestions that teachers of children aged three to eight would do well to consider. Enjoyment of the children, each and every day, is at the top of her list.

ENCOURAGING PARENTS TO BE CLASSROOM VOLUNTEERS

Parents can be involved in several ways in the preschool or primary grade program. They can:

1. Assist children with home assignments
2. Attend parent-teacher conferences
3. Attend parent meetings
4. Participate in home visits by staff
5. Contribute materials
6. Follow through with staff recommendations
7. Participate in "family journals"
8. Chaperone special events
9. Visit for observation purposes
10. Make presentations to the class
11. Volunteer to help on a regular basis
12. Help to organize special events
13. Assist other parents to volunteer
14. Sit on policy boards
15. Further their own development and education.

In their parent involvement programs, educators tend to focus on one or a few of these ways and measure success accordingly. Programs with a full range of family services, such as Head Start, might focus on all fifteen. Another method of gauging successful involvement is to first decide which of the ways are appropriate for the particular program, then assess success on a family-by-family basis (Rosenthal & Sawyers, 1996). For some parents, participation at levels 1–3 might constitute successful participation. For another family, criteria 1–7 might be used.

The number of parents working outside the home would seem to limit parent availability for in-class involvement (criteria 8–13). Nonetheless, with pleasant persistence, teachers can often prevail upon parents to find times when they can come into the classroom.

The present section focuses on those levels of involvement that pertain to the classroom, criteria 8–13. Specifically, the concern is how to help parents feel comfortable enough to volunteer on a regular basis. Previous chapters began the discussion about the importance of parent-teacher partnerships in the guidance approach. Gestwicki (1992) presents the following advantages of encouraging parents to be classroom volunteers:

Pat sees her role as not preparing children for first grade but as providing the best possible kindergarten experience for each child.

- Parents gain first-hand experience of a program, of their child's reactions in a classroom, and feelings of satisfaction from making a contribution;
- Children feel special when their parents are involved, feel secure with the tangible evidence of parents and teachers cooperating, and gain directly as parental understanding and skills increase;
- Teachers gain resources to extend learning opportunities, observe parent-child interaction, and can feel supported as parents participate and empathize with them (p. 246).

Roadblocks to Involving Parents

Despite these advantages, teachers sometimes encounter two road blocks: (a) other staff are dubious about the merits of using parent volunteers, and (b) parents cannot find the time or they are not sure they can contribute (Gestwicki, 1992). In regard to the first situation, few programs and schools have policies forbidding the use of parent volunteers; such a practice is ill-advised. As mentioned in Chapter 1, programs such as Head Start, cooperative nursery schools, and preschool/parent education programs have a rich tradition of including parents in the classroom. In a growing number of school districts, as well, parent volunteers are gaining in acceptance.

Parents volunteer in the classroom (and out) in many ways. Courtesy, *Bemidji Pioneer.*

The teacher interested in including parents needs to determine what is policy and what simply has never been done. Talking with sympathetic teachers and speaking with the administrator are important first steps. The teacher is more likely to experience success by starting on a small scale and keeping a low profile, so that the effort does not become a "burning teacher's lounge issue." As Gestwicki suggests, determination on the teacher's part is likely to be the main ingredient for success (1992).

Helping Parents Feel Comfortable

In regard to the second situation Rockwell, Andre, & Hawley (1996) suggest that teachers work carefully with parents and not push them to levels of participation beyond their comfort levels. Ideas for creating the climate for partnership with parents were illustrated in Chapter 4. The following suggestions help parents feel more comfortable about volunteering in the classroom.

1. Hold a "Greeting Meeting" for all parents. Distribute two fliers: (a) one that tells about your program, and (b) another that gives suggestions and guidelines for parent volunteers. (Samples in Appendixes C and D.) Go over each flier at the meeting. Stress that you encourage parents to visit and volunteer. Have a parent volunteer from the previous year share what he did. Mention that you know many parents work outside the home and that finding time to get away is difficult. If possible, state that you are open to visits on the parents' time schedules.
2. At or after the Greeting Meeting, ask parents to complete a questionnaire (samples are provided in Appendix B). On the questionnaire, ask parents to check different ways they would be willing to participate. Include choices pertaining to the classroom. Don't ask *if* they would like to volunteer. Provide choices of ways that previous parents volunteered and ask them to check as many as they would like.
3. If the teacher makes home visits, mention volunteering at the home visit. During the first parent-teacher conference, refer to the questionnaire and discuss volunteering in the classroom.
4. Establish with parents when they are welcome. If you choose not to have a general "open house" policy, specify in the flier and at the meeting when parents can visit. Be flexible: parents working outside the home have limited time availability.
5. Let parents know that they have three ways to volunteer: (a) parents can participate on a regular basis (They only need to call if they cannot make it); (b) parents can informally visit or initiate a special event, such as a family sharing activity. (It is important that they call you first); and (c) parents can help with field trips, picnics, etc.
6. A brother or sister brought with a parent probably will not be as disruptive as a teacher might think. For some parents, permission to bring a younger sibling is necessary for them to visit at all. Make clear your policy about siblings accompanying the parent.
7. Some parents might like to volunteer but don't have transportation. Help parents work this out, such as by having two parents "buddy up."
8. When parents visit your classroom, treat them as you would like to be treated if you were visiting a class. Stop what you are doing and privately greet the parent. If the parent seems comfortable with the idea, introduce him to the children. Have a place where the parent can store any belongings. Talk with the parent about what he would be comfortable doing, and help the parent get started. Observe how things are going and provide assistance if needed. When the parent is about to leave, thank him for visiting; let the parent know that he is welcome back; if possible, have the children say good bye.

The teacher assumes responsibility for relationships with parent volunteers. Teachers who view parent volunteers as a natural extension of the parent-teacher partnership will actively invite parents into the classroom. All stand to gain when parents become members of the teaching team (Stipek, Rosenblatt, & DiRocco, 1994).

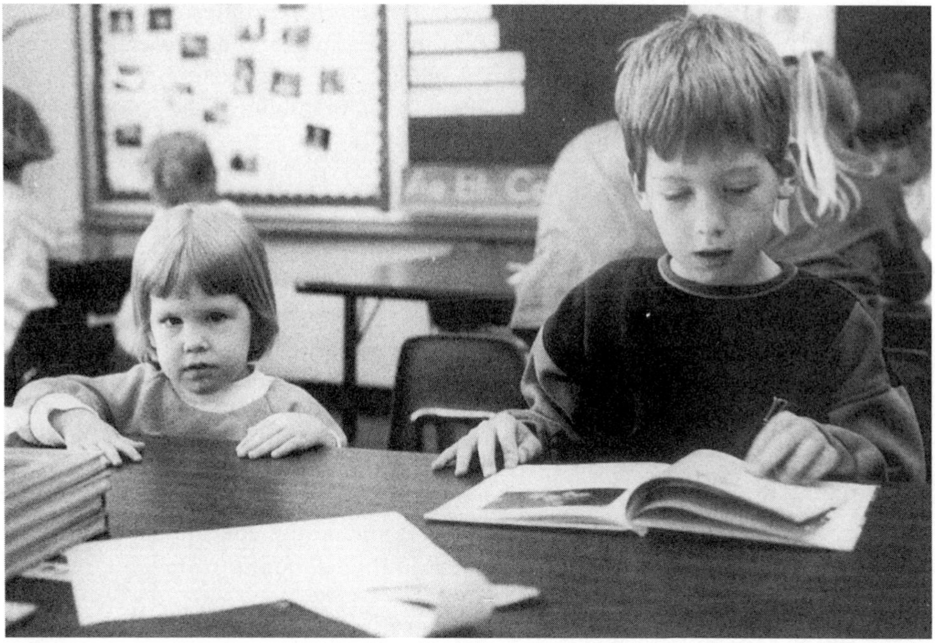

Because this first grader's class is used to visitors, his younger sister does not disrupt the daily program.

SUMMARY

What is the role of learning centers in the preprimary classroom?

Learning centers are distinct areas within the classroom that provide a variety of related materials for children's use. Traditional centers in preprimary classrooms are supplemented by modern variations. When teachers plan the layout of learning centers, they often use traffic flow patterns and noise levels as organizational factors. Through the large motor and perceptual-motor opportunities they provide, active play and carpentry are two important centers in a preprimary classroom. Center-oriented, self-directed play is critical in the preprimary program, including kindergarten. At least 45-minute time blocks—once during a half-day program, twice during a full-day program—are important.

What is the role of learning centers at the primary level?

The use of learning centers in elementary schools remains a progressive idea, though one that is unquestionably developmentally appropriate. Learning centers enable the active learning experiences such reformers as Dewey, Montessori, and Piaget have advocated, and the NAEYC Policy Document (Bredekamp, 1997) DAP recommends. Learning centers encourage a range of interactions, a variety of responses, and a wealth of learning opportunities. The values of self-directing/open-ended activity (play) for the encouraging classroom present a strong argument for this activity in the primary grades. Learning centers can be put to distinct uses and facilitate the use of integrated curriculum in the primary grade classroom.

How does theme-based instruction facilitate the operation of the encouraging classroom?

Integrated curriculum, through use of theme approach, is a teaching strategy that relies on the use of learning centers. Myers' & Maurer's model for three uses of learning centers fits well with the theme approach and indicates how centers can be used at the primary level. Themes enable instruction that touches the interests, backgrounds, learning styles, and needs of individual learners. Through webbing and the individual choices available in the thematic approach, children have opportunities for autonomous learning. By the use of authentic assessment, teachers can determine the effectiveness of themes as an instructional tool and the educational progress of the child. Themes allow for full engagement in the learning process and therefore reduce the need for mistaken behavior.

What is the place of routines in the encouraging classroom?

Pat Sanford, an experienced kindergarten and primary grade teacher, believes that the secret to management for the encouraging classroom lies in getting children used to routines. Pat begins teaching routines such as the location and use of restrooms and how to locate the classroom and the correct bus on the first day of school. She teaches how to stow outerwear so it will be where the children can find it. She models that making a mess during activities is fine, but returning materials and cleaning up are parts of kindergarten life.

Although Pat states that learning about routines is important, she believes in creating a warm classroom atmosphere, with a minimum of *institutionalization*. A sense of humor and respect for each child are important to her. She states that her job is not to prepare children for "next year," but to provide the best possible "present year" for the children in her class.

How does the teacher encourage parents to be classroom volunteers?

Parents can be involved in their children's education in fifteen or more ways. Teachers need to measure the success of the parent involvement program by looking at what is possible for each individual family. Parents, children, and teachers all gain when parents volunteer in the classroom. With a positive attitude and friendly persistence, teachers can overcome most roadblocks to involving parents. Eight suggestions were provided for encouraging parents to visit classrooms and become regular volunteers.

Centers lend themselves both to formal cooperative learning and informal table talk.

FOLLOW-UP ACTIVITIES

Note: In completing follow-up activities, the privacy of all involved is to be respected.

Reflection Activity

The reflection activity encourages students to interrelate their own thoughts and experiences with specific ideas from the chapter.

Recall from your experience as a student a theme or a classroom routine that you participated in and that means something to you in relation to your professional development. Compare or contrast that experience with relevant ideas from the chapter.

Application Activities

Application activities allow students to interrelate material from the text with real life situations. The observations imply access to practicum experiences; the interviews, access to teachers or parents. Students may compare or contrast observations and interviews with referenced ideas from the chapter.

1. **What is the role of learning centers in the preprimary classroom?**
   a. Observe learning center activity in use in a classroom. Watch particularly for one center at which children seem to be getting along easily. Watch for another center at which children may be having more difficulties. To what do you attribute the differences in the children's reactions?
   b. Interview a teacher about one or two of the more active centers in the classroom. Why does the teacher include them? What does he believe the children gain from being able to use them?
2. **What is the role of learning centers at the primary level?**
   a. Observe children who are using a center in one of the three uses described by Myers & Maurer. Which use is it? Why do you think so? In what ways is the children's behavior productive? What mistaken behavior do you observe? What do you think they are learning?
   b. Interview a teacher who uses learning centers in the classroom. Ask what a significant benefit is of using centers. Ask what a significant problem is about using learning centers. Ask what more the teacher might want to do with learning centers if space and resources were not an obstacle. How does what the teacher discussed compare or contrast with what the chapter says about learning centers at the primary level?
3. **How does theme-based instruction facilitate learning in the encouraging classroom?**
   a. Observe a teacher using thematic instruction with a preschool, kindergarten, or primary grade class. Identify and discuss how three practices you observed compare or contrast with the case study of the second grade theme in the chapter. What have you learned about teaching with themes from this experience that may help you in your professional development?

b. Interview a teacher about his use of thematic instruction. How does the teacher use centers when he teaches with themes? What does the teacher see as the advantages and drawbacks of using themes as a teaching strategy? How do the children behave when they are involved in theme activities? Discuss how the teacher's comments compare or contrast with ideas about teaching with themes in the chapter.

4. What is the place of routines in the encouraging classroom?

a. Observe a classroom where there are definite, well-accepted routines. What are the likely effects of the routines on the children? On the teacher? How do Pat's comments about routines compare or contrast with your observations? When you teach, would you use routines similarly to what you observed or differently? Why?

b. Interview a teacher about his use of routines. How does the teacher believe the use of routine assists with classroom management? Ask the teacher how he knows when insufficient use is made of routines in a classroom or when over-reliance is made on routines. How do Pat's comments in the chapter match with what the teacher said about routines?

5. How does the teacher encourage parents to be classroom volunteers?

a. Observe a classroom where one or more parents volunteer. Note what the teacher is doing to help the volunteer(s) feel welcome. Compare or contrast your observations with ideas from the chapter about encouraging parents to volunteer.

b. Interview a parent volunteer. What went into the parent's decision to volunteer in the classroom. What part did the teacher play in the parent's decision to volunteer? Compare what the parent said with ideas from the chapter about encouraging parents to be classroom volunteers.

RECOMMENDED RESOURCES

Diffily, D. (1996). The project approach: A museum exhibit created by kindergartners. *Young Children, 51*(2), 72-75.

Perlmutter, J. C. (1995). 'Play' as well as 'work' in the primary grades. *Young Children, 50*(5), 14-21.

Rosenthal, D. M., & Sawyers, J. Y. (1996). Building successful home/school partnerships: Strategies for parent support and involvement. *Childhood Education 72*(4) 194-200.

Stipek, D., Rosenblatt, L., & DiRocco, L. (1994). Making parents your allies. *Young Children, 49*(3), 4-9.

Willis, S. (1993, November). Teaching young children: Educators seek 'developmental appropriateness'. *Curriculum Update,* 1-8.

Workman, S., & Anziano, M. C. (1993). Curriculum webs: Weaving connections from children to teachers. *Young Children, 48*(2), 4-9.

REFERENCES

Abramson, S., Robinson, R., & Anenman, K. (1995). Project work with diverse students: Adapting curriculum based on the Reggio Emilia Approach. *Childhood Education, 71*(4), 197–202.

Beaty, J. J. (1996). *Preschool: Appropriate practices.* Fort Worth, TX: Harcourt Brace College Publishers.

Bredekamp, S., & Rosegrant, T. (Eds.). (1992). *Reaching potentials: Appropriate curriculum and assessment for young children.* Washington, DC: National Association for the Education of Young Children.

Bredekamp, S. (1997). *Developmentally appropriate practice in early childhood programs* (3rd ed.). Washington, DC: National Association for the Education of Young Children.

Brewer, J. A. (1995). *Introduction to early childhood education: Preschool through primary grades.* Boston, MA: Allyn and Bacon.

Diffily, D. (1996). The project approach: A museum exhibit created by kindergartners. *Young Children, 51*(2), 72–75.

Gestwicki, C. (1992). *Home, school, community relations.* Albany, NY: Delmar Publishers.

Gordon, A. M., & Browne, K. W. (1989). *Beginnings and beyond: Foundations in early childhood education.* Albany, NY: Delmar Publishers.

Hohmann, M., Banet, B., & Weikart, D. P. (1995). *Educating young children: Active learning practices in preschool and child care programs.* Ypsilanti, MI: The High/Scope Press.

Myers, B. K., & Maurer, K. (1987). Teaching with less talking: Learning centers in the kindergarten. *Young Children, 42*(5), 20–27.

Perlmutter, J. C. (1995). 'Play' as well as 'work' in the primary grades. *Young Children, 50*(5), 14–21.

Rockwell, R. E., Andre, L. C., & Hawley, M. K. (1996). *Parents and teachers as partners.* Fort Worth, TX: Harcourt Brace Jovanovitch College Publishers.

Rogers, C. S., & Sawyers, J. K. (1988). *Play in the lives of children.* Washington, DC: National Association for the Education of Young Children.

Rosenthal, D. M., & Sawyers, J. Y. (1996). Building successful home/school partnerships: Strategies for parent support and involvement. *Childhood Education, 72*(4), 194–200.

Stipek, D., Rosenblatt, L., & DiRocco, L. (1994). Making parents your allies. *Young Children, 49*(3), 4–9.

Schweinhart, L. J., Barnes, H. V., & Weikart, D. P. (1993). *Significant benefits: The High/Scope Perry Preschool study through age 27.* Ypsilanti, MI: High/Scope Press.

Wade, M. G. (1992). Motor skills, play, and child development: An introduction, *Early Report, 19*(2), 1–2.

Walmsley, B. B., Camp, A. M., & Walmsley, S. A. (1992). *Teaching kindergarten: A developmentally appropriate approach*. Portsmouth, NH: Heinemann Educational Books.

Williams, C. K., & Kamii, C. (1986). How do children learn by handling objects? *Young Children, 41*(8), 23–26.

Willis, S. (1993, November). Teaching young children: Educators seek 'developmental appropriateness.' *Curriculum Update,* 1-8.

Workman, S., & Anziano, M. C. (1993). Curriculum webs: Weaving connections from children to teachers. *Young Children, 48*(2), 4–9.

6

Managing the Encouraging Classroom

GUIDING QUESTIONS

As you read Chapter 6, you will discover answers to the following questions:

- **How does the teacher balance reliability and novelty in the daily program?**
- **What is the appropriate mix of active and quiet times?**
- **What part do large group activities play in the encouraging classroom?**
- **How does managing transitions reduce mistaken behavior?**
- **How can the teacher make use of parents and other classroom volunteers?**

In the encouraging classroom, the goal of the teacher is to empower children to grow toward **autonomy** in Piaget's terms; toward **initiative, industry,** and **belonging** in Erikson's; and toward the **encounterer relational pattern** level of social relations in Harlow's construct. In this effort, the teacher works to prevent some kinds of mistaken behavior and monitors, but does not necessarily prevent, other kinds. (Discussion about when and how to intervene when mistaken behaviors occur is the content of Unit Three.) One type of mistaken behavior that the teacher actively works to prevent is **institution-caused mistaken behavior.** This mistaken behavior is a result of a mismatch between the child and the expectations of the program—the education program is **developmentally inappropriate** (Bredekamp, 1997). Seven common sources of institution-caused mistaken behavior are:

- Teacher judges children's worth by the behaviors they show (conditional rather than unconditional acceptance).
- Teacher responds to misbehaviors instead of mistaken behaviors.
- Performance expectations for children are inappropriate (too demanding or not challenging enough).
- Lack of organization is shown in the classroom and teaching methods.
- Daily program lacks a balance of reliability and novelty.
- Large groups are too frequent, lengthy, and teacher-centered.
- Transitions lack planning and organization.

This second unit addresses creation of the encouraging classroom through the prevention of institution-caused mistaken behavior. Chapter 5 discussed organization of the physical space and the curriculum to achieve the **engagement** of children in the learning process. Chapter 6 continues the discussion by examining the daily program, the role of large groups, the management of transitions, and the use of parents and other volunteers.

THE DAILY PROGRAM

In the daily program, children need both a sense of reliability and the promise of novelty. Too little of the former results in a lack of predictability and anxiety. Too little of the latter results in tedium (Hendrick, 1996). A set schedule that children are familiar with provides a useful baseline for both the informal *teachable moment,* the gerbil having babies or the planned special event, a visit from Smokey Bear.

Over 100 years ago Montessori recognized that young children need a sense of order and continuity (Montessori, 1912/1964). A predictable schedule provides security (Brewer, 1995). Much of life is beyond children's control, from the time they get up in the morning to the time they go to bed. Some choices, like which of two sets of clothes to wear, are good for children and add to their self-esteem. Other choices, such as whether to go to school or not, children are not in a position to make. When they cannot decide a matter for themselves, children benefit from understanding about a decision that is made for them. Understanding reasons helps children find reliability in the relationship with the teacher and in the classroom environment—necessary basic needs for personal growth.

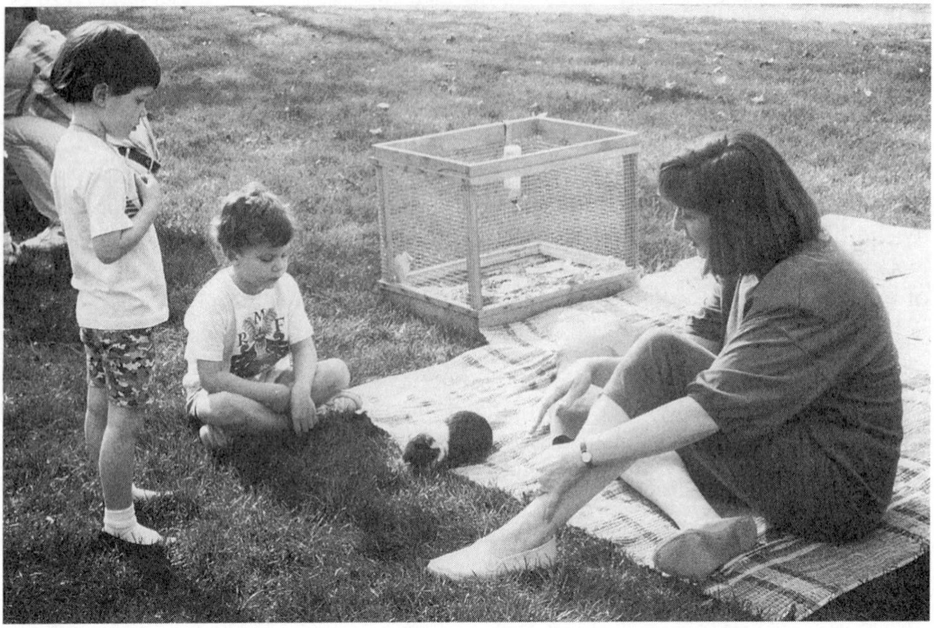

When unscheduled events enable positive results, they add to the everyday program.

The daily schedule is one of those decisions that young children don't make on their own but need to rely on. When unscheduled events enable positive results—celebration, delight, wonderment, enlightenment—they add immeasurably to the everyday program. An unpredictable program, however—whether it is just inconsistent or a continuous series of spontaneous teachable moments (basically unplanned)—makes children feel anxious and insecure. The teacher maintains a healthy balance in the schedule by monitoring the feeling level of the class—anxious, bored, interested, or engaged—and responding accordingly. By reading children's feelings and discussing reasons with them, the teacher may vary from the schedule. Returning to it allows children the security of knowing what is expected of them.

Three Sample Schedules

The sample schedules shown in Tables 6.1, 6.2, and 6.3 model developmentally appropriate programming, make full use of the classroom, and provide a daily program through which interesting experiences can happen. Use of volunteers, as in the teaching team concept, will facilitate some small group activities. Schedules such as these attempt to balance the novel and the predictable so that children are involved but not overloaded—making mistaken behavior less likely. As Walmsley, Camp, & Walmsley note, flexibility in the schedule is a prerequisite for a developmentally appropriate program (1992). The schedules are for a prekindergarten, kindergarten, and primary grade program.

Table 6.1
Prekindergarten Schedule

(Six-hour schedule, as in some Head Start programs. Half-day and full-day programs can be adapted.)

Time	Activity
8:15–8:30	Arrival. Teacher greets each child. Informal child-choice activity until all children arrive.
8:30–9:00	Breakfast in family groups of 8–10, each with a caregiver/teacher. At tables, the caregiver/teachers preview events; **Plan, do, and review** sequence used.
9:00–10:15	Center time. Self-directed/open-ended activity. All centers open. Clean up.
10:15–10:35	Snack in family groups. Review of "special things" done during center time.
10:35–11:00	Active play, inside or out.
11:00–11:15	Large group: music, story, movement activity, or occasional guest. (Sometimes replaced by longer small group activity that follows.)
11:15–11:45	Small group activities—art, cooking, creative drama, or walk outside.
11:45–1:00	Lunch in family groups. Rest.
1:00–2:00	Center time. Self-directed/open-ended activity. All centers open. Clean up.
2:00–2:30	Class meeting, song, and review of day. Get ready to go home.

Table 6.2
Kindergarten Schedule

(Full-day schedule. Half-day schedule can be adapted.)

Time	Activity
8:30–9:00	Arrival. Teacher greets each child. Breakfast for some children. Informal child-choice activity as children arrive.
9:00–9:15	Morning class meeting. Attendance, time and weather discussion. Quick preview of day.
9:15–9:30	Large group lead-in to theme activities through use of discussion, story, song, object, or picture. Teacher instructed/exploratory activities, with introductory instruction in large group.
9:30–10:10	Small group exploratory theme activities using learning centers.
10:10–10:40	Snack time. Balanced large group—movement, story, singing.
10:40–11:45	Center time. Self-directed/open-ended activity at centers. Clean-up.
11:45–12:30	Lunch and child-choice activity inside or active play outside, depending on the weather.
12:30–1:00	Story. Reading, relaxing, resting.
1:00–1:45	Special Activity—gym, art, music, library, or computer.
1:45–2:30	Self-directed/open-ended activity; all centers open. Clean up. Occasional special event during part of this time.
2:30–3:00	Afternoon circle time—songs, movement activities, finger plays, and review of day. Get ready to go home.

Table 6.3
Primary Schedule

Time	Activity	
8:15–8:45	Arrival. Teacher greets each child. Breakfast for some children. Informal child-choice activity as children arrive.	
8:45–9:00	Morning class meeting: business, discussion of important events and issues—brought up by either children or teacher. Preview of **language arts focus** (time block). Assignment of small groups to centers.	
9:00–10:00	Integrated language arts time block in small groups: book-read and share; journaling; language skills instruction; language skills follow-up; language arts choice—reading, journaling, or creative drama.	
10:00–10:30	Restroom, snack, and break/recess.	
10:30–10:45	Transition large group—active to quiet; review of language focus; preview of math focus.	
10:45–11:30	Math skill activities—manipulatives-based, in small groups; one small group each day has supervised computer use; every Wednesday, art specialist.	
11:30–11:45	Review of math focus, story, and transition to lunch.	
11:45–12:30	Lunch and recess.	
12:30–1:00	Relaxation—relaxation activity or another story, quiet music, and reading; sometimes option of educational video.	
1:00–2:05	Large and small groups work on integrative themes having a social studies/science emphasis. (See Mrs. Ryan case study in Chapter 5)	
2:05–2:15	Break, restroom, movement activity, and review of theme activities.	
2:15–3:00	Monday:	Continue work on themes; self-directing/open-ended activities.
	Tuesday:	Alternating music and physical education specialist.
	Wednesday:	Continue work on themes; self-directing/open-ended activities.
	Thursday:	Continue work on themes; self directing/open-ended activities.
	Friday:	Theme presentations by small groups to class; self-directed/open-ended activities.
3:00–3:15	Afternoon class meeting. Happenings of the day—problems and accomplishments, brought up by children or teacher; future events introduced; preparations to go home.	

Tracking the Daily Schedule

The daily schedule provides children with a sense of continuity and order regarding the education program. To maximize the benefits of the schedule for children, the teacher can use a visual tracking method. Two such devices are the horizontal or vertical **period chart** and the circular **day clock**; either can be used with or without a movable marker or "hand."

These visualizations serve multiple functions. One function is to acquaint adults new to the classroom—parent volunteers and substitutes—with the daily program. A second function is to assist young children to begin to understanding sequence and the passage of time. A third is to acquaint children with the idea of "telling time." Until they are seven or eight, children have difficulty understanding time concepts and frequently show *time confusion* (Elkind, 1976). In a helpful article on introducing time concepts, Van Scoy & Fairchild (1993) point out that in contrast to persons who are older:

> Young children's reasoning is tied to what they are seeing and experiencing; that is, young children are dependent on concrete, observable events . . . to help them 'figure things out.' Given this need for concreteness, it is understandable that time concepts—which cannot be seen, heard or felt—are difficult for young children to construct. . . . To help children understand the passage of time, we must relate time to physical objects and/or events that are meaningful to the children (p. 21).

When used with a marker or hand, the period chart or day clock helps children to track events that are real to them—snack, center time, rest, time to go outside. When each time block is displayed by an illustration and a name on the chart or clock, children have contextual clues for building functional literacy. The use of a marker or a single hand helps children to begin telling time in the natural way that time passes—without the complexity of the two handed clock (more appropriate for children who have passed into concrete operations during the primary grades). If the chart or clock has a marker or hand, the children can move it. The teacher can use the devise during the morning meeting to introduce events of the day, including any "special events." She can refer to it during the day to remind children about the order in which events will happen: "Remember? Snack time comes after what?" By constructing knowledge about time concepts that have personal meaning for them, children gain building blocks for the gradual mastery of the intricacies of chronology.

> About midway through the year a teacher introduced a one-handed day clock to her class of four-year-olds. Gradually, during the day, children began to ask her "What comes next again?" Her standard response was, "go read the day clock." She knew the day clock idea was registering when Sam, an "old" four, told her, "Teacher, I know what comes next. Snack. So we gotta go wash our hands." A few days later, a naturalist spoke during large group about protecting the environment. After about fifteen minutes, Sam, who was sitting by the teacher whispered, "Teacher, the clock says it's time for centers."

MIXING ACTIVE AND QUIET TIMES

In the words of that awestruck parent (previous chapter), young children are "active critters." They learn most effectively through movement of large and small muscles (Wade, 1992). Much of the daily program should include activity at a **busy activity level,** with occasional excursions into the **boisterous activity level** ("with exuberance and high spirits") and the **bucolic activity level** ("peaceful, simple, and natural"). The center approach, discussed in Chapter 5, defines busy activity. **Table**

talk and movement at and among centers are common in classrooms functioning at the busy level.

Boisterous activity is known to all—jumping on a mini-tramp, climbing on a climber, dancing to "The Pop Corn Rock," running, riding a trike. Bucolic activity includes attending in large groups, doing "seatwork," reading a book, watching a video, or resting.

Traditionally at the elementary level, educators have made bucolic the goal, with activity at the busy level occasionally acceptable, and boisterous activity only under special circumstances. The problem is that bucolic activity often lapses into *passivity,* the absence of engagement in the learning process. Without engagement children become bored and restless and mistaken behavior results.

When children experience difficulty in a program, adults often use common, sometimes trendy labels to describe their behavior: *immature, hyper, antsy, rowdy, strong willed,* or *attention-deficit disordered.* Sometimes these behavior patterns have a physiological or psychological basis that needs to be diagnosed and remediated. But often such labels result from the mismatch between the program and the child—the program tending toward the bucolic level, and children needing to be actively engaged, *busy.* Rather than suppress the active learning style of the young, teachers do better to guide it and empower children through it (Wade, 1992; Gronlund, 1995).

Rest and Relaxation

Although busy sets the tone of the developmentally appropriate classroom (Brewer, 1995; Gronlund, 1995), neither children nor teachers can function all day at the busy level. For some years, books by such authors as Clare Cherry (*Think of Something*

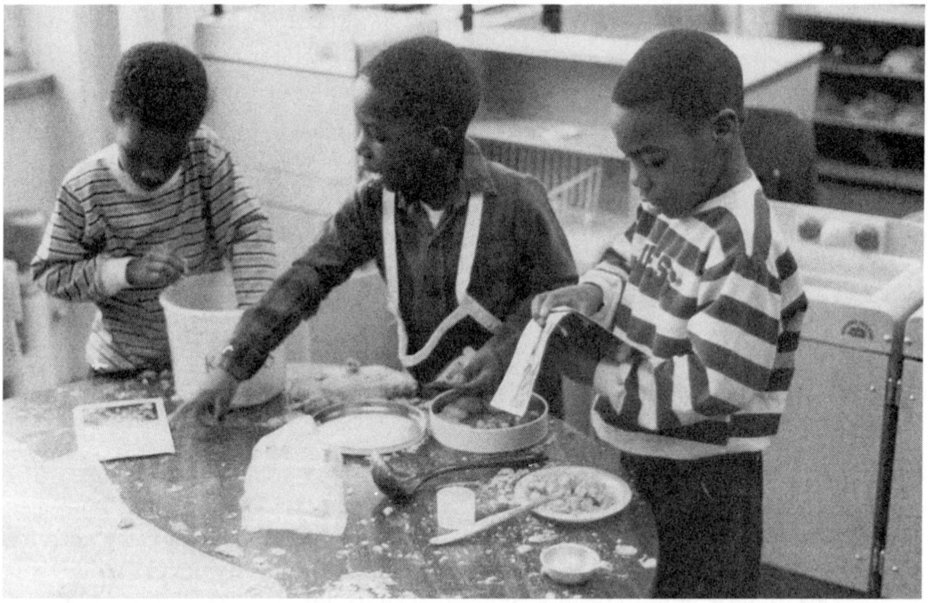

In the encouraging classroom, the normal activity level is busy.

Quiet, 1981) and albums by such musicians as Hap Palmer (*Sea Gulls,* 1978) and Greg and Steve (*Quiet Moments,* 1983) have been helpful in promoting relaxation in the classroom. With modern family life-styles and the pressures of school and community, children, like adults, become tense, angry, and anxious. Cherry (1981) and Honig (1986) have pointed out that children do not always have the ability to relax on their own. Marion (1995) discusses teaching children specific relaxation techniques to help them cool down and become more receptive to guidance talks (my term) with adults.

The traditional naps in preschool, the rest periods or naps in kindergarten, and quiet periods in elementary grades—when done nonpunitively—all serve to restore a sense of equilibrium for children and teachers. Stories too, when done on a daily basis in a relaxed atmosphere, have regenerating values. The relaxation materials mentioned previously go a step further, however, by providing activities to specifically reduce stress in young children. A few topics in the Cherry text, for instance, are:

- creating wholesome environments;
- responding to stress;
- developing inner awareness;
- learning to relax muscles (pp. v-vii).

Think of Something Quiet is now as old as some students reading this book. No work in the early childhood literature that I know of has replaced it; more attention needs to be given to the matter of relaxation and children at school.

In full-day programs for young children, nap times can be challenging. Children have different rest needs and show differing behaviors when adjusting to nap time (Saifer, 1990). When children of different ages share the same room for rest, problems can be compounded. The "finger tip guide" shown in Table 6.4 provides suggestions for helping staff meet nap challenge.

Adults help children to nap when they create a relaxing mood and setting. Maintaining a firm, friendly, and quiet response style is important. Staff who take a problem-solving approach to rest almost always improve the situation (Saifer, 1990), often within a week or two.

One class in a child care center had preschoolers from age three to five along with part-time kindergarten children who arrived from school each day at noon. The kindergarten kids felt they were "too old" for naps, and the younger children were affected each day by their arrival. "Rest" was proving difficult.

One day an assistant teacher asked a kindergarten child to rub the back of his younger brother to help the three-year-old get settled. It worked. The preschool staff got to talking about this and decided to try something new. They had each kindergarten child rub the back of a selected preschooler. After the preschooler fell asleep, the kindergartners lay down on their mats behind a long book shelf. On their mats the "k" kids looked at books or listened to relaxing music. In just a few days, rest time at the center changed completely.

Table 6.4
Fingertip Guide to Happy Napping

Challenge	Suggestion
Many children have trouble settling down.	Review: (a) Activity level prior to nap—relaxing, quiet? (b) Method of creating mood—story, music, relaxation activity used? (c) Environment—comfortable temperature, low lighting, enough space? (d) Role of adults—present, speaking quietly, lying with children, rubbing backs?
Children rest, but many ready to rise too early.	Assess length of nap time. Consider shortening. Start early risers doing quiet activities.
Older children don't sleep; ready to rise before others.	Move older children to different room or separate area. Allow to read books on mats. Allow to rise early and do quiet activities.
Individual child doesn't sleep; ready to rise. Doesn't seem tired.	Check with parent about priorities. If willing, try solution above for older children; note how child responds.
Individual child doesn't sleep; ready to rise. Does seem tired.	Separate from others. Primary caregiver rubs back, lies by child. At another time talk with child about problem. Talk with parent about child's sleeping habits.
Individual child not ready to rise with others.	Let child sleep. Monitor health of child. If pattern continues, talk with parent about possible reasons.
Early risers in buffer activity get too active.	Review selection of activities. Allow to read books, not just watch videos. Allow to read books or make pictures, but *not* watch videos. Review placement of children: too near sleepers? too close together? (Give children options for changing locations and activities, but within your limits of what is acceptable.)

Active Play

For teachers to use boisterous activity productively, three ideas are important.

1. Throughout the age range, movement to music activities refreshes participants and renews their ability to concentrate. A common practice in Asian programs, some American schools now begin the day with movement to music. Pieces by Steve and Greg, Hap Palmer, and various "aerobics for kids," artists are piped into classrooms over the loudspeakers. Teachers as well as the children move to the music. As enjoyment and not skill is the purpose, each person moves in her own way.
2. The teacher should not rely only on scheduled active play times or physical education periods to meet children's need for vigorous activity.

At the preprimary level, include an active play center—a climber, mini-tramp, etc.—that is open during at least one child-choice time per day.

3. Effective vigorous play activities involve children without the need to compete or take turns. Young children run for the sake of running, skip for the sake of skipping, and climb for the sake of climbing. The rules and complexities of competitive games tend to confuse young children and cause hurt feelings (Honig & Wittmer, 1996). As well, wait times between turns are often frustrating and limit the opportunity for physical activity that is the main reason for the activity. When all participate enjoyably, everybody wins.

> A Head Start teacher became tired of the usual active game in her class, Duck, Duck, Grey Duck. A large portion of the game was spent in squatting down. Once the children began running, the teacher noticed most did not want to stop. The inability of some children to catch the others also detracted from the fun. The teacher ended the game. Instead, she adapted Red Light, Green Light for her group by requiring different ways to move each time the "green light" showed and declaring the whole class winners as soon as the last child crossed the finish line. The game became the new favorite of the children, especially when the teacher taped a red light to her front and a green light to her back, jumped around, and enthusiastically called out directions.

Teachers who take the guidance approach need to consider the balance of active and quiet times in the daily programs. Distinct from traditional practices, the general noise level of classrooms should be *busy,* with planned periods that are *boisterous* and *bucolic.*

THE PLACE OF LARGE GROUPS

A hallmark of effective programs is that they accommodate the range of developmental responses that any group of children will show. A productive *center* such as a reading center accommodates developmental diversity by providing a variety of materials from picture books to "early readers" to elementary science tests. Productive *materials* such as blocks and clay accommodate developmental diversity by allowing children to construct whatever they will, from a simple stack to a castle, from a simple clay ball to a bird sitting on its nest of eggs. Productive *activities* also are developmentally inclusive. In the area of art, for instance, the teacher avoids photocopies and craft projects but instead motivates children to work creatively with the materials provided so that each child can succeed at her level (Bredekamp, 1997; Edwards & Nabors, 1993).

Likewise, productive **grouping patterns**—large groups, small groups, individual activities—encourage children to function effectively at their various levels of development. A problem with overreliance on large group, teacher-directed activities

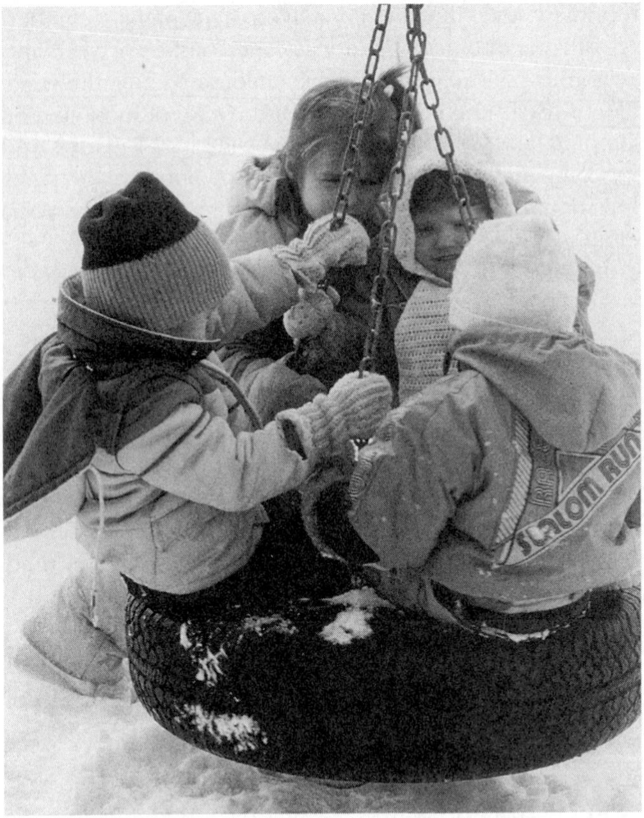

Children play actively without the need for adult direction, even under less than ideal conditions. (Courtesy Michael Crowley, Family Service Center, Koochiching-Itasca Head Start, Grand Rapids, Minnesota)

is that they easily exceed most children's developmental levels and attention spans (Brewer, 1995). Very few preschoolers, only some kindergarteners, and many—but not all—primary grade children are capable of sitting, listening, and following directions for any length of time (Bredekamp, 1997; McAfee, 1986).

An argument for frequent large groups is that young children need to get used to sitting and listening to succeed at school. However, the physiology of preprimary children prevents them from sitting comfortably for long periods. To the comment that young children must learn to sit and listen, the response is that young children are not developmentally ready; they will become more ready as they get older (Brewer, 1995). In fact, even though the development of primary grade children means that they attend longer, the DAP research indicates that even primary grade children learn more effectively when they are doing and interacting (Bredekamp, 1997; Dunn, L. & Kontos, S., 1997; Brewer, 1995; Gronlund, 1995).

On a sunny spring afternoon, a first grade class went to the library. While there, they silently read/looked at books, then heard the librarian read quite a long story. When they arrived back at the classroom, a parent who was scheduled to read a book that morning arrived and asked if he could read then. The teacher felt this was important and agreed. She and the student teacher sat with the children and worked hard to keep them focused on the story.

The next scheduled activity was another large group; the student teacher was to do a lesson on friendship with a puppet named Charlie. After three tries at starting the lesson, the student teacher whispered to the teacher. Then, the Puppet announced, "Boys and girls, Charlie thinks that listening is hard to do right now because you have had to sit so long. When I call your name, line up to go outside." An afternoon's pent-up energy expressed itself in a bedlam of activity. After a half hour outdoors, the teacher and student teacher again had "happy campers." The class came in and worked industriously on their daily journals.

Throughout this age range, children learn best when they engage in many independent activities, frequent small groups, and *occasional* large groups that are friendly, participatory, relevant to the children's experiences, and concise (McAfee, 1986). Brewer (1995) and McAfee (1986) recommend that teachers review standard

Primary grade children, like younger children, learn more effectively when they are doing and interacting.

large group practices for such criteria. From the perspective of the encouraging classroom, this section critically examines traditional large group practices: *taking attendance, calendar and the weather, show and tell, stories,* and *large group instruction.* To challenge these "circle time traditions" is a bit controversial. Teachers would do well, however, to reflect about the meaning of these activities for the children as well as themselves. Our mutual goal is to avoid the problem of *passivity* and actively engage the young learners in our charge.

Taking Attendance

Attendance can be done efficiently if teachers greet children individually when they arrive and ask them to "register" right away. One way of registering is to have laminated "mushrooms" with each child's name, a child-made design, and the child's photo. After learning their names, the children take their own mushrooms from slots in one tagboard sheet and put them in the slots with their names on a second sheet. At a morning class meeting, the teacher quickly reviews the charts with the class, and those absent and present are noted. Even three-year-olds quickly recognize their names.

Another alternative, which many teachers enjoy, is to sing an attendance song that mentions each present child by name. Such songs often have made-up words to familiar tunes and sometimes use name cards, such as the "mushrooms" to encourage functional literacy. Songs make taking attendance more participatory, an objective for successful large groups. Teachers who use greeting songs seem to overcome two minor difficulties with them: (a) with a large class, long verses take a lot of time; (b) some children get embarrassed and may not want their names sung. Short verses and a matter-of-fact approach with individual children make this method of greeting successful.

Calendar and the Weather

Calendar and weather activities easily become rituals rather than learning experiences (McAfee, 1986). As mentioned, until middle childhood, children experience **time confusion,** which means they have difficulty understanding time concepts (Elkind, 1976). A first grade teacher was amused to discover time confusion when she asked her students two questions: What season is the month of November in? and "How old they thought she was? She got answers that included *salty, 18,* and *62!* In their article about time, Van Scoy and Fairchild (1993) say this about typical time activities such as the daily calendar:

> Time is often taught to children by having them recite social labels such as the days of the week or months of the year. Children who recite labels in this way are being given an opportunity to construct **social knowledge** about time. . . . Social knowledge is knowledge of an arbitrary set of symbols and behaviors common to a society. Children who recite labels are not having experiences that will help them develop an understanding of the passage of time (p. 21).

Weather concepts also are more abstract to children than adults may realize. Two partly cloudy days following two cloudy days simply is not an every day topic of conversation for five-year-olds. When the selected "weather person" goes to the window and looks hard at what's going on outside, a passing truck or squirrel may be more natural interests than the cloud formation. If the child returns with the wrong report, the teacher has to engage in "damage control," especially with the two others who thought they should have been picked to be the weather person.

Many teachers use alternatives to the ritualistic treatment of the calendar and the weather. In a morning **class meeting,** an alternative is to ask four or five questions that encourage children to think about time and weather concepts in terms that have personal meaning for them. Sample questions include:

- Who can remember what you had for supper last night?
- Who knows what you will do after school today?
- Who can remember three things you saw on the way to school this morning?
- Was it hot or cold when you came to school today? How could you tell?
- It is windy today. Who saw the wind push something?
- It is raining today. Who hopes it is still raining after school today? Why? Why not?

These questions relate directly to the children's experience. If children know that all interpretations of questions are welcome and not just one answer that the teacher may have in mind, they will participate readily. Through engagement in interesting discussion, children gain in observation powers, thinking skills, and communication abilities (McAfee, 1986). They will have a foundation in personal experience that will help them master adult weather and time concepts later.

Despite the criticism that conventional calendar and weather tend to be more meaningful to teachers than children, many teachers would rather not give them up. They value the social development that occurs through a positive group experience and maintain that the exposure to weather, day, and date vocabulary has its own value. I remember visiting a classroom of three-year-olds in a child care center where the children clearly enjoyed singing a "days of the week" song, and the weather person's report was appreciated whatever it turned out to be. These activities helped the children feel a sense of belonging, reliability, and accomplishment—important for young ones away from home. The suggestion here is that young children may not understand as much of these activities as the teacher may think. A compromise is to do calendar and the weather in a way that is concise, positive, and as relevant as possible to the children's own experience. Then move on to activities that have more intrinsic interest for the audience.

Show and Tell

Show and tell often is criticized as "bring and brag" (Brewer, 1995). The thought behind show and tell seems to be that if children bring in familiar objects, they will feel comfortable showing them in a large group and so use communication skills. One problem with show and tell is that it is materialistic. Focusing on object possession, children expect one another to bring in interesting items. Then they judge each child on the basis of the items shown (Brewer, 1995). A second problem is that the child may not have a lot to say about the item. The teacher then has to become an interviewer, and the rest of the group may tune out. Passivity is likely to increase if all in the group share (Saifer, 1990) and after a few months of following the same routine (McAfee, 1986).

Teachers handle problems with show and tell in various ways. Most directly, some teachers have ended the practice. They spark discussions in the circle time instead that lead to a fuller sharing of thoughts and feelings. Open-ended questions that children can personally relate to are a superior medium for developing communications skills. The kinds of questions mentioned under the calendar and weather heading are examples. A few others include:

- Who can tell us about a time when you went swimming?
- Who can share about when you were in a snowball fight?
- Who knows about an interesting pet that someone owns?

Such questions lead well into themes and learning center activities that may follow the large group. They arouse interest and focus on *ideas* rather than *things*.

For teachers who do not wish to end show and tell altogether, Saifer (1990) provides ideas for dealing with "bored children during show and tell." Useful ideas include:

- Do show and tell in small groups (such as during center time, for those who are interested);
- Schedule show and tell on a rotating basis with only some children sharing each day;
- Directly encourage other children to ask questions; stand behind the child to direct the group's attention;
- "Have children share family experiences, a picture they made, or what they did earlier in the day at school. Sharing themselves rather than things, helps children who have no item to share; develops the children's ability to review; and makes for more personal, meaningful sharing" (Saifer, 1990, p. 22).

The main idea is to replace a competitive materialistic focus (on things) with a spirit of community that the sharing of thoughts and feelings can inspire.

4

Using Stories with Children

The traditional method of delivering stories is the large group. When doing stories in a large group, to preserve lines of sight, teachers frequently sit on low chairs. Children sit on rug samples or other markers, which reduces crowding and the frequent complaint that "I can't see." The technique is efficient but results in a separation between adult and children. An alternative in story delivery is the small group. With children on the adult's lap or all lying on stomachs around a book, an important closeness results, which the McCrackens term the lap technique (McCracken &

McCracken, 1987). Ideally, the lap technique begins early in the child's life at home. To encourage an appreciation of books and reading, the lap technique is an important method to use but difficult to accomplish in the large group. (See anecdote, page 170.)

Of course, a role remains for stories in large group settings (McCracken & McCracken, 1987). Thinking of two different purposes for using stories in large groups may be helpful. First, encourage appreciation; second, encourage personal expression. By focusing on the particular intention of the story experience, the teacher can reduce mistaken behavior.

Reading to Encourage Appreciation Teachers who wish to encourage appreciation of books and stories want the experience to be relaxing and engaging for the children. Usual times when the teacher reads to foster enjoyment are after sustained activity for a calming effect; and to set a relaxed mood for an activity to come such as lunch, nap, or going home. Adults can use various methods to establish an engaging story setting. The methods listed in Figure 6.1 are the author's top ten suggestions. (The list may be read up or down.)

Reading to Encourage Personal Expression While reading to children to encourage their receptive appreciation of stories is common in early childhood, there is a second function, *the encouragement of personal expression.* Some teachers are able to integrate the two functions quite effortlessly in the group setting, but others struggle especially with the second.

Reading for personal expression means encouraging discussion by the children during and after the story. At key points while she is reading, the teacher asks open-ended questions and welcomes children's responses. She uses a technique called **discussing inclusively.** Discussing inclusively means that when a child makes a comment that doesn't seem to relate to the discussion, the teacher realizes that the comment *does relate for the child.* The teacher responds in a friendly way and tries to include the comment in the conversation. When discussing inclusively, she does not focus on *correct* or *incorrect* answers but allows the discussion to build, based on the shared and unique experiences of the children. When the teacher thinks it is appropriate, she steers attention back to the book and continues to read.

Through the technique of discussing inclusively, the teacher fosters a number of desirable learner outcomes, including the practice of listening and speaking skills, comprehension abilities, engagement in the learning process, enjoyment of literature, and comfort at speaking in front of others. (As college students are aware, a fear of speaking in public is widespread and too often gets its start in classroom discussions that are handled insensitively.) Teachers need not, and should not, restrict inclusive discussions to the medium of children's books, but reading for personal expression provides an excellent opportunity to build a classroom where all feel their ideas are welcome.

Often, teachers use reading for personal expression as a lead-in for related expressive activity such as creative drama, journaling, story pictures, or more free-flowing discussion. Effective follow-up depends upon the teacher finding topics to which the children can relate. Often the most effective follow-up is in small groups, which the teacher has previously planned.

> After a snow fall, a kindergarten teacher was reading the classic, *A Snowy Day,* when Clarise raised her hand: "Teacher, me and Cleo went sliding and she got snow down her pants!" (General laughter.)
>
> Teacher: "That must have been cold. What did she do?"
> Clarise: "She went inside but Paul and me kept sliding. It was fun."
> Teacher: "Paul and you stayed outside so you could keep sliding. Thanks for sharing, Clarise; did anyone else go sliding last weekend?"
>
> After several children shared, the teacher commented, "You had lots of good times sliding and skiing. Now let's see what's going to happen to Peter."
>
> At the end of the book, the teacher announced: "It sounds as if you like to do lots of fun things in the snow just like Peter. Right now, when I tell you to, I would like each table group to take their seats. Use the materials that are laid out and make story pictures of your favorite thing to do when it snows." She dismissed the class by table groups, and each group chatted about snow adventures as they made their story pictures.

As a final note, make books you have read to the class available in the library center for children to look at by themselves and use in small group activities. When they use stories to spark follow-up activity, teachers further encourage personal expression and literacy development as well as a fuller appreciation of the literature they have shared.

Large Group Instruction

Teaching in large groups seems normal because it is the way most teachers themselves were educated, kindergarten through college. In traditional large group instruction, the teacher transmits information and then solicits repetition or application of the information from "volunteers" who give an indication of group understanding.

The basic criticism of this "didactic method" is that children are "over taught and under practiced" (McCracken & McCracken, 1987). They absorb the information but don't have the opportunity to construct their own knowledge from it. They are not fully able to "own" the learning, make sense of it, and value it. Common signs that children are unable to engage in the learning process include glassy eyes, inattentiveness, and restlessness. (Gronlund, 1995). With prolonged exposure to the

Figure 6.1
Top 10 Methods for Encouraging Appreciation of Books and Stories in Young Children

1. Select books appropriate for the age and backgrounds of the children and that will engage and hold their interest. Think about the children's attention spans and interests when previewing books you will read. Consider whether stories reinforce or go beyond stereotypes pertaining to culture, gender and disability.
2. Select books that match themes and special events. Many "read aloud," "story stretching," and theme books have bibliographies of relevant books. Preread such books for appropriateness to ages and interests of group.
3. Use large, oversized picture books so that all children can see the important details. Or, use filmstrips, but not necessarily with the sound cassette. Provide the narration yourself to personalize the story experience. Videos of children's literature *perhaps* also have their place, but they cannot be as easily personalized by the teacher.
4. Select books that you will be able to read with expression. If you are not familiar with the story, always practice it by reading aloud first. Use dramatic tones when you read; animate your usual speaking voice. When you are "into" the story, the children will be.
5. Station any co-teachers and volunteers near children in the group who may need extra support to stay engaged. If other adults are not available, quietly seat children who need extra support close to you. Establish that all children can see and that children need to stay seated where they are so that they can continue to see.
6. Use a brief finger play, movement activity, or interesting introduction to help children get ready for the story. If an **anticipatory set** is not established, some children may not focus enough to pick up the story line. Avoid simply starting the book without first gaining the children's attention; otherwise, you may never have it.
7. Allow children to read their own books while you read. Many children can attend to two things at once, and this will help *independent learners* keep occupied. The practice sounds unorthodox, but it is in line with the outcome of appreciation for reading and books. Typically, only some children choose to read their own books; these readers stay with their books until the teacher gets to a "good part." Then they look up and follow the teacher's story.
8. Tell stories as well as read them. Some current or historic folk tales of cultural relevance to your group may not be accessible in written form. Telling stories takes fortitude the first few times, but children adjust quickly to this "radio way of learning." Ask children to close their eyes and see the pictures in their minds. Having children spread out and lie down adds to the success of this experience and makes the technique useful at rest time.
9. Gauge your time. Avoid selecting books that will be too long for the available time block. You can sometimes shorten stories to fit the time but be prepared to be corrected if the children know the story already.
10. Have back-up activities planned. Be ready to shorten the experience, change books, or switch to another activity if many children loose interest.

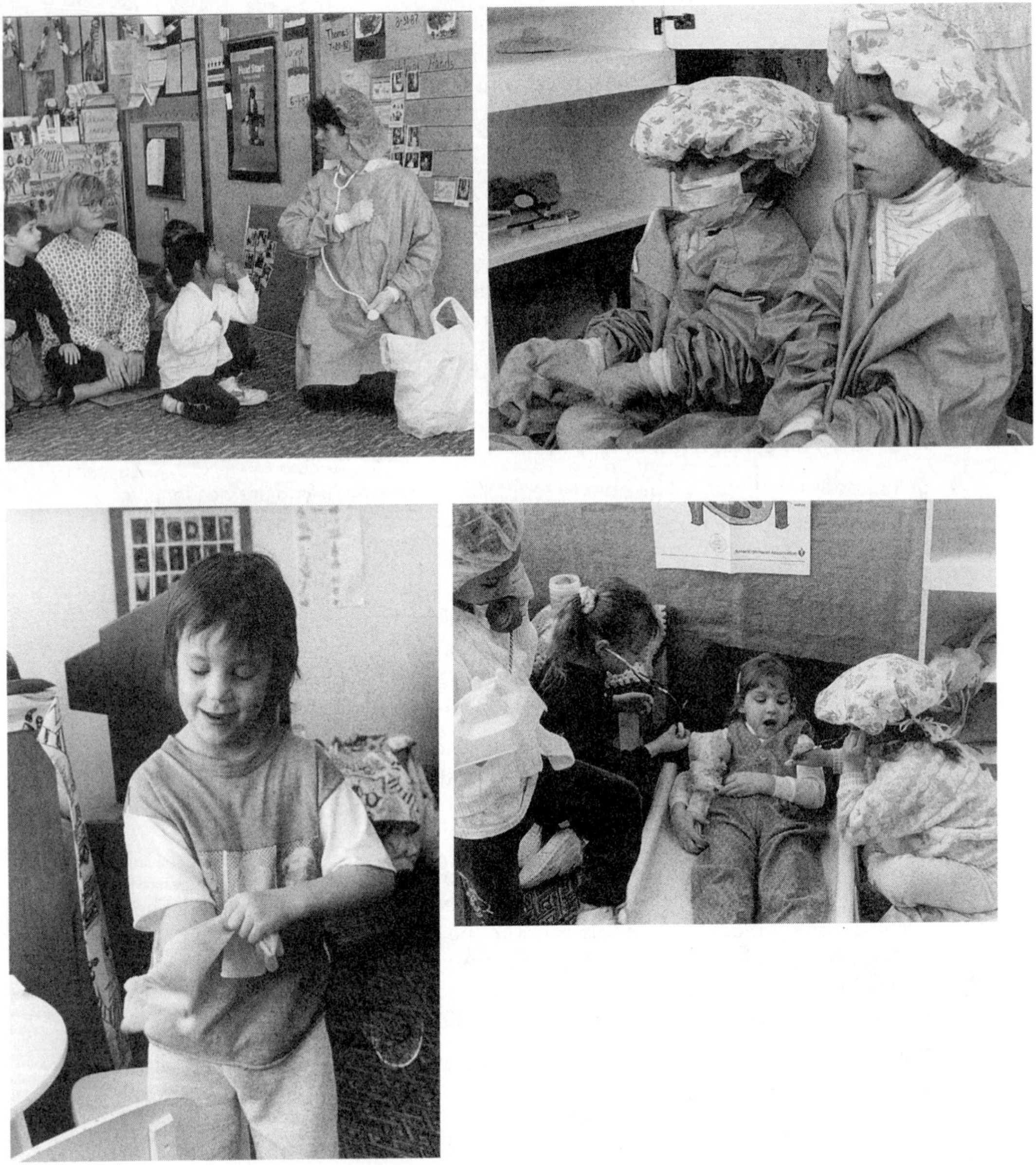

Stimulated by a teacher in surgical garb, children follow-up large group discussion with hospital play, complete with doctors, patients, and even a "new baby."

Large groups work well to orient children to interactive follow-up experiences on an individual basis or in small groups.

passivity of large groups, feelings of inadequacy build, and chronic mistaken behavior—tuning out as well as acting out—tend to result.

Contrasted with traditional large group instruction, the DAP position is that learning is *interactive*. The teacher provides opportunities for the child to integrate learning through expression in creative endeavor—art, music, play, creative drama, construction, and discussion (Bredekamp, 1997). Large groups work well for orienting children to an interactive learning experience (establishing an **anticipatory set**). The child then moves to a follow-up activity, either alone or in a small group. Using large groups to establish an anticipatory set *is* developmentally appropriate (Barbour & Seefeldt, 1992).

Whenever a large group is to be the sole vehicle for instruction, however, the teacher needs to proceed with caution (Bredekamp, 1997; McAfee, 1986). Successful large group experiences tend to include a series of short activities—a concise presentation or demonstration, a brief story, a movement activity or song, class business—each of which is less than five minutes. A quick pace to the large group, followed by a crisp transition, reduces passivity. To reiterate an earlier statement, for large groups to be a part of an interactive learning program, they should be friendly, participatory, relevant to children's experiences, and concise.

A teaching team in a Head Start class held three 20-minute large groups each day; as soon as all the children arrived, before lunch, and before time to go home. The team, frankly, was having problems with the large groups. The teachers tried preventive methods such as placing themselves strategically in the circle to help children stay focused. Still, many of the preschoolers grew restless, and the teachers found themselves calling for attention as much as conducting activities.

After reading this book (first edition), the lead teacher met with the team, and they reorganized the day. The teachers continued the morning large group but reduced it to singing a single attendance song and doing a "slow transition" game while children washed hands for breakfast. They dispensed with the large group just before lunch; instead, staff read stories to the children in three **family groups.** The groups also ate lunch together. Brief singing and a transition activity comprised the large group in the afternoon. The class went from one hour of large group each day to about 15 minutes.

With the change the teachers found that mistaken behavior decreased, and more children seemed engaged in productive activity. Though they had to "sell" the new program to a supervisor and parents, the team was pleased with the results, as was the author. As I remember, on the first day they reduced their large groups, the lead teacher commented: "This better work, Dan, *or else. . . .*"

MANAGING TRANSITIONS

Transitions, changes from one activity to the next, can be disruptive (Saifer, 1990). One classic transition dilemma occurs between individual activity and large group. A conventional approach is to get most of the children into the circle and then call out, "We're waiting for Ryan and Sonya." Such an approach embarrasses the targeted children and may make others in the circle wonder who is going to get "nagged" next.

Instead, the professional teacher uses alternative strategies that get children to the group on time but do not undercut self-esteem. Here are some basic guidance strategies for transitions. Some are more appropriate for preprimary classrooms; others pertain throughout the age range.

1. Give a notice five minutes before the transition. Some children—like adults—get so involved that they may need an additional "two-minute" notice.
2. Model enthusiasm for the clean-up process. Make the process a game with comments like, "I need some strong kids over here who can carry lots of blocks. Who is strong enough?" Participate in the clean-up.
3. "Give generous encouragement to the children who are conscientious about cleaning up" (Saifer, 1990, p. 32). Ignore or use matter-of-fact comments to children who are slow to participate. Avoid accusations and debates.

For large groups to be developmentally appropriate, they are friendly, participatory, relevant and concise. Courtesy, *Bemidji Pioneer.*

4. Sing a clean-up song with the children. Make up words and put them to a familiar tune. Children capture moods more easily than adults. Songs, or even popular pieces of recorded music, identify the transition and get children into the mood.
5. Make up and sing a song in the large group naming children who are there. (To your own tune:)

   We're happy to see you, see you, see you.
   We're happy to see you, Cathy, at circle time today.

   Be sure to include all children, including the late-comers when they arrive so that no one feels left out. The song is likely to speed up the transition and serves as a **buffer activity,** an activity that uses time productively while waiting. (One of the fringe benefits of teaching young children is they don't care if you can't carry a tune, just if you don't sing.)
6. With enthusiasm start the large group before all have arrived. The magnetism of an exciting large group will attract the rest of the children. No comment about anyone who is late is needed.

Wait Times A primary consideration in managing transitions is the reduction of time children spend waiting. Young children live totally in the here and now

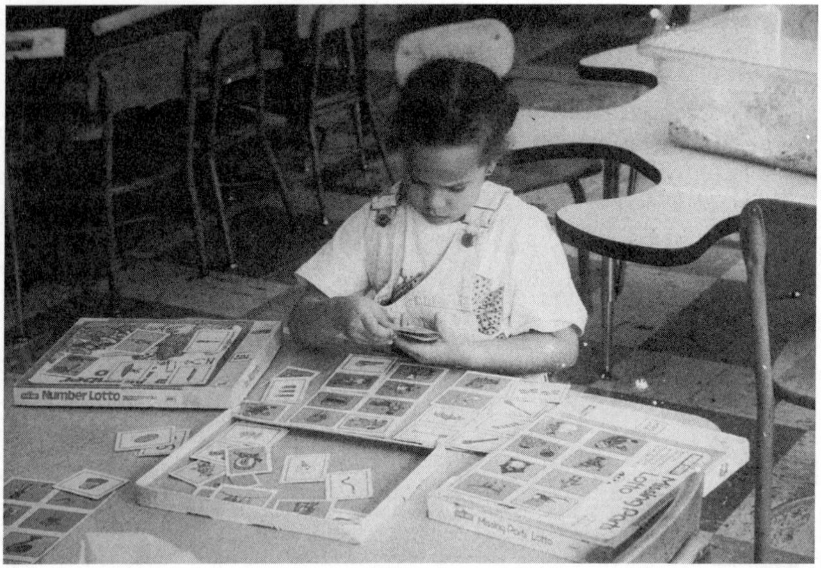

Recognize that even after a five-minute notice, children sometimes will need a bit longer to finish.

(Elkind, 1976). Although most will do it better as they get older, children under seven or eight years do not wait well. Strategies the teacher uses to reduce wait times prevent many problems.

A student teacher was in charge of "art time" in a kindergarten class. Her projects were all open-ended and creative (and so developmentally appropriate). She ran into problems, though, with the wait time before the children could do the projects. First, she had the children sit at the tables while she gave directions. Then she handed out the materials to each table. The problem was the children grabbed for the materials at the same time and mini-chaos resulted.

Next, she had all materials out on the tables when the children came in from recess. This time they began using the materials before she could introduce the project, so the theme was lost.

Finally, she used a two-step approach. She set out the materials on the tables but had the children sit at the large group circle when they came in. She discussed the project with them at the circle. Then she dismissed them to their tables a few at a time by the color of clothing they wore: "All wearing purple or yellow may get up and slowly walk to their tables." The student teacher did not interrupt the flow by challenging children who had interesting interpretations of purple or yellow; the purpose was to get them to the tables efficiently without a stampede or hurt feelings.

Buffer Activities

Buffer activities keep children occupied during wait times. A song in a large group before everyone arrives is an example. At the primary level, a teacher often has alternative activities for children who finish first. Such activities range from "working quietly at your desk" to use of selected learning centers. Although these types of buffer activities are useful, they should not be so attractive that they encourage hurried completion of the main lesson. Such a pattern discourages thorough work habits and discriminates against children who work slowly or find the task difficult. Activities used as buffers should be available at another time of day as well for all to enjoy. With thought, the teacher can use buffer activities to reduce significant amounts of mistaken behavior:

> Children at a Head Start center were having problems each day just before lunch. The schedule called for them to come in from outdoor play, line up to use the restroom, and wash hands. During this time, the lead teacher prepared the tables for lunch, and the assistant teacher monitored the lines. Waiting in line with nothing to do was difficult for many of the children. Pushing and fights were becoming more frequent.
>
> The teaching team reviewed the situation and tried a new arrangement. The teacher brought in a few children early. They washed their hands first and helped the teacher set the tables and bring in the food on carts. When the rest of the children came in, they sat at the reading center near the restroom and sink where they looked at books together. During this buffer, the assistant teacher had small clusters of children use the facilities and rotate back to their books until lunch. The waiting in line was eliminated and with it the mistaken behavior.

A first step in creating a successful buffer activity is awareness that mistaken behavior can be situationally caused, such as by prolonging the time that children are waiting. With this awareness, the second step follows: adapting the program to better accommodate the children's development. Buffer activities, sometimes planned, sometimes spontaneous, help in this effort.

Learning to Live with Lines

Young children and lines—like large groups—are not a natural match. Moving big groups of little people is always a hazardous business. In many preschools, formal lines are not used. Out-of-building excursions are safest when the ratio of adults to children is about 1:4 and lines are not needed. This ratio is so important, especially on busy streets, that staff should do their utmost to recruit additional volunteers for these occasions. An unsafe alternative is the old-time use of ropes with loops that each child holds. Besides the "chain gang" appearance, anyone who has seen one child stumble and all lose their balance knows this is one piece of equipment that should be retired.

Preschools located in public school buildings sometimes experience difficulty with movement of the group through halls. The concept of two-by-two lines is not a natural one for three- and four-year-olds. School administrators should not expect the same "hall expertise" of preschoolers that they expect of third graders. Discussions with administrators about their expectations are important even before preschools locate in school buildings.

When having children line up, teachers learn quickly that more is needed than simply stating, "Everyone line up at the door." Instead, teachers need "creative alternatives," methods for lining up in a quick but orderly fashion. The methods should *not* violate the principle of unconditional positive regard—"Millie, you've been quiet; you can line up first today." This practice results in hurt feelings among the others who have been quiet and weren't selected. "Chance-based" criteria such as "Everyone whose first name begins with a C or K may quietly line up," are more appropriate. Chance-based criteria remove the appearance of favoritism from the line-up procedure and get the job done efficiently.

A common point of contention is who will be the "leader" (and sometimes "trailer") when lines form. Some programs have a Very Important Kid or Star of the Week who leads the lines for a designated period. Another method is to have a large chart with each child's name. A marker, moved each day, indicates who will lead. (Perhaps the child who led the previous day could be the "caboose.") Other

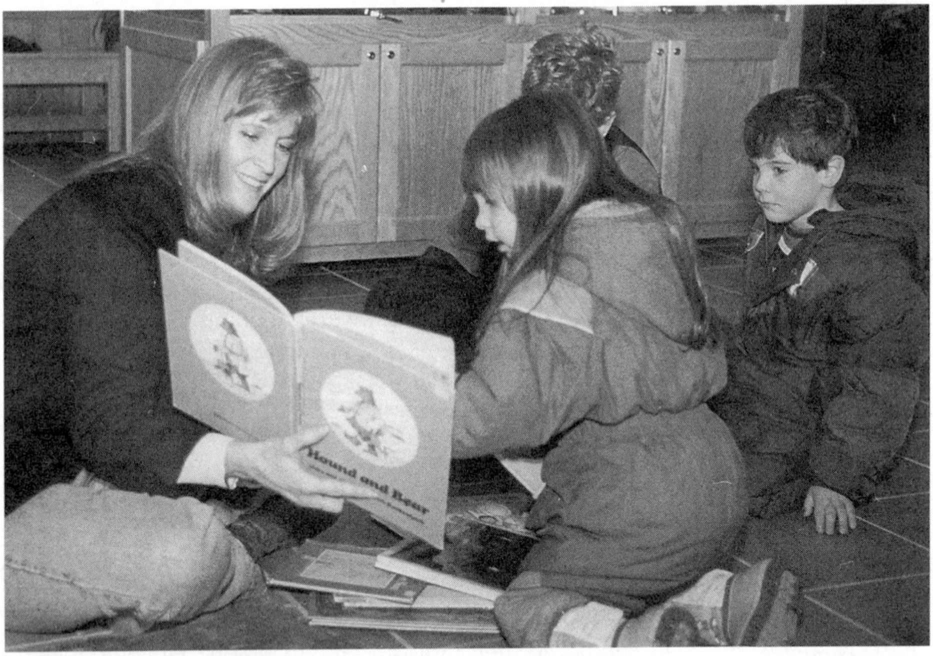

Buffer activities, sometimes planned, sometimes spontaneous, reduce the mistaken behavior caused by waiting. Courtesy, *Bemidji Pioneer.*

markers could be placed on the chart to identify other "classroom helpers." This practice makes selection systematic and visible and eliminates "I was first!" "No, it's my turn!" controversies.

Here are two other considerations about line procedures, one controversial, the other, "common sense." In agreement with the ideas of anti-bias curriculum (Derman-Sparks, 1989), the author recommends lines that do not pair girls and boys. This practice needlessly exaggerates differences between the sexes in an era when cross-gender cooperation needs to be encouraged. Healthy cross-gender interactions become more difficult in programs that institutionalize gender differences (Derman-Sparks, 1989).

Instead, the teacher should work to create an atmosphere in which gender is accepted as just another element in who each child is. As *Anti-Bias Curriculum* points out, teachers have more say about reducing sexism in the classroom environment than they might think (Derman-Sparks, 1989). Comfortable cross-gender relations are in keeping with the encouraging classroom and should be reflected in line-up procedures as well as in all other parts of the program.

The common-sense suggestion is in relation to helping young children wait and move in lines cooperatively. Whenever a teacher can make such time an enjoyable experience, she is showing skill at preventing mistaken behavior. Having finger plays and songs ready for when children in line must wait is sound preventive practice. Simple songs that use the children's names are effective buffer activities.

Similarly, when children walk in lines, stimulating their imaginations can work wonders.

> A particular kindergarten teacher used the children's imaginations to move her class efficiently. On one day she whispered: "Today, we are the elephant mommies and daddies. We need to tiptoe quietly so we don't wake up the sleeping baby elephants. Let's very quietly tiptoe down the hall." When the principal came out of her office to compliment the class, one of the children told her, "Ssh, you'll wake up the babies."

PARENTS AND OTHER CLASSROOM VOLUNTEERS

A premise of this chapter is that the shift away from large groups toward small group and individual activities promotes a developmentally appropriate program. Moving to a **multidimensional environment** though, does pose challenges for the teacher. In the multidimensional environment, the teacher is a manager of the daily program as well as the lead teacher. The teaching team concept, discussed in Chapter 4, is not an absolute requirement in this classroom environment, but it does make the teacher's tasks easier.

The teacher has two sources of adults to comprise the teaching team, paid staff, and volunteers. In the preschool classroom, typical paid staff members are assistant teachers and aides. In the elementary classroom, paid staff are paraprofessionals, special education personnel, team teaching partners, and specialists. Volunteers in either setting are likely to be "foster grandparents" (from federal or state-sponsored programs for retired citizens), college students, older students from the school system, private citizens, and parents.

Depending on the skills and comfort level of the teaching team members, staff and volunteers perform a variety of functions in the classroom. The teacher's goal is to have volunteers working with individual children, reading stories, leading small groups, being in charge of centers, and presenting on occasion to the full group. Children gain from the role modeling, encouragement, support, and teaching that caring adults can provide.

In a kindergarten with an effective volunteer program, five parents visit the class once a week at center time. (One attends each day.) They usually help with the same center each week, where an index card (work card) provides them with instructions. Occasionally, Mona (the teacher) will ask a parent to go to a different center or help with a particular project, like making cookies with a small group. Several other parents have visited to share a hobby, interest, or item of family heritage with the class. Many parents have come in on their child's birthday and on monthly class field trips. Parents know they are welcome, and some have brought younger brothers or sisters when they have visited.

Mona is an exception in her school, and developing the program has taken a few years. Some parents each year have chosen not to participate. Not all the teachers approve, though more are including parents than in prior years. It has taken extra work, but Mona believes firmly that involving parents in the classroom is worthwhile for the increased individual attention the children receive.

Helping Parent Volunteers Feel Welcome

A key to working successfully with parents is to help them feel welcome. At whatever point a parent enters, she should be greeted by the teacher and usually introduced to the children. Taking time to orient the parent briefly is important. A "parent's corner," though not always possible in the classroom, provides a great home base. A bulletin board, check-out library, pamphlets and fliers, a collection of newsletters, and a place the parent can leave belongings should be included. One teacher set up a corner behind a tall book stand in the reading center. When not used by the teacher at story time, a rocking chair was kept in the "corner."

In addition to parent helpers with parties and field trips, parents who share knowledge or skills with a class are important "special events" volunteers. One teacher asked three families per month to share a favorite dish, the vocation of a family mem-

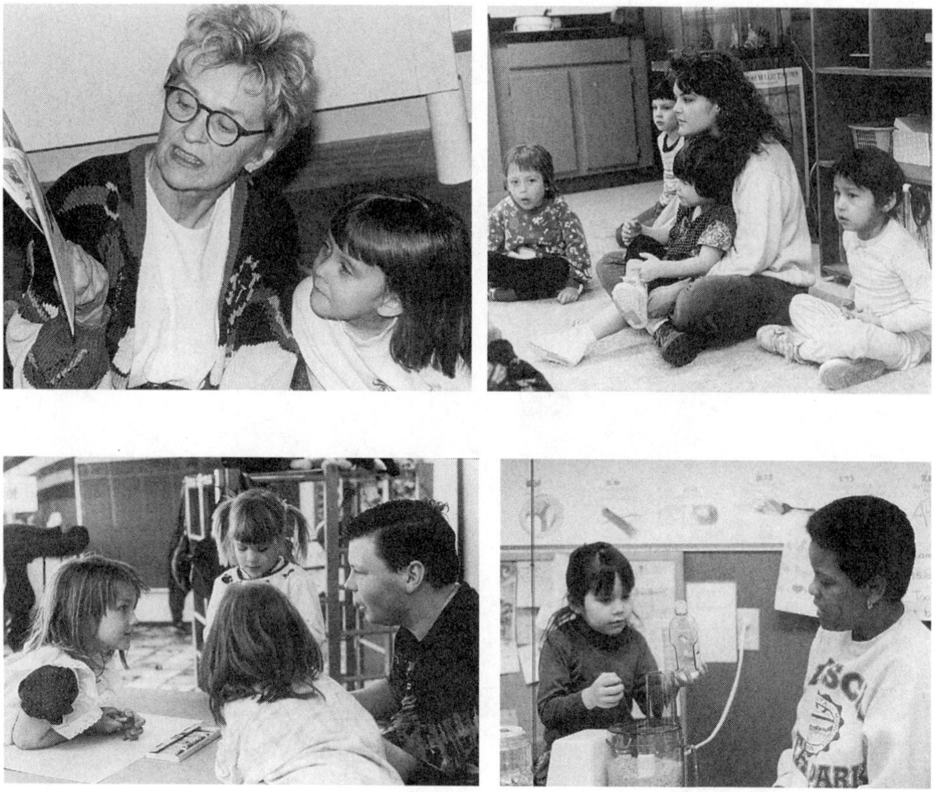

Classroom volunteers often include foster grandparents, college interns, students from older grades, and parents. Top left photo courtesy, *Bemidji Pioneer.*

ber, a family interest (including the interest of an older brother or sister), and/or a bit of family heritage. The social studies program for the year was taken care of on this basis. Parents working in nontraditional gender roles are a particularly important resource. A male nurse, a female firefighter or police officer, an in-home working dad all raise children's consciousness levels and horizons.

On the first visits for parents who may become regulars, the teacher encourages the parent to walk around, interact, and observe but not take on undue responsibility (Gestwicki, 1992). The teacher is aware that the busyness of the developmentally appropriate classroom will draw in the parent. Sitting and talking with a group as they work, reading a book to children, and helping a child get a coat on closely resemble parenting tasks—tasks that parents generally find nonthreatening in a home or classroom.

Some children feel strong emotions when parents enter the room or leave for the day. Teachers often cite this drawback for not encouraging parent involvement (Gestwicki, 1992). The teacher addresses this possibility before hand by providing reassurance that she will work with the parent to handle any problems that arise (Gestwicki, 1992). Allowing the child to sit with the parent shows sensitivity to the

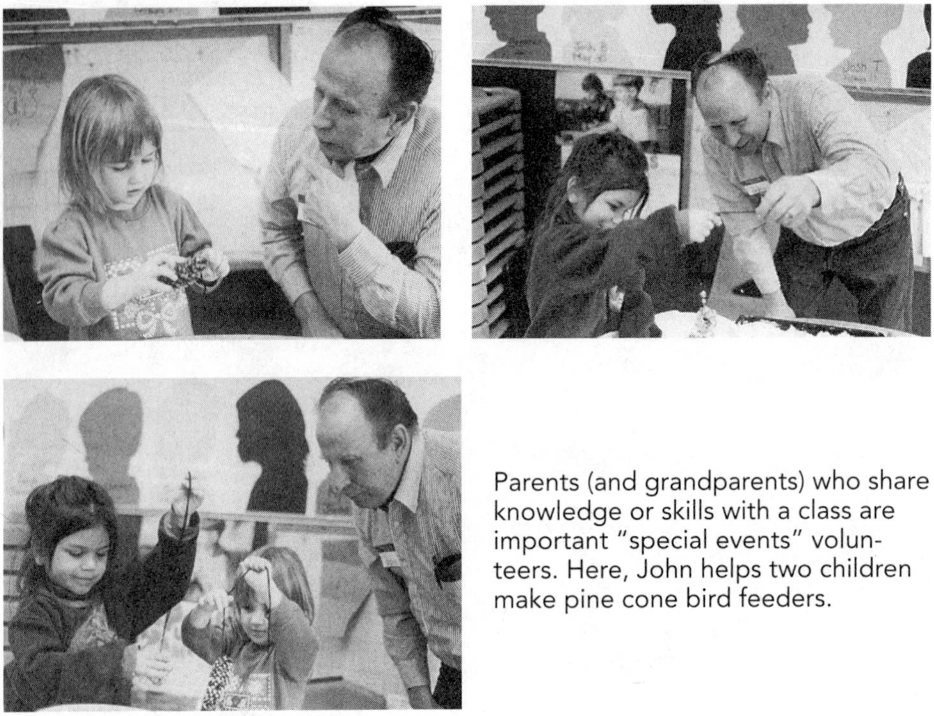

Parents (and grandparents) who share knowledge or skills with a class are important "special events" volunteers. Here, John helps two children make pine cone bird feeders.

child's feelings. Reassurance and diversion to activities are standard at the time of separation. As children adjust to frequent visitations by parents, their own included, the need for their parents' undivided attention subsides.

Working with Regulars

When a few parents have begun to volunteer regularly, the teacher may want to meet with them after school. Such meetings can be useful in further acquainting the parent with the education program or with observation techniques to better understand children's needs (Kasting, 1994). "Old hands" might be invited to attend to share suggestions and sometimes to educate about DAP as well as the teacher. (An important example is educating parents to let children do their own artwork.) If a parent needs extra guidance about volunteering, the teacher needs to find a way to provide it (Gestwicki, 1992). Open and frequent communication can prevent the unusual circumstance of asking a parent to come in less often.

The teacher will know that a volunteer is a true "regular" when ongoing communication becomes unnecessary. Teachers then can begin to rely on the skills of the volunteer by assigning a center and providing a work card, as Mona did in the anecdote on p. 176. Gestwicki sums up the process of helping parents become productive in the classroom by stating:

The most important reason for involving parents is that it encourages them to become more active in their children's education.

> As teachers invite parents to participate in classroom learning activities, they need to concentrate on their skills for working with adults. Teachers need to be able to relax and enjoy the contribution of others to their classrooms and not feel threatened by any attention transferred from themselves to a visiting adult. It is important to remember that as more specific information is given to parents, parents will feel more comfortable knowing what is expected of them (p. 259).

Perhaps the most important reason for involving parents in the classroom is that it encourages them to be active in their children's education (Rockwell, Andre & Hawley, 1996). Each year as a result of parent involvement, families become more interested in their children's success at school—and the children respond. This reason is enough, but annually as well, many parents become interested in personal and professional advancement as a result of a successful volunteering experience.

> Parents like feeling that they're making a valuable contribution to a classroom. Many parents will try to find the time for a visit if they feel truly needed and wanted. A note of appreciation from the teacher and children afterwards, pictures of the event displayed on a bulletin board, a mention of the event as a classroom highlight in the next newsletter—all these convey to parents that their time was well spent (Gestwicki, 1992, p. 260).

SUMMARY

How does the teacher balance reliability and novelty in the daily program?

Programs that lack consistency are unpredictable and cause anxiety for children. Programs that never change or incorporate the teachable moment result in tedium. The schedule provides a base line of predictability for the children about the program. When unscheduled events enable positive results for children, they add to the everyday program. The teacher maintains the balance between predictability and novelty by reading children's behaviors and discussing reasons for changes with them. Developmentally appropriate schedules for prekindergarten, kindergarten, and the primary grades provide reliability but still allow for novelty.

What is the appropriate mix of active and quiet times?

In the encouraging classroom, much of the daily program is at a *busy* level with occasional excursions into the *boisterous* and the *bucolic*. Teachers sometimes stigmatize a child who does not fit the sedentary activity level of their classrooms. Rather than suppress the innate activeness of the young, teachers do better to empower children through programs that are more active and allow for a better developmental match.

Though "busy" sets the tone for the classroom, children and teachers also need periods of rest and relaxation. Relaxation activities and a thoughtful approach to rest times rejuvenate spirits in children and adults alike. Three ideas boost the benefits of boisterous activity. First, the teacher needs to supplement formal active play times with opportunities for vigorous activity during other periods of the day. Second, throughout the age range, movement-to-music during large group activities refreshes children and renews their ability to concentrate. Third, effective vigorous activities avoid formal rules, competition, and taking turns.

What part do large group activities play in the encouraging classroom?

A problem with overreliance on large groups is that they easily exceed children's developmental levels and attention spans. For this reason, large groups should be used selectively and not as a matter of institutional routine. Teachers who want to use large groups effectively do well to re-assess the effectiveness of traditional large group practices: taking attendance, calendar and the weather, show and tell, reading, and large group instruction. A developmentally appropriate use of large groups is to establish an *anticipatory set* for interactive follow-up activities done either independently or in small groups. For large groups to be a part of an interactive learning program, they should be friendly, participatory, relevant to children's experiences, and concise.

How does managing transitions reduce mistaken behavior?

Transitions, changes from one activity to the next, can be disruptive. The professional teacher develops and implements strategies for transitions that get the job done but do not undercut self-esteem. A primary consideration in managing transitions is

Movement activities fit the criteria for developmentally appropriate large group experiences.

the reduction of time that children spend waiting. One strategy to reduce waiting is through buffer activities. When lines prove necessary, teachers need to plan strategies for lining up and waiting in lines that support each member of the group and capture children's imaginations.

How can the teacher make use of parents and other classroom volunteers?

In the *multidimensional learning environment* the teacher is a manager of the daily program as well as a lead teacher. The use of staff and volunteers as a *teaching team* contributes to the success of the program. Depending on the skills and comfort level of the team members, staff and volunteers perform a variety of functions in the classroom. A first step in working with volunteers in the classroom is to make them feel welcome. The teacher helps the volunteer find tasks she is comfortable with such as fastening coats or reading to a small group that a parent might do at home.

Leadership by the teacher at trouble points such as separations adds to the parent's comfort about volunteering. The teacher maintains ongoing communication with the parent but recognizes when the parent has become a regular and needs less support. The most important reason for involving parents in the classroom is that the experience encourages them to become more active in their child's education, although the parent stands to benefit in other ways as well. The teacher who involves parents and other adults in the classroom has an added role to perform and additional tasks to do. Because the entire program stands to gain, the extra effort is worthwhile.

FOLLOW-UP ACTIVITIES

Note: In completing follow-up activities, the privacy of all involved is to be respected.

Reflection Activity

The reflection activity encourages students to interrelate their own thoughts and experiences with specific ideas from the chapter.

Think about a classroom you have visited as a part of your preparation program. Recollect a regular activity or routine during the day in which more mistaken behavior occurred than at other times. Referring to the chapter for possible ideas, how would you change this part of the daily program to reduce the mistaken behavior and make the classroom more encouraging?

Application Activities

Application activities allow students to interrelate material from the text with real life situations. The observations imply access to practicum experiences; the interviews, access to teachers or parents. Students may compare or contrast observations and interviews with referenced ideas from the chapter.

1. **How does the teacher balance reliability and novelty in the daily program?**
   a. Observe an instance of the "teachable moment" when a teacher deviated from the schedule to provide a special experience. How did the teacher manage the change of routine? What did you notice about the children's behavior before, during, and after the special event?
   b. Talk with a teacher about the daily schedule she uses. What parts of the schedule is the teacher pleased with? If the teacher were going to modify the schedule, what parts would she change? Why?
2. **What is the appropriate mix of active and quiet times?**
   a. Observe three activities, one each that is bucolic, busy, and boisterous. Note typical interactions in the classroom in each type of activity. Did you notice instances of mistaken behavior? How was the mistaken behavior similar at the various levels? How was it different?
   b. Interview a teacher about how she conducts a rest time, a busy activity, and a vigorous activity. What potential problems is the teacher alert to in each kind of activity? How does she work to prevent difficulties from arising?
3. **What part do large group activities play in the encouraging classroom?**
   a. Observe children in a large group activity. If most children are positively involved, what about the large group seems to be holding their attention? If several children look distracted, or are distracting others, what do you think are the reasons?

b. Interview a teacher about large group activities. How does the teacher plan large groups to hold children's attention? While teaching, what techniques does the teacher use to hold children's attention?

4. **How does managing transitions reduce mistaken behavior?**
   a. Observe a transition to or from an organized activity. How does the teacher prepare the children? How does the teacher manage the physical movement of the children? How does the teacher get the new activity started?
   b. Interview a teacher about how she handles transition situations. Ask about what she does when some, but not all, children have finished an old activity and are ready to begin the new activity. What suggestions does the teacher have for when she and the class have to wait for an event; when she and the class have to walk in a line?

5. **How can the teacher make use of parents and other classroom volunteers?**
   a. Observe a teacher working with staff or volunteers in the classroom. What is typical in how the teacher communicates with the other adults? How much of the teacher's attention is directed to working with the other adults? How much to working with the children?
   b. Interview a teacher about having other adults, staff, and volunteers, in the classroom. What benefits does the teacher see in the arrangement? If there are difficulties, what are they? What would the teacher recommend for working through some difficulties that might arise?

RECOMMENDED RESOURCES

Barbour, N. H., & Seefeldt, C. A. (1992). Developmental continuity: From preschool through the primary grades. *Childhood Education, 68*(5), 302–304.

Cherry, C. (1981). *Think of something quiet.* Belmont, CA: David S. Lake Publisher.

Educational Productions Inc. (1990) Video: Give yourself a hand: "Guidance techniques for successful group times," Program 2 in video training series: Super Groups: Young children learning together. Portland, Ore: Educational Productions Inc.

Edwards, L. C., & Nabors, M. L. (1993). The creative art process: What it is and what it is not. *Young Children, 48*(3), 77–81.

Gronlund, G. (1995). Bringing the DAP message to kindergarten and primary teachers. *Young Children, 50*(5), 4–13.

Kasting, A. (1994). Respect, responsibility, and reciprocity: The 3Rs of parent involvement. *Childhood Education, 70*(3), 146–150.

Rockwell, R. E., Andre, L. C., & Hawley, M. K. (1996). *Parents and teachers as partners: Issues and challenges.* Fort Worth, TX: Harcourt Brace College Publishers. (See Chapter 10, Parent and Community Volunteers.)

Van Scoy, I. J., & Fairchild, S. H. (1993). It's about time! Helping preschool and primary children understand time concepts. *Young Children, 48*(2), 21–24.

Willis, S. (1993, November). Teaching young children: Educators seek 'developmental appropriateness.' *Curriculum Update,* 1–8.

REFERENCES

Barbour, N. H., & Seefeldt, C. A. (1992). Developmental continuity: From preschool through the primary grades. *Childhood Education, 68*(5), 302–304.

Bredekamp, S. (Ed.). (1997). *Developmentally appropriate practice in early childhood programs* (3rd ed.). (Washington, DC: National Association for the Association of Young Children.

Brewer, J. A. (1995). *Introduction to early childhood education: Preschool through primary grades.* Boston, MA: Allyn and Bacon.

Cherry, C. (1981). *Think of something quiet.* Belmont, CA: David S. Lake Publisher.

Derman-Sparks, L. (1989). *Anti-bias curriculum: Tools for empowering young children.* Washington, DC: National Association for the Education of Young Children.

Dunn, L., & Kontos, S. (1997). What have we learned about developmentally appropriate practice? *Young Children, 52*(5), 4–13.

Edwards, L. C., & Nabors, M. L. (1993). The creative art process: What it is and what it is not. *Young Children, 48*(3), 77–81.

Elkind, D. (1976). *Child development and early childhood education: A Piagetian perspective.* New York: Oxford University Press.

Gestwicki, C. (1992). *Home, school, community relations.* Albany, NY: Delmar Publishers.

Gronlund, G. (1995). Bringing the DAP message to kindergarten and primary teachers. *Young Children, 50*(5), 4–13.

Hendrick, J. A. (1996). *Whole child.* Columbus, OH: Merrill Publishing Company.

Honig, A. S. (1986). Research in review. Stress and coping in children. In J. B. McCracken (Ed.), *Reducing stress in young children's lives* (pp. 142–167). Washington, DC: National Association for the Education of Young Children.

Honig, A. S., & Wittmer, D. S. (1996). Helping children become more prosocial: Ideas for classrooms, schools, and communities. *Young Children, 51*(2), 62–70.

Kasting, A. (1994). Respect, responsibility, and reciprocity: The 3Rs of parent involvement. *Young Children, 70*(3), 146–150.

McAfee, O. D. (1986). Research report. Circle time: Getting past 'two little pumpkins'. In J. B. McCracken (Ed.), *Reducing stress in young children's lives* (pp. 99–104). Washington, DC: National Association for the Education of Young Children.

McCracken, R. A., & McCracken, M. J. (1987). *Reading is only the tiger's tail.* Winnipeg, Canada: Perguis Publishers Limited.

Marion, M. (1995). *Guidance of young children.* Columbus, OH: Merrill Publishing Company.

Montessori, M. (1912/1964). *The Montessori method.* New York: Schocken Books.

Palmer, H. (1978). *Sea gulls.* Topanga, CA: Hap-Pal Music.

Rockwell, R. E., Andre, L. C., & Hawley, M. K. (1996). *Parents and Teachers as partners.* Forth Worth, TX: Harcourt Brace College Publishers.

Saifer, S. (1990). *Practical solutions to practically every problem: The early childhood teacher's manual.* St. Paul, MN: Redleaf Press.

Scelsa, G., & Millang, S. (1983). *Quiet moments with Steve and Greg.* Los Angeles, CA: Youngheart Records.

Van Scoy, I. J., & Fairchild, S. H. (1993). It's about time! Helping preschool and primary children understand time concepts. *Young Children, 48*(2), 21–24.

Wade, M. G. (1992). Motor skills, play, and child development: An introduction. *Early Report, 19*(2), 1–2.

Walmsley, B. B., Camp, A. M., Walmsley, S. A. (1992). *Teaching kindergarten: A developmentally appropriate approach.* Portsmouth, NH: Heinemann Educational Books.

7

Leadership Communication with the Group

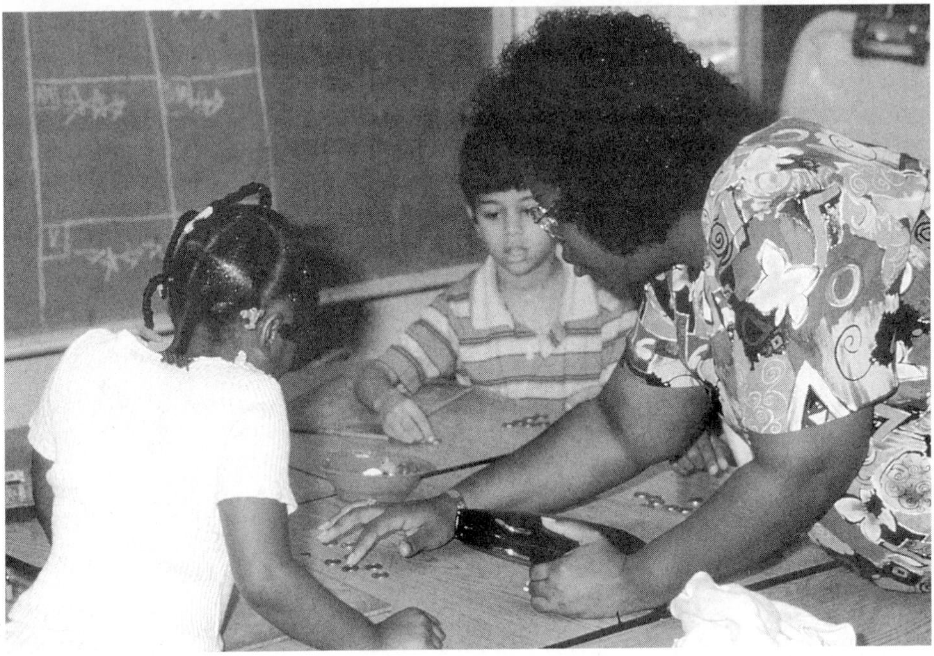

GUIDING QUESTIONS

As you read Chapter 7, you will discover answers to the following questions:

- **How does the teacher establish leadership in the encouraging classroom?**
- **Why are guidelines, not rules, important in the encouraging classroom?**
- **Why is encouragement more appropriate than praise?**
- **Why is discussing inclusively important?**
- **How do class meetings reduce the need for mistaken behavior?**
- **How does leadership communication with parents build and maintain partnerships?**

Much mistaken behavior is the result of a mismatch between the child and the education program and of miscommunication between the child and teacher. Previous chapters discussed reducing this *institution-caused* mistaken behavior by using a developmentally appropriate educational program. While retaining the main idea of the unit, that "prevention is the best medicine," Chapters 7 and 8 shift focus to the communication skills of the teacher. In these chapters, **leadership communication** defines the communication techniques used by the teacher to build the encouraging classroom by reducing the need for mistaken behavior.

Chapter 7 examines leadership communication that is *group-focused*. Another term for group-focused leadership communication is **proactive group management.** Elements of group-focused leadership communication include:

- Establishing leadership by being firm and friendly
- Creating guidelines instead of rules
- Using encouragement instead of praise
- Discussing inclusively.

The chapter concludes with a discussion of communication techniques teachers use to build and maintain partnerships with parents.

ESTABLISHING LEADERSHIP

Chapter 3 established the need for positive teacher-child relations as a guidance principle. The teacher works to accept each child unconditionally, even as he endeavors to help children learn socially acceptable alternatives for mistaken behavior. The environment in which children feel individual acceptance and growing social capability is the encouraging classroom. The ability to create this feeling of community in the classroom takes particular leadership on the part of the teacher, leadership that is democratic and authoritative (Dreikurs, 1968; Wittmer & Honig, 1994).

Building an encouraging environment in the classroom begins in the first few days. The teacher establishes leadership by acquainting the class with routines and guidelines. Children benefit from knowing what is expected of them and what the limits of acceptable behavior are. The teacher is clear, firm, and friendly in this communication effort. When teachers blur the distinction between *firm* and *strict,* friendliness drops out of the formula, and teachers work against their own best intentions. In this matter, the guidance approach differs from conventional discipline.

Conventional thought about discipline holds that the teacher is *strict* at the beginning of the school year, in order to "take charge of the classroom" (Canter, 1988). Then, with the teacher's "right to teach" established, he eases up in demeanor. From the guidance perspective, this position holds pitfalls. The teacher may fixate on the assertion of will and lose faith in more positive teaching practices. Children and teacher alike get used to the teacher in the role of disciplinarian. He becomes a disciplinarian as part of a permanent teaching style. This unfortunate situation is epitomized by the proverbial teacher who meant only "not to smile until Christmas"—and didn't smile for forty years (Gartrell, 1987).

Through the program and the communication skills used, the teacher reduces the need for mistaken behavior.

Even if the strict teacher gradually does "lighten up," children suffer from negative encounters in the interim. Working with limited experience to develop feelings of initiative and belonging, children who have conflicts early in their school careers may receive lasting damage to self-esteem (Gartrell, 1995). A "law and order" environment in the classroom affects even model children who do not normally "get into trouble."

Early in September, a parent who was also a health professional noticed her first grader seemed bothered by something. Shirley asked her daughter what was the matter. The first grader, an early reader, had seen a word on the chalkboard and asked what it was: "D-E-T-E-N-T-I-O-N." Shirley explained, and her daughter then asked several other questions:

"Where is detention?"
"Do the children get to go home?"
"Why do Jarrod and Paula go there?"
"Are they bad children?"
"Will the teacher put me there?"

Shirley commented later that she saw concern in her daughter's face that she had never seen during kindergarten. Shirley went in and talked with the teacher who said, "The children need to know that I am here to teach, and they are here to learn. I will not let individual children keep this from happening."

Shirley wondered about a classroom where the first words children learned to read were the names of friends being punished. She monitored her daughter's feelings closely and talked with the teacher several more times that year. The following spring she worked with the principal to place her daughter with a second grade teacher whom Shirley knew to be more positive.

Guidance and Routines

No matter how anxious a teacher is about beginning the school year, children are more anxious. In the first days, the teacher starts a course for children's education that makes it either a welcome event, or an event arousing ambivalence and negative feelings.

During the first week of kindergarten, two teachers responded to a similar situation differently. Trying to acquaint their groups with desired routines, each teacher instructed children to put away the materials they were using and come to the circle for large group instruction.

Teacher one reminded Juan, who was building a road, to put away the blocks; she then directed the group into a circle. She was set to begin when she noticed that Juan was still quietly building. From her place at the head of the group, the teacher said loudly, "Get over here, young man. In this classroom, children listen to the teacher." After waiting for Juan to join the group, she explained the daily schedule to the children.

When *teacher two* was about to begin the large group instruction, she noticed that Darnell—to whom she had just spoken—was still building with Legos. The teacher walked to Darnell, smiled, and held out her hand to him. She said quietly, "You can finish your building after circle time. We need you to join us now." Back in the large group, she introduced the children to the daily schedule.

Teacher two was showing leadership no less than teacher one. She reacted differently, though, to the notion that the teacher must "be tough from the beginning." Teacher two recognized that children in the first days of school can become overloaded and that they readily identify with materials that seem "safe." Teacher two did not equivocate with a guideline for her classroom, but took a guidance approach by educating children to the guideline. She used guidance measures so that Darnell (and the rest of the class) would not develop doubts about themselves and fears about school, but they would learn classroom routines.

GUIDELINES, NOT RULES

A point of agreement about guidance over the years is the importance of establishing clear expectations with children. Standards for behavior, understood by all, are important in any educational setting. Insufficient attention has been given, however, to differences between rules and *guidelines.* In making the case for guidelines as a part of the guidance approach, this section looks anew at the conventional use of rules.

Rules tend to be stated in negative terms: "No running in the classroom"; "No gum chewing in school." Frequently, punishments are predetermined for the transgression of a rule:

- No talking out of turn or your name goes on the board;
- No unfriendly words or you sit in the time-out chair;
- No homework and you stay after school.

The conventional thinking about rules with known consequences is that they convey clear conditions of citizenship and teach children about governance by law in adult society (Dreikurs & Cassel, 1972). This view presents two difficulties.

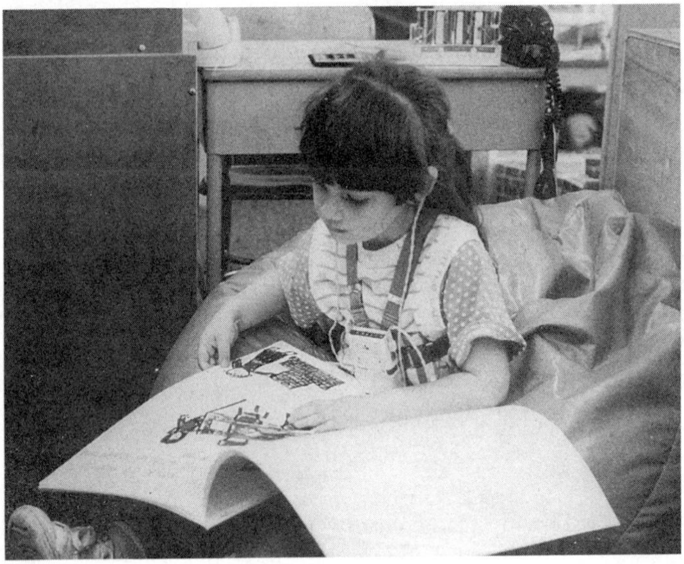

In the first days of school, children identify with materials that are familiar and seem safe.

First, rules with defined consequences institutionalize the use of punishment in the school or center. The negative phrasing of rules suggests that teachers expect children to break them. Spelled-out consequences underscore this perception. Reason, cooperation, and caring become secondary when educators enforce preset standards that may or may not fit actual situations. The teacher who reacts with an automatic response often shows less than full understanding of the event. If teachers choose "to make an exception" and not enforce a predetermined punishment, their leadership comes into question. In either case, the teacher is functioning as a technician and not as a professional (Chapter 4).

A second problem lies in the effects of punishment itself. Punishment tends to reduce human interaction from the educational to the moralistic. The factor of developmental egocentrism in young children makes this issue critical. Developmental egocentrism means the younger the age, the less the child understands about social expectations (Elkind, 1976). Because of lack of experience and development, young children have difficulty understanding that when they are punished for breaking a rule, the punishment is the result of their *actions*. They tend instead to internalize the shame associated with the punishment and to feel that they are being punished because they are "bad children." Diminished self-esteem results (Gartrell, 1995; Kohn, 1993). The child has been influenced away from feelings of initiative, belonging, and industry, and toward shame and self-doubt. (Elkind, 1987).

Logical Consequences

With his writings, Dreikurs raised discipline practice to a level above the reliance on punishment (Dreikurs, 1968; Dreikurs & Cassel, 1972). Dreikurs suggested that misbehavior has **logical consequences,** responses taken by adults that "fit" a child's mistaken act. Logical consequences differ from punishment because the redress imposed is a logical extension of the misbehavior itself. For example, if a preschooler marks on a table, he cleans it off. It a second grader neglects doing homework, he completes it before going out at recess. This consequence contrasts with the punishment of detention whether the child finished the assignment during the day or not.

The use of logical consequences fits a guidance approach if two conditions are met: (a) the consequence is logical to the child as well as the adult; and (b) the consequence is *not* set out beforehand.

In reference to the first condition, note the difference between these statements:

"You get a sponge and wipe that mark off the table right now."

"It's OK, your marker just went off the paper. Let's get a sponge and clean it off." An adult may have thought the first statement was a "logical consequence," but it probably sounded like punishment to the child.

In reference to the second condition, a primary grade child may have legitimate reasons for not completing homework such as a family emergency. In a guidance approach, a teacher uses professional judgment to evaluate an event before

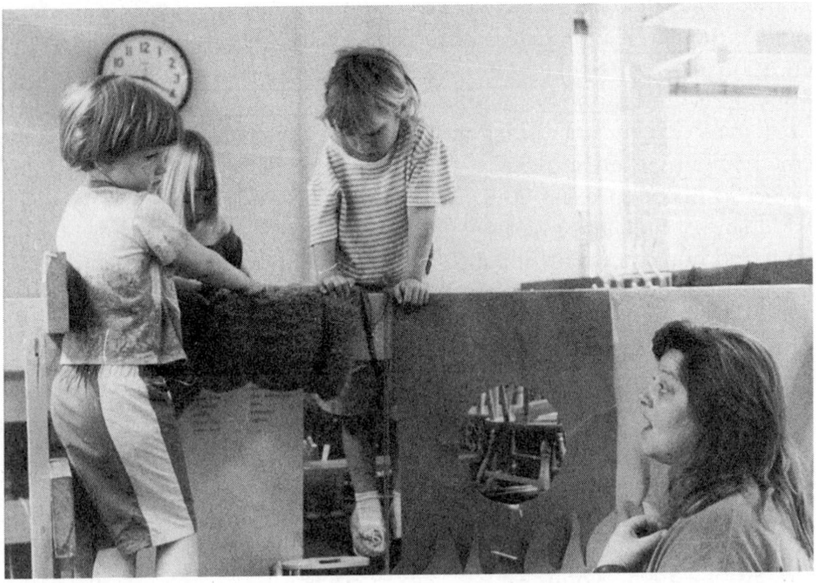

A logical consequence of climbing on a divider is to choose between staying on the floor in the same area or moving to the "real climber" that is safe.

deciding upon a logical consequence. The teacher acting as a professional recognizes that every situation is different.

In a foremost current interpretation of Dreikurs' theories, Linda Albert (1996) handles very carefully the use of logical consequences. The method is included more as a last resort than the "first line of defense," as it was treated in the past (Charles, 1996). Dreikurs maintained that his approach to discipline was a democratic one. In new interpretation of his work, emphasis is placed on communication *before* problems arise—an effective use of democratic leadership. Albert's work is in line with the guidance approach and is titled well: *Cooperative Discipline: How to Manage Your Classroom and Promote Self-Esteem* (1996). Guidelines fit with current interpretations of Dreikurs' concept.

The Benefits of Guidelines

For children in the classroom standards are necessary to build understanding about the requirements of social living. Like rules, guidelines set those standards. Unlike rules, guidelines accomplish this understanding in a positive way. As suggested in the previous section, an admonishment such as "Don't talk," (run, hit, etc.) is likely to make a child feel that he is "bad" in the teacher's eyes. Moreover, from this enforcement of the rule, young children often fail to recognize what the teacher is really asking them to do. *By using guidelines, teachers explain what productive behavior is; they do not just admonish against mistaken behavior.* Because their message is positive and instructive guidelines are more developmentally appropriate in educational settings than are rules.

Guidelines contribute to the encouraging classroom of the guidance approach. Contrast the following guidelines with conventional classroom rules:

- We use words to solve problems;
- We use friendly touches only;
- Sometimes we need to stop, look, and listen;
- We walk when we are inside, except at special times;
- We all help to take care of OUR room;
- We appreciate each other and ourselves;
- Making mistakes is OK—we just try to learn from them.

Guidelines and Different Age Levels

Teachers at various levels work with guidelines differently. In the first edition of the National Association for the Education of Young Children guidebook on developmentally appropriate practice (DAP) (Bredekamp, 1987) recommends that standards not be used formally with children under four:

> Adults know that three-year-olds do not usually understand or remember the rules. Guidance reasons [guidelines] that are specific to a real situation and that are demonstrated repeatedly are more likely to impress young children (p. 50).

Teachers of three-year-olds keep guidelines in mind ("guidance reasons") as reference points to make communication consistent in different situations and on different days. Though not on a formal basis, teachers of threes who use guidance, model and reinforce guidelines in their communications. An example is, "Use your words. Ask him, 'Are you done?'"

A difference at the preschool, kindergarten, and primary levels is the number of guidelines used. Teachers often comment that there should not be too many rules. This recommendation applies as well for guidelines. The exact number of guidelines depends on the teacher and the group, but usual practice is 2–3 guidelines in prekindergarten classes; 3–4 in kindergarten; and 4–6 in the primary grades. These figures are arbitrary, however. Pat Sanford, the kindergarten teacher mentioned in Chapter 6, uses three: "Be kind," "Be safe," and "Be smart."

Creating Guidelines

Castle & Rogers (1993) present many benefits of having children create rules in a democratic classroom atmosphere. The authors point out that children usually make the same rules that adults would, but respect the rules more because they feel ownership of them. They comment that "Engaging children in classroom discussions on creating rules leads to: "active involvement, reflection, meaningful connections, respect for rules, sense of community, problem solving through negotiation, cooperation, inductive thinking, and ownership" (pp. 77–78)—certainly all attributes of the encouraging classroom community.

Although the authors do not distinguish between rules and guidelines, the same benefits of guideline formulation certainly apply. With preprimary children, the teacher may need to take more of a lead in the discussion process. Even if very young children do not actually formulate the guidelines, they develop ownership of a guideline like "Friendly touches only" by discussing it—why the guideline is important; why we might not always remember to follow it; what procedure we can use when a mistake is made. Certainly primary grade children, the main focus of the Castle & Rogers article, can take more of the lead in the formulation process. The idea is that by reducing external control, from a context of democratic leadership, children are likely to take more responsibility for their own (and each other's) behavior. Castle & Rogers conclude:

> Teachers who commit time and effort to the process have found it benefits children's relationships and increases understanding of what it means to participate as a constructive member of a classroom community (1993, p. 80).

In this text, the procedure of holding group discussions to formulate and monitor the use of guidelines is called *a class meeting.* Class meetings are a versatile guidance technique, especially in connection with the use of guidelines. Class meetings can be used with preschoolers (Hendrick, 1992) and older adolescents, and can be held both on a regularly scheduled and "special occurrence" basis. Class meetings are further discussed later in this chapter.

A first reason for using guidelines is that they supportively educate children to standards of behavior. A *second reason is that guidelines allow teachers a range of choices and so empower them to be professionals.* Rules with set punishments force teachers to act as technicians. Rules fail to encourage teachers to be professionals who can use their store of experience to help children settle problems wisely. In contrast to rules, guidelines create neither hierarchies of authority that young children feel compelled to challenge nor lines of morality that children feel pressed to cross. Guidelines contribute to an environment where mistaken behavior is seen by the leader as a problem to solve. Note the difference in the teachers' roles in the following anecdotes:

> (Teacher working with rules.) At recess on a rainy day, second graders Clarence and Rubey first argued, then fought over a "friendship bracelet." Mrs. Cleary came into the room, separated the children, and declared, "You know the rule in here about fighting. I am taking you both to the principal's office."
>
> The principal asked Mrs. Cleary what the punishment was for fighting. Mrs. Cleary stated that it was detention and sitting out the class's next popcorn party. When the two children returned, others in the class made fun of them. The two looked miserable as they sat in detention. Rubey did not attend school the next day when the class party was held.

(Teacher working with guidelines.) At recess on a rainy day, a second grade teacher, Mrs. Drewry, entered her room to find two children fighting. She separated the children and had them each cool down at their desks. She then asked Cosby and Marla to "a private meeting" to each tell their side of the problem. Marla said she brought some cookies to eat at recess, and Cosby tried to take them. Cosby said he didn't either. The teacher acknowledged what each child said and felt. She then requested to hear how they would keep from fighting next time. Marla told Cosby he should bring his own stuff to eat. Cosby said his mom wouldn't let him.

The teacher paused and said to Cosby: "Our guideline says 'We use words to solve problems.' If you want Marla to share, you need to ask with words. Cosby, I've got an idea. Why don't you save an apple or roll from breakfast in the lunch room? Then, you will have something to eat at recess." Cosby shrugged and Marla looked relieved. The teacher ended the meeting by stating firmly, "Remember, in this class we use words to solve problems." Mrs. Drewry made a mental note to talk with the kitchen staff the next morning, and follow-up with Cosby.

When young children have disputes, they gain if they are helped to talk through the difficulty. To the complaint that the teacher should not be a "referee," the response is that the adult is teaching conflict management skills, the ability to solve problems with words. The use of guidelines enables the teacher to act as a mediator and teach conflict management. Effective conflict management may be the most important life skill in the 21st Century.

ENCOURAGEMENT

Perhaps the most basic guidance technique is that of *encouragement*. It bridges two dimensions of the teacher's communications in the classroom—with the class and with the individual child. How the teacher uses encouragement in the one dimension influences the other. For this reason, both dimensions of encouragement, group focused and individually directed, are discussed here.

Encouragement More than Praise

A basic difference between encouragement and praise is that encouragement acknowledges the efforts of the child; praise highlights the achievements (Hitz & Driscoll, 1988). With the process-orientation young children bring to activities, encouragement is important if only for this reason. As introduced in Chapter 3, however, encouragement is preferable to praise for other reasons as well.

A typical example of praise is, "Children, see what a good worker Joshua is." Writers such as Dreikurs (1968), Ginott (1972), Hitz & Driscoll (1988), and Kohn (1993) believe that a comment like this one creates several problems:

1. The statement is made more to elicit conformity from the group than to recognize the individual child.
2. Others in the group who were working as hard as Joshua feel slighted because they were not praised.
3. Class members feel resentment toward Joshua for being praised.
4. All children in the class are reinforced toward dependency on the teacher for evaluation of their efforts rather than being taught to evaluate efforts for themselves.
5. The class is uneasy about whom the teacher will single out next and what he will say.
6. Joshua experiences mixed emotions: pride at being praised, embarrassment at being publicly recognized, worry about how others will react, uncertainty about exactly what he did that was *right,* and concern about what the teacher will say to him next time.

Typically, praise stresses the adult's definition of successful achievement such as "winning" or "doing the best." When this emphasis is strong, children become anxious about the possibility of not living up to the adult's expectations—of becoming "losers" or "failures" (Kohn, 1993). This use of praise leads to a classroom with an environment of conditional acceptance: Children who meet the teacher's criteria for success feel like winners and enjoy the social trappings of winning; other students feel the humiliation and resentment that accompanies their more marginal social status. Teachers who use encouragement comfortably have learned that support is usually needed more during a task than at its completion—the accomplishment frequently being its own reward. They have learned that all children in a class deserve full acceptance and support and that is what an encouraging classroom is about.

Encouragement happens in two primary ways, publicly directed to the entire group, privately directed to the individual. A teacher says to her kindergarten class, "You are working very hard on your journals today. Many special story pictures are being made. I am proud of you all." Strengths in **public encouragement** include:

1. The group has received clear feedback and knows their efforts are being appreciated.
2. The teacher has not made a value judgment about "the class personality" but has given a **self-report:** She has described the event being recognized and given an **I message** or personal response to it.
3. No children feel the ambivalence of being singled out.
4. The teacher has avoided institutionalizing "winners" and "losers," (in-groups and out-groups). He has eliminated the negative social dynamic of differential treatment.

The child knows that encouragement given privately is truly meant for him.

5. The group feels a positive group spirit, a sense that "we are in this together and we are succeeding."
6. While being supportive of their work, the teacher has allowed room for children to evaluate their efforts for themselves (Ginott, 1972). He is empowering a sense of competence in the members of the class.

Many of the same benefits apply to **private encouragement** given to an individual child. Note this teacher's response to Julia when the four-year-old mentions she is building a castle: "You *are* building a castle, Julia. It has towers and walls and windows and doors. I am impressed."

In all likelihood from this one comment, Julia knows what the teacher has noticed in her work. Because the comment was in private, Julia sees that encouragement really was meant for her. Julia was allowed to draw her own conclusions about her building ability, without undue expectations on her for the next time. Julia feels that she and her work are appreciated by the teacher. She feels positively about building again.

(From the journal of a student while completing a practicum in a kindergarten classroom.) I decided to use both types of encouragement, publicly directed to the entire group and privately directed to the individual. In the second observation, I use (C) for the specific child, and (S) for me.

Public Encouragement, Directed to the Entire Group

Students were working on story pictures to send to some survivors of the Oklahoma City bombing disaster. I made a point of going around to look at each child's creation, not making any specific comments; then I stood in front of the class and said, "You are all working very hard on your story pictures. I'll bet that you are proud of your work." Some children smiled, and they all seemed pleased with this comment. They worked very hard. I noticed a few children even made comments to other children on how nice their story pictures were. By saying something positive to the group, they all wanted to share in that feeling; it was like the domino effect.

Private Encouragement, Directed to the Individual

Later the children were involved in play, and one child in particular was drawing. I went over to him and looked at his creation.

S: You are really working hard on that picture.
C: Yeah, I'm using brown, 'cause that's the main color of it. Can you smell it? (giggle)
S: (Smile) No, does it smell?
C: No, not for real. It's a piece of garbage under a microscope. I'm gonna color it lots of colors cause that's how it looks.
S: Wow! You have drawn an enlarged piece of garbage. I see that it has many points, curves, and corners. It really looks like it would look under a microscope. Your picture is impressive.

After this last comment the child gave me a very large smile and continued to draw using lots of colors all mixed together. Later I learned the child had been exposed to a microscope by an older sibling, but he applied the idea of garbage under the microscope by himself. I was impressed.

Encouragement—What to Say

When they are beginning to use encouragement, teachers sometimes do not know what to say. If a child's product is "pre-representational" or is not what was expected, teachers find themselves especially at a loss for words. A strategy is to use a **starter statement** that elicits a response from the child; the encouragement then comes from the interaction.

An effective starter statement used by the practicum student in the previous anecdote was "You are really working hard on that picture." The idea is to begin a starter statement with *you* or *we* and then describe what the teacher sees that indicates effort or progress. The teacher is developing skill in the use of encouragement when he can pick out details in the child's or group's efforts and positively acknowledge them. **In fact, the ability to notice and comment positively about details ends the "loss for words" problem.**

Encouraging statements are simple, but they can have an immediate and positive effect:

In the course of a day there are many opportunities to offer encouragement.

Cartoon courtesy of American Guidance Service, p. 8 of "Teaching and Leading Children" by Dinkmeyer, McKay et al. © 1992.

- You have made a real start on that puzzle.
- You have printed almost your whole name.
- Everyone is working so hard to clean the room today. We're almost ready for the story.
- You got eight of the ten problems correct.
- You have all the letters right in that word but one.
- You slid down the slide all by yourself.
- You didn't get upset even once today.

An effective starter sentence tells a child that the teacher is interested, cares, is willing to help. Listening is a big part of the act of encouragement. Frequently, the child's response will be a smile, new resolve in the continuation of the activity, or discussion of a problem encountered.

The support has registered when the child says something like:

Yep, that's a picture of my baby brother. You can't see him 'cause he's hiding under the covers.

or

Yes, but I'm not sure I did it right.

In contrast to encouragement, statements of praise like "good job" neither give specific feedback nor invite interaction (Bredekamp, 1997). Such statements do not take as much concentration by the teacher and are mental shortcuts; they are quick and easy "fixes" for the teacher (Kohn, 1993). Mastering specific encouragement requires conscious practice over time. The boost in student self-confidence, persistence on-task, and acceptance of others' efforts makes the effort worthwhile.

Stickers and Smiley Faces: Extrinsic Rewards

Stickers and stamped smiley faces have become traditions in early childhood education. The following *nontraditional* comments are intended to provoke thought about the use of these *reward tokens.* In the discussion, the term *stickers* is used to include stamped smiley faces.

Stickers in most uses, are praise rather than encouragement (Kohn, 1993). They reward achievement rather than acknowledge effort. They fail to tell the child exactly what the teacher likes about the achievement. Keeping the use of stickers private is quite difficult. If they are given to some but not all, children make mental comparisons about who gets how many, how often. When used in evaluation of behavior or achievement, stickers reinforce an impression of differential treatment by the teacher—"who the teacher likes". They are easily interpreted by young children as judgments about personality. Because they are extrinsic rewards, stickers build dependency upon the teacher. They demean the intrinsic worth of the learning activity (Bredekamp, 1997). (If it is developmentally appropriate, no external reward should be necessary. If the activity is not developmentally appropriate, the teacher should not be doing it.)

Personal encouragement instead, either spoken or written, is more appropriate for young children. To a first grader, the teacher could either whisper or write, "You got all of your Ms on the line." If written, the teacher might read the notation to the child; *that* will be a paper likely to be taken home. Written encouragement, even to kindergartners, is a sure inducement to functional literacy. As the previous anecdotes illustrate, specific, nonevaluative feedback supports an environment in the classroom in which each child is encouraged to try.

Interestingly, no other section of the first edition of this text has been more controversial than this one with students in my classes. Stickers and smiley faces are a popular tradition indeed. For students and teachers insistent on the use of these reward tokens, here are two suggestions:

1. **With individual children, save the use of stickers for those who have particular needs** (and who are perhaps showing Level Three mistaken behaviors). Use the stickers in defined situations to help the child master a specific behavior such as not taking home small figures in play sets. Give the stickers as privately as possible and explain to the child why you are giving them each time. (Explain the reason as well to children who notice; they can understand more than teachers sometimes realize.) Discontinue the stickers as soon as the child is making noticeable progress but keep giving encouragement.

2. **Use stickers to celebrate not evaluate.** Give everyone in the class a sticker when you are proud of the group's accomplishments. Celebratory use should not be every day, just on special occasions. Older kids will compare stickers, so make them as equivalent as possible—not smelly stickers to some and not to others. Use stickers that do not glorify violent "super heroes," but convey friendly and happy themes.

When Praise Is Appropriate

Praise is not *always* inappropriate, though it does need to be given with care. As mentioned in Chapter 3, on occasion a solid rationale exists for having the class recognize an individual child. One reason is to acknowledge achievement after a child has struggled publicly and persevered. The class can appreciate in any child a hard fought victory.

A second example is the practice in some classrooms of recognizing a "Star of the Week" or "Very Important Kid." If using this practice, the teacher needs to ensure that children know they will all have a turn. One way to designate turns is the chart with each child's name and a movable marker. The children might be listed in order of age, with the youngest child the first Very Important Kid. When praise is done carefully in select situations, both the individual and the group benefit. The child receives a boost in self-esteem, and the class a boost in empathy levels toward individual members. Praise and encouragement both take conscious thought and decision-making by the teacher.

DISCUSSING INCLUSIVELY

Chapter 6 introduced the idea of discussing stories inclusively with children. In discussions of all kinds, of course, the teacher listens. He does not discard comments that seem out of context. On the surface, what sounds like inattentiveness may indeed be careful listening and hard thought—but from a perspective different than the teacher's.

> With the coming of spring, a kindergarten class had finished a dinosaur unit and was well into hatching chicken eggs. In a discussion the class talked about how baby chickens know to peck for food. The teacher asked if anyone knew what the word *instinct* meant. One child raised her hand and announced, "That's like dinosaurs 'cause they're not alive any more." The teacher started to call on another child, then turned to the first child and thanked her for the comment. With an impressed smile, the teacher explained to the class the difference between *instinct* and *extinct*.

The teacher in this anecdote knew that the kindergarten class would not gain a full understanding of the terms from her brief explanation. (Some children may even have heard the word *extinct* as *eggstinct.* However, she never could have anticipated the association made by the child. The teacher might have passed over the remark as having no connection to the present discussion—in fact she almost did. Instead, the teacher's open-ended expectation of progress was rewarded because of her willingness to listen. The teacher was discussing inclusively.

What can the teacher do, however, when children really do *not* listen? The conventional practice has been to call on a child who is "chatting" or daydreaming to force renewed focus. The implication of the guidance approach is that the teacher **needs to make the discussion interesting so that children will want to participate.** On average, by the time children have begun kindergarten, they have watched nine months to a year of television, including perhaps a month of Sesame Street. From television—as well as from the family—they have acquired a host of receptive experiences to work through and share.

The days are fading when teachers could force compliance to didactic instructional methods, focused on retrieval of a series of "right answers." Fewer children now come from "children are seen and not heard/think before you speak" home environments that prepared them for the traditional classrooms of the past.

Children learn willingly when ideas are interesting to them. They fail to learn, in significant ways, if content and delivery have no relevance (Wing, 1992). When discussions require a right answer that children may not know, many develop defensive strategies—playing "dumb," making jokes, acting belligerent—to escape the embarrassment of public correction (Holt, 1964). Discussions that accommodate a diversity of ideas and opinions mean that the teacher has mastered the skill of discussing inclusively. The atmosphere in such classrooms is likely to be both encouraging and intellectually stimulating. The two go together.

> A teacher was reading the classic *Harry the Dirty Dog* to her new first grade class. A girl the teacher hadn't gotten to know yet raised her hand and said, "Teacher, we got a canary at our house."
>
> The teacher decided to use reflective listening and repeated the girl's comment, "Rita, you have a canary?"
>
> "Yes," said Rita, "And last night it was dirty so me and my dad gave it a bath, and then it was cold, so we put new newspapers in its cage and put it by the radiator, and this morning its feathers was soft and warm and fluffy."
>
> Another child then chipped in, "Guess what, teacher, we have two canaries!"
>
> The teacher, who knew this, said, "Yes, Ramon, you do." She then added, "You know what, everybody? Let's see what's going to happen to Harry, because he needs a bath just like Rita's canary did. As soon as we finish the book, we'll talk more about pets and whether you give them baths."

She finished the book, and resumed the discussion, beginning with Ramon. She then had the class write and/or draw in their journals about when they gave or might give a pet a bath. The children worked hard on their journals, and shared them at language arts time the next day.

In reflecting about the activity, the teacher was pleased with Rita's comment. The experience gave Rita a chance to have a successful sharing experience in front of the class. Rita had to use comprehension, sequencing, syntax, and vocabulary skills (canary, cage, newspapers, feathers, fluffy) in telling her story. At a receptive level, the rest of the class similarly gained. In addition, a teachable moment occurred that made the book come alive for the children in a way that the teacher had not anticipated. What was to be a simple literature activity became a multidimensional language arts experience.

This teacher modified a traditional practice when reading books to children: The teacher reads and the children listen. She commented that if less time was available or the story had been more compelling, she might have reacted to Rita the way she did to Ramon, accepting the comment and gently steering attention back to the book. She would have made a point, though, to return to Rita, either in the large group or later individually. Not all teachers would react as this one did, of course, but she showed that she knew the importance of discussing inclusively.

THE CLASS MEETING

Glasser is credited with popularizing the use of *class meetings* (1969). In Glasser's model, class meetings are held to identify problems and work toward solutions. The meetings center around behavior issues, curriculum matters, or student concerns. Glasser is adamant that the class meeting occurs without blame or fault-finding by participants. Honest opinions stated and respected are the keys that make the method work. When children know they have a say in how the program goes and how it can be made better, they feel like they belong and want to contribute.

In a 1989 account of the writing of Glasser on building "a sense of togetherness" within the class, Charles states:

> To foster a sense of togetherness, the teacher should continually talk with the class about what they will accomplish *as a group,* how they will deal with the problems they encounter as a group, how they will work together to get the best achievement possible for every individual in the group. In order to bring this about, responsibilities are given and shared, students are encouraged to speak of their concerns while the class attempts to find remedies, and the teacher takes special steps, when necessary, to incorporate every student into the ongoing work of the class (p. 142).

Teachers use class meetings to establish a sense of belonging, conduct class business, and to solve problems that arise. Whatever the purpose, during class meetings guidelines such as these apply:

- Anyone can talk;
- Take turns and listen carefully;
- Be honest;
- Be kind.

The teacher might also have personal guidelines for class meetings, such as: "Maintain a positive group focus"; "Individual situations require private remedies"; "Class meetings are to solve problems, not create them." A class meeting is usually one of two types: scheduled or unscheduled.

Scheduled Class Meetings

A common time for holding scheduled class meetings is each morning after the children have arrived. The *morning meeting,* introduced in Chapter 6, might include attendance, class business, orientation to the day, and a high-interest discussion. As mentioned in Chapter 6, personally relevant time and weather questions can spark the discussion; or, the teacher can ask other questions that tie in with a theme, area of study, or special event. Special event discussions usually focus on an event not in the everyday routine, but also may relate to members of the group such as a stay in the hospital,

Teachers use class meetings to establish a sense of belonging, conduct class business, and to solve problems that arise.

a missing tooth, or perhaps the death of a pet. Special event discussions should be handled with sensitivity. If they directly involve a class member, the teacher may wish to discuss the circumstances with the child and parent before "going public."

A second time for holding scheduled class meetings is just before going home. The purposes of the meeting are to review the day and discuss coming events. Children might share something they learned or enjoyed doing, or something that did not go right. When a teacher or child experiences a problem, the end of the day meeting is a time to discuss it (Greenberg, 1992). The teacher, or a child, may bring up the messy restroom or inappropriate behavior involving members of the group. If an afternoon meeting becomes too involved, the teacher asks the class to think about it overnight so that "we can discuss it in the morning when we are fresh." The teacher works to end class meetings on a positive note.

Unscheduled Class Meetings

Usually, the teacher calls unscheduled class meetings to address mistaken behavior that cannot wait. Examples include when an activity gets out of hand, or a word like *butt head* is catching on and driving a teacher "bananas."

According to Glasser (1969), the teacher models and teaches during class meetings the following discussion skills:

1. The dignity of individuals is protected;
2. Situations are described, not judged;
3. Feelings are stated as *I* messages;
4. Suggestions for solutions are appreciated;
5. A course of action is decided, tried and reviewed.

Class meetings that focus on problems provide an excellent opportunity for learning human relations and conflict management abilities. Some of the most important learning that the class and teacher will do occurs during class meetings:

> In Vicki's kindergarten class, Gary wet his pants. A volunteer took Gary to the nurse's office where extra clothes were kept. Vicki overheard some of the children talking about Gary and decided it was time for a class meeting. She explained to them what had happened. She then told a story about when she was a little girl, she wet her pants too and felt very embarrassed. She said people sometimes have accidents, even adults, and it's important that we be friendly so they don't feel badly. Vicki then paused and waited for a response.
>
> The children began to share similar experiences they remembered. When Gary came back to the room, another child smiled at him and said, "It's OK, Gary; last time I wet my pants too."
>
> Other children said, "Me too." Looking greatly relieved, Gary took his seat. The class got back to business.

The reader may assume that the discussion of class meetings is directed more to the elementary than to preschool levels, which is not the case. Hendrick (1992) discusses using class meetings to teach "the principles of democracy in the early years" (p. 51). She comments that one part of the process is "learning to trust the group" (p. 52). Hendrick states, "Even four-year-olds can participate successfully in making simple group decisions that solve social problems" (p. 52). She goes on to say:

> Together, for example, they might plan ways to stop children from running through the room. They might also discuss which special outside activity to do—would they rather take a snack and ride their trikes around the block or get out the wading pool for a swim? As children move on to kindergarten and first grade, opportunities of greater magnitude arise (pp. 52–53).

Class Meetings and Circle Times

Class meetings transcend the academic curriculum and deal with life in the classroom. Circle times, in contrast, tend to emphasize the traditional academic pursuits of early childhood: singing, finger plays, stories, creative movement, visits from guests, theme-related discussions, and anticipatory set activities. Class meetings on occasion flow into circle times and vice versa. Whatever type of large group, the teacher should remain vigilant to attention spans and interest levels.

Circle times go back to Froebel's first kindergarten programs in Germany. For Froebel, the circle represented the nonbeginning/nonend of the universe and the unity of humankind with God. Whether modern teachers work from this symbolism or not, the circle suggests the equality and worth of each individual and lends itself to the community spirit of the class meeting. Class meetings that are cooperative in tone can be held successfully with classes of preschoolers and high school students alike. Such meetings are a staple in the encouraging classroom.

LEADERSHIP COMMUNICATION WITH PARENTS

The responsibility for communication with parents lies with the teacher (Sturm, 1997). Parents depend on teachers, even those younger than themselves, to initiate contacts and maintain relations. Most parents respect and appreciate even beginning teachers who enjoy working with young children and take pride in their programs. This section discusses the use of leadership communication with parents to keep communications open and solve problems before they become serious.

Previous chapters discussed the uses of leadership communication with parents to encourage greater involvement in the education of their own children and increased participation in the educational program of the class. Specific activities toward these goals included the following:

1. Send welcome letters (Appendix B) to children and parents before the start of school. When possible, make home visits. When a visit is not possible, make introductory telephone calls to the home.
2. Begin the program on a staggered schedule with half the parents and children attending each of the first two days or on alternating days for the first week. Give a special invitation to parents to attend on these days.
3. Telephone each family on the first night of school. Check with the family about any problems the child had that the teacher might help resolve.
4. Hold an orientation meeting (greeting meeting) on two occasions during the first week or two—ideally on a late afternoon and evening. Invite parents to attend either meeting. Go over a brochure about your education program (Appendix C) at the meeting; discuss policies and highlight opportunities for parent involvement. Ask parents to complete optional surveys during or after the meeting to provide information about the child and family and their preferences for how to be involved (Appendix B).
5. Have parent conferences during the first month. Use the conferences to get to know each parent, referring to the survey if appropriate.
6. Invite parents to be involved in the program. Make sure parents know they are welcome to volunteer in the classroom. Help them feel welcome and useful when they visit (Appendix D).
7. Assist parents to find tasks in the classroom that they are comfortable doing so that they will return.

For parents to feel comfortable with any of these activities, they must feel comfortable in their relationship with the teacher (Sturm, 1997). Rosenthal & Sawyers (1996) refer to building positive relations with parents as **joining.** Joining means establishing the idea in parents' minds that the teacher accepts them and is working together with them on behalf of the child. Leadership communication is the tool of the teacher in building partnerships. Discussion now focuses on the four basic types of leadership communication helpful in maintaining positive parent-teacher partnerships and preventing serious problems: (a) written notes, (b) telephone calls, (c) parent meetings, and (d) parent-teacher conferences.

Written Notes

Many parents associate notes home with criticisms of children's behavior. In the guidance approach, notes home are neither for the purpose of punishment nor correction. The reason is straightfoward: notes do not allow for discussion. The written message is, as it were, cast in stone. When a critical note arrives, the parent has a limited range of responses which frequently come down to doing nothing, becoming upset with the child, and/or feeling "dumped on" by the school.

When sending personal notes that discuss a child, the teacher uses *encouragement.* The note is either an occasional, unsolicited "happygram" or a statement of progress, perhaps as follow-up to a conference. In the latter case, the logical format is often the **compliment sandwich.** Because children wonder about the content of personal notes from the teacher, he does well to read them to the child beforehand. If the tone of the note is encouraging, most children will take pride in seeing that it is delivered. If the matter is serious, it probably is best handled not by a note but by a conference.

To alleviate any anxiety about notes home the teacher may send a happygram or two home with each child during the first few weeks, reading the note to the child beforehand. Such notes give the child a "real idea" about what the teacher thinks; lets the parent know that the teacher is "on the child's side"; and helps children feel positively about carrying notes home in general. Those early happygrams actually may improve the rate of note delivery for the rest of the year.

Regarding routine notes about events, the teacher needs to be aware of three factors: (a) delivery rates by children are seldom 100 percent; (b) some parents will forget or misplace the note; and (c) some parents are nonreaders. The teacher can use newsletter items and repeat notes to remediate factors (a) and (b). Regarding (c), the teacher needs to make an effort to learn if parents are nonreaders. When he knows that illiteracy is a factor, the teacher can either telephone or deliver the message personally. If he has a relationship with nonreading parents, the teacher may be able to send home taped messages or coded picture graphs.

Telephone Calls

Telephone calls allow for personal conversation but not for physical proximity and face-to-face contact. For this reason, unless the teacher knows the parent, telephone calls should be used in a similar fashion as notes home. In other words, under normal circumstances a teacher should not attempt a serious conference on the telephone. Telephone conversations are helpful in underscoring the need for special conferences. They are excellent for personally delivering happygrams, following-up conferences, and inviting parent participation in special events.

When requesting a conference regarding a child's behavior over the telephone, the use of a *compliment sandwich* is important. If the teacher is upset, the compliments help the teacher put the behavior in perspective. For the parent, they convey the message that "my child is not a total problem because the teacher sees at least some 'good' in him." Note the difference between these two calls home regarding Jeremy, a four- and a half-year-old.

Call One: Jeremy was a total monster today. He hit two children, bit one, and threw a book at me. We will have to talk about his behavior tomorrow because I've had it. How is eight o'clock?

Call Two: Jeremy has been working hard on his behavior, but he had a rough day today. He had conflicts with two children this morning. After that he settled down, and the rest of the day went better. He's making progress, but I think we need to talk. What are some times that would be good for you tomorrow?

Phone calls and conferences are two important ways to communicate with parents.

Telephone calls also are well suited to giving positive feedback after a conference. If the teacher wants to communicate more directly than with a note, a call like the following would mean a lot:

> I just wanted to let you know how Jeremy did this week. No hitting or kicking at all. He only got upset once, but he used words. He was also playing more with the other children. I'm really pleased. How are things going for him at home?

Parent Meetings

Regular meetings offer an important vehicle for parent involvement, but they can be difficult to accomplish with complete success. Foster (1994) provides several ideas for successful parent meetings, incorporated into the six suggestions shown in Figure 7.1. (See Foster's article, "Planning Successful Parent Meetings" in Recommended Resources.)

As Figure 7.1 illustrates, meetings add to the time demands on busy staff as well as busy parents. Parent meetings should be held for a reason, not just because they *should* be held. Once the purposes for the meetings are clear, the work in planning and carrying them out becomes worthwhile. With successful meetings, the classroom community expands to include home and school together.

Parent-Teacher Conferences

Conferences provide the most direct link between teacher and parent, and much has been written in recent years about them. Gestwicki devotes a chapter to conferences

Figure 7.1
Suggestions for Successful Parent Meetings

1. Consider convening a parent committee to help plan meetings. Teachers might ask parents who are familiar with the program to serve on the committee. This step is not an automatic guarantee of success, but it shows respect for parent involvement and helps build parent ownership of the meetings (1994). Some teachers prefer to plan the topic and have the committee help to make the logistical arrangements. Others prefer to make the arrangements themselves.
2. Assess parents' interests and needs. Asking parents to complete the optional questionnaire, contacting parents at the beginning of the school year, and polling the parent committee can help with this determination. Topics selected should be high priorities for the parents.
3. Make specific arrangements for the meetings by considering the following:
   a. Date, time of day, and length of the meeting; plan for when most parents can attend. Specify both a starting and ending time so that parents know when the meeting will be over. Keep the meeting concise; under an hour and a half.
   b. Meeting location; an informal location comfortable to the parents is best.
   c. Transportation options; bus line availability; car pool possibilities.
   d. Free onsite child care; takes work to arrange, but it makes a difference. (As Foster points out, "Babies should be welcomed and allowed to stay with their parents if need be" (p. 79).)
   e. Refreshments; good food brings people together and helps bring them back (1994).
4. Get the word out about the meeting. A useful advertising strategy is to have a "hook" that will draw in people. Teachers need to use their imaginations to attract parents. One center borrowed a camcorder, videotaped the children in activities, and sent home notices saying, "See your kids on TV." Other ideas often used are pot luck meal meetings held early in the evening and activity nights where parents, or parents and children together, do typical class activities or make-and-take projects.
5. Keep in mind key elements of the meeting:
   a. A short greeting is given that includes thanks to presenters, meeting organizers, and parents in attendance. Include a concise overview of the program.
   b. An icebreaker activity—perhaps parents telling stories about their children—helps participants relax.
   c. Whether it is a lecture, panel discussion, open discussion, or video, the presentation needs to be interesting and keep in mind fatigue levels. A useful technique is to follow a concise presentation with small group discussions. The large group then reconvenes for small group sharing, questions of the presenter, and a summary statement. Refreshments and informal conversation follow.
   d. Parent go out the door with make-and-take projects or handouts, fliers about the next meeting, and many thanks for attending.
6. Include the parent committee and/or all involved in the planning to assess how the meeting went and decide any changes for future meetings.

Serious discussions occur best in the face-to-face setting of the conference.

in her text, *Parent, Teacher, Community Relations* (1992). Others who have written about conferences are Bjorklund & Burger (1987); Rockwell, Andre, & Hawley (1996); and Rosenthal & Sawyers (1996). (See Recommended Resources.) This section discusses using conferences to build partnerships for the prevention of problems. Conferencing to remediate problem situations is discussed in Chapter 8.

Gestwicki suggests that successful conferences consist of three phases: *preparation, conduct,* and *evaluation* (1992). In preparing, the teacher needs to make sure the parent knows the reasons for the conference. A statement about conferences might be included in a brochure about the program (Appendix C) and repeated in a note home. Time options are helpful for the parent, including both night and daytime slots if possible. An informal private setting, in which parent and teacher can sit side by side at a table, is preferable to conversing over a desk. Likewise, adequate time is preferable to the "get them in; get them out" atmosphere common in some schools.

The teacher should have a folder for each child with samples of the child's work over time. Dated observational notes are helpful. A form to record notes from the conference, in preparation for a later written summary, rounds out preparation (Gestwicki, 1992).

There is considerable agreement about the *conduct* of the conference. The teacher begins with a positive *I* statement about the child, such as: "I really enjoy having Maybelle in class. She works hard and has such a sense of humor." The teacher goes over materials he has prepared, and invites parent discussion about them. He asks about items the parent would like to discuss. The teacher paraphrases comments the parent makes and uses **reflective listening,** which means repeating back the thoughts and feelings the parent is expressing (Gestwicki, 1992). The compliment sandwich is another useful communication technique. If a follow-up plan comes out of the conference, the teacher writes it out and sends it to the parent for approval. The teacher ends the conference on a positive note (Gestwicki, 1992).

Gestwicki includes a list of pitfalls to avoid during conferences:

- Technical terms and jargon. Use terms parents can understand.
- The "expert" role. Describe events and trends rather than make broad judgments.
- Negative evaluations of a child's capabilities. (Use compliment sandwiches.)
- Unprofessional comments: talking about others, becoming too personal or, taking sides. Respect the principle of confidentiality.
- Parental advice. Offer alternative suggestions "that have worked for other parents," for the parent to consider.
- Instant problem-solving. Decide instead on a cooperative plan of action that will be reviewed (1992, p. 221).

Gestwicki concludes her discussion of conferences with this important paragraph:

> It should be remembered that nonattendance at a conference does not necessarily indicate disinterest in the child or the school. Instead, it may be a reflection of different cultural or socioeconomic values, of extreme pressures or stress [on the] family or work demands. A teacher's response to nonattendance is to review the possible explanations . . . see if different scheduling or educational action will help, persist in invitations and efforts, and understand that other methods of reaching a parent will have to be used in the meantime (p. 222).

Following the conference, the teacher reviews notes and completes a brief summary, perhaps on a prepared form. He files the original form and when a cooperative plan has been decided upon, sends a copy to the parent. The teacher also reflects in personal terms about the success of the conference, takes agreed upon follow-up actions, and notes possible changes in approach for conferences to come (Gestwicki, 1992).

SUMMARY

How does the teacher establish leadership in the encouraging classroom?

An encouraging classroom is one in which the teacher sets and maintains clear limits at the same time as reinforcing self-esteem and self-control. The combination of these two qualities in children empowers autonomy, the ability to make intelligent, ethical decisions. From the beginning of the school year, the teacher is firm and friendly, establishing leadership, but in a way that values children and teaches them to value each other. In such an environment, much mistaken behavior becomes unnecessary. A key difference between guidance and conventional discipline is that while the teacher is friendly and firm, he avoids being strict or harsh.

Why are guidelines, not rules, important in the encouraging classroom?

Rules tend to be stated in negative terms and have preset consequences. Rules institutionalize the use of punishments, fail to respond adequately to the complexities of situations, and reduce the role of the teacher to a technician. Guidelines educate children toward productive behavior. Helping to formulate guidelines increases children's ownership of the guidelines and their sense of belonging in the class. Guidelines allow the teacher the range of choices appropriate for a professional. Guidelines mean that the teacher works to solve problems and mediate disputes. In the process, the teacher models conflict management skills, crucial in the 21st Century.

Why is encouragement more appropriate than praise?

Praise rewards achievements, often is used to manipulate the group, and fails to distinguish between personalities and deeds. Encouragement recognizes effort; does not single out or evaluate personalities; gives specific, positive feedback; and builds an encouraging environment. Encouragement is public when directed to the group and private when directed to an individual. Teachers are mastering the technique of encouragement when they comment on details in children's efforts in ways that encourage interaction with the child. As reward tokens, stickers and smiley face stamps constitute praise. Teachers need to be conscious of this when they are using either praise or encouragement.

Why is discussing inclusively important?

In group situations, as well as with individuals, the teacher listens. He goes beyond a preoccupation with *right* or *wrong* answers and who is and is not listening. Instead, the teacher works to make class discussions opportunities for engagement by children through welcoming all perspectives in a mutually respectful atmosphere. By discussing inclusively with children, the teacher is building an encouraging environment in the classroom.

How do class meetings reduce the need for mistaken behavior?

Class meetings are held to maintain a sense of community, carry on the business of the class, and solve classroom problems. Scheduled class meetings occur most often at the beginning and end of the day. The teacher calls unscheduled meetings when events cannot wait. Guidelines for class meetings such as the need to be respectful of others make class meetings positive and productive experiences. Preschoolers and high school students alike can participate in class meetings.

How does leadership communication with parents build and maintain partnerships?

Leadership in communication with parents lies with the teacher. An overriding goal of the teacher in communication with parents is *joining,* or establishing with parents that the teacher wishes partnership with them on behalf of the child. Four types of leadership communication with parents were highlighted: notes home, telephone calls, parent meetings, and parent-teacher conferences. Notes and telephone calls are best used to deliver happygrams that recognize children's progress, provide necessary information to the parent, and set up conferences. Telephone calls can also be used as conference follow-ups.

Parent meetings take planning, often done with a parent committee. The program, as well as general meeting arrangements, need to be worked out in advance for meetings to be successful. Parent conferences have three phases: preparation, conduct, and evaluation. The teacher starts and ends the conference positively, attempts to put the parent at ease, shares specific information about the child and is receptive to parent input. After the conference, the teacher reviews notes, assesses how it went, and follows up.

FOLLOW-UP ACTIVITIES

Note: In completing follow-up activities, the privacy of all involved is to be respected.

Reflection Activity

The reflection activity encourages students to interrelate their own thoughts and experiences with specific ideas from the chapter.

Think of a time when you were embarrassed by praise a teacher gave you, or when you embarrassed a child by giving praise. Compare or contrast that experience with what the chapter says about praise. How might the teacher, or you, have given encouragement in that situation instead? What difference do you think giving encouragement might have made?

Application Activities

Application activities allow students to interrelate material from the text with real life situations. The observations imply access to practicum experiences; the interviews, access to teachers or parents. Students may compare or contrast observations and interviews with referenced ideas from the chapter.

1. **How does the teacher establish leadership in the encouraging classroom?**
   a. Observe an example of what you believe to be positive leadership shown by a teacher. What was the situation? What did the teacher say and do? What did the children say and do in response? Using ideas from the chapter, why do you believe this was an example of leadership communication?
   b. Interview a teacher who shows what you believe to be positive leadership in the classroom? Ask the teacher to share how he goes about establishing leadership at the beginning of the school year. How do the methods of the teacher agree or disagree with what the chapter says about leadership communication?
2. **Why are guidelines, not rules, important in the encouraging classroom?**
   a. Whether he uses the term *rules* or *guidelines,* observe how a teacher uses standards in the classroom. Is the use of standards closer to that of *rules* or *guidelines?* Document your conclusion.
   b. Interview a teacher about how he uses standards with young children. (The use of the term *guidelines* is new, so he may use the term *rules.*) What developmental considerations does the teacher make in creating and using the standards? How is the class involved?

3. **Why is encouragement more appropriate than praise?**
   a. Observe a teacher giving feedback to a child or to the class. What did the teacher say and do? How did the children respond? Was what you observed more like praise or encouragement? Why do you think so?
   b. Interview a teacher about his priorities when giving positive feedback to an individual child and to the class. Write down what the teacher said. How do his ideas correspond to the text ideas about encouragement and praise?
4. **Why is discussing inclusively important?**
   a. Observe a teacher in a discussion or activity with the class. How does the teacher respond to questions or comments that do not seem to "fit"? How has your understanding of discussing inclusively changed by what you observed and read in the text?
   b. Interview a teacher about his priorities in discussions with the class. Ask how the teacher generally responds to comments that do not seem to "fit" the topic or activity. How do the teacher's comments correspond to the text ideas about discussing inclusively?
5. **How do class meetings reduce the need for mistaken behavior?**
   a. Observe a class meeting as distinct from a "Circle Time". Determine whether the meeting was scheduled or unscheduled and the purpose of the meeting. How do the purposes and conduct of the meeting correspond with ideas from the chapter?
   b. Interview a teacher who uses class meetings. Does the teacher use scheduled class meetings, unscheduled, or both? What does the teacher believe to be the reasons for holding class meetings? How do the reasons identified by the teacher correspond with ideas from the chapter?
6. **How does leadership communication with parents build and maintain partnerships?**
   a. Observe how a teacher uses notes, telephone calls, meetings, or conferences with parents. How does the teacher's use of these communication methods correspond with ideas from the chapter?
   b. Interview a teacher about using notes, telephone calls, meetings, or conferences as communication techniques with parents. How do the teacher's priorities correspond with ideas from the chapter?

RECOMMENDED RESOURCES

Castle, K., & Rogers, K. (1993). Rule-creating in a constructivist classroom community. *Childhood Education, 70*(2), 74–80.

Foster, S. M. (1994). Planning successful parent meetings. *Young Children, 50*(1), 78–81.

Kohn, A. (1993). *Punished by rewards: The trouble with gold stars, incentive plans, A's, praise, and other bribes*. New York: Houghton Mifflin Company.

Rockwell, R. E., Andre, L. C., & Hawley, M. K. (1996). *Parents and teachers as partners: Issues and challenges.* Fort Worth, TX: Houghton Mifflin Company.

Rosenthal, D. M., & Sawyers, J. Y. (1996). Building successful home/school partnerships: Strategies for parent support and involvement. *Childhood Education, 72*(4), 194–200.

Wing, L. A. (1992). The interesting questions approach to learning. *Childhood Education, 69*(2), 23–26.

REFERENCES

Albert, L. (1996). *A teacher's guide to cooperative discipline.* Circle Pines, MN: American Guidance Service.

Bjorklund, G., & Burger, C. (1987). Making conferences work for parents, teachers, and children. *Young Children, 42*(2), 26–31.

Bredekamp, S. (Ed.). (1987). Developmentally appropriate practice in programs serving children from birth through age 8. (2nd ed.) Washington, DC: NAEYC.

Bredekamp, S. (Ed.). (1997). *Developmentally appropriate practice in early childhood programs* (3rd ed.). Washington, DC: National Association for the Education of Young Children (NAEYC).

Canter, L. (1988). Viewpoint 1: Assertive discipline and the search for the perfect classroom. *Young Children, 43*(2), 24.

Castle, K., & Rogers, K. (1993). Rule-creating in a constructivist classroom community. *Childhood Education, 70*(2), 74–80.

Charles, C. M. (1989). *Building classroom discipline.* New York: Longman, Inc.

Dreikurs, R. (1968). *Psychology in the classroom.* New York: Harper and Row.

Dreikurs, R., & Cassel, P. (1972). *Discipline without tears.* New York: Hawthorn Books, Inc.

Elkind, D. (1976). *Child development and education: A Piagetian perspective.* New York: Oxford University Press.

Elkind, D. (1987). *Miseducation: Preschoolers at risk.* New York: Alfred A. Knopf.

Foster, S. M. (1994). Planning successful parent meetings. *Young Children, 50*(1), 78–81.

Gartrell, D. J. (1987). Assertive discipline: Unhealthy to children and other living things. *Young Children, 42*(2), 10–11.

Gartrell, D. J. (1995). Misbehavior or mistaken behavior? *Young Children, 50*(5), 27–34.

Gestwicki, C. (1992). *Home, school and community relations: A guide to working with parents.* Albany, NY: Delmar Publishers.

Ginott, H. (1972). *Teacher and child.* New York: Avon Books.

Glasser, W. (1969). *Schools without failure.* New York: Harper and Row.

Greenberg, P. (1992). How to institute some simple democratic practices pertaining to respect, rights, responsibilities in your classroom without losing your leadership position. *Young Children, 47*(5), 10–21.

Hendrick, J. (1992). Where does it all begin? Teaching the principles of democracy in the early years. *Young Children, 47*(3), 51–53.

Hitz, R., & Driscoll, A. (1988). Praise or encouragement? New insights into praise: Implications for early childhood teachers. *Young Children, 43*(4), 6–13.

Holt, J. (1964). *How children fail.* New York: Pitman.

Kohn, A. (1993). *Punished by rewards: The trouble with gold stars, incentive plans, A's, praise, and other bribes.* New York: Houghton Mifflin Company.

Rockwell, R. E., Andre, L. C., & Hawley, M. K. (1996). *Parents and teachers as partners: Issues and challenges.* Fort Worth, TX: Houghton Mifflin Company.

Rosenthal, D. M., & Sawyers, J. Y. (1996). Building successful home/school partnerships: Strategies for parent support and involvement. *Childhood Education, 72*(4), 194–200.

Sturm, C. (1997). Creating parent-teacher dialogue: Intercultural communication in child care. *Young Children, 52*(5), 34–38.

Wing, L. A. (1992). The interesting questions approach to learning. *Childhood Education, 69*(2), 23–26.

Wittmer, D. S., & Honig, A. S. (1994). Encouraging positive social development in young children. *Young Children, 49*(5), 4–12.

8

Leadership Communication with the Individual

GUIDING QUESTIONS

As you read Chapter 8, you will discover answers to the following questions:

- **How do teachers' listening skills encourage young learners?**
- **How are contact talks a useful guidance method?**
- **What is a compliment sandwich and how does it work?**
- **Why is humor an important guidance strategy?**
- **Is touch still a viable guidance technique?**
- **How do teachers use leadership communication in the parent-teacher conference?**

Children show mistaken behavior because they do not know how else to act; others have influenced them to act in a particular way; or they are driven to act out because of strong unmet needs. When adults get beyond **childism,** the naive belief that childhood is a rosy time without stress and hardship, they realize that sometimes the opposite is the case. Without the strong role definitions and social supports of families in the past, many children come to school with pronounced needs and are unsure of how to cope with the uncertainties of the classroom. When children understand that the teacher will listen to their needs and cares about them, they can feel that they belong in the class. They want to be there, fit in, and do well. Almeida (1995) phrases the idea this way:

> Teachers need to care more about their students as the focal point of the classroom, and less about the curriculum. Without question, the curriculum is important, but if students sense that you're more concerned about finishing a spelling lesson than you are about them, they'll be less likely to behave the way you'd like them too. . . . Teachers must care about their students as children (p. 89).

Chapter 8 presents five skills for leadership communication with individual children. The five skills are: listening to life experiences, contact talks, the compliment sandwich, humor, and (although controversial) the careful use of touch. The skills build upon the general guidance priority of encouragement, introduced in previous chapters. In contrast to Chapter 7, the skills focus on leadership communication with the individual child. The chapter concludes with a discussion of leadership communication with parents in the setting of the parent-teacher conference.

LISTENING TO LIFE EXPERIENCES

The educational values that support the encouraging classroom indicate a teacher who cares about children. A teacher using the guidance approach recognizes that young children who are unhappy cannot easily express their anxieties in words and that pent up feelings tend to show themselves as serious mistaken behaviors. Two co-existing environments of the child, the school and the home and neighborhood, each and together can be sources of child stress. In listening to children, to help them cope with stress, the teacher must be attuned to problems emanating from each source.

Listening for School-Related Stress

In many children, the symptoms of school-related stress manifest themselves in feelings of ill-health. Symptoms range from the twice-a-year stomach ache to actual ulcers, from occasional headaches to hypertension and depressive reactions. The causes of school anxiety can be related to specific situations, such as the morning bus ride or the afternoon "power test," or be more pervasive—a child's general feeling of being a failure or being disliked. A remedy for many school-related anxieties is making the education program more developmentally appropriate. At an interpersonal level, as Almeida (1995) suggests, the teacher who understands school-related stress is alert to the individual support that children sometimes need (Furman, 1995).

> (From the journal of a student teacher.) We were cleaning the tables for breakfast when Jamal walked into the room. He stood over by his cubby with his head down. Tami [the teacher] went over, knelt down beside him, and said, "It looks like you might be a little tired this morning." Jamal shook his head no. She asked him if anything was wrong. He told her that someone on his bus hit him with a backpack and he felt really bad. Tami affirmed that wasn't a good way to start the day and asked if they could do something together. She suggested a book and he agreed. They sat down on the bean bag chair and read. She really encouraged him to say the words from the book with her. He smiled and helped her read the book.

Listening for Stress Related to the Home and Neighborhood

Many writers have discussed the increasing complexity of family life today. The rising numbers of dual working parent families, single parent families, blended families, and dysfunctional families are by now well known. In previous times, grandparents, aunts, uncles, and other family members were available to support parents in times of need. Now, not only are many children without access to the extended family, but they are experiencing the trauma of unsafe and violent conditions outside in their neighborhood, as well as within their home. Children can be *resilient,* but they need, at minimum, at least one significant adult who cares about them. That caring adult more and more is the teacher.

Bullock (1993), Furman (1995), Rich (1993), and Sang (1994) discuss in practical terms the effects of unsafe home and neighborhood situations on children in the classroom. Bullock (1993) discusses factors that lead to children being lonely and rejected. She says that "Observing is the key to detecting feelings of loneliness in children" (p. 56). Assisting children to express their feelings through open-ended activities and helping them to build social skills can make a lasting difference in their lives.

Furman (1995) suggests that stresses are unavoidable and may offer opportunities for education. He states that, in turning the challenge into an opportunity, teachers can help children deal with their feelings and develop cooperative working relations with parents.

Sang (1994) describes her mental health consultation role in a kindergarten class as the "worry teacher." She recounts how working with children who need help immediately relieves behavioral demands on the teachers, gives the children in need the opportunity to express and work through their feelings, and models for the teacher's therapeutic teaching techniques. Today, the values of ongoing mental health consultation in a classroom cannot be underestimated.

In the most direct suggestion for teachers, Rich (1993), discusses how she worked with "Harry," who showed perpetual disruptive behavior in her kindergarten classroom. Rich was able to get another adult to cover her class for the first ten minutes of each day, and spent the time "for more than a month" talking with Harry in a quiet corner of the hall. They sat in two chairs, and as time went on, Harry began "thinking of things that he wanted to talk about" (p. 52). As a result of this "talking time," the relationship grew and Harry's impulsive talking and acting out in the class diminished. Rich concludes that "talking time" might not work for every child like Harry, but for him, "talking time was the simple, positive nudge into a calmer, more richly communicative life" (p. 52).

On any given day, teachers do well to "read" children's feelings when they first enter the classroom. If the teacher prepares for the day ahead of time and allows for open activity when children first arrive, she is able to listen to as well as greet her students. The teacher may then be able to give a little attention to the child, or ask other members of the teaching team—assistants, volunteers, or other staff—to do so. When the teacher is able to show caring at the beginning of the day, the teacher and child may be able to reduce or avoid serious mistaken behavior that may show up later on.

In a first grade class, the children each drew in their own way three faces—happy, sad, and angry—on large paper plates. With help, they labeled each face and attached dials to their "face plates." When children came in each morning, they set the dials according to their moods. The teacher and an assistant made a point of noticing each child's setting and attended to those children who might need an adult to listen. In a class meeting, the children talked about how sometimes they felt more than one mood. They decided they could put their dials in between faces on these days. (One said that between sad and angry, though, "was the worsetest.")

When a third grade teacher witnessed Jesse tear up his arithmetic paper and say, "I hate this damn stuff," he reacted with a friendly hand on the shoulder and some kind words. The teacher might have reacted differently except for a talk he had with Jesse earlier that morning:

"Hi, Jess, you're not smiling today." When Jesse looked down and shook his head, the teacher asked, "Something you'd like to talk about?"

Jesse said no, then fighting back tears shared, "Last night a guy hit Bumpers with his truck. We thought he was gonna be OK, but we took him to the vet. The vet took X-rays and said his whole back end was broken. We had to put him to sleep. That guy did it on purpose too."

The teacher said, "Oh, Jesse, I'm so sorry. I know what Bumpers meant to you. Do you want to talk more about it?" Jesse said no, but the teacher knew that for Jesse this would be a long day.

Boyer (1991) comments that an increasing challenge to our schools is the pressure on personnel to be social workers as well as educators. In agreement with Almeida (1995), the four authors mentioned above argue that individual support and social development are a central part of the modern teacher's role. The early childhood teacher is not licensed to be a psychologist or a social worker, but every day, she or he does perform some of these functions. In the presence of Level Three mistaken behaviors caused by stress within or without the school setting, the teacher collaborates with parents, colleagues, and other professionals to help the child solve the problem. Whether comprehensive collaboration is needed or not, the teacher uses a listening ear to assist children to work through anxieties, build social skills, and gain self-esteem.

CONTACT TALK

Contact talk is a variation of the practice of "quality time," adapted for the classroom. Teachers seldom have more than a minute or two to make personal contacts. The point is that even a very short time matters to children; it tells them they are valued so much that their busy teacher takes time to talk with them.

On the surface, contact talk may sound similar to the tactic of "catch them being good," but the two are different. The "catch them" practice involves a one-way conversation with the teacher giving praise. Specific recognition of productive behavior (using encouragement) *is essential* with children, but it is not the main reason for contact talk.

With contact talk, the teacher has the motive of getting to know a child. The teacher initiates, or allows the child to initiate, a conversation. She responds as the

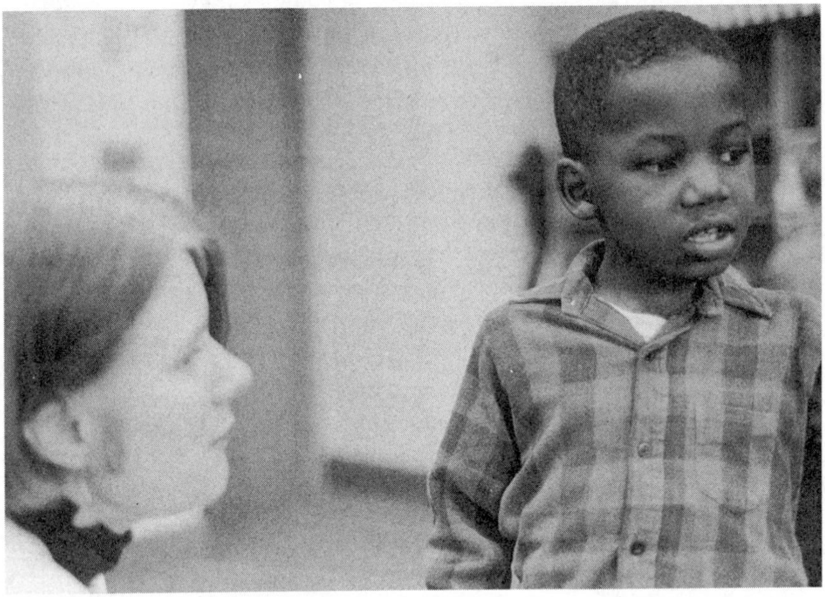

The teacher uses a listening ear to assist children to work through anxieties, build social skills, and gain self-esteem.

The teacher decides that a contact talk will happen by putting aside other work, moving to the child's level, and conversing openly.

child defines the course of the conversation. For the time that the teacher can give, she is a good listener. Children are generally eager to have contact talks with adults. The teacher's role is pivotal in deciding that a contact talk will happen. She does so by putting aside other work, moving to the child's level, and conversing openly with the child.

Examples of contact talks were given in the previous section, at the preschool level with the teacher who helped Jamal get over an unhappy experience on the bus, the kindergarten level with the teacher who scheduled talking time with Harry, and the primary level with the teacher who gave Jesse permission to express his feelings about the experience with his dog. Contact talks need not be of great length. They do not even have to be of a serious nature, but they do need to happen with each child in the class on a regular basis.

Mavis bounded in the door of Head Start, ran a circle around the teacher, and announced, "Me gots new shoes, teacher!"

Looking down at Mavis' pulled up pants, the teacher exclaimed, "Oh, Mavis, those are sure some colorful sneakers."

Indignant, Mavis replied, "Not sneakers. 'Lectic shoes!"

Grinning broadly, the teacher corrected herself, "I'll bet you can sure run fast in those athletic shoes." With a nod over her shoulder, Mavis galloped out the door to the playground.

As time is precious during the day, the teacher must look for opportunities for contact talks to occur. Some likely moments in the daily program include:

- before other children arrive,
- during a choice time,
- at recess (inside or out),
- at lunch,
- during a break in the day,
- after a self-directing activity has begun,
- after school.

Contact Talks at the Preschool Level

The following anecdotes, from the journals of student teachers, illustrate contact talks at lunch and during choice time in two separate Head Start centers.

> (Lunch time) Karly and I were eating at the lunch table. Some children at the table were talking about what they had done on Easter, where they had gone, etc. Karly quietly said, "I didn't see my Daddy at Easter."
>
> I said, "Oh?"
>
> She then said, "He isn't good with kids. He doesn't like them either. My Grandma and Grandpa don't like kids either."
>
> I said, "I'm sorry, Karly. I'll bet you have other grown-ups who like kids."
>
> She smiled and said, "Yes, I do! My other Grandma and Grandpa love me. And Uncle Tim and Aunt Judy like to play with me. And my Mom really loves me."
>
> I said, "Then you are a very lucky girl to have so many people who love and care for you." she nodded seriously, and that ended the conversation.

> (Choice time) I heard the words, "Shut up," and walked around the corner to the restroom to find out who said them. Shayna was sitting in the corner crying. I asked, "Shayna, why are you crying?"
>
> She said, "Amanda and Christina said they aren't my friends anymore." I asked her if she told them to shut up. Shayna said yes.
>
> I told her I was sorry that what they said made her feel sad and angry, but we don't use those words in our classroom because they hurt people's feelings. (Amanda and Christina had been watching and listening to us talk.) I added that maybe next time she could tell the girls that hearing that they didn't want to be her friend made her sad. I told Amanda and Christina that Shayna was feeling sad. They came over to Shayna and gave her a hug and said they were sorry.

> Shayna walked over to the table where I was sitting. She started crying again. I asked, "Is something making you feel sad, Shayna?"
>
> She said, "I miss my daddy." (Her father was killed in a car accident a few months before.)
>
> I asked if she would like to sit on my lap, and when she did, I said, "Shayna, my daddy died when I was a little girl, and I was very sad too. I am so glad you told me why you were crying." We sat by each other until snack.
>
> Shayna went to the housekeeping area after snack. Later in the day, she came up to me and said, "I'm over my daddy now."
>
> I said, "Shayna, feeling sad about missing your daddy is OK. I still miss my dad. If you need a hug or want to talk, you come and tell me."

The advantage in staffing arrangements of preschools is that contact talks can occur more easily. In the supportive prekindergarten classroom, a reasonable goal is *at least* one contact talk with each child every day. Teachers of three- to five-year-olds can hardly escape contact talks, and of course shouldn't.

Contact Talks in the Primary Grades

Contact talks are more difficult on a regular basis at the elementary school level. A system that allows every child to be reached is critical. Here is where use of the teaching team can help. If the teacher can bring other adults into the classroom, more contact talks can occur (Rich, 1993). With only one adult in the room, a teacher might only be able to have a few conversations a day—still better than none at all. Elementary grade teachers who work to increase the number of contact talks tend to be rewarded.

> In his first year of teaching, Clay felt hampered because he was only able to relate to his thirty third graders as "students." He decided to try an after school program that he called "Get to Know Our City." He got approval from the principal and sent home letters with permission forms. One day each week, he took a carload (five) of the third graders to visit interesting places.
>
> By the end of the school year, all children had gone with him at least once. Most had gone a few times. Clay found the experience had helped him gain new understanding about the children. When one child who usually did not say much asked him if his toothache was better, Clay discovered that the other children were also getting to know him. Of course, the entire class learned more about the city. And, quite important to Clay, the program especially helped his relations with a few children he had mainly known before as "strong willed."

For a workshop assignment, Gayle, a kindergarten teacher, made a chart of the children's names set against a four-week calendar. Daily, the teacher made a point of having two-minute personal conversations with at least five children and noted these conversations on the chart. With alternate day programming, Gayle was able to have at least one contact talk with each child every two weeks—and with most children more than one.

After the month, Gayle decided to continue the practice. The teacher discovered she was becoming more receptive to the children, especially those who were less outgoing. She found she was not only getting to know the children better, but they were also getting to know her. Gayle felt there was a change of atmosphere in the classroom.

The value of contact talks is that as teachers and children get to know each other, trust builds, and the need for mistaken behavior lessens. Studies have shown that teachers tend to talk most with children who are talkative and from backgrounds similar to their own (Derman-Sparks, 1989; York, 1991). A chart may seem mechanistic, but it ensures that all children (and the teacher) receive the benefits of contact talks.

The value of contact talk is that as teachers and children get to know each other, trust builds, and the need for mistaken behavior lessens.

THE COMPLIMENT SANDWICH

At a workshop, Dr. Julie Jochum came across the idea of the **compliment sandwich.** Jochum developed the concept as a feedback technique for teacher education majors when journaling with children (Jochum, 1991). As adapted from Jochum's usage, the compliment sandwich provides a focused way of giving encouragement. The technique is useful with children or adults for preventing or resolving problems. (The technique even works with family members, though sometimes a "triple decker" is needed.)

The compliment sandwich has three parts: *two* statements of encouragement; *one* suggestion, recommendation, request, or question. The two encouragements recognize effort, progress, or interim achievement. (They are the two pieces of "bread.") The peanut butter in the middle guides the child toward further progress. The ratio is important as some research has shown that two positives per negative is the barest minimum for a child to feel supported (Kirkhart & Kirkhart, 1967). In other words, three pieces of bread ("triple-decker encouragement") is desirable. If the teacher considers adding a second request or recommendation, she makes a new sandwich.

What do compliment sandwiches sound like? The reader can tell very quickly what is and is not a compliment sandwich. Let us "overhear" two second grade teachers, one during language arts, the other during math time.

> *Language arts:* You are being careless again. Look at how those sentences wander over the page. You forgot your periods. This is messy work. You will need to do it again.
>
> *Math:* You have seven of the problems exactly right. This assignment is hard, and you are really staying with it. Use your counters again and see if you can get different answers for the other three. You can do it.

By using the compliment sandwich—as opposed to "character assassination"—the second teacher was probably helping to prevent math anxiety. The technique is self-explanatory—for whatever change the teacher requests, she recognizes two or more indicators of progress or effort. The math teacher's use of the technique was in an academic situation. The compliment sandwich also applies in other classroom situations. Here are some examples of compliment sandwiches, first with a group and then with an individual child:

> *Preprimary:* You have put away all the blocks and the books. We just have the table toys to finish and then we can go outside.
>
> Jamie, you have your coat hung up and your boots off; you just need to put the boots under your coat, and you're all set.
>
> *Primary:* Class, you read lots of books in the library today, and you sat very quietly for the story. Coming back through the hall, though, was a little too noisy. Who has ideas for how to make the walk back more quiet?

Sondra, you stayed in your seat and didn't have any problems with your neighbors. That's real progress! Now, how can we help you to remember to use that "inside voice"?

Encouragement that is a part of the compliment sandwich reassures children that the teacher is on their side. (It is always easier to improve when the coach is pulling for you.) With serious mistaken behavior, the compliment sandwich also helps to remind the *teacher* of this fact. In meetings with parents, the compliment sandwich helps establish a spirit of cooperation, that the parent and teacher are working together for the benefit of the child. The technique is an important one, an essential ingredient of leadership communication.

HUMOR

The sensitive use of *humor* affirms positive relations with children and affords a friendly atmosphere in the classroom. An attraction of teaching young children is the delightful unpredictability in their responses. Teachers who find themselves refreshed by the reactions of young learners know why they are practicing at this age level. In light of the difficulties classroom teachers face each day, the ability to find humor in situations adds to the positives of the profession.

A student kept a journal of her practicum experiences throughout her teacher education program. A few of the enjoyable statements she recorded:

When I was helping a boy in kindergarten fold his paper in half,
Cody said, "I can't fold very good because I'm from Tenstrike, and people in Tenstrike don't know how to fold."

While I was helping a four-year-old button her coat,
Ashley said, "My grandpa can't snap the buttons very good because his hands are old."

As I read kindergartners a story,
Amanda said as I paused to catch a breath to keep reading, "Miss Curb, you have bags under your eyes." (Kids are so honest—you gotta love it!)

During a practicum at St. Philip's Preschool,
While five of us education majors were doing a theme project with the children, the teacher asked the three- to five-year-olds if they could do anything to help us. One little boy piped up and asked, "Should we pray?" We all laughed because it wasn't such a bad idea.

> At a practicum in a day care center,
> A little girl arrived late, just in time to pass the "Easter Bunny" on the sidewalk. The Bunny, who had just visited our center, was in a hurry to get to his next visit. The little girl watched wide eyed as the Bunny got in his car and drove off. She walked into the center shaking her head and muttering, "I didn't know the Easter Bunny could drive a car"!

Different kinds of situations are apt to make teachers smile. One such occasion is when teachers hear their own words echoed by children:

> A teacher was at first amazed, then amused when a four-year-old made the following request: "I am having a difficult morning, so I need kindness." The teacher remembered making a similar comment in jest earlier in the week.

The fact that children interpret words quite literally can be a source of enjoyment for adults and children alike:

> It began raining heavily outside the windows of a kindergarten class. The teacher exclaimed, "Why, it's raining cats and dogs out there."
> The children looked out of the windows intently. Then one child turned to the teacher and said with a smile, "Teacher, it's raining elephants even."

A classroom atmosphere in which humorous moments are enjoyed by all is a positive atmosphere. Teachers who see humor even in trying moments can defuse problems effectively. Curwin & Mendler suggest the use of mildly self-effacing humor as a remedy for power struggles (1988). This use of humor can be challenging for a teacher, but it has its rewards.

> In front of the class, a fearless third grader said to his male teacher, "Boy, Mr. D., you sure are hairy."
> The teacher, who had forgotten to shave, said, "You're right, Willie. I couldn't find my razor today, so I hit my whiskers in with a hammer and bit them off inside. Guess I missed some." The class, including Willie, shook their heads and laughed. The moment was quickly forgotten as Mr. D. started a project.

Humor helps in sustaining positive teacher-child relations. However, humor can also be used against children, by a teacher who needs to control through humiliation. Dr. John Halcrow, an education professor in human relations, has this to say about the use of humor:

> We need humor in the classroom but let's be careful about it. Humor can be a two-edged sword. Some rules for humor: Never use it as a weapon, nor to chastise or correct. Never make a student the butt of a joke, and remember not to take yourself too seriously.
>
> We need fun, hope, even frivolity in the classroom. If we put too much focus on the mechanics of what we're teaching, we kill the joy. Work students hard, then let them play with what they've learned. Let them talk to each other, try out their ideas and correct their own errors along the way (1988).

A sense of humor in teachers is much appreciated by learners of all ages. Humor makes learning meaningful because it makes it fun.

TOUCH

Along with humor, another practice that conveys warmth in relations is the use of **touch.** Unfortunately, the use of warm physical contact (hugs and friendly touches) by teachers, so accepted in times past, has become controversial today. Now in some school districts, teachers must ask permission of a child before giving a pat on a shoulder or a hug. In many situations, teachers must communicate with fellow staff, administrators, and parents before doing what before came so naturally. Every teacher must make personal decisions regarding touch. This section cites Curwin & Mendler (1988) and Hendrick (1996) in supporting the use of friendly physical contact within the limits of reasonable policy.

Curwin & Mendler (1988) recommend the use of hugs and touching in communicating with children. They decry the fallacy of prohibition against touch because of sexual misunderstanding, but they seem to assume that this proscription pertains only to teachers of older students (1988, p. 16). Yet, Hendrick points out that recent sensationalized court cases have made early childhood teachers as well "uneasy about touching or cuddling youngsters lest they, too, be accused" (1996, p. 107). The article, "Vanishing Breed: Men in Child Care Programs," (Robinson, 1988) points out that male teachers of young children are particularly susceptible to such suspicions.

Given the value of nurturing touches for children, physical closeness should not be deleted from the teacher's repertoire. Rather, as Hendrick points out (1996), educators need to maintain written policies that allow open visitation by parents, require clear understanding among all staff regarding physical closeness, and conduct criminal background checks for prospective employees. The rationale for the guideline "friendly touches only" needs to be fully communicated to children, parents, and staff. Such practices are becoming necessary for the continuation of this important teaching technique.

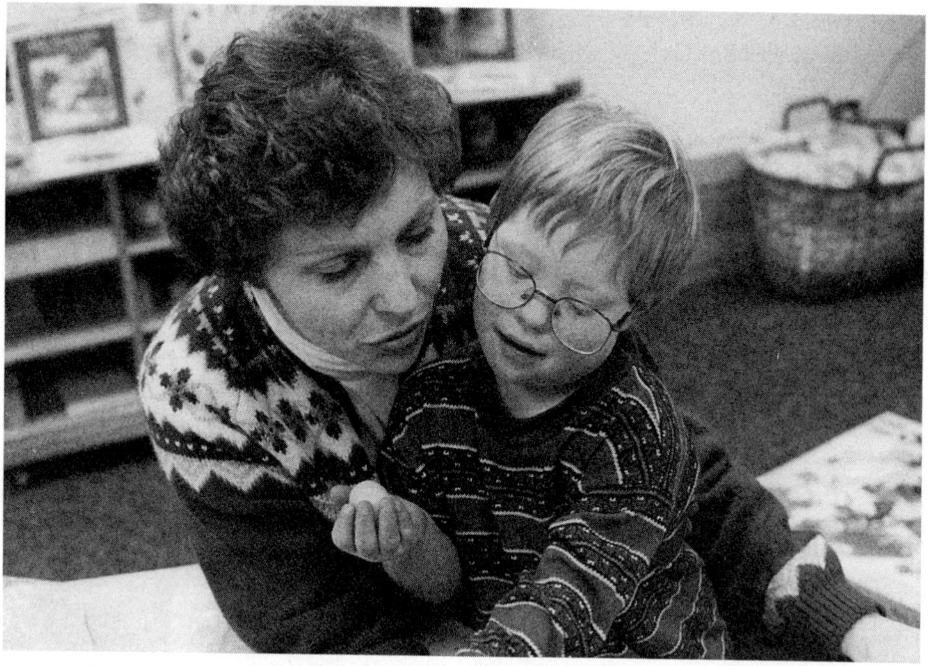

A practice that conveys warmth in relations is the use of touch.

New to a school, a teacher worked to develop a sense of belonging with her class. In her own words, she was "a hugger," and talked with the principal early in the year about the school's policy regarding physical closeness. The principal commented that the policy was, "Friendly physical contact is acceptable in the public confines of the classroom with the written permission of the parents and the verbal permission of the child." Bothered but undeterred by the policy, the teacher explained the situation to parents at the September orientation meeting for them. Almost all the parents signed the written permission slips allowing the teacher to use "friendly touches, hugs, and sitting on my lap."

With her kindergartners, the teacher held a class meeting. The class decided that at arrivals and departures if children wanted a hug, they would give two thumbs up; if they wanted a friendly wave or comment only, they would put up one thumb. The teacher also made sure that they knew they could put up one or two thumbs during other times of day, if they needed to.

Stationing herself by the door each morning, she greeted each child with a one thumb or two thumb hello. She noticed that some children were "every day huggers," and some children wanted a hug seldom or once in a while. All the children, though, responded warmly to her daily greeting. Although the teacher did not like having to prepare for the day earlier, she believed that putting her preparations aside for the greetings helped the day go better.

The teacher also gave a one or two thumb farewell at the end of the day. She noticed that more children elected a hug at the end of the day than at the beginning. She talked with the one or two children whose parents had not signed the slips, and gave these children special smiles and verbal comments. Though she saw the policy as a bother, she concluded that it was worth it to make her classroom a friendly place.

Physical closeness accomplishes what words cannot in forming healthy attachments with children (Curwin & Mendler, 1988). As Hendrick points out, children "require the reassurance and comfort of being patted, rocked, held, and hugged from time to time" (1996, p. 107). Hendrick states:

> Research as well as experience supports the value of close physical contact. Montagu (1986) has reviewed numerous studies illustrating the beneficial effect of being touched and the relationship of tactile experience to healthy physical and emotional development. Investigations documenting the link between touching and the development of attachment confirm those findings (1996, p. 107).

The use of friendly touches by teachers has become controversial. Considering the benefits of touch for children, teachers should not dismiss this technique out-of-hand, but use it carefully and with open communication to the extent that program policies allow.

LEADERSHIP COMMUNICATION IN THE PARENT-TEACHER CONFERENCE

Chapter 7 emphasized four basic teacher-parent communication techniques useful in creating positive relationships: notes home, telephone calls, parent meetings, and parent-teacher conferences. Chapter 8 focuses specifically on the parent-teacher conference and what Rosenthal & Sawyers argue is the overriding goal of conferences, the accomplishment of *joining,* or helping parents understand that the teacher accepts them and wants to work with them on behalf of the child (1996).

Joining with Parents

The traditional setting for the conference is the classroom, though sometimes parents feel more comfortable with the teacher in a setting outside the school—the home, a community center, a child care or Head Start building, or a restaurant. (One

A main purpose of the conference is to help parents understand that the teacher accepts them and wants to work with them on behalf of the child.

of my favorite stories is of the teacher who, after several attempts at reaching a single mom, finally located her at a lounge where she worked as a cocktail waitress. The two had the conference in a booth during the mom's coffee break.) The teacher needs to give consideration to the site of the conference and its likely meaning for parents.

> In her second year of teaching first grade, a teacher created a "parent corner" in her classroom by placing a cardboard divider, decorated by the children, between her desk and a corner of the room. The corner was small, but it had enough room to squeeze in two chairs, a table and coffee pot, a bulletin board, a fledgling resource library, and a coat hook with a carton below where volunteers could stow their belongings. After talking with one volunteer, the teacher decided to have her conferences in the parent corner. She noticed that the parents felt quite comfortable having the conferences in "their" area. Unlike the previous year, many of the conferences proved downright fun, and holding the conferences in the corner seemed to increase the number of parents who came into the classroom to volunteer. Two other teachers set up parent corners the next year and conducted their conferences in them.

Wherever the site of the conference, Rosenthal & Sawyers offer a list of suggestions important for the process of joining (building partnerships) with parents:

1. Speak the language of the family; use their words and definitions.
2. Understand the family's rules and rituals.
3. Try to keep jargon to a minimum—especially at first.
4. Monitor your own level of discomfort; do you resort to becoming the "expert" when you become uncomfortable?
5. Try to build a collaborative, rather than an adversarial, system.
6. Ask the family to suggest solutions [and contribute ideas].
7. Recognize signs of a power struggle (1996, p. 197).

Listening to Parents

In an article included in the Recommended Resources, Studer (1993) offers suggestions to better enable teachers to "listen so that parents will speak." The following discussion incorporates Studer's ideas.

An essential part of communication is listening. Studer points out four reasons for why teachers may not listen as effectively as they might (1993). First, the teacher may have negative attitudes about the parent. For instance, if the teacher believes that the parents do not care about their child's education, she may not even attempt communication intended to build partnerships. Second, when persons such as teachers are in "power" positions in conversations, they tend to think ahead to the next point they want to make. Instead, the teacher needs to listen to what the other is saying. Third, in a similar fashion, the teacher may finish the comments of parents, or otherwise "politely" interrupt, rather than give the respect of fully listening. Fourth, prejudging a person and anticipating what that person is going to say may keep the teacher from listening effectively (p. 74).

For teachers to be effective in communications, they need to listen fully and reflectively (what Studer terms *active listening*). Real listening involves both body placement and the honest effort to understand (Studer, 1993). The teacher sits side by side with the parent or in chairs across from one another; faces and even leans toward the parent in an open posture; and when culturally appropriate, makes eye contact and uses light touch.

In listening, the teacher acknowledges what the parent says in respectful ways, avoids giving quick advice, and involves the parent as a full partner in the discussion. Notice the difference in the following dramatized reactions of two teachers when Mrs. Dillworth comments that her son, Cory, has complained about two children picking on him.

> *Teacher one* sits behind a desk with arms folded, leans away, and looks out the window. Interrupts when he has heard "enough." Speaks in a "lecture" voice: "You know, Mrs. Dillworth, when I was a kid, I had that problem and what I did was join a karate club. Get Cory enrolled in a karate club, Mrs. Dillworth. Your kid just has to learn to take care of himself."
>
> *Teacher two* sits next to Mrs. Dillworth, faces her, and lets her fully express what is on her mind. He reflects back what he has heard, how Mrs. Dillworth must be feeling, and what she probably would like to see happen (Studer, 1993). "Cory has shared that two boys in the class have been picking on him? You must be bothered by that idea, and I'll bet you'd like this problem addressed. Tell me more about what Cory has said and then we'll figure out what we can do about this problem."

In the first scenario, a parent might well assume they weren't going to get very far, thank the teacher for the time (maybe), and leave still feeling upset. In the second, the teacher has listened to what the parent has said and involved the parent as a team member. By doing so, she has improved the chances that a positive action will result from the conference and that a problem with the parent will be prevented.

One of the first reactions of many teachers to situations like the one in the anecdote is defensive: "Doesn't happen in my classroom." "Your kid's a trouble-maker anyway." These thoughts, the result of feeling threatened by the parent, usually are not directly expressed, but they come through indirectly in defensive communication styles. By staying calm and remembering that the parent, child, and teacher are all on the same team, the teacher is in a better position to invite cooperation from the parent and prevent problems in parent-teacher relations. Studer concludes her article in this way:

> Teachers must remember that parents have special needs and special concerns. Conferences need to be approached with an attitude of sharing and learning, as well as a willingness to consider parents' observations. Such a cooperative attitude between home and school can be paramount to a child's achievement (1993, p. 76).

Such an attitude will also result in parents who are not adversaries but allies, because the conference has allowed joining to occur.

SUMMARY

How do teachers' listening skills encourage young learners?

With the complexities of modern life, many children feel tension, stress, and anxiety. These feelings may be school-related or related to the child's experiences in the home or neighborhood. Unless they are able to express their feelings and concerns, and therefore understand them better, their unmet needs may cause children to show Level Three mistaken behavior. With larger problems, the teacher works with other adults in a collaborative approach. In many cases, however, by listening and helping children to express and cope with the stress they feel, teachers bolster self-esteem, boost feelings of belonging with the class, and promote the development of life skills.

How are contact talks a useful guidance method?

Contact talk is the concept of quality time adapted to the classroom. The purpose of contact talks is neither to preach nor to "catch the student being good." Rather, contact talks are for the purpose of the teacher and the child getting to know each other. Contact talks need not be long nor especially serious, but the teacher needs to find the time and take an action such as moving to the child's level to ensure that the talk happens. Some elementary level teachers chart contact talks to make sure they reach each child. With a conducive staff to child ratio, preschool teachers should endeavor to have at least one contact talk with each child each day. In the process of the contact talk, the teacher learns more about the child and how to work with the child more effectively. The child learns that the teacher cares and that the classroom is an encouraging place to be.

What is a compliment sandwich and how does it work?

Research long has indicated that children need more positive interactions than negative for healthy personal and social development. The compliment sandwich allows teachers to make a request for change or further progress in line with this research by coupling the request with two or three statements of encouragement. When a teacher is bothered by a child's behavior, the compliment sandwich assists the teacher to phrase the concern positively. Adults as well as children respond more easily to requests for change when the listener concludes that both individuals are on the same side. For this reason, the compliment sandwich has uses with colleagues and parents as well as with children.

Why is humor an important guidance strategy?

For children and teachers alike, good natured humor eases tense situations and makes classroom transactions more enjoyable. One important benefit of being a teacher of young children is the delightful things that they say. The ability to enjoy the freshness and unpredictability of children adds much to the profession. When laughter is not used against children but with them to create a feeling of community, humor becomes an important guidance strategy. Learners of all ages appreciate teachers who use friendly humor.

Is touch still a viable guidance technique?

Some teachers reject using touch with children because they fear the innuendo of sexual abuse. Such attitudes are unfortunate. Children experience the world through touch even more than other senses. For younger children and older ones alike, appropriate touch is fundamentally reassuring; it tells children in ways that words cannot that the teacher cares. Programs need to be clear about their guidelines for touch, when and what kind of touch is appropriate, and they need to negotiate these guidelines with parents. Within those established guidelines, touch tells children that they are cared for and they belong.

How do teachers use leadership communication in the parent-teacher conference?

The main purpose of communicating with parents is *joining,* or helping parents understand that you are working with them cooperatively on behalf of the child. A main vehicle in the process of building partnerships is the parent-teacher conference. The teacher endeavors to make the conference setting comfortable for the parent. In the conference, the teacher must be sensitive to any prejudices toward the family and listen without interrupting or giving quick advice. Listening to parents is crucial in the communication process of the conference. To listen effectively, the teacher takes an open body position and uses eye contact and light touch as culturally appropriate. In a supportive tone, the teacher reflects back what the parent says and states what she thinks the parent is getting at. With confirmation, the teacher involves the parent in a shared resolution of the issues at hand.

FOLLOW-UP ACTIVITIES

Note: In completing follow-up activities, the privacy of all involved is to be respected.

Reflection Activity

The reflection activity encourages students to interrelate their own thoughts and experiences with specific ideas from the chapter.

Think about a time when a child needed to say something to you and you listened. Compare the dynamics of this experience with what the chapter says about listening skills and contact talks. What did you learn about working with young children by making the decision to listen?

Application Activities

Application activities allow students to interrelate material from the text with real life situations. The observations imply access to practicum experiences; the interviews, access to teachers or parents. Students may compare or contrast observations and interviews with referenced ideas from the chapter.

1. **How do teachers' listening skills encourage young learners?**
   a. Observe an adult in the classroom who is sympathetically listening to a nonacademic experience a child is sharing. What do you notice about how the adult is using listening skills. What seems to be the child's demeanor at the start of the conversation, at the end?
   b. Interview a teacher about the priority she gives to listening to individual children's personal experiences. Ask the teacher if she can remember an experience when she helped a child by listening? How does the teacher cope with the "time problem" that listening to individual children entails?
2. **How are contact talks a useful guidance method?**
   a. Observe a teacher having what appears to be a contact talk with a child. What did the teacher do to be available for the talk? Who is doing more talking? Do you still believe that the talk was a contact talk? Why or why not?
   b. Interview a teacher about contact talks. Explain the term if necessary. What does the teacher believe the place of contact talks should be in the daily program? How does the teacher's position agree or disagree with the discussion of contact talks in the text?
3. **What is a compliment sandwich and how does it work?**
   a. Observe a teacher talking with a child about a behavior that the teacher would like the child to improve. Did she use a compliment sandwich? Why or why not?
   b. Interview a teacher about the compliment sandwich. Explain the term if necessary. When does the teacher believe the compliment sandwich would be appropriate to use? When not?
4. **Why is humor an important guidance strategy?**
   a. Observe an instance of humor used by a child in a classroom. How did the other children respond? The teacher respond? Observe a second instance of humor, this time used by the teacher. How did the children respond? What have you learned about humor in the classroom from these observations?
   b. Interview a teacher that you believe to have a sense of humor. What is important to her about using humor in the classroom? Ask for an example or two of events that the teacher found humorous. Compare what the teacher says about humor with the text position.
5. **Is touch still a viable guidance technique?**
   a. Observe two instances when a teacher used touch in the classroom. What seemed to be the effect on the child in each case? How does each child's reaction correspond to what the text says about touch?
   b. Interview a teacher that you know uses friendly touch. Ask the teacher how she deals with the concerns that some adults have about touch. Ask if the program has any policies or guidelines regarding touch.

Ask what the teacher believes to be important about the use of touch with children.

6. **How do teachers use leadership communication in the parent-teacher conference?**
   a. Observe a parent-teacher conference. Identify some listening behaviors used by the teacher. How do the behaviors used by the teacher correspond to the recommendation for effective listening in the text?
   b. Interview a teacher experienced in parent-teacher conferences. Ask the teacher to discuss how she communicates during the conference to make it productive for both the parent and the teacher. How do the communication ideas mentioned by the teacher correspond to the recommendations for effective listening in the text?

RECOMMENDED RESOURCES

Almeida, D. A. (1995, September). Behavior management and "the five C's." *Teaching prek-8,* 88–89.

Bullock, J. R. (1993). Lonely children. *Young Children, 48*(6), 53–57.

Furman, R. A. (1995). Helping children cope with stress and deal with feelings. *Young Children, 50*(2), 33–41.

Rich, B. A. (1993). Listening to Harry (and solving a problem) in my kindergarten classroom. *Young Children, 48*(6), 52.

Robinson, B. E. (1988). Vanishing breed: Men in child care programs. *Young Children,* 43(6), 54–57.

Sang, D. (1994). The worry teacher comes on Thursdays. *Young Children 49*(2), 24–31.

Studer, J. R. (1993). Listen so that parents will speak. *Childhood Education, 70*(2), 74–77.

Sturm, C. (1997). Creating parent-teacher dialogue: Intercultural communication in child care. *Young Children, 52*(5), 34–38.

REFERENCES

Albert, L. (1996). *A teacher's guide to cooperative discipline.* Circle Pines, MN: American Guidance Service.

Almeida, D. A. (1995, September). Behavior management and "the five C's." *Teaching prek-8,* 88–89.

Boyer, E. L. (1991). *Ready to learn: A mandate for the nation.* Princeton, NJ: The Carneigie Foundation for the Advancement of Teaching.

Bullock, J. R. (1993). Lonely children. *Young Children, 48*(6), 53–57.

Curwin, R. L., & Mendler, A. N. (1988). *Discipline with dignity.* Alexandria, VA: Association for Supervision and Curriculum Development.

Derman-Sparks, L. (1989). *Anti-bias curriculum: Tools for empowering young children.* Washington, DC: National Association for the Education of Young Children.

Furman, R. A. (1995). Helping children cope with stress and deal with feelings. *Young Children, 50*(2), 33–41.

Halcrow, J. (1988). *Laughter in the classroom.* (Professional education document). Bemidji, MN: Bemidji State University.

Hendrick, J. (1996). *The whole child.* Englewood Cliffs, NJ: Merrill/Prentice Hall.

Jochum, J. (1991). Responding to writing and to the writer. *Intervention, 26*(3), 152–157.

Kirkhart, R., & Kirkhart, E. (1967). The bruised self: Mending in the early years. In K. Yamamoto (Ed.), *The child and his image: Self concept in the early years.* Boston: Houghton Mifflin Company.

Rich, B. A. (1993). Listening to Harry (and solving a problem) in my kindergarten classroom. *Young Children, 48*(6), 52.

Robinson, B. E. (1988). Vanishing breed: Men in child care programs. *Young Children, 43*(6), 54–57.

Rosenthal, D. M., & Sawyers, J. Y. (1996). Building successful home/school partnerships: Strategies for parent support and involvement. *Childhood Education, 72*(4), 194–200.

Sang, D. (1994). The worry teacher comes on Thursdays. *Young Children, 49*(2), 24–31.

Studer, J. R. (1993). Listen so that parents will speak. *Childhood Education. 70*(2), 74–77.

York, S. (1991). *Roots and wings: Affirming culture in early childhood programs.* St. Paul, MN: Redleaf Press.

Unit Three

Solving Problems in the Encouraging Classroom

Chapter Overview

9 Guiding Children to Solve Social Problems

Chapter 9 explores how the teacher can teach mediation and negotiation skills to children so that they can solve social problems. Discussion is given to: the factor of societal violence; teacher understandings about social problem-solving and conflict management models, and teaching problem-solving skills. The final section explores how parent involvement at St. Philip's School in northern Minnesota helped to build a peaceable school community.

10 Problem-Solving Mistaken Behavior

Chapter 10 presents strategies for the teacher to use to resolve mistaken behavior. Strategies include applying the concept of mistaken behavior, making the decision to intervene, responding to behaviors reported by children, using quick intervention techniques, and intervening when follow-up is necessary. A question answered is, "Why take the time to find solutions"? The final section discusses building cooperation with parents through nonbiased communication.

11 Guidance Through Intervention

Chapter 11 offers information to help prospective and practicing teachers cope with and remediate strong needs mistaken behavior. Conditions that make intervention necessary are examined. Methods of crisis management and of handling feelings of anger are discussed. Strategies and case studies in working with Level Three strong needs mistaken behavior are presented. The chapter concludes with considerations for when teachers and parents disagree.

12 Liberation Teaching

Chapter 12 develops the concept of liberation teaching. The chapter links liberation teaching and resiliency; and liberation teaching and antibias curriculum. A section examines the connection of liberation teaching to the elements of guidance including peace education. The chapter ends with application of the concept of liberation teaching to relations with parents.

9

Guiding Children to Solve Social Problems

GUIDING QUESTIONS

As you read Chapter 9 you will discover answers to the following questions:

- **Does violence in society affect how children handle conflicts in the classroom?**
- **What understandings about social problem-solving do teachers need?**
- **What understandings about conflict management models do teachers need?**
- **How does the adult teach conflict-management skills to children?**
- **How have parents helped to shape the peaceful problem-solving program at St. Philip's School?**

Thanks to Sarah Pirtle of the Discovery Center, Shelburne Falls, Massachusetts, and to Sue Liedl of the St. Philip's School, Conflict Management Program, Bemidji, Minnesota for contributing to this chapter.

(From the journal of a student teacher) *Observation:* Starre came to Head Start one day with a buzz haircut—quite a change from her longer hair. Starre went up to her friend, Aisha, and asked, "Do you like my hair?"

Aisha looked at her and started to say that she didn't like it, but caught herself and with a quizzical smile said, "I'm not used to it yet."

Starre replied, "Yeah, me neither."

No less than parents, educators want children, as they mature, to be able to make *autonomous* (ethical and intelligent) decisions. With young children such as Aisha this social problem-solving includes a bit of self-control and beginning empathy for the other person. In adolescence, when faced with peer pressures regarding vandalism, cigarettes, alcohol, drugs, and premature sex, the young person's ability to make autonomous decisions requires individual strength, a healthy conscience, and well-practiced problem-solving skills.

Slably et al. (1995) define *social problem-solving* as "The skills needed to manage social conflict successfully. . . . " Sometimes, as in Aisha's case in the previous anecdote, the management of conflict means having the skills to prevent conflict from happening. In fact, this ability might be considered a central "learner outcome" of teaching social problem-solving skills. More often, though, and especially with young children, social problem-solving is needed after one child has objected to an action of another, and the conflict is escalating. This is when the teacher steps in to model and teach conflict management skills.*

Chapter 9 discusses teaching conflict management to children so that they can solve social problems. The subject of conflict management is a complex one with many works written about it. Chapter 9 surveys numerous recent materials and provides an overview of conflict management as it relates to guidance in the encouraging classroom. Topics include two conflict management basics: mediation/negotiation and peace education; violence in the society and its effects on children; what every teacher needs to know about social problem solving and conflict management models; and teaching conflict management skills to children. The chapter concludes with the case study of a school in northern Minnesota that, as a result of parental input, has made conflict management and peace education its way of life.

TWO CONFLICT MANAGEMENT BASICS

In exploring social problem-solving from a guidance perspective, the teacher needs a firm grounding in the *mechanics* of conflict management, the use of **mediation, peace, props,** and **child-negotiation** to solve social problems; the teacher also

* The term conflict management is regarded by many as more inclusive than the similar term "conflict resolution." Conflict management is the term used in this text.

needs understanding about the *dynamics* of conflict management, the place of the approach in the broader context of **peace education.**

Mediation/Negotiation

In the text, when a teacher intervenes to assist children to solve a social problem, the teacher is referred to as the *mediator* who is *mediating* a solution with children unable to resolve a problem on their own. The terms *mediator, mediating,* and *mediation* refer to this solution-oriented teacher intervention in which all participants win. The literature on conflict management tends to define the mediation procedure and qualifications of the mediator more formally than in this text (Girard & Koch, 1996). Mediation training is desirable for teachers to have; however, in the encouraging classroom, any adult who assists two or more children to work out a problem is engaging in mediation.

Over the last ten years, numerous models and programs for conflict management have arisen. Pirtle (1997) and Porro (1996) make the case that more similarities than differences exist in methods for assisting children to resolve a conflict. One functional distinction is between models that use a consistent step-by-step procedure and models that use a set procedure but also incorporate a formal area or prop to facilitate the problem-solving process. *Talk-and-listen chairs, a conflict corner* (Porro, 1996), *a peace table, peace puppets,* and the *talking stick* (Janke & Penshorn Peterson, 1995) are examples of **peace props.**

Formal areas and props can indeed enhance the mediation process, but the teacher who uses a set procedure alone to help children "work it out" is still using mediation effectively. Pirtle (1997) points out that all set procedures are only guideposts for the professional teacher in guiding children to learn to solve social problems. In the encouraging classroom, the objective is to move children from a reliance on the teacher for mediation to where the children *negotiate,* or work out a problem on their own (Wichert, 1989). Negotiation skills and autonomy are the interrelated social and personal aspects of democratic life skills, the goal of the guidance approach.

For the teacher to guide children to use social problem-solving, a fundamental change in his role must be accomplished. The teacher no longer acts in the traditional role of a moral authority who determines who is right and wrong in a situation and then prescribes consequences. The teacher instead functions as an ethical leader who, by modeling and instruction, guides children to solve problems in ways in which all involved gain. Much of the text to this point has developed this progressive view of the teacher's role. The remainder of the text explores how the teacher using guidance responds in the event of conflict.

Peace Education

Social problem-solving is often taught as a part of a philosophical approach called **peace education.** Peace education is an important reference point for prospective and practicing teachers. In their adaptation of Harris' 1988 work on the subject,

Janke & Penshorn Peterson (1995) set out eight tasks of peace education. Peace education:

1. draws out from people their desires to live in peace;
2. provides awareness of alternatives to violence;
3. consists of teaching skills, content, and a peaceful pedagogy;
4. examines the roots and causes of violence;
5. empowers students to confront their fears of violence;
6. helps build a peaceful culture to counteract militarism;
7. challenges violent ways of thinking and acting;
8. promotes loving behavior towards oneself, others, and the environment.

Readers may react to some of these issues as being political as much as philosophical: such an interpretation is definitely the consumer's right. Nonetheless, the tenets of democratic life skills have much in common with the priorities of peace education. Given the violence prevalent in modern life, teachers today can hardly engage in character education without addressing the issues of peace and the need for peace education.

THE FACTOR OF SOCIETAL VIOLENCE

Whatever the specific views of writers regarding social problem-solving, they generally agree on these facts: (a) Social conflicts—disagreements, disputes—happen all the time; they are a part of life for children and adults. (b) Popular culture tends to glorify the violence in our society in ways that make civil problem-solving difficult to teach and learn. (c) If we as a society are to increase our capacity to resolve conflicts peacefully, using negotiation rather than violence, then we need to provide a comprehensive educational program for our children, beginning while they are young in the home and in the school (Carlsson-Paige & Levin, 1992; Girard & Koch, 1996; Kriedler, 1984; Levin, 1994; Slaby et al., 1995).

In the encouraging classroom, children learn many social problem-solving skills from each other (Slaby et al., 1995). In fact for reasons of similarity in development, experience, and social role, an important strategy is to specifically empower children to "take charge for themselves" and resolve their own disputes (Carlsson-Paige & Levin, 1992; Wichert, 1989). However, the adult role in getting children to this point is one of active leadership (Carlsson-Paige & Levin, 1992). In the past, and in some cultures of today, the reason that children show aggression has been attributed only to the immaturity of the young. Carlsson-Paige & Levin (1992) and Levin (1994) point out, however, that ours is an exceedingly violent society, and few children escape the influence of exposure to violence. For too many children, the factor of developmental immaturity is aggravated by the prevalence of societal violence.

Modern children experience violence through television and related recreational activities. On average, American children between the ages of three and six view four hours of television each day, often including a diet of violent cartoon shows (Levin, 1994). By age 18, they will have watched the equivalent of 7 years of TV,

Adults teach conflict management as an integral part of the education program.

not including videotapes and video games (Levin, 1994). Between the ages of 5 and 15, children will have viewed more than 13,000 TV murders (Carlsson-Paige & Levin, 1992).

Although parents often believe they are screening what their children watch, a large portion of shows, videotapes, and video games that children are exposed to are designed for older viewers. In addition, toys and books based on action figures flood the market for children to play with and read when they are not at a television or computer screen. As they get older, children become aware as well of popular youth culture and the violence attendant to it (Carlsson-Paige & Levin, 1992).

Most children in the society experience violence at least indirectly by viewing television. Through her construct, "the continuum of violence in children's lives," (Figure 9.1), Levin points out that smaller numbers of children have more direct and intense exposure to violence. For instance, children from low income situations tend to view more television than their middle income counterparts (Levin, 1994) and experience more direct violence in the neighborhood (Carlsson-Paige & Levin, 1992). Some children at all income levels are exposed to violence in the home. Levin comments:

Figure 9.1
The Continuum of Violence in Children's Lives

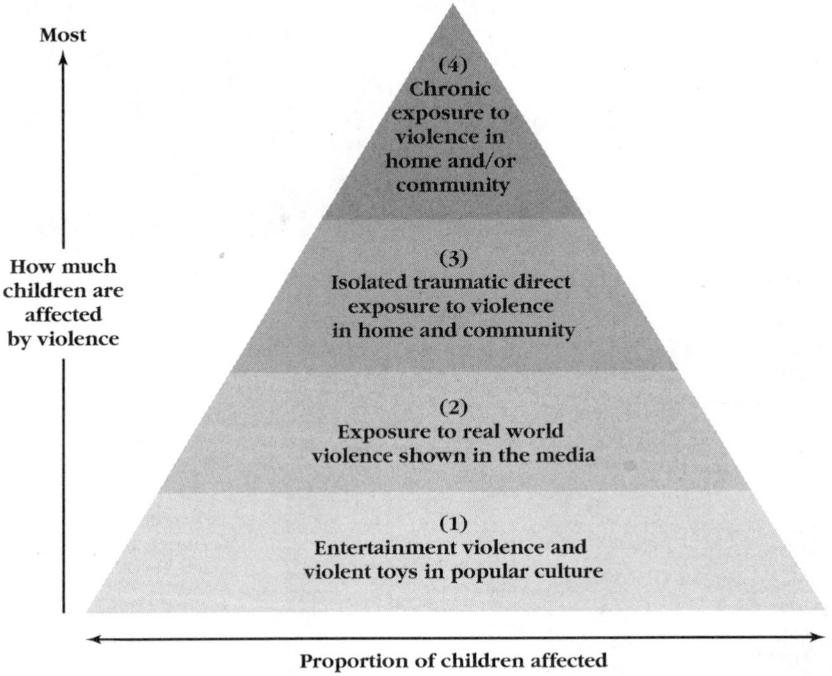

Reprinted with permission from *Teaching Young Children in Violent Times,* by Diane E. Levin © 1994 Educators for Social Responsibility. For more information call 1-800-370-2515.

> The more frequent, varied, and extreme the violence children experience, the more likely their ideas and behavior will be affected by that violence, and the more help they will need from adults in working through the harmful effects of that violence in learning how to be nonviolent themselves (p. 15).

With a still developing ability to understand, young children face conflicting messages about violence, experiencing it through television, and receiving contradictory messages from adults: "don't hit," "play nice," "stand up for yourself" (Levin, 1994). Pirtle (1997) points out that along with the increase in television viewing, parents are having young children participate more in formal, organized activities such as ice skating, gymnastics, and music lessons. Less time is then available for the informal neighborhood play that in the past has been so important for children to learn social problem-solving abilities (Pirtle, 1997). Unless taught otherwise by adults, children today easily acquire "unrealistic and superficial beliefs" about violence as the way to handle conflicts (Slaby et al., 1995).

For children to learn social problem-solving skills, they need a coordinated, encouraging learning environment and specific, positive teaching. While this instruction needs to happen in the home, through the encouraging classroom teachers too have an important role in it. New educational programs such as *Linking Up* (Pirtle, 1997) are designed to help educators use the expressive arts to assist children in developing positive social skills. Literature, music, movement, art, and creative drama are useful instructional tools for educating about feelings, cooperation, and problem-solving.

UNDERSTANDING SOCIAL PROBLEM-SOLVING

To be effective in modeling and teaching conflict management skills, the teacher needs some important understandings about social problem-solving:

1. *Social problem-solving and guidance are connected.* The goal in each approach is to develop an individual's ability to think autonomously. Teachers from both the conflict management and the guidance perspectives believe that they can help children reach this goal. Educators from both perspectives teach children that making mistakes is all right; we just have to learn from them and mistaken behaviors are synonymous concepts. The personal acceptance and encouragement toward growth that constitute guidance provide the encouraging classroom in which problem-solving skills can be learned. The role of the teacher as strong but responsive leader in the guidance classroom includes: the mediation of conflicts and the teaching of negotiation (social problem-solving) skills. (As mentioned previously, **mediation** occurs when a third party assists the "conflicted" parties to solve problems; **negotiation** occurs when the parties resolve the conflict themselves) (Girard & Koch, 1996).

2. *While teachers work to prevent institution-caused conflicts, they realize that conflicts are inevitable and can be important learning opportunities.* Through a developmentally appropriate curriculum, many conflicts leading to mistaken behavior can be prevented (Dinwiddie, 1994). The prevention of especially institution-caused mistaken behavior is a priority of the teacher and was the theme of Unit Two. Of

course, even in the developmentally appropriate classroom, conflicts will still occur. As an experienced teacher once remarked, "You know, for a large part of almost every day, a large number of small bodies and a small number of large bodies inhabit a very small space together. Of course, there will be conflicts."

Most writers in conflict management (Girard & Koch, 1996; Slaby et al., 1995) argue that conflicts are not negative, which is the common perception, but that they are opportunities for learning and progress, depending on how they are handled. Traditionally, teachers impose "solutions" on problems because of the emotional discomfort conflicts cause, the need for general teacher control, the need to put "certain" children "in their place," and/or the distraction from time-on-task (Carlsson-Paige & Levin, 1992; Dinwiddie, 1994). They fail to see that social problem-solving skills are an appropriate part of the social development (social studies) and communications skills (language arts) curriculum. Learning social problem-solving skills is significant learning; learning that stays with individuals long after their formal education ends.

Teachers who regard social problem-solving skills as basic to the developmentally appropriate curriculum are committed to approaching conflicts as learning opportunities and strive to respond to such situations positively and effectively. Taking the time to intervene is not time "off task" for such teachers. For them, conflict management is a part of the curriculum. These teachers know that as children learn social problem-solving skills, conflicts will take up less of their classroom time, and the classroom community will become a more effective learning environment for the effort (Levin, 1994).

3. *When a problem occurs, the teacher avoids blame and retribution and works with the children to find a winning solution* (Dinwiddie, 1994). A guidance principle is that the teacher addresses the behavior and protects the personality, solves the problem but does not punish the child for having a problem. Scolding a child who hit another in the stomach "for not sharing" is tempting indeed. A better outcome occurs for both children, however, if the adult mediates a solution in which all parties gain from the experience (called a *win-win* or a *winning solution*).

To achieve this better outcome, the adult helps the children focus on the immediate problem, generate nonviolent solutions to it, and decide on one that is mutually satisfactory. The process allows for the child who was hit to tell the other child how it made him feel. Evidence suggests that victim-centered techniques, which help children understand the consequences of their hurtful actions, tend to increase prosocial behaviors (Wittmer & Honig, 1994). Being told by a peer in a conference situation that he didn't like it when he was hit is a powerful message to a young child. The adult would then talk with the children about what they could do to solve this problem that caused the hitting and what they could do differently next time (Wichert, 1989).

4. *The teacher need not mediate an ideal settlement every time for children to learn social problem-solving skills* (Wichert, 1989; Dinwiddie, 1994). In matters of high emotions with young children, the adult cannot expect to resolve every problem perfectly. By bringing even an imperfect mediation process to problems in a positive manner, children will still be learning the following problem-solving skills: (a) The ability to evaluate immediate consequences; (b) the ability to generate

nonviolent, alternative solutions; and (c) a growing ability to predict the consequences of their behavior in advance (Dinwiddie, 1994).

Besides, although the basic process of mediation is widely agreed upon, which is important, almost as many separate steps exist as do writers (Pirtle, 1995). Following the four steps suggested by Kreidler (1994), would not be following "perfectly" the six steps suggested by High/Scope (1996), or the tens steps suggested by Slaby et al., (1995). To their credit, Slably and his colleagues point out that expecting children to master each of several specific conflict-management steps is unrealistic. They suggest that adults gradually teach the steps and during conflicts focus instead on the general approach.

5. *Teachers need to understand the developmental characteristics of young children that lead to conflicts and successful resolutions*. Dinwiddie (1994) points out that:

> Children have conflicts over property, territory, or privilege. The younger the child, the more likely the conflict is to concern property: toys, clothes, even people can be viewed by young children as their own personal property (p. 15).

Property tends to be the most frequent source of conflict in the preprimary years, and the kind of dispute adults most often have to mediate. As teachers know, the concepts of sharing materials or taking turns with them are not natural ones for preprimary children. These concepts take time and understanding to teach.

When children begin to play in groups, problems of **territory** arise (Dinwiddie, 1994). These problems involve whether a child gets to join others in the dramatic play area, where a third child can play when joining another two, and so on. In some ways, territorial disputes seem easier to mediate than property disputes because "negotiable" space rather than a single object is the issue. However, a child already in an area tends to define fairly shared spaced differently than the other child *and* the adult. In territorial mediation, the adult frequently has to work hard to see the issue as the child already in the area does.

Problems of **privilege** emerge as children's awareness of social subtleties continues to grow. Privilege issues such as who gets to line up first or who gets to sit next to the teacher are often seen in sophisticated preschoolers as well as in primary grade children. Dinwiddie (1994) points out that conflicts can be over a combination of these issues, and different issues can be at work with different children. The challenge for the teacher is to understand the issue for each child in a dispute, and thereby mediate a successful solution for all.

Carlsson-Paige & Levin (1992) frame the developmental factor in teaching social problem-solving as follows. Young children

> tend to see problems in the immediate moment and in physical terms. They also see problems from their own point of view. Only with age and experience do children slowly learn to see problems in a larger context; in more abstract terms that involve underlying motives, feelings, and intentions; and from more than their own point of view. Until they are able to do this on their own, therefore, the teacher needs to help (1992, p. 7).

Carlsson-Paige & Levin (see Recommended Resources) suggest guidelines for teaching social problem-solving to young learners (1992). The object of such mediation is to present problems encountered in terms that make sense to each child. The following items are an interpretive summary of their suggestions:

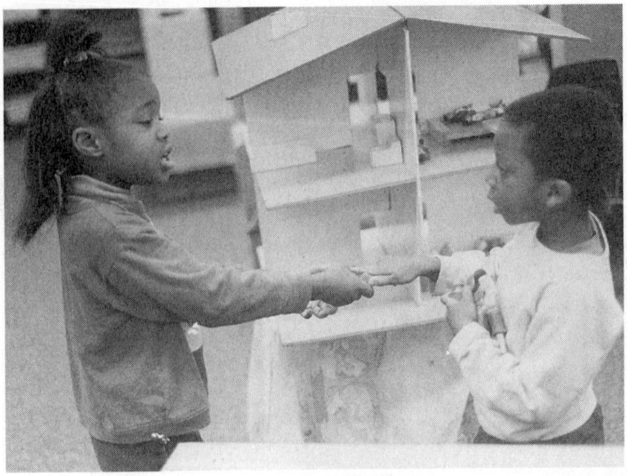

If children cannot think of winning solutions, suggest alternatives and help them find, try, and evaluate the solution suggested.

- Help children define problems in simple terms: physical objects and concrete actions.
- Use the concrete situation to reinforce that their problems have two sides.
- Encourage children to see the whole problem and how their behavior contributed to it.
- Encourange children to suggest their own solutions. Adult solutions tend to be "fair," but they are cast from an adult's point of view. Often children's solutions are more creative than the adults. Although not always as fair in adult terms, they may be more satisfactory because the children arrived at them themselves. Carlsson-Paige & Levin call these *inclusive solutions.*
- If children cannot think of winning solutions, suggest alternatives and help them find, try, and evaluate the solution selected.
- Nudge children from mediation (the teacher serves as mediator) to negotiation in which children resolve problems by themselves. The teacher

provides only as much mediation as the children need to negotiate the rest for themselves (pp. 7–10).

One morning in a day care center, two three-year-olds decided they both wanted to use scissors for free form cutting in the art center.

Only one chair was at the table, and they raced to the chair and began pushing each other for possession of it. Both children were getting increasingly upset as the teacher arrived.

She knelt down, put an arm around each child, and said, "You two are upset because you both want this chair."

Sheila said, "Me had it, and her tried to take it."

Button didn't say anything, but she continued the wailing she had just started. The teacher comforted Button and then said, "What can we do so that you can both have a chair?" The girls just frowned at each other so the teacher suggested, "Sheila, there's another chair right over there. Why don't you get it? Then you can both have one." Sheila didn't move, she just bit her lip. Just then, Button (in a complete mood change), exclaimed, "We could both use this one"!

The teacher was about to say this wouldn't work when to her amazement, the two girls sat side-by-side, each on half of the chair. They cut together for 15 minutes.

6. *Social problem-solving is taught not just through conflict intervention but through the instructional program and the climate of the classroom and school.* Social problem-solving is taught at three levels: conflict mediation, the instructional program, and the climate of the center or school. Much of this text focuses on building the encouraging classroom, or in Kreidler's term, the peaceable classroom (1984).

Going beyond the classroom to the school, Bodine, Crawford, & Schrumpf (1994) discuss *creating the peaceful school,* a school environment that teaches nonviolence, compassion, trust, fairness, cooperation, respect, and tolerance (Girard & Koch, 1996). Pirtle (1995) mentions creating in the school, "a strong cooperative community where people feel affirmed." Adult participants model nonviolence in problem-solving, but more than that, they create an inclusive school community in which participants—teachers, administrators, parents, and children—cooperate to further the social progress of the institution.

At the level of the instructional program, teachers incorporate skills for social problem-solving into the curriculum. A clear and useful example is Kreidler's 1994 handbook, *Teaching Conflict Resolution through Children's Literature.* (See Recommended Resources.) Kreidler integrates conflict management activities with such classics in children's literature as *Alexander Terrible, Horrible, No Good, Very Bad Day,* and *The Grouchy Ladybug.* The book indicates Kreidler's vision as an educator.

Many management skills programs are available commercially, often referring back to Kreidler's 1984 landmark work, *Creative Conflict Resolution: More than 200*

Activities for Keeping Peace in the Classroom. Another book, written particularly for the preschool level is Wichert's *Keeping the Peace* (1989). This book offers useful strategies for mediation and negotiation, suggestions for setting up learning centers, and ideas for activities.

One of the more original programs is *Peacemaker's A, B, Cs for Young Children: A Guide for Teaching Conflict Resolution with a Peace Table* (Janke & Penshorn Peterson, 1995). The program provides ideas ranging from mediation to *peacemaking* philosophy, includes lessons with illustrative stories, and uses props to educate and problem-solve. In the last few years, the proliferation of peacemaking activities, songs, and materials testifies to the timeliness of this grassroots movement in society. The integration of social problem-solving concepts with guidance principles is a natural union as educators enter the 21st century.

UNDERSTANDING CONFLICT MANAGEMENT MODELS

As the reader may be aware, a *model* is a consistent procedure designed to resolve a social or educational problem and attain a specific goal. The variety of conflict management models available provide a sometimes confusing array of priorities, procedures, activities, and lessons. Fundamental differences, however, are relatively few, and can be considered "variations on a theme" (Pirtle, 1995). One functional difference, mentioned previously, is between those conflict management models that use a physical prop as part of their procedure and those that do not. The first section to follow discusses some of the more popular peace props and their uses; the second section explores seven core elements shared by conflict management models, and the third section lists and itemizes features of five widely used models of conflict management.

Peace Props

One feature in some conflict mediation models is the use of *peace props* to teach lessons and facilitate mediation efforts. An established peace prop is the use of *talk-and-listen chairs*. Other common props are the *Peace table*, the *talking stick*, and *problem puppets* (Kreidler, 1984; Janke & Penshorn Peterson, 1995).

Talk-and-listen chairs and the peace table are both formally designated places in the classroom where children and adults go to resolve disputes. Children follow established guidelines such as: *respectful words only; explain; don't attack; take turns talking;* etc. The talk-and-listen chairs assist in the taking turns guideline by having as a policy that the children actually switch chairs to talk and listen.

A prop popularized by Janke and Penshorn Peterson (1995) is the talking stick. Teachers introduce the talking stick as a "sacred tool" for helping children talk and listen to one another. Often, it is passed around in class meetings, where the person holding the stick expresses thoughts and feelings, and all others listen. The stick is passed until the problem or issue facing the group is resolved, or the group decides they have "counseled" enough for one sitting. Another use is in an exchange between individual children locked in a dispute. The teacher calms and mediates as necessary to remind the children that the stick is a peace prop and not a weapon. With modeling and practice, even preschoolers will seek the talking stick and resolve a problem on their own.

> During April, a student teacher in a Head Start classroom recorded in her journal an anecdotal observation of two children, "Charissa" and "Carlos":
>
> *Observation:* Charissa and Carlos were building with blocks. Charissa reached for a block, and Carlos decided he wanted the same one. They both tugged on the block and then Carlos hit Charissa on the back. Charissa fought back tears and said, "Carlos, you're not s'posed to hit, you're s'posed to use the talking stick."
>
> Carlos said "yeah" and got the stick. I couldn't hear what they said, but they took turns holding the stick and talking while the other one listened. After only a minute, the two were playing again, and Charissa was using the block. Later I asked her what the talking stick helped them decide. She said, "That I use the block this time. Carlos uses it next time." (Smile.)
>
> *Reflection:* I really got concerned when Carlos hit Charissa, and I was just about to get involved. I was surprised when Charissa didn't hit back but told Carlos to get the talking stick, and he did! Then, they solved the problem so quickly. "DeeAnn" [the teacher] told me that she has been teaching the kids since September to solve their problems by using the talking stick. Usually she has to mediate, but this time they solved the problem on their own. It really worked!

Puppets are another conflict management prop that Kreidler discussed (1984) and that are still in use today. Whether they are called *peace puppets, power puppets,* or *problem puppets* (Kreidler, 1984; Janke & Penshorn Peterson, 1995), hand puppets have almost magical properties and can instruct in ways that adults by themselves could only hope to do. Like the talking stick, puppets can be used both to instruct and to help resolve problems. Because puppets "come alive" for young children, they can draw children into communication in ways that other props cannot. Kreidler (1984) and Janke and Penshorn Peterson (1995) have many suggestions for their use. (See Recommended Resources and anecdote, p. 265.)

Core Elements in Conflict Management Models

Pirtle (1995) has studied conflict management models for similarities and differences in approach. Although procedures differ in the steps followed and vocabulary used, Pirtle found seven core elements were widely shared.

First, a common goal is for children to learn communication skills. For children to gain in communication development, they must know that they will not be punished for mistaken behavior but that they are expected to learn from their mistakes. The connection between conflict management and guidance is again made.

Second, the models help children learn that they have options and choices when conflicts arise. As children learn social problem-solving skills, they rely less on the conventional reactions of hitting back, discrediting the other child verbally, retreating, or telling the teacher. The programs support alternative *creative* responses that manage the conflict without violence.

Third, management models help children recognize what will escalate a problem and make it worse. Typical escalating reactions are described in Figure 9.4; reactions that include name calling, blaming, yelling, and put downs. Many of the programs particularly identify *you statements* accompanied by attack words (as distinct from *you statements* with descriptors that supportively reflect a child's words or feelings).

Fourth, the models assist children to learn de-escalating responses such as listening, paraphrasing, and expressing feelings without insult. A commonly mentioned idea is the *I statement,* which expresses needs in a way that invites collaboration and tends not to make the other person feel blamed or defensive (Pirtle, 1995).

Fifth, the models assist children to seek win-win (mutually successful) solutions. In our society, adults, including some teachers, have difficulty grasping the concept of resolving problems so that both parties are satisfied. Children are just beginning to understand this possibility. Nonetheless, when programs are well implemented, teachers see the capacity for conflict management grow in children's responses.

Sixth, the models provide concise mediation methods, often with acronyms, to assist with recall and use. Pirtle (1995, p. 5) comments that an "acronym calls up a clear mental picture of the kind of communication that is the goal." As an introduction to the kinds of acronyms the models use, two procedures floating around Minnesota are **S O D A S:**

S Stop and say what happened
O Look at options
D Discuss if you disagree
A Agree on some options
S Try the solution

and **P O P S:**

P Put the problem into words
O Consider options
P Put out a possible solution
S Simply do it

(Please note that the acronyms above are not a subliminal advertisement for the soft drink of your choice.) Pirtle adds "Whatever you call it, we want to be able to say to children, 'Try an I to I' or 'Try SODAS' or 'Try talking it out' and have them know what we mean" (1995, p. 5).

Seventh, educators generally agree that children (and adults) need time to master social problem-solving skills, so that whatever model is used, it must be used consistently (Pirtle, 1995). Children progress in the use of mediation skills in the presence of four conditions: (a) an encouraging classroom in which children know that they will not be punished for mistakes; (b) teachers who model guidance and problem-solving in their general classroom transactions; (c) formal class activities that teach component problem-solving skills; (d) experience in conflict situations with teachers who take the time to use resolution skills and encourage children to use them.

Broad support from teachers, peers, administration, and families is needed to create a climate for lasting change in a school and the full internalization of problem-solving skills by children. (It takes an entire school and home community to teach social problem-solving to a child.)

Sample Management Models

Five conflict management samples are found in Figure 9.2 through Figure 9.6. The intent in this presentation is to allow the reader to see similarities and differences in

Figure 9.2

Educators for Social Responsibility use Kreidler's **ABCD** procedure (1994):

- **A**sk what's the problem.
- **B**rainstorm solutions.
- **C**hoose the best.
- **D**o it.

Strengths: The procedure is one of the most basic, easy to remember and use. It works well with preschoolers. This procedure is well supported by publications and other resources that teach it in the broader context of creative conflict resolution as a curriculum area.

Figure 9.3

Peacemakers A, B, Cs of Conflict Resolution (Janke & Penshorn Peterson, 1995) uses a *peace table, power puppets,* and the *talking stick* to assist in the mediation/negotiation process.

Step A, Part 1:	Always stop right now (cool off).
Step A, Part 2:	Ask to work it out.
Step B, Part 1:	Become communicators.
Step B, Part 2:	Brainstorm solutions.
Step C:	Choose a solution.
Step D:	Do it.
Step E:	Evaluate how it went.

Strengths: The procedure adds Step A, Part 1, a calm down phase, and Step E, an evaluation phase, to the steps. The request to *stop and calm down* is often needed to help children focus. *Evaluation* allows the teacher to do some affirming and teaching about alternatives for the future. Each step has its own "lesson" taught to the group outside the conflict situation. The peace table, power puppets, and the talking stick are props that tend to make the process more significant for young children.

Figure 9.4

St. Philip's School and schools in the Bemidji School District use a popular program in northern Minnesota, the *I to I*. Developed by the Mid-Minnesota Women's Center (Guth, 1995), the *I to I* has three rules that children are taught before attempting to resolve a problem.

1. Agree to work hard to solve the problem.
2. Take turns listening and speaking.
3. Speak truthfully and respectfully. Avoid
   Name calling
   Blaming
   Yelling
   Put downs

As slightly modified, steps in the *I to I* include:

1. What Happened?
2. How Do I Feel About It?
3. What Is My Part in What Happened?
4. What Did the Other Person Say?
5. What Is My Plan to Solve This Problem?

Strengths: Mediators carry small cards that have *I to I* rules on one side and the questions on the other. They can easily refer to the rules and questions during the mediation. The rules and procedure are straightforward enough that *I to Is* are used with kindergarten children through eighth graders. Guth comments, "These guidelines are just that. . . . They are not meant to inhibit your creativity in devising solutions. The only principle that applies to potential solutions is that they are respectful of all parties, including you" (1995, p. 30).

the models in a concise fashion. Strengths of each model are identified in each figure. The models are important enough that they are presented in the text rather than as an Appendix. Additional information about each model is accessible through the Recommended Resources at the conclusion of the chapter.

TEACHING CONFLICT-MANAGEMENT SKILLS

The goal in social problem-solving is to move children from dependency on the teacher to reliance on themselves. Although Wichert's *Keeping the Peace* (1989) is not the most recent work on the issue, the text provides a clear introduction to three levels of teacher response designed to achieve this objective. In an adaptation of Wichert's terminology, the teacher guides children to progress from **high-level mediation** to **low-level mediation** to **child negotiation.** *High level mediation* involves direct, guiding intervention by the adult, including, if necessary, articulation of the problem, possible solutions, and the solution—agreed to by the children. At

Figure 9.5

The Massachusetts-based Discovery Center uses a four-step procedure called *Talk It Out* (Pirtle, 1995):

1. Stop and think.
   a. Greet children and offer to help.
   b. Have participants agree to ground rules.
2. Say what happened.
   a. Ask one person to start by saying, "What's the problem?" Or, "Tell me your side of the story."
   b. Summarize how they describe the problem.
   c. Ask each person until each has had a turn.
   d. Summarize so that each speaker feels that the teacher understands.
   e. Remind about the ground rules. Wrap up by describing the problem in a fair way that doesn't take sides.
3. What would you like?
   a. Ask each person: "What can you do to solve this?" Or, "What do you want to have happen now?"
   b. If they can't think of action steps, suggest two or three choices but don't tell them what to do.
   c. Ask each person which ideas they liked the best.
4. Make a plan.
   a. Keep working until all parties have agreed to action steps.
   b. Make sure the plan is the children's and not the teacher's.
   c. If the plan seems unrealistic, help them look at it again.
   d. Determine whether it is a win/win situation for all.
5. Launch the plan.
   a. Help them launch the first step of the plan.
   b. End the mediation: "Thanks for working together to talk it out."

Strengths: The *Talk It Out* system is designed for use by student (peer) mediators as well as adults. The Discovery Center trains prekindergarten to sixth graders in communication skills, including peer mediation, and specializes in incorporating music and movement games. The procedure here is the form for kindergarten to second grade.

the high mediation level, the adult does not impose interpretations and conclusions, but offers them as suggestions agreed to or not by the child. The adult provides active leadership in the resolution process.

In *low-level mediation,* the adult suggests that children negotiate the conflict, but stands by to offer assistance as needed. Low-level mediation has been achieved when the children in dispute are able to define the problem, generate a solution, and bring about a resolution with minimum adult assistance but clear encouragement from the adult.

Child Negotiation occurs when children take charge of resolving a conflict by themselves. An illustration of negotiation was the anecdote about Charissa and Carlos on page 255. An irony in the field of social problem-solving is that many

Figure 9.6

Wichert's six-step problem-solving model, with an emphasis on calming children and focusing them on solving the problem (1989, pp. 54–56).

1. Calming and focusing
   Sample responses:
   "There is a problem here. Please hand me the [object] while we talk about it. You'll both have a chance to talk. Let's take a deep breath and be quiet for a minute."
2. Turning attention to the parties concerned
   Sample responses:
   "Now, I'm going to ask you to talk first, but you're going to have your turn, too." "It will help me if you don't interrupt." "And now you."
3. Clarifying/stating the problem
   Sample responses:
   "So, the problem is that you . . . and you. . . . Is that right?"
4. Bargaining/resolving/reconciling
   Sample Responses:
   "Tell her what you want." [If child doesn't come up with language, adult models by saying, "Tell her that you want (adult gives language)." Or, "Why don't you ask her. . . . [adult gives language]." [Adult clarifies bargaining comments of each child and prompts children toward their own resolution.]
5. Preventing
   Sample comments:
   "It's usually a good idea to ask people if. . . . "
   "Next time, it might be better if you ask people instead of. . . . "
   "Next time, what could you do so there is not a problem?"
6. Affirming
   Sample comments:
   "Thank you for working so hard at [talking to each other, not interrupting, listening to each other, or solving the problem]."

Strengths: The procedure gives important attention to calming and setting up the process so that each party has a chance to express feelings and explain what happened. The solution is sometimes effective reconciliation rather than action; the procedure takes this possibility into account. The prevention and affirmation steps are particularly useful, as the adult helps each child anticipate future consequences, think of alternatives, build empathy, and feel affirmed for successful participation.

young children, guided in the conflict management process, can negotiate conflicts successfully while many older students, who have not been so guided, cannot.

The discussion now turns to a case study analysis of the three levels of resolution at work: high-level teacher mediation, low-level teacher mediation, and child negotiation. The case studies begin by illustrating each level of resolution through

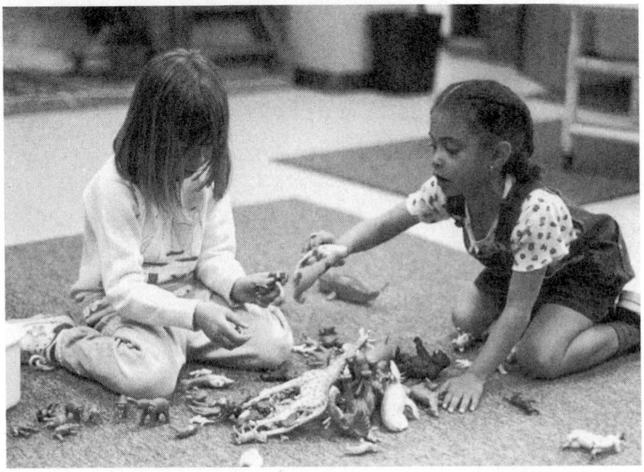

Guided in the conflict management process, many young children can negotiate conflicts.

journal entries of student teachers in two kindergarten and one prekindergarten classroom. Analysis of each anecdote then proceeds in three phases:

Defining the Problem

Reaching the Solution

Bringing Successful Closure

The journals of student teachers have been used (with appropriate permissions) to document that extensive teaching experience is not necessary in guiding children to solve social problems. Notice that the three student teachers and the children did not use a specific conflict resolution model, but instead flowed through the three phases listed above quite informally. A point made earlier bears repeating: Conflict management skills need not be used perfectly to assist children with conflict resolution.

High-Level Teacher Mediation

During a project with seeds, the teacher instructed kindergarten children to wrap a bean inside a saturated paper towel and place it into a plastic baggie with their name on it. After doing this, the children were supposed to take their baggies over to the window and tape them on the window. About half the class had their baggies taped on the window when I noticed two boys arguing about putting their baggies in the same spot. I listened for about a minute and decided to intervene because I felt that the arguing was becoming more heated (they were pushing each other), and they would not be able to resolve this issue without outside guidance.

Heather: I think we have a problem. You both want your baggies taped up in the same spot.
Justin: Yeah! (nodding).
Brian: I was here first, and Justin just came up and stuck his right there too.
Heather: Okay, we need to think up some ideas to try and solve this problem. Can you boys help me think of something that we can do?
Justin: We could put the bags on top of each other.
Heather: We could, but then I don't think we would be able to see whose baggie is whose, and you wouldn't be able to see your bean grow. Let's try it and see.
Brian: Now I can't see my name.
Heather: We should see if we can try something different. Can you think of something else?
Brian: He could put his on the wall next to mine.
Heather: That might work, but remember about what we learned this morning about what plants need in order to grow. Do you think that Justin's bean would get any sunlight if it was taped up on the wall?
Brian: No.
Justin: I know! He can tape his up here, right above mine.
Heather: What do you think, Brian?
Brian: Okay.
Heather: It's settled. We will tape Brian's baggie right above Justin's. I'm so glad that you boys can use your words to solve problems. Thank you.

The boys didn't seem to be upset with each other after they talked out their conflict. Later that morning I saw them playing with the plastic zoo animals together.

Defining the Problem Heather recognized that the conflict was over territory. She approached the situation calmly and neutrally. She stated that "we" have a problem and identified it for the two children in a way that they could accept. The way that she described the situation gave the children confidence to proceed to the step of sharing information.

Some procedural models have the mediator ask permission of the children to conduct the mediation. In the Peacemaker program, the children agree to participate in mediation as a part of the program. In the *I to I* program, children are given the choice of *using their power* to solve the problem by mediation or *giving up their power* to adult authorities who would then solve the problem for them. As in the case of the anecdote, children in classrooms where the choice of mediation is not a formal issue are usually relieved to participate in the process. If one or all involved children are too agitated, the teacher may give other choices, or request a **cooling down time.**

The mediation procedure of High/Scope (1996) stresses the acknowledgement of feelings at the beginning of negotiation as a way to calm down children. If the mediator believes children need to cool down before "talking it out," options are Wichert's suggestion, "Take a deep breath and be quiet for a minute," or reflective statements suggested by the High/Scope procedure, such as:

"You don't like it that. . . ."

"You feel . . . because. . . ."

"You feel . . . because . . . and you feel . . . because. . . ."

The acknowledgement of feelings releases emotions so that the children become calm enough to discuss the problem.

Reaching a Solution In the anecdote, the accurate statement of the problem by Heather enabled the children to share the details of what happened. A formal restatement of the problem did not seem necessary. She moved them directly to thinking about solutions by asking, "Can you boys help me think of something that we can do?" She then helped them test two solutions they came up with without imposing her own, often the mark of effective mediation.

Gaining information and achieving an objective restatement of the conflict serves two purposes. Sometimes the adult will not know what the issue is, and of course he needs that information to facilitate a solution. As well, when children are given an opportunity to explain what happened from their own perspectives, they feel that their side has been heard, and they are more willing to participate in the process.

A challenge for many teachers in high-level mediation is to *avoid imposing a solution*. By the time the mediation has progressed to the point when the problem is identified and the participants accept the description, the teacher has an idea of how to solve the problem. Often by this point the participants also have reached a degree of reconciliation, and the problem has become less of "an issue." An imposed solution by the teacher allows the children to get on with things they would rather be doing, often together. As mediation unquestionably takes time, imposing a solution also saves time for the teacher.

The reason for encouraging children to come up with their own solutions is that the resolution process becomes that much more empowering for them. The children more fully realize that they can solve their own problems. If the teacher does decide to help with solutions, he needs to be conscious about whether the solution is only suggested or imposed. This difference is reflected by asking, "Now, how do you think you can help him feel better?", instead of demanding, "Now, shake hands and say you're sorry."

Bringing Successful Closure Heather confirmed the solution with both children and then affirmed their use of management skills by saying, "I'm so glad that you boys can use your words to solve problems. Thank you." She also was undoubtedly prepared to give follow-up if needed, but it was not, confirmed by her observation that they played together later in the morning. The success of this experience is likely to reinforce their continuing willingness and ability to use problem-solving skills.

Low-Level Teacher Mediation

Dakota and Chante were in the classroom store. Dakota was using the cash register, and Chante was talking "to a customer" on the telephone. Dakota picked up another telephone and started talking to her. Chante turned to him and yelled, "Shut up!"

Dakota looked very sad. I knelt down and asked if he could tell Chante how that made him feel. He turned to her and said, "I felt really, really sad and bad when you yelled at me."

Chante responded, "I'm sorry, Dakota. I didn't mean that, I guess. I was talking to a 'custmer.'"

I asked, "Chante, I think Dakota wants to talk on the telephone with you."

Chante said, "Yeah, but he's not a 'custmer.'"

I suggested, "I wonder if Dakota could take the telephone to the house and be a customer?"

"I could call you from the house," Dakota said.

"Yeah, you need lots of stuff," said Chante (getting into it). "Go over and tell me what you need."

Dakota, smiling, "phoned" from the house. Chante had the "stuff" ready for him when he came to pick it up. He gave her some "make believe" money, and she even gave him change!

Defining the Problem Camille (the student teacher) approached the situation calmly and had a calming effect on Dakota by kneeling down and speaking directly to him. She acknowledged his feelings, then encouraged him to tell Chante how what she said made him feel.

The student teacher did not begin a formal conflict resolution procedure that involved acknowledging Chante's feelings and asking each child to describe what happened. Some educational programs prefer the teacher to follow the mediation procedure more formally so that the steps in the mediation would not be lost. Instead, Camille made the decision that encouraging Dakota to express himself was important and that the chances were good that a satisfactory resolution would occur if he did.

Reaching a Solution Again, the student teacher did not follow the formal steps of gathering information, restating the problem, and asking for possible solutions. Both children understood the situation. When Dakota let Chante know how he felt, Chante offered a first solution: apologize. When Camille helped Dakota understand how Chante was using the telephone, Dakota enabled a second solution: talk on the telephone in a way that fit Chante's purpose. The third part of the solution was that they continued the activity together in a way meaningful for both.

Camille did not follow conventional mediation procedure. She observed the children as they negotiated and made one suggestion, but she let them reach the solutions by themselves.

Bringing Successful Closure Typical of a successful low-level mediation, the children basically solved the problem themselves and went back to playing as if nothing had happened. The reflection portion of Camille's journal indicated how pleased she was that they solved the problem. Camille states, "These kinds of instances just prove to me that these children will solve their own problems. Sometimes all they need is a little guidance."

Child Negotiation

Nakisha and Suel Lin were caring for a variety of dolls in the kindergarten housekeeping area. They both reached for the last doll that had to be fed, bathed, and put to bed. They started yelling that they each had it first, and Suel Lin took Nakisha's arm and started squeezing it.

"Stop, that hurts," exclaimed Nakisha. "Use your words"!

"I can't," yelled Suel Lin.

"Then get Power Sock," Nakisha demanded. Both girls, still holding part of the doll, walked over and got Power Sock. "I will wear him, Suel Lin, and you tell Sock."

Suel Lin said to Sock, "Baby needs a bath, but we both want to do it."

"Both do it," said Sock.

The two girls put back Power Sock and returned to the housekeeping area, both holding the doll. One girl washed the top half, the other the bottom half. Then Suel Lin held the doll and fed it while Nakisha read a story to the other dolls already in bed. Suel Lin said, "Here's baby, do you want to read another story?"

"Yeah," said Nakisha, who read another story while Suel Lin rubbed the babies' backs as they lay in their beds.

Defining the Problem Nakisha acknowledged her feelings calmly enough that Suel Lin could agree to negotiate with her by using the Power Sock. Suel Lin broke a guideline by squeezing Nakisha's arm. Conventional discipline would call for a punishment such as sitting on a time-out chair. The result would have been Suel Lin feeling upset and Nakisha feeling victimized. Because the student teacher refrained from intervening, she opened the door for negotiation and the opportunity for the children to find a win-win solution.

Reaching a Solution Nakisha and Suel Lin used a prop introduced by the teachers to reach a solution. Nakisha was more experienced with Power Sock than Suel Lin and took the initiative to request Sock to help in the negotiation. The solution did not involve a high level of verbal articulation and probably evolved as the children got back into the situation. Nonetheless, their solution was creative and peaceable and would have made many teachers smile. The self-esteem of each child seems to have been sustained.

Bringing Successful Closure The two children continued to play together and did so with a high level of cooperation. A common outcome in the successful

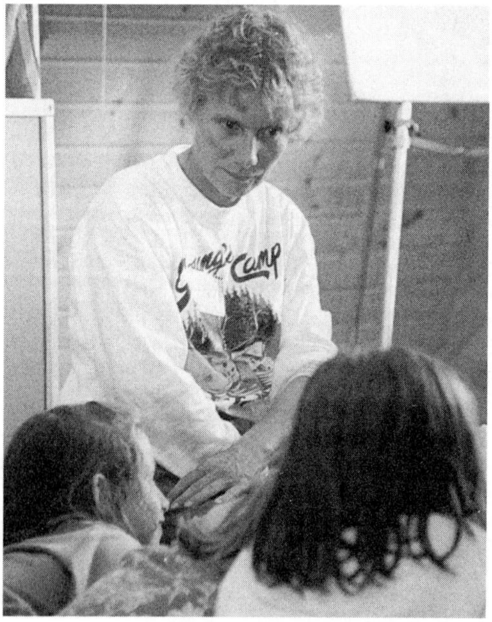

Sue and fellow parents introduced summer leadership camps to orient new third graders to conflict-management projects.

settlement of conflicts is that children are no longer upset with one another, but they are again friends. Successful negotiation eliminates any buildup of residual resentment. The ability of children to negotiate conflicts makes the goal of an encouraging classroom attainable.

PARENT INVOLVEMENT AT ST. PHILIP'S: BUILDING A PEACEABLE SCHOOL COMMUNITY

The story told in this section illustrates how one parent worked with other parents, teachers, administrators, and children to bring a comprehensive conflict management program and the spirit of peace education to a parochial school in northern Minnesota. The program being profiled is not a typical one. The parent provided extraordinary leadership, the school is not a public school, and the community is more rural than urban. Still, as a case study, the story illustrates what can happen when parents, teachers, and children see peace education as a goal, accept it, and work toward it. The account that follows is a summary of interviews with the parent, Ms. Sue Leidl about the project.

First Year (1992–1993)

St. Philip's is a prekindergarten through eighth grade school of 270 students in downtown Bemidji, a town of 15,000, including tourists, university students, and truck drivers passing through. One spring day, Sue Liedl's second grade son told her of a playground game called, "smear the queer." It was a kind of dodge ball game in which if you hit others with the ball, you got to call them names. The game bothered her son, and it bothered Sue. A social worker having several years of experience with youth-at-risk, Sue looked at the problem as a chance to prevent some of the life situations that she saw oppressing the kind of youth she worked with.

Shortly thereafter Sue left her job and began to volunteer hours at the school, on the playground and in classrooms. In the school office she came across a brochure on conflict management, read it, and located more materials. During May with the support of the principal, Sue met with the 23 staff members to discuss whether they would be interested in a **peer mediation** program at St. Philip's the following year. The staff expressed interest in Sue's beginning the program. *Peer mediation* is a system of conflict management in which trained upper elementary students assist other students who may be having conflicts, such as on the playground. Sue reports that peer mediation was the most popular form of conflict management used at the time of this story.

Second Year (1993–1994)

In September, Sue called a meeting of the 190 families in the school; 70 parents attended. She introduced them to peer mediation and asked for and received their support for a program at St. Philip's. She recruited a core committee of three parents, all interested in working with the teachers and children. Sue attended peer mediation training and then trained the parent committee. The committee wrote grant proposals, collected resources, contacted other Minnesota schools, and mapped out a plan for sharing the training with staff and students.

Over the winter the committee prepared the teaching staff for the program, and on Martin Luther King Day, January 19th, the four parents introduced the idea to the third through eighth grade classes by presenting a play. (Drama has been a continuing part of the St. Philip's program. This play, like most, actively involved the students and illustrated the importance of respectful communication skills.)

The upper elementary children (by themselves) selected 2 peer mediators per classroom for a total of 24 peer mediators. The peer mediators had two days of training away from the school. To supplement the work of the peer mediators, the parent committee returned to each classroom once a week for four weeks to present the program. The peer mediators were active at the school throughout the spring and conducted 35 mediations; about half the cases seemed to be students "testing the system."

Third Year (1994–1995)

Over the summer, Sue held the first of what have become annual leadership camps, attended by the peer mediators and teachers, and conducted by St. Philip's parents. In September, the committee reviewed the peer mediation program and came to a surprising conclusion: They decided that the focus of peer mediation was too specialized to meet their goals for the school. The committee's goal was to make every student a "peaceful problem solver." The peer mediator program continued into the school year, but the parent committee, with some new members, discussed their conclusion with the school staff. The staff agreed, and over the third year the conflict management program began to take a new direction.

The parent committee held a series of meetings during the year with families to discuss the new emphasis. At the same time, two of the parent committee went into each of the classes weekly for eight weeks, involving all the students actively in conflict management instruction. Puppets frequently were used to teach such skills as communicating feelings productively, using the *I to I* process, achieving win-win solutions, and keeping friends despite disagreements.

During the third year, each of the upper elementary classes took a specialized topic and method of presentation. In teams of four or five, they rehearsed their puppet play, real life skit, or game sequence. The older students presented their plays for younger students, frequently involving them in the productions, and the whole school got involved. On a night in mid-winter, the school put on their program for the families, and over 90 percent of the parents attended. Each team put on their performance for their own parents; then the family—children and family together—would visit other classrooms and participate in other productions.

Sue reported that the family night more than any other activity sparked parent interest in the conflict management philosophy. She commented, "Every child in the school participated. If their children are involved, parents will attend; that's what gets parents involved."

Fourth Year (1995–1996)

Over the summer, the new third grade class again participated in the summer "leadership training." The teacher attended the training with the class, which made for strong attachments right from the beginning of the school year. In September the third grade teacher began by reviewing with the children the skills they learned at the leadership camp. The class then received additional training over ten weeks and attended a two-day retreat. The third graders learned to do puppet plays illustrating the basics of conflict resolution. They performed the plays for the younger children, actively involving the younger children in discussion about the plays. This emphasis on active participation, with children teaching other children, has been a hallmark of the program. By this time, the *I to I* model, developed by Guth (1995) had replaced the peer mediation model, and the whole school was participating.

During the fourth year, an initiative was also started with the seventh graders. Another St. Philip's parent began a media literacy program, educating these older students about the effects of violence and commercialism in the public media. Guests from outside the school helped students at various levels connect peacemaking efforts with music and the martial arts (Liedl, 1996). Sue and the planning committee actively wrote grant proposals to support bringing in guests for brief residency periods. Another grant enabled St. Philip's School to make a video documenting elements of the program, to be shown as a demonstration piece in other schools in the region.

Fifth Year (1996–1997)

This past summer, the new third grade again attended leadership camp. A special project is being prepared for the coming year. The fourth graders will be teamed in groups of four or five with parent volunteers. The teams will specialize in a topic and prepare participation-productions relating their topic to conflict resolution. After much practice, the teams will serve as trainers for other classes at St. Philip's and other schools in the area.

A second project, begun over the summer in a two-day "theater camp," will continue this fall. Sue, with a group of fourth through eighth graders, have created a six-scene play illustrating differences between families with high and low social problem-solving skills. Aided by a professional director, the players are polishing their production for performances this fall.

One performance in particular will be a special one, because it will include a role created for Arun Gandhi of the M. K. Gandhi Institute For Nonviolence in Tennessee. Mr. Gandhi will be in the area participating in a three-day community-wide residency to include events scheduled at Bemidji State University, in the Bemidji Schools, with local law enforcement and human service personnel, as well as St. Philip's School. The unique cooperation for organizing and funding this event, including both public and private agencies, was begun with efforts by Sue Liedl and other parents at St. Philip's.

The "peaceful problem-solving" project still continues at St. Philip's. Sue mentions that she receives inquiries each week from educators throughout the upper Midwest wanting to know about the St. Philip's program. She emphasizes that she is but one person who wished to make a difference as a parent at her local school. The lesson is instructive for all educators and parents. When schools choose to involve parents, and use their particular skills, there are few limits as to what can happen.

SUMMARY

Does violence in society affect how children handle conflicts in the classroom?

The prevalence of violence in society means that few children escape its influence. Between the ages of 5 and 15, for instance, children on average view about 13,000 television murders. Although this indirect exposure is widespread, some children, are exposed to violence more directly in the home and neighborhood. The more intense and prolonged the exposure, the more heightened the effects of violence are likely to be. Young children are just beginning to develop the cognitive equipment they need to understand and overcome the effects of violence in their lives. They need consistent and comprehensive programming to learn skills in solving problems peacefully.

What understandings about social problem-solving do teachers need?

Six key ideas are the following:

1. Social problem-solving and guidance are connected.
2. Teachers work to prevent institution-caused conflicts, but they realize that conflicts are inevitable and can be important learning opportunities.
3. When a problem occurs, the teacher avoids blame and retribution and works with the children to find a mutually satisfactory solution.
4. The teacher need not mediate an ideal settlement in order for children to learn social problem-solving skills.
5. Teachers need to understand the developmental characteristics of young children that lead to conflicts and successful resolutions.
6. Social problem-solving is taught not just through conflict intervention but through the instructional program and the climate of the classroom and school.

What understandings about conflict management models do teachers need?

Some models augment their procedures with peace props; others do not. Seven core elements in conflict management models are the following:

1. A shared goal in the models is for children to learn communication skills.
2. The models help children learn that they have options and choices when conflicts arise.
3. The models assist children to seek out win-win (mutually satisfactory) solutions.

4. Management models help children recognize what will escalate a problem and make it worse.
5. The models assist children to learn de-escalating responses such as listening, paraphrasing, and expressing feelings without insult.
6. The programs provide concise mediation methods, often with acronyms, to assist with recall and use.
7. Children (and adults) need time to master social problem-solving skills so that they can use them effectively.

Five widely used conflict management models were presented, including features of each. The models are Kreidler's ABCD procedure, the Peacemaker's ABCs, the Minnesota *I to I* model, the Talk It Out model of the Massachusetts-based Discovery Center, and Wichert's six step problem-solving model.

How does the adult teach conflict-management skills to children?

Through modeling and encouragement, the teacher moves children from high-level mediation, with children dependent on the teacher, to low-level mediation, with the teacher providing support, to child-negotiation in which children take charge of solving problems for themselves. A "developmental timetable" does not exist for learning social problem-solving skills. With training four-year-olds negotiate many conflicts themselves; without training many eight-year-olds do not.

Communication in the problem-solving process occurs in three phases: identifying the problem, reaching a solution, and bringing successful closure to the process. In identifying the problem, children need to be calm and accept the problem-solving process. In reaching the solution, children need to share information to understand each other's viewpoints and the whole picture, generate possible solutions, and try one. In reaching successful closure, parties again engage in productive activity and acknowledge that a successful solution and/or reconciliation has been attained.

How have parents helped to shape the peaceful problem-solving program at St. Philip's School?

An interview/case study discloses how a parent, Sue Liedl, brought the spirit of peace education and practicality of conflict management to a small northern Minnesota school. A parent at St. Philip's School, Sue Leidl became uncomfortable with a playground game her son told her about. Rather than complain, she began in this first year to volunteer her time to introduce the basic concept of conflict management to other parents, the staff and students. In year two of the program, parents and staff became better educated about conflict mediation, and a peer mediation program began. In the third year, the peer mediation program was replaced with a whole school emphasis, in which all classes were actively involved in teaching conflict management skills to each other, using the *I to I* model.

In the fourth year, third graders were trained in teams to perform puppet and other skills demonstration activities that they performed for and with the younger classes and other schools. The older children participated in a media literacy project and continued training sessions in conflict management. In the fifth year, third graders will expand their visits to other schools, and upper elementary students will put on a play production that includes the noted peace educator, Arun Gandhi.

The program began and has developed as a result of the receptivity of the staff of St. Philip's School to working closely with parents. St. Philip's has become a center for conflict management and peace education in northern Minnesota.

FOLLOW-UP ACTIVITIES

Note: In completing follow-up activities, the privacy of all involved is to be respected.

Reflection Activity

The reflection activity encourages students to interrelate their own thoughts and experiences with specific ideas from the chapter.

Recall a conflict situation in a classroom resolved by the use of conflict management. Referring to the chapter, was the process used high-level teacher mediation, low-level teacher mediation, or child negotiation? Analyze the possible effects for each individual involved (including the teacher if present) in relation to self-esteem and life skills.

Application Activities

Application activities allow students to interrelate material from the text with real life situations. The observations imply access to practicum experiences; the interviews, access to teachers or parents. Students may compare or contrast observations and interviews with referenced ideas from the chapter.

1. **Does violence in society affect how children handle conflicts in the classroom?**
   a. Observe instances of play that you believe to be quite aggressive. Does the aggressive activity seem to be influenced more by media superheroes or by life experiences? Why do you think so?
   b. Interview a teacher about a child or two whom he believes to be aggressive in play or violent in other behaviors. What does the teacher think might be some possible causes for the behavior?
2. **What understandings about social problem-solving do teachers need?**
   a. Observe an instance of social problem-solving in a classroom that involves a teacher. Which of the six understandings listed in the summary did you see operating in the situation? Which of the six did you not see?
   b. Interview a teacher about what he believes to be important in encouraging the use of social problem-solving by the class. Which of the six understandings listed in the summary did the teacher mention as important? Which did he not mention?

3. **What understandings about conflict management models do teachers need?**
   a. Observe an instance of conflict management in a classroom. Which of the seven core elements listed in the summary did you see operating in the situation? Which of the seven did you not see?
   b. Interview a teacher about his experience with conflict management. Which of the seven core elements listed in the summary did the teacher mention as important? Which did he not mention?
4. **How does the adult teach problem-solving skills to children?**
   a. Observe an instance of high-level mediation, low-level mediation, or child negotiation. Which do you believe it is? Why? How effective was the process of social problem-solving that you observed? How successful was the solution reached?
   b. Interview a teacher about his views on the relative importance of mediation with children versus encouraging children to negotiate. What surprised you about the teacher's comments? What of his comments were what you expected?
5. **How have parents helped to shape the peaceful problem-solving program at St. Philip's School?**
   a. Observe an instance of any program in a classroom (simple or comprehensive) put on by one or more parents. What did you learn about parent-led programs from what you observed? How did what you observe compare or contrast with events in the chapter?
   b. Interview a teacher or a parent about a specific parent program in a classroom. What does the person think is important for successful parent programs? How did the ideas shared compare or contrast with events in the chapter?

RECOMMENDED RESOURCES

Carlsson-Paige, N., & Levin, D. E. (1992). Making peace in violent times: A constructivist approach to conflict resolution. *Young Children, 48*(1), 4–13.

Crary, E. (1984). *Kids can cooperate: A practical guide to teaching children problem solving* [in the family]. Seattle: Parenting Press, Inc.

Dinwiddie, S. A. (1994). The saga of Sally, Sammy, and the red pen: Facilitating children's social problem solving. *Young Children, 49*(5), 13–19.

Guth, J. T. (1995). *Teacher P.A.L.S. A classroom guide to the peaceful alternatives and life skills program.* Brainerd, MN: Mid-Minnesota Women's Center, Inc.

Head Start Bureau, (1997). *Head Start Bulletin: Conflict Management Issue,* Spring 1997 (61). Washington, DC: U.S. Department of Health & Human Services.

Janke, R. A., & Penshorn Peterson, J. (1995). *Peacemaker's A, B, Cs for young children.* Marine on St. Croix, MN: Growing Communities for Peace.

Kreidler, W. J. (1994). *Teaching conflict resolution through children's literature.* New York: Scholastics Professional Books.

Pirtle, S. (1997). *Linking up: Building the peaceable classroom with music and movement.* Boston: Educators for Social Responsibility.

Slaby, R. G., Roedell, W. C., Arezzo, D., & Hendrix, K. (1995). *Early violence prevention.* Washington, DC: National Association for the Education of Young Children.

Wichert, S. (1989). *Keeping the peace.* Philadelphia: New Society Publishers.

REFERENCES

Bodine, R. J., Crawford, D., & Schrumpf, F. (1994). *Creating the peaceable school.* Champaign, IL: Simon & Schuster.

Carlsson-Paige, N., & Levin D. E. (1992). Making peace in violent times: A constructivist approach to conflict resolution. *Young Children, 48*(1), 4–13.

Dinwiddie, S. A. (1994). The saga of Sally, Sammy, and the red pen: Facilitating children's social problem solving. *Young Children, 49*(5), 13–19.

Girard, K., & Koch, S. J. (1996). *Conflict resolution in the schools.* San Francisco: Jossey-Bass Publishers.

Guth, J. T. (1995). *Teacher P.A.L.S. A classroom guide to the peaceful alternatives and life skills program.* Brainerd, MN: Mid-Minnesota Women's Center, Inc.

Harris, I. M. (1988). *Peace Education.* Jefferson, NC: McFarland and Co.

High/Scope (1996). *Problem-solving approach to conflict: Two-day workshop participant guide.* Ypsilanti, MI: High/Scope Press.

Janke, R. A., & Penshorn Peterson, J. (1995). *Peacemaker's A, B, Cs for Young Children: A Guide for Teaching Conflict Resolution with a Peace Table.* Marine on St. Croix, MN: Growing Communities for Peace.

Kreidler, W. (1984). *Creative conflict resolution: More than 200 activities for keeping peace in the classroom.* Glenview, IL: Scott, Foresman.

Kreidler, W. J. (1994). *Teaching conflict resolution through children's literature.* New York: Scholastics Professional Books.

Levin, D. L. (1994). *Teaching young children in violent times: Building a peaceable classroom.* Cambridge, MA: Educators for Social Responsibility.

Liedl, S. (1996). *We dream; mediation news.* [Spring 1996 Newsletter]. Bemidji, MN: St. Philip's School.

Pirtle, S. (1995). *Conflict management workshop guide.* Shelburne Falls, MA: The Discovery Center.

Pirtle, S. (1997). *Linking up: Building the peaceable classroom with music and movement.* Boston: Educators for Social Responsibility.

Porro, B. (1996). *Talk it out: Conflict resolution in the elementary classroom.* Association for Supervision and Curriculum Development.

Slaby, R. G., Roedell, W. C., Arezzo, D., & Hendriz, K. (1995). *Early violence prevention.* Washington, DC: National Association for the Education of Young Children.

Wichert, S. (1989). *Keeping the peace.* Philadelphia: New Society Publishers.

Wittmer, D. S., & Honig, A. S. (1994). Encouraging positive social development in young children. *Young Children, 49*(5), 4–12.

10

Problem-Solving Mistaken Behavior

GUIDING QUESTIONS

As you read Chapter 10, you will discover answers to the following questions:

- **How do teachers apply the concept of mistaken behavior?**
- **What goes into the decision to intervene?**
- **What are five quick intervention strategies?**
- **How does the teacher respond to mistaken behaviors reported by children?**
- **What are five strategies when interventions require follow-up?**
- **Why take the time to problem-solve mistaken behavior?**
- **How does the teacher build cooperation with parents?**

Chapter 10 continues the theme of Unit Three: **Rather than punish children for having problems, guidance teaches children to solve them.** Chapter 9 explored a general strategy for guiding children to solve social problems. Often when mistaken behavior occurs, mediation is the guidance strategy of choice. Sometimes, however, the teacher may not be sure that mediation is feasible in a particular situation. Chapter 10 considers the full range of decisions teachers make when they encounter all but the most serious mistaken behavior. Dealing with serious, strong needs mistaken behavior is the focus of Chapter 11.

A beginning note needs to be made about a matter of vocabulary. In Chapter 9, the word *conflict* was often used. **Conflict** is a disagreement over an action, verbal or physical, one or more parties has taken (Girard & Koch, 1996). In the case of children, the action usually involves property, location, or privilege (Dinwiddie, 1994). We also learned in Chapter 9 that conflicts need not be negative. If through mediation or negotiation children come to a solution peacefully, the conflict actually had a positive result.

In guidance terms **mistaken behavior is a conflict** where the action usually is taken by a child or children, and the person disagreeing with the action usually is the teacher. The teacher may react with punishment, in which case the mistaken behavior has a negative outcome, or with guidance, in which case the mistaken behavior is more likely to have a positive outcome.

Another possibility also exists, of course, that the teacher may initiate a conflict, and the child may object to the *teacher's* mistaken behavior. This remote possibility with readers of this book (smile) is also addressed in Chapter 10.

MISTAKEN BEHAVIOR: APPLYING THE CONCEPT

The ability to understand the level of a child's mistaken behavior helps with intervention decisions. When teachers perceive the motives at work, they can respond effectively. Yet, most interventions cannot wait for the teacher to make a "formal diagnosis." The teacher has to act on the basis of a quick judgment. Often she will be right, but whatever the consequences of the intervention, reflection about the level after the event assists the teacher to work with the child in the future. For these reasons, a return to the three levels of mistaken behavior begins the discussion of problem-solving mistaken behavior.

Level One Mistaken Behavior

Children show Level One, experimentation mistaken behavior, in the course of interactions with others and the environment. The mistaken behavior might be the result of a spontaneous situation or an intentional act. (The child is acting out of involvement or curiosity.) In either case, the behavior is an attempt to learn about the limits and realities of daily life (Gartrell, 1995). Examples include:

- a child who "uncharacteristically" uses an expletive and watches for a reaction;
- a child who is not finished with an activity and does not want to put materials away;
- two children who quarrel over a material;
- a child who randomly marks on a table;
- a preschooler who wanders from a playground;
- a kindergartener who talks to a neighbor after large group has begun;
- a second grader who forgets to do an assignment;
- third graders who giggle at a photo from *National Geographic*.

Experimentation mistaken behavior is common and should be expected by teachers even in developmentally appropriate education programming. Mistakes in social living are a natural part of the total learning of children. An environment that allows children to learn from their mistakes helps them to build personal resources ("individual strength" and "character"). The teacher supports the dynamic of development that leads to Level One mistaken behavior even while she teaches children skills to manage their behavior more productively (Gartrell, 1995).

The teacher who understands experimentation mistaken behavior takes a balanced approach toward it. On the one hand, the teacher recognizes that a "mistake-free" classroom is a sterile place. Being intolerant or fearful of the mistakes of childhood undermines children's confidence in learning healthy lessons from life (Gartrell, 1995; Greenberg, 1988). On the other hand, the teacher does not impose

A carpet square as a "hat" is not what the teacher had in mind. No one is being bothered by this Level One mistaken behavior, however, and the teacher is proceeding with the activity.

problems or conflicts on children. Challenges enough arise from everyday classroom living. Failure is one thing if it is the result of a child-directed activity and another if it is a teacher-directed activity. In the later situation, the emotional stakes are higher for the child. The teacher accepts that mistakes naturally will occur in the classroom, and does not force them. She expects, and guides, the child to learn from those mistakes.

With experimentation mistaken behavior, unless a danger of actual harm or serious disruption exists, teachers generally "soft pedal" their responses. They may remind about guidelines or assist to solve a problem, but they recognize that children are learning through their behavior, mistakes as well as accomplishments. Especially if the Level One behavior involves "testing," the teacher acts as a leader and reinforces a guideline. Still, when a teacher overreacts to Level One mistaken behavior, the child feels hurt and resentment and may sense power in the act. Innocent behaviors become socially reinforced and more calculated. Unless the child is secure, stifled emotional needs become a factor, and she may act out, showing mistaken behavior even at Level Three. The teacher works to keep Level One mistaken behavior from having more serious consequences.

(From a student teacher journal) Jarren and Rory were playing with the trains on the floor. Rory kicked the tracks by Jarren, and Jarren mumbled something, frowning. I said to Rory, "You know what, Rory? I think Jarren is trying to tell you something." Can you repeat what you said, Jarren?"

Jarren replied, "Quit kicking my stuff—I don't like that."

I turned to Rory reminding him that Jarren was using the tracks. Rory apologized to Jarren, but Jarren started to walk away. I asked Jarren where he was going, and he said, "I don't like him anymore."

I knelt down and said, "Jarren, Rory made a mistake in his behavior, but he's still a nice person."

Rory said, "I still like you."

"OK," said Jarren. He went back to play with the trains, and they played together like before.

Level Two Mistaken Behavior

Level Two, socially influenced mistaken behavior, is learned behavior. Children show Level Two mistaken behavior when they are reinforced by significant others to show the behavior (Gartrell, 1995). Socially influenced mistaken behavior shows itself in distinct ways, such as:

- preschoolers who hear a word used to make fun of another and repeat it: "poopy-butt" or "butt-head";
- a kindergarten child who is used to roughhousing at home wrestles and engages in super-hero play at school;

- a first grader who hears explicit language and uses it as an older person would;
- second graders who shun another child, following the lead of others;
- third graders who "act up" to get their names written on the board as "the 'in' thing to do."

The influence by the other can be intentional or unintentional, but the result is the same: the child behaves as a result of that influence. Common authority sources that reinforce Level Two behavior include:

- parents
- other family members
- friends of the family
- children who are playmates
- classmates
- teachers and other school staff

Unfortunately, through their own mistaken behavior, educators too can model and reinforce Level Two mistaken behaviors in children.

Angelina loved to draw with markers. An only child, she used markers frequently at home, and her parents enjoyed her pictures. During art time at Thanksgiving, the teacher showed the children how to make a turkey using their hands as an outline and three "Thanksgiving colors." Angelina had seen a "real turkey" on Sesame Street. She drew the turkey from memory using a variety of bright colors. The teacher noticed Angelina's turkey and told her in front of her table group that she hadn't followed directions and that her picture was messy. After the teacher was done, her seatmates told Angelina, "You can't draw," and "Yeah, you don't know how to make a turkey." Angelina went home from school a sad little girl.

The teacher in the anecdote caused Level Two mistaken behavior in Angelina's classmates. She also interpreted creative behavior on the child's part as unacceptable, instead reinforcing conformity and diminishing self-esteem.

Responding to Level Two Behavior in Individual Children

When teachers encounter socially influenced mistaken behavior, they make some quick determinations. First, they decide whether the behavior is unique to one child, a habit such as using inappropriate language, or collective, "contagious" name-calling. When an individual child has shown a Level Two behavior, the teacher then determines whether the behavior was directed to another specific person, or was expressed more generally.

If the behavior involved another child or children, the teacher collects the parties and engages in mediation. The reason is that both children, and not just the child who showed the behavior, can gain in social skills (Carlsson-Paige & Levin, 1992; Gartrell, 1995). If the behavior is directed "to the world at large," the teacher has a **guidance talk** with the child in which she reinforces a guideline, teaches an alternate acceptable action, and affirms the child's worth. Note that the guidance talk is also the way mediation often ends. Wichert refers to this closure process as *prevention* and *affirmation* (1991).

Responding to Level Two Behavior in the Group

With socially influenced mistaken behavior in the context of a group, the teacher holds a *class meeting* to mediate a solution to the problem. She involves children in the discussion about the relevant guideline and requests that children share their perception of the problem. The teacher and class then generate possible solutions. They develop a plan for preventing the mistaken behavior in the future, and the teacher helps the class to implement the plan (Hendrick, 1992).

Over the years, the kinds of *contagious* mistaken behaviors that affect groups have been well known: targeting a child with name-calling, shooting spit balls, making obnoxious sounds, etc. As indicated in Chapter 9, the prevalence of violence in contemporary society means that social pressures and media violence have caused some Level Two mistaken behavior to become more aggressive.

Class meetings—sometimes more than one are needed—are effective in addressing group-centered socially influenced mistaken behavior. They certainly are more productive than the traditional punishments of an entire class for the actions of some—incidents of which readers can probably remember. Begun when children are young and continued through the elementary years, class meetings change how teachers and children conventionally have viewed "contagious" Level Two behaviors.

As teachers long have known, however, socially influenced mistaken behavior in the group is often stimulated, and sometimes organized, by one child who tends to be labeled the "instigator" or the "ring leader." Usually, the child who influences others toward mistaken behavior has acted from Level One motivations. (Leadership skills, like other life skills, are complex and take experience and development to learn.) Increasingly, due to societal violence, children who show *mistaken leadership* seem to be acting from a strong emotional set, and, in fact, are showing Level Three, strong needs mistaken behavior. When one child has inspired, or otherwise significantly contributed to, socially influenced mistaken behavior, the teacher combines a class meeting with guidance talks and other actions necessary to guide the child and the group. In the case of both individual- and group-centered mistaken behavior, the teacher follows-up interventions with *encouragement* and the *compliment sandwich*.

> In a first grade class, a teacher noticed that Josh seemed totally consumed with the Mighty Morphin Power Rangers. This came to her attention when another teacher commented that Josh was organizing friends to "play" Mighty Morphin Power Rangers on the playground. The teacher

observed that other children were being drawn into the play; some were being pushed and "karateed," and others were being taken prisoner. The teacher realized that lately Josh had been identifying with the "Rangers" to an extent she thought unhealthy. In from the playground, the teacher decided to have an unscheduled class meeting.

She mentioned that she had seen some activity on the playground that bothered her and, she thought, other children as well. She held a *talking stick* while she spoke and then passed the stick to others who expressed strong feelings about the play. In keeping with a guideline, no one mentioned Josh's name, but the teacher noticed that he put his head down and looked at the floor during the discussion. He said nothing. After all who wanted to discussed the situation, the teacher reminded them of a guideline of the class, "Friendly touches only," and summarized the input by saying that the game was making people forget that guideline. She asked for ideas about how to solve that problem.

Some children said that the game should not be allowed. Others said that maybe only the ones that wanted to should play, "but only fight the invisible space marauders." Several liked this idea. The teacher asked Josh what he thought and he said, "OK." The solution they tried was three days of this new way to play, with everyone monitoring how it went. Progress was discussed daily at the afternoon class meeting.

The teacher knew this solution would be hard on Josh. She talked with Josh individually and encouraged him to write about the Power Rangers in his journal. Over the next few days, all of the invisible foes must have been defeated because interest in the game waned. On the other hand, Josh got several other children writing Power Ranger stories in their journals, an outcome the teacher decided everyone could live with.

Level Three Mistaken Behavior

Level Three, strong needs mistaken behavior, is serious. The primary difference between Level Three and Level One or Two mistaken behavior is the strong emotional content of Level Three reactions. All children (and even teachers) are entitled to a "Level Three day" now and then—due to health or psychological circumstances. When a child continues to act atypically ("strangely") or in an extreme fashion, the teacher should suspect trouble in the child's life and the presence of strong unmet needs. In acting out as a result of those needs, the child shows Level Three behavior (Gartrell, 1995).

Typically, Level Three mistaken behavior shows itself in any of the following ways, when a child:

- loses control and acts out over seemingly minor frustrations;
- noticeably changes social patterns such as from sociable to withdrawn;
- displays a pattern of nonparticipation, inattentiveness, or sadness (depression);

- exhibits fear or hostile reactions to adults or other children;
- is continuously active and cannot concentrate;
- lies, takes things, or manipulates others toward Level Two mistaken behavior;
- shows inappropriate interest in or knowledge about sexuality;
- is continually competitive, showing a need to do things perfectly, or to dominate others.

Mediation, guidance talks, and class meetings reduce mistaken behavior at the first two levels. However, these methods are only components of a more comprehensive approach that is necessary with children showing Level Three (Curry & Arnaud, 1995; Heath, 1994). Discussed in Chapter 11, the comprehensive approach includes:

1. nonpunitive intervention at the point of crisis;
2. effort to increase understanding about the child and the situation;
3. a comprehensive plan of action developed with parents, the child, and others concerned;
4. work at building a relationship with the child;
5. coordinated implementation and review of the plan.

Teachers cannot always solve the problems that cause strong needs mistaken behavior. By being proactive and nonpunitive, however, the teacher can make life easier for the child, the rest of the class, the family, and herself.

THE DECISION TO INTERVENE

Beginning teachers especially feel concern about the decision to intervene because of fear of alienating the children in their charge. In response to a basic question about the role of the early childhood teacher, she *is* a friend to children—but as an adult and a child must be friends—with the adult as leader and guide.

In intervention situations, the adult retains the element of friendliness, even if circumstances call for responses that are firm and that children may not like. Feelings change, and there will be time after the intervention for the adult and child to "make things right." Writers about child behavior from Glasser (1969) to Reynolds (1996) share the view that children need to know the limits of acceptable behavior.

The teacher acts with firmness if guidelines protecting safety or well-being are endangered. Guidance rests upon the authority of the teacher to protect the learning environment for all. Children feel secure when clear limits are reinforced consistently. Note, however, that punitive discipline practiced with consistency is still punitive discipline. Teachers using guidance need to appreciate the difference between firmness and harshness (Clewett, 1988; Gartrell, 1997; Greenberg, 1988).

As well, firmness as an *overriding* personal characteristic of a teacher limits other important personality dimensions, such as flexibility. The professional teacher is sometimes permissive and sometimes firm, depending on judgments about the situation. (From this perspective, the saying "Don't smile until Christmas" is better

By being proactive and nonpunitive, the teacher makes life easier for the child.

expressed perhaps as "Don't smile in this situation.") If children know when the teacher will smile and when she will be firm, *consistency* has been achieved.

Kounin's concept of *withitness* (synonymous with "eyes in the back of the head") is an important teaching skill (1977). Yet, in a guidance approach, teachers recognize that the judgments they make are more appropriately thought of as *hypotheses*. Teachers must react quickly and firmly to situations, but the professional teacher does not hold judgments as infallible. Instead, she attempts to learn from the situation.

In a Head Start classroom, a four-year-old named Sharisse was playing with Kiko, also four, at the water table. After a few minutes, Sharisse stormed over to the teacher and said, "Kiko spilt water on me." She had a spot of water on her overalls. Upset, the teacher walked over to the water table. Kiko turned around. His shirt and pants were soaked and he was crying silently. The teacher got down to Kiko's level and asked what happened. After listening to him and talking with Sharisse, she figured out that Kiko had dropped a bottle and it splashed up on Sharisse. Sharisse then dumped a bowl of water on his front.

The teacher helped Kiko get a change of clothes. She then talked with Sharisse and Kiko together. Kiko had been having a rough week with frequent displays of mistaken behavior. The teacher felt fortunate that she had gotten additional facts.

In this situation the teacher was able to collect information that helped her modify her original hypothesis. Anytime a teacher can act less like a police officer on the street and more like a mediator, she is in a better position to make informed decisions.

Another important part of *withitness* decision making is to determine the number of children involved in a situation. With only a few children, **child guidance** responses are called for; with several, **group management** responses are needed. Child guidance responses involve intervention in the least obtrusive way possible to bring the child's behavior within guidelines while protecting self-esteem. Frequently, the teacher uses mediation to solve the immediate problem and *guidance talks* to guide toward alternative behaviors in the future.

Group management responses address the entire group and avoid calling attention to individuals. The key to group management, of course, is prevention of *institution-caused* mistaken behaviors by using the ideas discussed in previous chapters. The class meetings and intervention techniques discussed later in Chapter 10 augment the many prevention aspects of positive group management previously discussed. When a teacher is able to keep the class busily on-task, she is better able to give extra guidance to those few children who seem to require so much of a teacher's time—the children facing Level Three difficulties.

Withitness is an important skill that, even for "gifted" teachers, takes continual effort. Daily, professional teachers make immediate decisions about the ever-changing situations that they face. In addition to judgments about the level of mistaken behavior and whether child guidance or group management responses are necessary, the teacher makes two other important determinations now discussed:

1. Whether to intervene at all;
2. The degree of firmness to use in the intervention.

Whether to Intervene

A first decision is whether to intervene. In cases of serious mistaken behavior, the teacher has no choice; she must enter the situation. In other cases, the decision is not so clear. Three situations that require thought about whether to intervene are **marginal mistaken behaviors,** *"bossy" behaviors,* and *arguments.*

Marginal Mistaken Behaviors. Teachers have different comfort levels with minor mistaken behaviors. One teacher intervenes; another does not. Because no one way is the only way to use guidance, this human difference is to be expected.

An important question to ask is if the behavior is bothersome only to the teacher and not particularly to the group. When this is the case, care should be taken in the intervention decision. Unless the intervention is matter-of-fact and nonthreatening, the intervention may constitute more of a disruption than the mistaken behavior itself. In such a case, the degree of firmness is mismatched with the situation.

During rest time in a day care center, a teacher witnessed the following event. Four-year-old Missy, who "never misbehaved," reached out and tugged a neighbor's hair. Then, she rolled over and pretended that she was asleep. The neighbor, a three-year-old, sat up, rubbed his head, and complained. He then lay back down and closed his eyes. The teacher *did not* wade through the sleeping bodies and scold Missy. Instead, she smiled at this unusual event and commented later to a colleague that she thought Missy was finally feeling comfortable at the center.

The day care teacher decided that Missy's Level One mistaken behavior did not warrant intervention. To do so would have embarrassed a child with high personal standards and disrupted a group of sleeping preschoolers. The teacher did make a point of watching Missy's behaviors more closely, involving Missy in more activities, and building the relationship with her.

Marginal mistaken behaviors are the sort that some teachers may react to one day but not the next. *Consistency* in teacher response is needed both by the child and the group. Consistency provides reliability in the environment and facilitates trust between child and teacher. In determining whether to intervene, the teacher references behavior to the guidelines that have been established, the specifics of the situation, and the personalities of the children involved. Ultimately, the teacher must make intervention decisions by relying on her professional judgment. Reflection after the event helps the teacher decide whether adjustments are necessary for "next time."

Bossiness. Many teachers experience negative feelings about the marginal mistaken behavior of bossiness. A democratic society depends on citizens with leadership abilities. When young children show beginning leadership behaviors, they do so with the developmental egocentrism that they show in all behaviors. As a sense of fair play is strong in most teachers, they need to check tendencies to come down quickly on "bossy" behavior.

At choice time four kindergarten girls were playing cards. The game went like this: Lisa, who frequently organized play situations, stacked and dealt the cards. All four children picked up their hands and giggled, then put them back in the deck. Lisa stacked the cards again and re-dealt.

The teacher, who was watching, fought a tendency first to teach the children a "real game" and second to have each girl get a turn stacking and dealing. As it was, none of the other children pressed to have a turn, and the game went on as it was for almost half an hour.

Children learn about leadership and group participation from experience with peers. Teachers may need to remind a child to give others a chance; this is understandable. At the same time, they should positively acknowledge and encourage instances of "beginning leadership." The children themselves provide an indication of

Teachers positively acknowledge and encourage beginning leadership.

how leadership is showing itself. If others willingly associate with the leading child, intervention should be minimal. If other children shy away, the child probably needs guidance. Teachers frequently can help a child feel less need to dominate by building a personal relationship and helping the child feel more secure and accepted by the group.

Arguments. Teachers generally feel a need to intervene when children quarrel. In the guidance approach, the teacher uses withitness skills to analyze the situation and takes any of several possible courses of action, as Table 10.1 suggests.

Head Start teachers, Tammy and Connie, had a stock phrase whenever children had a disagreement: "We have a problem. How can we solve this problem?" At the beginning of the year, they helped children settle arguments on a daily basis with the phrase. As the year went on, the two needed to use it less and less. The reason was that other staff (including a teenage assistant) and the children themselves began to say: "We have a problem. How can we solve this problem?"

As presented in Chapter 9, children who learn to solve problems with words are gaining a life skill of lasting value (Wichert, 1991). Using words to solve problems can be learned by prekindergarten children no less than by third graders.

Table 10.1
Problem-Solving Classroom Arguments

Situation	Teacher Response
1. Reasonable chance children can work out difficulty.	Monitors, but may not intervene. If needed, uses low-level mediation.
2. Argument proving disruptive to a focused group activity.	Teacher intervenes. Redirects parties to class activity. States that she will help them solve problem later. Teacher follows up.
3. Argument becoming heated. Children don't seem able to resolve on own. Perhaps one child dominating.	Teacher mediates. May use props like talking stick or talk-and-listen chairs. Has each talk in turn and uses high-level mediation to assist children to resolve problem.
4. One child reports argument to teacher; wants assistance.	Teacher avoids taking sides. Determines whether #1, #2, or #3 above applies. Responds accordingly.
5. One or both have lost control; children are yelling or fighting.	Teacher intervenes. Separates children for cool-down time. Uses high-level mediation when tempers have cooled.

Firmness of Intervention

Besides deciding whether to intervene, the teacher must determine the level of firmness to use if intervention is necessary. Matching firmness to the seriousness of the mistaken behavior is a practice usually taken for granted. Part of practicing withitness should be conscious thought about the degree of firmness to use.

As Ginott points out, "Children are dependent on their teachers, and dependency breeds hostility. To reduce hostility a teacher deliberately provides children with opportunities to experience independence" (Ginott, 1972, p. 76). The teacher avoids communication that pits her authority against children (Greenberg, 1988). Instead, she **invites, requests,** or **commands choices.** The teacher does so in factual nondemeaning ways, because children "resist a teacher less when his communications convey respect and safeguard self-esteem" (Ginott, 1972, p. 77).

Putting choices to children illustrates how to use degrees of firmness in teacher responses. A first degree is **inviting cooperation:**

"I need some strong helpers to put the blocks away."

For some teachers, a mild invitation in situations like this is all that is needed. For others (and in other situations for all teachers) increased firmness is needed. A second degree is **requesting cooperation:**

"As soon as the blocks are picked up, we can go outside."

or

"The blocks need to be picked up before we can go out."

Suggesting a reward after a task has been done is known as the "grandma principle" (Jones, 1993). (As Grandma says, "Eat your peas, and then we can have dessert.") When requesting cooperation, the tone of voice as well as the words convey a matter-of-fact determination that the task be done.

The third degree of firmness is **commanding cooperation:**

> "Children, I am bothered that the books are still on the floor. You need to put the books away so that you don't miss some of your recess."

When commanding choices, the teacher often includes an *I message* to underscore the seriousness of the situation. Notice use of the *I* message, factual report, and firm direction in the teacher's statement. The teacher has avoided the "me-against-you" pitfall evident in the contrasting statement, "Either you pick up the book now, or I will keep you in at recess." Posing choices respects the autonomy of the learner by giving the responsibility to the child.

When putting choices to children at any degree of firmness, an objective is to make the *in-choice* attractive. (The *in-choice* is the one the teacher hopes the child will make.) The teacher must be prepared, though, for the occasional selection of the *out-choice*. (The *out-choice* is the less preferred option for the teacher, but one she can still live with.) Sometimes, even in guidance classrooms, children select the out-choice because they need to feel in control of the situation. Other times, the out-choice just plain sounds better. If a child does select the out-choice, the teacher accepts this option, figures out how to reinclude the child, and works on phrasing for next time.

(From a student teacher journal) *Observation.* Eric [a new child at Head Start] was climbing over the playground fence. By the time the lead teacher realized what he was doing, she only had time to grab and hold him until I went around to bring Eric back. Eric didn't want to go back. He said, "Teachers don't make the rules. The kids decide what to do." I explained to him how the kids get a choice in some situations, but not in all of them.

Meanwhile, the lead teacher had come around the fence and taken over. She said, "Eric, you have two choices: One, you can walk back into the playground by yourself or, two, you can be carried back in."

I could tell the lead teacher expected Eric to say walk, but he replied, "Carried."

The lead teacher didn't miss a beat. She said. "You want me to carry you over my shoulder like a sack of potatoes?" Eric confirmed this statement, so the lead teacher picked him up and carried him over her shoulder like a sack of potatoes back into the playground. While carrying Eric, she made jokes about him being a sack of potatoes. Eric enjoyed being carried back into the playground. He didn't try the "trick" again, but played for awhile, and then the lead teacher talked with him about the incident. When it was time to go in, they walked in together.

Reflection. The lead teacher gave Eric a choice of what he wanted to do and responded to the choice he made. Since he picked a way that might have caused him embarrassment, the teacher decided to make carrying him fun and nonthreatening. It saved him from being embarrassed in front of the other kids and didn't allow him to get upset at the teacher for carrying him back into the playground. I think this was a respectful and appropriate way to handle this situation.

Offering choices is basic in the guidance approach, but the skill takes practice. Sometimes, beginning teachers offer a choice that is too open-ended, or where choosing really is not warranted; for example: "Do you want to wash your hands for lunch?" Children need to know what the teacher wants them to do in order to cooperate. Sometimes a task gets done with minimum fuss if, instead of a choice, a friendly suggestion or request is given: "It's time to wash hands for lunch now."

QUICK INTERVENTION STRATEGIES

Unlike marginal mistaken behaviors, teachers generally agree that serious classroom situations require intervention. When teacher-time is limited, the resolution of problems becomes more difficult. Nonetheless, the objective is still to solve the problem, and effective techniques for resolving problems quickly are among the most important for teachers to learn. With quick and effective intervention, little problems tend not to become big ones, and the spread of mistaken behavior to other children—socially influenced mistaken behavior—is prevented. Quick intervention strategies to be considered are: **negotiation reminders, humor, nonverbal techniques, brevity,** and **being direct.**

Negotiation Reminders

When a child complains about a conflict with another, a common teacher phrase is

> "If that bothers you, use your words to tell him."
>
> or
>
> "Did you tell him how you feel?"

When a teacher is making conflict management a part of the everyday program, this friendly reminder is often enough to stimulate child-negotiation. Though it might not seem so, the message to a child in these statements seem to be, "I had a complaint, and the teacher listened." Having told the teacher and been heard, children often feel less need to press the issue with the other child. If a child does confront the other, it is often with righteous indignation rather than belligerence. The other child, usually taken aback (and aware that the teacher has been consulted), tends to respond in interesting ways:

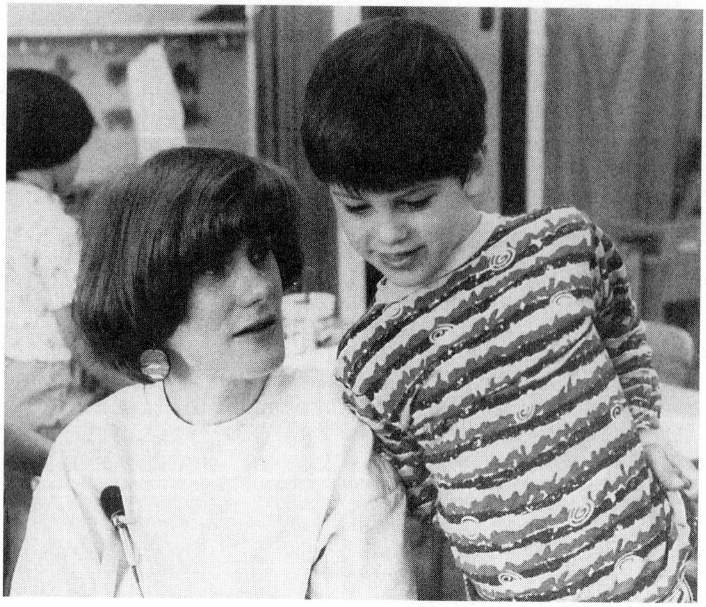

With quick intervention, little problems tend not to become big ones.

(From a student teacher journal) *Observation.* Aureole, Amber, and Kendra were decorating doilies with sequins and other materials. After a couple of minutes, Amber came up to me and said, "Teacher, Aureole keeps telling me what to do. She's bossy."

I got down on my knees, looked her in the eye, and said, "Could you tell her how that makes you feel?" Amber nodded her head, returned to Aureole, and said, "I don't like when you tell me what to do. That makes me sad."

"Sorry," replied Aureole, "I won't be bossy no more, OK?" Amber smiled, "OK."

Reflection. These children are very used to using their words and are comfortable with it. It was extremely effective for Amber to explain how she felt instead of telling me about it. I was very happy that Aureole was receptive of her feelings and that they were able to continue working together.

A stock phrase like the student teacher used is not a panacea, but it does tend to remind children that they can handle many issues for themselves.

Sue Liedl, in the case study at the end of Chapter 9, has reframed a classic negotiation reminder attributed to Marshall Rosenburg (Pirtle, 1995). Designed more for elementary than for preschool children, Liedl's **sentence frame** is as follows:

I feel__________

when____________________ .

Next time________________________ .

Sue points out that many accidental or mostly accidental things happen when groups of children are in confined spaces for long periods of the day. She teaches the children to use this response before getting more serious, such as by asking a teacher to mediate. This way of framing the statement opens the door to solving the problem in a relatively nonconfrontational way; for example:

Sentence frame: "*I feel* really sad *when* you bumped my arm 'cause I'm writing. *Next time* try to be more careful, OK?"

Response: "Well, I didn't mean to, but OK."

Sometimes, children just do not know what to say or how to respond in a conflict situation. Taking the time to teach a specific response like this (perhaps as a part of a communication arts lesson) gives the elementary teacher another helpful reminder to use: "Did you use your sentence frame?"

Humor as Problem-Solver

Just as good-natured humor prevents mistaken behavior, it also diffuses problems that do occur. The ability to see humor in a difficult situation relieves tension. When not at the expense of a child, humor compliments well the firmness teachers show, and helps children and teachers alike put mistaken behavior in perspective.

In a child care center, the preschoolers were making a footprint mural. An assistant at one end of a five-foot strip of butcher paper helped children step into a bin of red paint and pointed them in the right direction. The teacher at the other end assisted as the children stepped into a bin of soapy water and onto an absorbent towel.

Two children waiting in line began to push, and the assistant went back to mediate. A three-year-old decided not to wait for the assistant's help. She stepped into the paint, walked onto the paper, and took an abrupt left turn. The teacher at the receiving end was busy with another child and looked up to see red tracks leading to the restroom, just as the door closed. The two adults looked at each other, grinned, and shook their heads. The assistant stayed with the waiting line while the teacher, still smiling, retrieved the three-year-old.

A teacher in an elementary school classroom was also the part-time principal. The children knew that when she was out of the room, silence was to reign. On one occasion when Mrs. Kling returned, she was dissatisfied with the noise level and demanded, "Order, please!"

From the back of the room a reply was heard: "Ham and eggs!" The young man (whose voice sounded a lot like the author's) was greatly relieved at the teacher's response: She laughed with gusto.

Using humor in a difficult situation is the teacher's choice. For some teachers, humor comes easily and helps all to function comfortably in the classroom. For others, humor takes work; it requires that the teacher look freshly at events when "the pressure is on." Young children, because they look freshly at all situations, make humor an obvious tool to use. The challenge is for teachers not to take themselves too seriously and to remember that shared laughter can make long days seem not quite so long.

Nonverbal Techniques

The advantage of using nonverbal techniques (also called **body language**) is that they remind children about guidelines without causing undue embarrassment. Charles comments that nonverbal techniques typically include eye contact, physical proximity, body carriage, gestures, and facial expression (1996). Smiles and a friendly facial expression are, of course, the basic nonverbal technique. Also important, **physical proximity** is useful both in prevention and intervention with young children. In the active, developmentally appropriate classroom, the teacher is constantly moving about and establishing physical proximity. Locating by children who have a problem is frequently enough to refocus attention. The skillful teacher often does so without disrupting the flow of the activity or lesson.

Fredric Jones is known for his writing about body language as a method in positive classroom discipline (1993). For purposes of intervention, Jones' nonverbal techniques apply mainly to children in the *primary grades and up*. Preprimary children are so involved in situations that they tend to be oblivious to all but the most direct nonverbal techniques—physical proximity and friendly physical contact. A second proviso about nonverbal techniques is that eye contact and some touches, such as a pat on the head, may be appropriate with European American children, but not with children of some other cultural backgrounds. Knowledge of the cultural expectations of the families one works with is important.

As they progress through the primary grades, children become attuned to the teachers' use of body language. Appropriate with this age group, a multistep strategy for addressing mistaken behavior follows, building from the work of Jones (1993). Although the final steps involve words, the words are carefully chosen and follow from the nonverbal foundation.

Step one: *Eye contact*
The power of eye contact, the age-old stare, is remembered by most adults from their own school days. Generally, making eye

contact involves less embarrassment than if the teacher calls out a child's name or writes it on the board. A slight smile lessens the intensity of Step one.

Step two: *Eye contact with gestures*
A slow shake of the head with a gesture such as the palm up or an index finger pointed up at about shoulder height reinforces the message of the eye contact. Jones maintains that holding eye contact until the child resumes attention is important (1993).

Step three: *Physical proximity*
Mistaken behavior occurs most often away from the teacher. An important finding of Jones (1993) was that nearness of the teacher to children is effective at reestablishing limits.

Step four: *Proximity with general reminder*
Having moved close to children, the teacher makes a general reminder such as "I need everyone's attention for this." (A quick glance at the children makes this step more emphatic.)

Step five: *Proximity with direct comment*
After establishing proximity, the teacher makes eye contact and firmly requests the behavior expected. (The teacher protects self-esteem by speaking in a low but determined tone.) A follow-up conference sometimes is warranted.

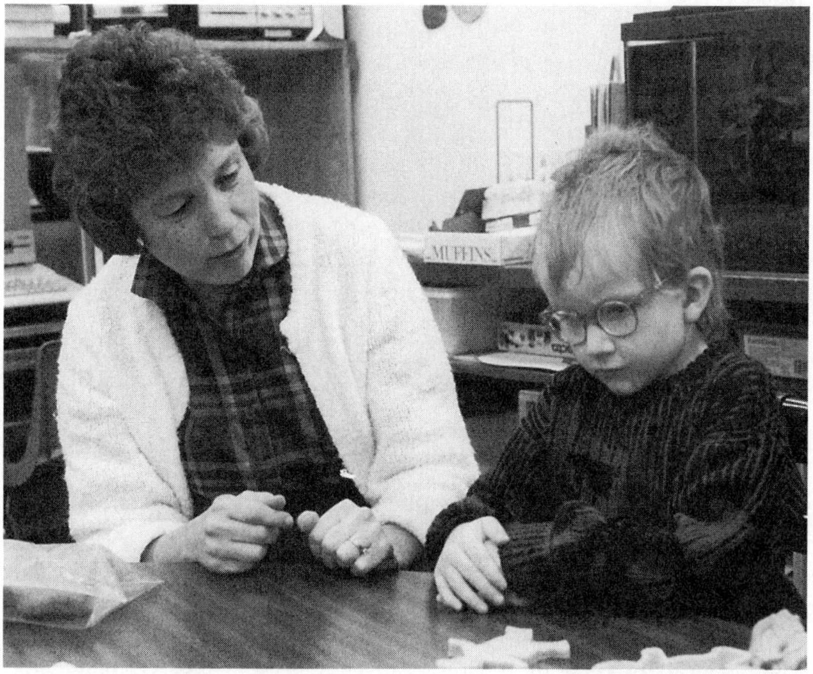

A caring expression communicates acceptance and support for a child in need.

Jones has contributed to intervention practices with his emphasis on body language. According to Jones, body carriage even more than spoken words tells children about the teacher's sureness of professional calling and comfort level with the group (1993). The basic element of body language, of course, is facial expression. About facial expression, important for all teachers of young children, Charles (1996) says the following:

> Like body carriage, *facial expressions* communicate much. Facial expressions can show enthusiasm, seriousness, enjoyment, and appreciation, all of which tend to encourage good behavior; or they can reveal boredom, annoyance, and resignation, which may encourage misbehavior. Perhaps more than anything else, facial expressions such as winks and smiles demonstrate a sense of humor, the trait students most enjoy in teachers (p. 133).

Brevity

Among writers about teacher-child relations, none discusses the use of language more constructively (or elegantly) than Ginott (1972). Ginott states:

> Teachers like parents, need a high degree of competence in communication. An enlightened teacher shows sensitivity to semantics. He knows that the substance learned by a child often depends on the style used by the teacher (1972, p. 98).

About the use of language during intervention, Ginott speaks of the importance of **brevity.** Young children have difficulty understanding lengthy explanations. Concise statements by the teacher that address the situation and motivate toward change are the objective.

> When Justin spoke to a neighbor for the third time during a class discussion, the teacher moved over to him and did **not** state: "Justin, you certainly have a lot to say today. Your mouth and your ears can't work at the same time. When you're talking, others can't hear either, and the class can't have important discussions. Do you think you could sit quietly for the rest of the group? You can talk all you want to the other children when you're out on the playground. Now, let's see you use your listening ears. Do you have them on? I am certainly glad that you do."
>
> Establishing proximity, the teacher **did** say (quietly but firmly), "Justin, only one person talks at a time. You have good ideas to share, but you need to raise your hand."

The brief use of encouragement while reinforcing a guideline captures well Ginott's sense of the positive power of words.

Being Direct

Confrontation as an intervention technique must be used with care. The line between earned authority and forced authority is crucial in the guidance classroom. This is why the use of negotiation reminders, humor, and nonverbal strategies anchor quick guidance interventions. When the teacher does not have time for mediation, matching firmness to the behavior by using choices (previous section) is a key concept. A set of ideas from Ginott (1972) provides yet another alternative when situations are so serious that harm or serious disruption are imminent, and the teacher is on the verge of becoming upset. Ginott suggests the following trio of ideas (1972):

- Describe without labeling;
- Express displeasure without insult;
- Correct by direction.

Describe Without Labeling. The teacher accepts the individual, but she need not accept the individual's mistaken behavior. In a paraphrase of other Ginott words: address the situation, do not attack personality. The teacher describes what she sees that is unacceptable, but does so without labeling personalities, because "labeling is disabling" (1972). *Example:* "Stefan, you have a right to be upset, but we don't hit in our classroom. Hitting hurts. Use words to tell him how you feel."

Express Displeasure Without Insult. Anger leads to mistaken behavior, in children and in adults. For this reason, even obedience discipline models maintain that "teachers should never act out of anger." As Ginott points out, anger is an emotion that all teachers feel; they either manage it or are controlled by it (1972). Since they assist children to express emotions in acceptable ways, professional teachers need to model the management of anger themselves. The careful use of displeasure, to show that you mean business but will not harm, is a necessary teaching skill. Ginott advocates the use of *I* messages, to report feelings without condemnation. *Example:* "I am really bothered that you two are fighting. You will sit down in different places. We will use words to talk as soon as both of you and I have cooled down."

Correct By Direction. This statement echoes another guidance basic: "Don't just tell children what not to do; tell them what to do instead." Direct children to alternate, acceptable behaviors. The difference is between intervention that is punitive and intervention that is educational. Young children are still learning "what to do instead" and have a need for and a right to this guidance. *Example:* "Voshon, I cannot let you hit anyone, and I will not let anyone hit you. You need to use words to tell him how you feel. He doesn't know until you tell him."

Using the Ideas Together. The describe-express-direct intervention techniques recommended by Ginott need to be used with care. They are guidance-oriented only when they address mistaken behaviors and at the same time support self-esteem. Note that the teacher expresses displeasure only when she feels bothered by events and needs to get personal feelings "on the table." *Describe* and *direct* are sufficient to move many behaviors back within guidelines, and to sustain an

Table 10.2
Examples of Describe-Direct Intervention

- Many outside voices are being used. Inside voices only please.
- It sounds like the battle of the Sumo wrestlers over here. Please solve the problem peacefully.

Table 10.3
Examples of Describe-Express-Direct Intervention

- I have difficulty listening when many children are using outside voices. I am bothered by the noise. Inside voices please.
- You two are arguing like cats and dogs. I am really upset about this. You choose; solve the problem peacefully or do things separately. Which will it be?

encouraging classroom. Expressing the teacher's feelings tends to "up the ante." Notice the difference shown in Tables 10.2 and 10.3.

BEHAVIORS REPORTED BY OTHER CHILDREN

"Tattling" bothers most teachers. They would prefer that children "attend to their own affairs" and solve their own problems. In some classrooms, children are punished for tattling. In others, a child who chronically tattles acquires a label such as "tattle tale" or "busy body."

Child-report (an alternate term for *tattling*) is difficult to deal with because the motives of children are not always what they seem. The reasons for a child-report range from a legitimate concern to a need for attention to a desire to manipulate the teacher. From a guidance perspective, teachers have two reasons for neither banning nor disparaging child-report.

First, sometimes a teacher wants a child to report, for instance, when:

- a child has strayed from the playground;
- children are fighting, and one has been seriously hurt;
- a child has been injured in an accident;
- a child is having a seizure or is otherwise ill;
- others are acting inappropriately toward a child.

Children should be encouraged to report such incidents. In a class meeting, the teacher may discuss with children what such an emergency is and what children should do in the event of an emergency. The well-being of children and the professional integrity of the teacher are supported by children acting as "concerned citizens."

Second, a report by a child is a request for a response by the teacher. Children need positive contact with teachers even if they don't always know how to ask for contact appropriately. The teacher models acceptance of the child by responding even when she sees an event differently than the child. One technique that attempts to balance the priorities of teachers and the needs of children is a "report box." Children who have concerns that are not emergencies can write or draw out the problem on prepared "report forms" and put them into the box. The teacher consults the box daily, reads the name the child has put on the "name line," and talks with the child about the concern. Follow-up actions to address the concern, such as a class meeting, may result, though often a little individual attention is enough to resolve the situation.

When children report, the teacher does well to take a moment and consider which of several possible motives may be operating. A first motive is that they have experienced a problem and have come to the teacher for assistance. A second motive is that they have witnessed a problem and believe the teacher should know about it. A third motive is that they report to find out what the teacher will do. A fourth motive is more to make contact with the teacher than to express a concern. A fifth motive is that they wish to control the teacher's reactions. A sixth motive is that they wish to put another child in a difficult situation.

As Table 10.4 indicates, teachers respond differently depending on the suspected motive of the child.

Why should teachers bother with the complex, troublesome interactions that are a part of child-report? By using guidance when they respond, adults teach children to resolve their own conflicts; to respect others' efforts at problem-solving; and to come to the aid of peers who are genuinely in need. These capabilities will be desirable in citizens of any age in the 21st century. From this perspective, "tattling" too becomes a teaching opportunity.

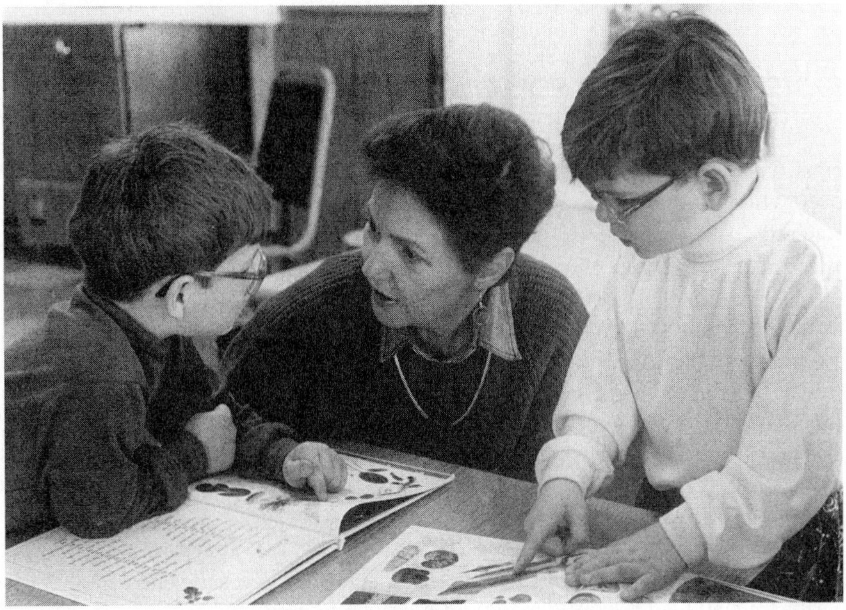

Child-report can be for many reasons—including a legitimate request for assistance.

Table 10.4
Suggested Responses to Child Report

Suspected Motive of the Child	Suggested Response of Teacher
Child has legitimate difficulty in relations with another child.	Teacher encourages children to solve on own—"tell him how you feel about that"—or mediates to extent necessary.
Child honestly reports problem situation involving other children.	Teacher thanks child for being a "caring citizen." Monitors situation. If necessary, intervenes taking a guidance approach.
Child reports to get teacher's attention or see what teacher will do (Level One mistaken behavior).	Teacher reassures child that things are under control. Monitors situation in low profile manner "just in case." Notices whether reporting child seeks attention in other ways. Works on building relationship with child.
Child reports minimal problems on a regular basis (Level Two mistaken behavior).	Teacher thanks child for concern but explains that other children can take care of themselves. Tells child what the serious problems are that child can report. Builds relationship.
Child reports either to manipulate teacher or get another child into "trouble" (Level Three mistaken behavior).	As in all cases, teacher avoids "charging into the situation." Keeps open mind about children involved. Monitors "reporter" for other Level Three mistaken behavior. If necessary, follow procedures for working with this level. (See Chapter 11)

INTERVENTION WHEN FOLLOW-UP IS NEEDED

When adults disagree, the immediate resolution of differences is not assured. Yet, with children who lack the resources and experience of adults, instant resolution frequently is expected. In academic settings that emphasize decorum and academic achievement, many view teachers who mediate difficulties as using time unproductively.

Time is required if differences are to be settled in ways from which all can benefit. In the mutually satisfactory resolution of problems, all learn (Wichert, 1991). In the peaceful resolution of difficulties, teachers enhance children's self-esteem and their faith in school—their will for educational success (Greenberg, 1988).

Ginott (1972) recognized that in many situations there should be "no hurried help." He wrote that when the teacher quickly "solves" problems for children, they feel inadequate. In anticipation of the conflict management movement to come, Ginott states:

> The teacher listens to the problem, rephrases it, clarifies it, gives the child credit for formulating it, and then asks, "What options are open to you?" "What are your choices in this situation?" Often the child himself comes up with a solution. Thus, he learns that

> he can rely on his own judgment. When a teacher hastily offers solutions, children miss the opportunity to acquire competence in problem-solving and confidence in themselves (p. 92).

Sometimes, situations can be addressed quickly with nonverbal or verbal responses that sustain self-esteem and increase understanding. In these cases, follow-up is not necessary. In other cases, speedy resolution is not realistic. When the teacher must give time to a situation, she does so either at the moment of the occurrence or later in the day. (Response at a later time is due to conflicting demands on the teacher at the moment, or to the need for a *cooling down time* if emotions are high.)

This section addresses teacher responses when follow-up is necessary. Five follow-up strategies are explored: *teacher-child negotiation, reflective listening, including children's ideas, guidance talks,* and *reconciliation.*

Negotiating Teacher-Child Conflicts

Chapter 9 primarily addressed social problem-solving among children. Child-child conflicts tend to be the main focus of writers about social problem-solving. With the active learning characteristic of developmentally appropriate practice, child-child disputes are a natural focus. Yet, a higher concern among many beginning teachers are teacher-child conflicts.

Teacher-child conflicts occur more frequently when the education program is less responsive to the developmental needs of children. Such programs place an expectation on children that they may not be ready for, and create a mismatch situation that frequently leads to defiance, anxiety, and frustration. The teacher reduces this mistaken behavior, of course, by making the program more developmentally appropriate.

Still, even in encouraging classrooms, differences of opinion will occur between teacher and child. Moreover, children with serious needs will show some Level Three mistaken behavior regardless of classroom climate, and sometimes the teacher will be the target.

When two individuals resolve a conflict between themselves without an outside mediator, they have *negotiated* a solution. The idea of *teacher-child negotiation* makes some teachers uncomfortable because the term seems to imply communication at a peer-to-peer level. This line of reasoning is that if negotiation can only happen between peers, teachers would have to relinquish their leadership role and compromise their standards! In fact, probably the leaders that most people look up to—whether they are teachers, administrators, bosses, or political figures—frequently negotiate.

The choice to negotiate is the teacher's, and she may elect not to negotiate depending upon the circumstances. But sometimes, the best action a teacher can take *is* to negotiate. When the teacher so decides, she does not give up the mantle of leadership, just uses it with dignity and mutual respect. The *thought* of negotiating with a child can be unsettling. However, for many teachers who use guidance, the action is not a "big deal"; teachers negotiate routinely.

(From a student teacher journal) *Observation.* It was the end of free time in a first grade class. Miles had been running around for most of free time already. He ran over to the window and noticed that some wheat berries, planted by the class, had sprouted. "Look, teacher, they're growing," he screamed. He then went around showing the sprouts to anyone who would look.

When he was back by the window, the teacher met Miles, kneeled down, and said, "Miles, I can see you are very interested in the wheat berries that are starting to grow. If you come to the writing table where your group is starting, maybe we can write down how we could plant some more seeds tomorrow." Miles went to the table with the teacher.

Reflection: I was impressed with the teacher's response. Miles, who gets enthusiastic about a lot of things, just noticed the sprouting seeds for the first time. The teacher realized that and let him know she understood what he was feeling. She was then able to get him back on task at the writing table by writing a plan that he was very interested in making. (Later, I asked her if she had been planning to plant more seeds the next day. She smiled and said, "We are now.")

When a teacher disagrees with a child's behavior, she uses the same problem-solving steps as in child-child conflicts. A consolidation of the conflict management models given in Chapter 9, along with some others, yields a process of at least 14 steps. The steps are listed for review in Table 10.5, but in practice, negotiation with children has the basic components of mediation in general: (a) agreeing on what the problem is; (b) cooperatively arriving at a solution to try; (c) implementing and (d) supportively evaluating the solution. These steps are the same used when a teacher is mediating between children or negotiating with a single child. The advice of several writers on conflict management is worth heeding in negotiation. Stay calm and attempt to be calming. If remaining calm is difficult, just as the teacher might ask two children to take a cooling down time, the teacher might need to cool down as well.

Reflective Listening

A key tool in mediation and negotiation is *reflective listening,* referred to several times in the text. In a conflict situation, reflective listening has both a *release* and a *guidance* function. First, reflective listening means that the teacher articulates or rephrases the child's feelings and perceptions. By having feelings and perceptions affirmed by the teacher, the child feels less need to act out and is more open to dialogue. The release function is illustrated in many of the text anecdotes and is the common use of reflective listening.

In the *guidance* function, the teacher guides to a self-calming strategy. Slaby et al. point out that many children lack a strategy to help themselves calm down in order "to talk to others about what they want and what they can do" (1995, p. 106). After

Table 10.5
Steps in Problem-Solving Conflicts

A. Identify the problem.
   1. Decide that time should be taken to solve the problem.
   2. Establish that the purpose is to resolve a problem, not blame or label individuals.
   3. Enable each party to express views and feelings about the problem, using reflective listening to clarify points.
   4. Summarize differing viewpoints, checking for accuracy of interpretation with participants.

B. Generate possible solutions.
   1. Request cooperation in seeking a solution.
   2. Encourage the suggestion of solutions.
   3. Appreciate that each suggestion was made, even if others have difficulty with it.

C. Agree on a solution to be tried.
   1. Work for consensus on a course of action.
   2. Avoid accusation of vested interest. Instead, point out that "others see the situation differently" and encourage further discussion.
   3. If necessary, point out that perfect solutions are not always possible, but this one is worth trying.

D. Reach successful closure.
   1. Facilitate implementation of the solution.
   2. Provide encouragement (compliment sandwich if necessary).
   3. Affirm the participant(s) for reaching the solution.
   4. Discuss alternative behaviors for next time.

Including children's ideas during negotiation sustains their involvement in the problem-solving process.

helping the child acknowledge that she is upset, the teacher then gives a self-calming suggestion, such as

"Take some deep breaths";

"Count to ten on your fingers."

With older children, the teacher might say,

"Stop and think what you can do";

"Think aloud."

The teacher will need to use the guidance function consistently before children who tend to act out begin to pick up on the cuing. Still, practicing these *self-calming* skills "provide[s] a foundation for more independent self-control skills in later childhood and adulthood" (p. 107).

Les was building a barn with blocks when Craig accidentally knocked it over. Les had fists clenched and teeth set when the teacher arrived. The teacher said, "Craig didn't mean to, Les, but it's too bad about your building, and it's OK to feel upset about it." Les remained upset and kicked the remaining blocks, a half unit smacking the teacher on the ankle. Les saw what had happened and looked like he was about to cry.

The teacher grimaced silently, then said, "Les, take deep breaths please so that you will feel better . . . in and out, that's right." She put her arm around Les' shoulder and continued, "It's OK, Les, that only hurt a little, and I'm not upset because I know you didn't mean to. You're not having a very good day, are you?" Then Les did cry. The teacher held him until he felt better, and the two picked up the blocks together. Later they talked about what he could do next time when he felt upset.

For the teacher to use reflective listening effectively, she must remain calm. As the anecdote illustrates, *I messages,* which some writers refer to as *self-report,* serve as a self-reflective listening technique that helps the teacher focus on the situation. (Sometimes, teachers themselves have to practice both the release and guidance functions to remain calm and objective.) The teacher who uses the two functions of reflective listening is practicing a sound strategy in problem-solving mistaken behavior, both in terms of immediate consequences and in the long-range life skills the child is learning.

Including Children's Ideas

Another tool helpful in both mediation and negotiation is *involving children in the solution process.* When children contribute to the solution, they feel capable as problem-solvers. Including some suggestions of Ginott, questions like these empower children to "work things out":

- What options are open to you?
- What are your choices in this situation?
- How can we solve this problem?
- Who has an idea about what we can do?
- What can we do about it?
- How could you solve this differently?
- Maybe the two of you can solve the problem together?
- What words could you use next time?

When children are asked for their views, ideas, and assistance, they are encouraged to show initiative and to work for a cooperative solution. The leadership of the adult here is critical (Wichert, 1991), as the following example of teacher-child negotiation illustrates.

Third-grader Elaine had a difficult time concentrating during large group activities. She visited with neighbors and showed inattentiveness to topics being discussed. At a break-time, the teacher talked with the child:

Teacher: Elaine, we need to talk about a problem we are having during large group. I have to remind you to pay attention too many times.
Elaine: Well, the other kids are always talking to me.
Teacher: Yes, I know; it is hard to listen when too many people are talking. What can we do about it?
Elaine: (long pause) Maybe I could move.
Teacher: That sounds like an idea. Why don't you choose? Where could you sit where you wouldn't be bothered by other children?
Elaine: By Renee, maybe.
Teacher: All right, let's try it. But remember our guideline, one person talks at a time, OK?
Elaine: OK, teacher

The teacher followed through by making sure Elaine sat where they agreed and by using nonverbal techniques, including smiles, to hold her attention. Two days later the teacher complimented the progress that Elaine has shown.

Negotiation can be used with groups as well as individual children. In fact, many class meetings are called so that teachers and children can negotiate solutions to problems together. The leader is the teacher, who is perhaps bothered by an event, and calls a class meeting to problem-solve the conflict situation (Hendrick, 1992).

A kindergarten teacher brings together the class for a serious discussion.

Teacher: We need to talk about a problem during choice time. A child was hurt on the climber today. Play there is getting too rough, and I am disturbed about it.
Louise: Yeah, and I nearly fell off, too.
Dennis: The kids was going down the slide wrong.
Elsabet: Too many of them and it's loud.
Teacher: Well, Mr. Stone (the janitor) and I could put the climber away for a while, or maybe you have some ideas for what we could do.
Allen: Don't let so many on.
Louise: No pushin' on top, and go down on your seat.
Elsabet: No pushing and yelling.
Teacher: It sounds like we have some guidelines for the climber the way we do for class. I will write them down. (She prints what the children have told her and reads the guidelines aloud.) We will give the climber another try, but everyone needs to remember the guidelines.

The teacher posted the guidelines near the climber. Though the children could not decode every word, they did remember the guidelines and reminded their friends about them. Play on the climber became safer and the equipment stayed up in the room.

The ability to settle differences cooperatively is a cornerstone both of individual mental health and the functioning of a democracy. The teacher who takes time to negotiate is modeling social problem-solving in the way most likely to impact children. When the situation involves the teacher as a participant, she must model caring leadership despite emotional involvement. One of the challenges for teachers who use conflict management is that it is often easier to resolve problems that are between children. The teacher can be the objective (and authoritative) third party who mediates or encourages child-child negotiation. When the teacher is directly involved in the conflict, the emotional stakes are higher for all concerned. The outcome is not assured, as it is (at least on paper) in traditional classroom discipline. The measure of teachers' commitment to the civil resolution of classroom conflicts, and to guidance, is their growing ability to use teacher-child negotiation, as opposed to traditional discipline.

Guidance Talks

Teacher use mediation and negotiation to solve classroom problems. They utilize *guidance talks* to empower children to handle difficulties more effectively in the

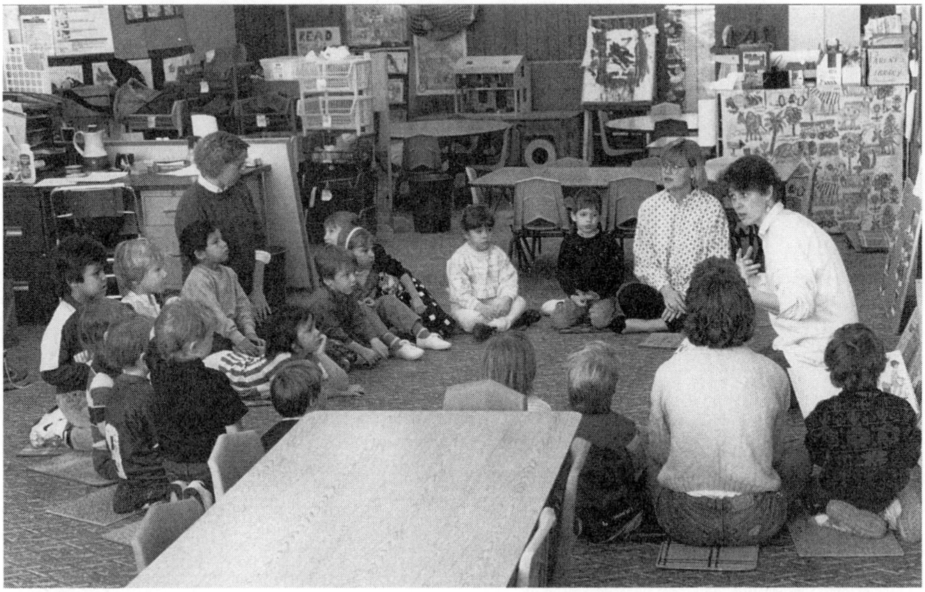

In a group setting, a request to solve a problem becomes part of a class meeting, or a negotiation between the teacher and the class.

future. Guidance talks are not needed after every intervention. They are needed when conflicts have been serious, and a child could benefit from additional teacher contact. The teacher uses guidance talks after a problem has been resolved, but it is still fresh in the child's mind.

The reader is familiar with three communication techniques helpful in guidance talks: *encouragement,* the *compliment sandwich,* and *reflective listening*. The teacher uses these tools informally and supportively in the guidance conversation. Guidance talks differ from another kind of talk discussed in Chapter 8, *contact talks*. Contact talks are used to get to know a child better. In contact talks the teacher follows the line of conversation of the child, respecting the child's interests and background, and listening.

In guidance talks, the teacher has topics that she wishes to discuss: (a) an update as to how the child is feeling; (b) ideas about what the child might do differently next time; (c) suggestions about how the situation might be reconciled, if not accomplished fully during mediation. A teacher and child should have both kinds of talk, of course. Contact talks allow a teacher to continue to build a relationship after a guidance talk has occurred.

A second distinction is the difference between a guidance talk and "the lecture." The disciplinary lecture tends to convey a "shape up or else" message and is only marginally a discussion. The guidance talk accepts the child's perceptions and feelings, educates about the consequences of behaviors, and guides toward more productive possibilities. Its tone is supportive and conversational.

When Curtis hit Glen, the child he was playing with, the teacher conducted high-level mediation. Afterwards, Curtis and the teacher had the following conversation:

Teacher: How are you feeling now, Curtis?
Curtis: Still mad.
Teacher: Sometimes it takes a while to feel better. Curtis, why do you suppose you hit Glen?
Curtis: 'Cause he wouldn't play.
Teacher: If you hit kids, will they want to play with you?
Curtis: Yeah, maybe.
Teacher: (Smiles.) I've been around a long time, Curtis, and I've noticed that kids mainly want to play if you're friendly. How could you be friendly to Glen?
Curtis: Not hit?
Teacher: That's an idea. You are really thinking. What else?
Curtis: Get something so he could play.
Teacher: Those are friendly ideas, Curtis. When you play with Glen, what do you and he like to do?
Curtis: Play with trucks and stuff, and he likes puzzles.
Teacher: Those are some good ideas. Glen told us he was feeling sad that you hit him. When you both are ready, I wonder how you could help him feel better.
Curtis: Maybe do puzzles.
Teacher: That sounds like something friends can do together.

Curtis rejoins the children, but stays away from Glen. Later, the teacher notices Curtis and Glen together, not doing a puzzle, but reading a book.

Reconciliation

Reconciliation is an important part of the guidance talk. Note that the teacher did not impose a reconciliation in the Curtis and Glen situation. **The teacher does not force apologies.** Children no less than adults know when they are ready to apologize and when they are not. (To their credit, children tend to forgive more easily than most adults.) Instead, the adults asks the child for ideas about "how to help the other child feel better." Children come up with creative solutions when they are encouraged to make amends on their own. Teachers often hear ideas like:

"Tell her I'm sorry."

"Tell him I would be his friend again."

"Put a wet towel on it."

The teacher then encourages the child to act to get the relationship back on even ground. Children are more willing to apologize when they know that their feelings and points of view have been respected—what the guidance talk is about.

In the most serious conflict situations, teachers physically restrain or remove children to prevent harm (see Chapter 11). In these cases, the primary focus of the child's anger may be the teacher. Whatever the focus of blame for a conflict, the teacher is the one who initiates reconciliation. The principle of unconditional positive regard means that the teacher works for reconciliation as a part of daily practice. In the guidance approach, the teacher recognizes that the act of reconciling comes not from weakness, but from strength. Guidance differs from punitive discipline in this regard.

The guidance talk may not turn around mistaken behavior instantaneously. The lessons of getting along with others and expressing strong emotions acceptably take time to learn. Nonetheless, supportive conversations help children in many ways, not the least of which is the modeling of human compassion.

WHY TAKE THE TIME?

Researchers such as Mitchell have noted a steady decline in the self-esteem of children as they progress through the grades. To quote Curwin and Mendler:

> Mitchell found that 80 percent of children enter first grade with high self-esteem. By the time they reach fifth grade, only 20 percent have high self-esteem. By the time they finish high school, the number having positive self-esteem has dropped to a staggering 5 percent (1989, p. 26).

Mitchell's finding suggests that school experiences such as failure, embarrassment, and other facets of conditional acceptance have a deleterious effect.

In a *Newsweek* feature on early childhood education, Katz referred to the need for a "1st R" in educational practice: *Relationships* (Kantrowitz & Wingert, 1989). As we enter the new millennium, the personal and social skills of democracy need to be considered components of the curriculum no less than the academic basics. Guidance, including the problem-solving of mistaken behavior, is a part of an interactive teaching approach that includes the "1st R." Through the use of guidance to solve problems, adults are teaching children essential life skills. Children are learning:

- acceptable ways of expressing strong emotions;
- positive alternative behaviors to act out;
- conflict resolution skills;
- consideration for the viewpoints and feelings of others;
- positive self-regard;
- appreciation for the teacher as a helping person;
- respect for the role of the teacher;
- acceptance of the role of student.

Put into terms of broad developmental outcomes, the child gains in:

- emotional development through the ability to express feelings acceptably and resolve problems constructively;
- language development through the vocabulary, phrasing, and functional communication necessary for the resolution of difficulties;
- cognitive development by the critical thinking inherent in problem-solving;

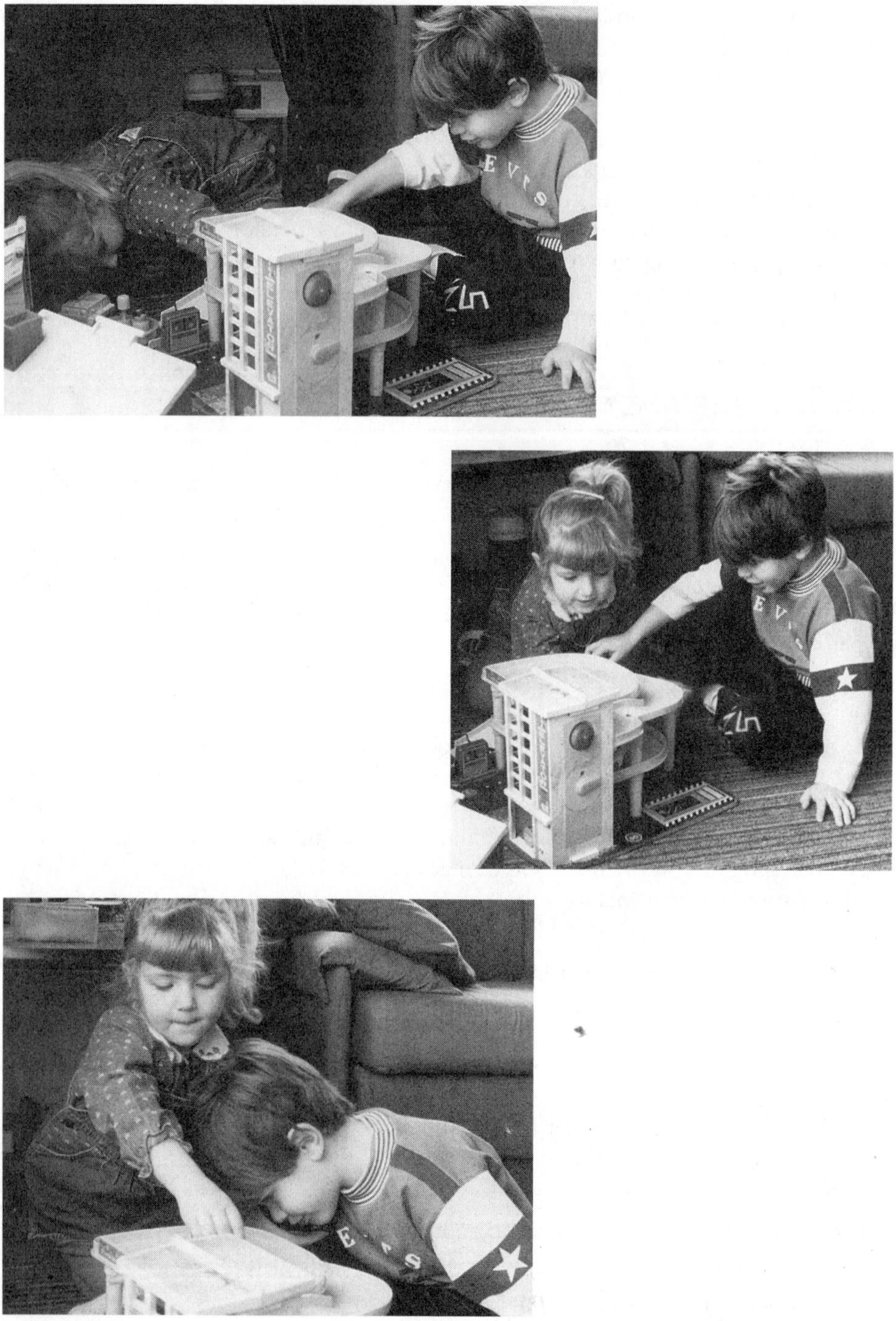

Guidance discipline is a part of an interactive teaching approach that includes the "1st R," relationships.

- physical development through freedom from the effects of stress, tension, and hostile feelings when problems remain unresolved or become aggravated;
- social development by learning life skills important for productive functioning as a member of the group and a democratic society.

The time commitment adults give to problem-solving mistaken behavior is an investment in the personal and educational success of the children in their care.

COOPERATION WITH PARENTS

As a professional, the teacher cooperates with parents in the education of the child. Many factors make cooperation with parents a challenge (Galinsky, 1988). Parents and teachers have distinct roles and so perspectives and values differ from each other. Parents:

- have a strong emotional investment in their own child;
- at times question their own effectiveness (Morgan, 1989);
- have views about acceptable behavior and discipline methods influenced by their backgrounds more than formal education (Galinsky, 1988);
- may view the teacher as a "superior" who will be unreceptive to efforts at communication (Greenberg, 1989).

Unless they come to understand these role-based qualities, teachers may take personally contacts with parents that seem defensive or unfriendly.

To accommodate the difference in roles and viewpoints, Galinsky recommends: "Rather than the dispenser of correct information, the professional builds an alliance in which the parent's own expertise is strengthened" (1988, p. 11). Galinsky (1988) and Morgan (1989) provide useful suggestions for taking this collaborative approach. The following discussion builds upon points made by the authors. These six steps can guide the teacher toward achieving cooperation with parents.

Create a Team Concept

This step, mentioned in other chapters of the book, provides a foundation for cooperation if problems arise. The step cannot begin too early in the program year. As Morgan (1989) suggests, work with parents' emotional ties to their children, not against them.

Be Aware of Feelings Toward the Family

Some teachers may feel uncomfortable around some children, as well as some families. One reason for negative feelings toward a family is the view that a family has not met implicit expectations about parenting (Galinsky, 1988). In this event, the teacher needs to understand circumstances within the family that may make the expectations unrealistic. Cultural, economic, and social factors all contribute to life styles and values potentially different than the teacher's. The teacher who identifies and accepts the fact of cultural diversity is in a better position to understand and work with the family, and the child.

Understand Parent Development

About this topic Galinsky states:

> It is much easier to understand parents if you know the normal course of parental growth and development. For example, before decrying the superbaby phenomenon, it helps to know that all new parents want perfection for their children—that is normal. It is their definition of perfection you want to alter, not their desire for the best (1988, p. 10).

Choose Words That Avoid Value Judgments

Describing without labeling is a basic of the guidance approach that pertains to parents no less than children. Galinsky and Morgan use examples that may sound familiar. Here is a variation of an example used by Morgan (1989, p. 56):

Understanding parents is much easier if the teacher understands the normal course of parental growth and development.

Instead of: Karla was a real terror this afternoon. It was "isolation corner" for her today. After that she shaped up, and she is being a good girl now.

Say: After nap today, Karla had a problem with two children. She needed a cool-down time, but then we read books and she is having an easier time now.

Note the nonjudgmental tone and the recognition of progress included in the second statement, which is approaching a compliment sandwich. As a contrast, in the first statement the use of "value laden" language is clear (Morgan, 1989). The compliment sandwich, *I* message, and reflective listening all provide alternatives to value judgments, and are useful in communications with parents as well as with children to encourage cooperation.

Use Support Services

Galinsky identifies a crucial role for the teacher as referring families to other services (1988). She states, "It is just as important to know when to say no and to refer as it is to know when to say yes" (p. 10). The teacher is not a therapist or a social worker, but she can refer a family to a needed service and be supportive through the referral process.

Head Start has led the way in assisting families to access health and social agencies as well as educational services. Increasingly, schools and other programs are coming to realize that not just the child, but the family is the unit of service in early childhood programs (Boyer, 1992; Heath, 1994). The ability to work with families to remove the stigma of special education or social service assistance is a goal of the teacher (Coleman, 1997).

In making referrals, to the extent possible teachers should know the agencies in their area and individuals at the agencies who will be helpful. Rosenthal & Swayers (1996) provide a list of steps important in making a referral:

1. Know the agencies in your area.
2. Know competent people with whom you can work at these organizations.
3. Refer to specific people, not just an organization.
4. Get agreement from the family that they will participate.
5. Ask the family to predict what might prevent them from participating and ask for solutions (such as transportation and child care).
6. Check on families' ideas about solutions and arrangements.
7. Make sure you provide for a follow-up meeting (p. 199).

A teacher in a Head Start program might be comfortable helping with more of these steps; a child care professional or an elementary school teacher might be comfortable with fewer of the steps. Often, the individual teacher should not think in terms of taking referral actions on her own. Instead, working with other staff as a team, teachers can and should endeavor to make referrals, including the preliminary step of learning as much as possible about the services available. Families who are helped with successful referrals tend to strengthen their commitment both to their children and to the staff.

Problem-Solving with Parents

Teacher-parent negotiation often becomes necessary when a child's mistaken behavior grows serious. Galinsky suggests a six-step approach to *teacher-parent problem-solving*. The goal is to convert "unhealthy tension" to "healthy tension" in relations (1988). The six steps are similar to the processes suggested earlier for helping children solve problems in the classroom. The steps include:

1. Describe the situation as a problem to be solved. Avoid accusations or the implication that the source of the problem resides in the personality of the parent or the child.
2. Generate multiple solutions. Parents and professionals should both do this, and no one's suggestions should be ignored, put down, or denounced.
3. Discuss the pros and cons of each suggestion.
4. Come to a consensus about which solutions to try.
5. Discuss how you will implement these solutions.
6. Agree to meet again to evaluate how these solutions are working so that you can change your approach, if necessary (p. 11).

On occasion, communication with parents may prove difficult and negotiation needs to give way to third party mediation. As Galinsky comments, "Having others to turn to when there are tensions is crucial in working effectively with parents" (1988, p. 10). Seeking a senior staff member to assist in the problem-solving process is a mark of maturity for the guidance teacher. A source of support for the teacher outside of the immediate situation—preferably both a fellow staff member and a friend or family member—is equally important. The person serving as the support base should recognize the need for a teacher to privately "vent" with no repercussions. Hopefully, the source of support can also assist the teacher to plan a constructive course of action regarding the situation.

The teacher cannot separate the child's life at school from the child's life at home. The child's life at home is the family. Through cooperating with the family, the teacher optimizes chances of gaining the parents' trust and assistance in helping the child.

SUMMARY

How do teachers apply the concept of mistaken behavior?

Ability to understand the level of a child's mistaken behavior helps the teacher with intervention decisions. Children show Level One, experimentation level mistaken behavior, as a result of involvement in situations or curiosity. The teacher responds in a matter-of-fact manner to educate toward alternatives without reinforcing the behavior. Children show Level Two mistaken behavior, socially influenced, when they have been reinforced toward mistaken behavior by significant others. The teacher uses guidance talks or class meetings to re-establish an applicable guideline and to teach alternative behaviors. Level Three, strong needs mistaken behavior, occurs when trouble in the child's life is beyond the child's capacity to cope with and understand. The teacher uses the comprehensive approach to addressing Level Three mistaken behavior introduced earlier and discussed in Chapter 11.

What goes into the decision to intervene?

The teacher is a friend to children, but she is an adult friend who accepts the responsibility of leadership. The adult works to understand situations by practicing "withitness." She determines the level of mistaken behavior, and whether problem situations involve one or two children or a number of children. The teacher then decides whether to intervene and the degree of firmness of the intervention. The strategy of inviting, requesting, or commanding choices illustrates the use of different degrees of firmness and at the same time grants children a measure of independence.

What are five quick intervention strategies?

Quick intervention strategies that resolve problems but still protect self-esteem are important in guidance. Negotiation reminders that cue children to use their own developing social skills are a first strategy. Humor is a second strategy by which the teach can relax nerves in tense situations. A third strategy is nonverbal communication that includes using facial expressions and establishing proximity. Brevity is a fourth strategy, an effective alternative to moralizing and "lectures." A fifth strategy is direct intervention through the "describe, express, and direct" and the "describe and direct" sequences.

How does the teacher respond to mistaken behaviors reported by children?

Child-report (an alternate term to *tattling*) is difficult to deal with because the motives of children are not always what they seem. Teachers should neither ban nor disparage child-report for two reasons. A teacher wants a child to report when safety is threatened. Also, child-report is a request for contact with the teacher. Children need positive contact even if they don't always know how to ask for the contact appropriately. Suggestions were provided to help teachers determine motives for child-report and take an appropriate course of action.

What are five strategies when interventions require follow-up?

Time is required if conflicts are to be settled in ways in which all can benefit. In the event of teacher-child conflict a first strategy is to negotiate. This negotiation is not at a peer level; the teacher uses her authority to problem-solve civilly with the child, using the principles of conflict resolution. A second strategy, reflective listening, is an effective tool in both negotiation and mediation. The technique assists children with emotional control by helping them express their feelings in ways acceptable both to themselves and to other children.

A third strategy is to include children's ideas in the problem-solving effort. By including children's ideas, children feel ownership of the resolution process and are more likely to participate fully in it. A fourth strategy is the use of guidance talks with the child after a conflict has been resolved. Guidance talks help children understand the consequences of actions, alternative future actions, and the possibilities of reconciliation. The fifth strategy, the reconciliation process, is a chief point of difference between guidance and conventional discipline. Through reconciliation, the child is able to make amends in ways that she feels comfortable with help, so enabling a mutual sense of compassion and re-establishing her place in the group.

Why take the time to problem-solve mistaken behavior?

Assisting children to develop democratic life skills is a valid part of the curriculum for the 21st century. Individual children and the society both benefit when teachers take the time to problem-solve mistaken behavior.

How does the teacher build cooperation with parents?

Collaboration with parents is sometimes difficult for teachers because of differences in perspective and values. To accommodate these differences, Galinsky (1988) suggests that the role of the teacher is to foster an alliance in which the parents' own expertise is strengthened. To do so, the teacher builds positive relationships, monitors feelings toward the family, understands parent development, chooses words that avoid value judgments, and uses referrals for support services. The teacher uses a six-step problem-solving approach in collaboration with parents to solve problems that may arise. When communication becomes difficult, third party assistance both in problem-solving and providing a support base for the teacher are important. Through cooperation with the family, the teacher reaches the child.

FOLLOW-UP ACTIVITIES

Note: In completing follow-up activities, the privacy of all involved is to be respected.

Reflection Activity

The reflection activity encourages students to interrelate their own thoughts and experiences with specific ideas from the chapter.

Recall an incident when you or a teacher intervened in a situation that required follow-up. What strategies did you or the teacher use that are identified in the chapter? What strategies were used that were not mentioned in the chapter? Was reconciliation a part of the intervention strategy used? Why or why not?

Application Activities

Application activities allow students to interrelate material from the text with real life situations. The observations imply access to practicum experiences; the interviews, access to teachers or parents. Students may compare or contrast observations and interviews with referenced ideas from the chapter.

1. **How do teachers apply the concept of mistaken behavior?**
   a. Observe a teacher who intervenes in an instance of Level One, Two, or Three mistaken behavior. Respecting the privacy of the teacher, how did the intervention comply with or deviate from the recommended guidance approach for that level?
   b. Interview a teacher about the kinds of mistaken behavior that she finds most troubling. Ask the teacher to discuss why. At what level or levels was the mistaken behavior that the teacher described?
2. **What goes into the decision to intervene?**
   a. Observe a situation when a teacher had to decide whether to intervene. Respecting the privacy of the teacher, how did the decision correspond to the discussion about intervention in the chapter? Refer to the issues of withitness, the intensity of the mistaken behavior—marginal to serious—and the degree of firmness of the intervention.
   b. Interview a teacher about how she decides whether intervention in a situation is needed. Does having one or two children or a larger group involved in an intervention make a difference? How does the teacher decide how firm to be during the intervention?
3. **What are five quick intervention strategies?**
   a. Observe one of the five strategies in use. How did the teacher use the strategy? How did the child or children respond? What did you learn from the observation about the intervention strategy?
   b. Interview a teacher about which of the five strategies she has used. How conscious is the teacher of using the strategy? How often does she use it? How comfortable is the teacher with the strategy? Why?
4. **How does the teacher respond to mistaken behavior reported by children?**
   a. Observe an instance of child-report. Referring to the section as a guide, what seemed to be the motivations of the child in making the report? How did the teacher handle the situation? What seemed to be the effect on the child who reported?
   b. Interview a teacher about tattling. How does the teacher handle child-report? How do the teacher's views compare or contrast with the material on child-report in the text?
5. **What are five strategies when interventions require follow-up?**
   a. Observe an instance of serious mistaken behavior. Which of the strategies did the teacher use? How did she use them? What did you learn about working with serious mistaken behavior from your observation?
   b. Interview a teacher about her approach when intervening during serious mistaken behavior. What does she try to accomplish at the point of the conflict? After the parties involved have cooled down? Which of the five strategies did the teacher discuss? What did she have to say about them?

6. **Why take the time to problem-solve mistaken behavior?**
   a. Observe an instance when you believe a teacher took a problem-solving approach to mistaken behavior. What was the outcome for the children involved? What was the outcome for the teacher? What did you learn from the observation about using problem-solving strategies with mistaken behavior?
   b. Interview a teacher who takes a problem-solving approach to mistaken behavior. What are the priorities of the teacher when she intervenes? What does the teacher want children to learn when she intervenes? How do the teacher's priorities compare with those of the chapter?
7. **How does the teacher build cooperation with parents?**
   a. Observe, and if possible participate in, an instance of teacher-parent communication outside the classroom—a conference, parent meeting, home visit, etc. How did the teacher's priorities compare with those of the chapter? What seemed to be the result in terms of teacher-parent cooperation?
   b. Interview a teacher about a family that she was uncomfortable with or had trouble understanding. How did the teacher communicate with the family to build cooperation? How satisfied was the teacher with the success of the effort?

RECOMMENDED RESOURCES

Curry, N. E., & Arnaud, S. H. (1995). Personality difficulties in preschool children as revealed through play themes and styles. *Young Children, 50*(4), 4–9.

Galinsky, E. (1988). Parents and teacher-caregivers. Sources of tension, sources of support. *Young Children, 43*(3), 4–12.

Morgan, E. L. (1989). Talking with parents when concerns come up. *Young Children, 44*(2), 52–56.

Rosenthal, D. M., & Sawyers, J. Y. (1996). Building successful home/school partnerships: Strategies for parent support and involvement. *Childhood Education, 72*(4), 194–199.

Wichert, S. (1991, March). Solving problems together. *Scholastic Prekindergarten Today,* 46–52.

REFERENCES

Boyer, E. L. (1992). *Ready to learn: A mandate for the nation.* Princeton, NJ: The Carnegie Foundation for the Advancement of Teaching.

Carlsson-Paige, N., & Levin, D. E. (1992). Making peace in violent times: A constructivist approach to conflict resolution. *Young Children, 48*(1), 4–13.

Charles, C. M. (1996). *Building classroom discipline.* White Plains, NY: Longman, Inc.

Clewett, A. S. (1988). Guidance and discipline: Teaching young children appropriate behavior. *Young Children, 43*(4), 26–36.

Coleman, M. (1997). Families and schools: In search of common ground. *Young Children, 52*(5), 14–21.

Curry, N. E., & Arnaud, S. H. (1995). Personality difficulties in preschool children as revealed through play themes and styles. *Young Children, 50*(4), 4–9.

Curwin, R. L., & Mendler, A. N. (1989). *Discipline with dignity*. Alexandria, VA: Association for Supervision and Curriculum Development.

Dinwiddie, S. A. (1994). The saga of Sally, Sammy, and the red pen: Facilitating children's social problem-solving. *Young Children, 49*(5), 13–19.

Galinsky, E. (1988). Parents and teacher-caregivers: Sources of tension, sources of support. *Young Children, 43*(3), 4–12.

Gartrell, D. J. (1995). Misbehavior or mistaken behavior. *Young Children, 50*(5), 27–34.

Gartrell, D. J. (1997, September). Beyond discipline to guidance. *Young Children.*

Ginott, H. (1972). *Teacher and child.* New York: Macmillan Publishing Company.

Girard, K., & Koch, S. J. (1996). *Conflict resolution in the schools.* San Francisco: Jossey-Bass Publishers.

Glasser, W. (1969). *Schools without failure.* New York: Harper and Row.

Greenberg, P. (1988). Ideas that work with young children. Avoiding 'me against you' discipline. *Young Children, 44*(1), 24–29.

Greenberg, P. (1989). Ideas that work with young children. Parents as partners in young children's development and education: A new American fad? Why does it matter? *Young Children, 44*(4), 61–75.

Heath, H. E. (1994). Dealing with difficult behaviors—Teachers plan with parents. *Young Children, 49*(5), 20–24.

Hendrick, J. (1992). Where does it all begin? Teaching the principles of democracy in the early years. *Young Children, 47*(3), 51–53.

Jones, F. H. (1993). Instructor's guide: Positive classroom discipline. Santa Cruz, CA: Fredric H. Jones & Associates.

Kantrowitz, B., & Wingert, P. (1989, 17 April) How kids learn. *Newsweek,* 50–56. New York: Newsweek, Inc.

Kounin, J. (1977). Discipline and group management in classrooms. From first edition, (p. 259) New York: Holt, Rinehart and Winston.

Morgan, E. L. (1989). Talking with parents when concerns come up. *Young Children, 44*(2), 52–56.

Pirtle, S. (1995). *Conflict management workshop guide.* Shelburne Falls, MA: The Discovery Center.

Reynolds, E. (1996). *Guiding young children: A child-centered approach.* Mountain View, CA: Mayfield Publishing Company.

Rosenthal, D. M., & Sawyers, J. Y. (1996). Building successful home/school partnerships: Strategies for parent support and involvement. *Childhood Education, 72*(4), 194–199.

Slaby, R. G., Roedell, W. C., Arezzo, D., & Hendrix, K. (1995). *Early violence prevention: Tools for teachers of young children.* Washington, DC: National Association for the Education of Young Children.

Wichert, S. (1991, March). Solving problems together. *Scholastic Prekindergarten Today,* 46–52.

11

Guidance Through Intervention

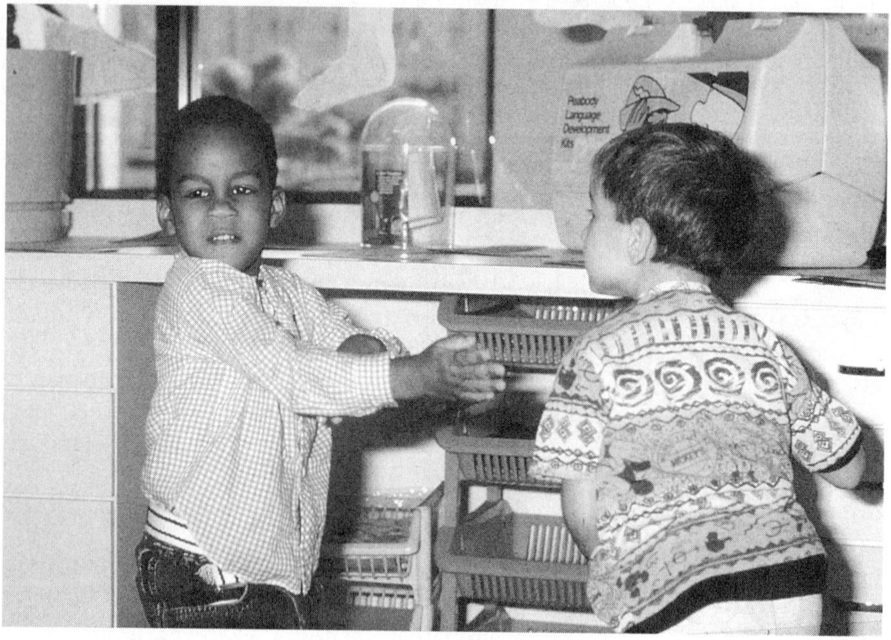

GUIDING QUESTIONS

As you read Chapter 11, you will discover answers to the following questions:

- **What conditions make intervention necessary?**
- **What are three methods of crisis management?**
- **What techniques assist the teacher to manage personal feelings of anger?**
- **What are strategies for working with Level Three strong needs mistaken behavior?**
- **What are considerations when teachers and parents disagree?**

From early experiences in baby-sitting or high school child development classes, some young adults gravitate toward early childhood education in college. After teaching in the upper grades, other adults shift to early age groups, feeling they can relate more comfortably with young children. The opportunity to be fully nurturing within the teaching role, and the rewards for being so, motivates many women and a small but growing number of men toward early childhood education.

Teachers want to be friendly and supportive toward young children. Aware of the trust that is placed in them, early childhood teachers take seriously the decision "to discipline." They worry about hurting feelings and losing children's friendship. They are concerned about what they or a child might do when emotions run high. They wonder how intervention will affect other children and the atmosphere of the class. They fear the self-doubt and shame that occurs if they overreact. They may feel anxiety as well about what a child may say to a parent, and what the parent may do in response.

Still, sometimes intervention is necessary, and timely intervention is the measure and foundation of the authenticity of the teacher (Gartrell, 1997). Enforced limits provide security for the child, other children, and the teacher (Slaby et al., 1995). To paraphrase Dreikurs (1972), reluctance to intervene in the face of harm or serious disruption marks an unproductive level of teacher permissiveness, as distinct from democratic discipline [guidance].

A premise of Unit Three is that even in crisis situations, intervention techniques remain problem-solving in nature, intended to guide and not to punish. Chapter 10

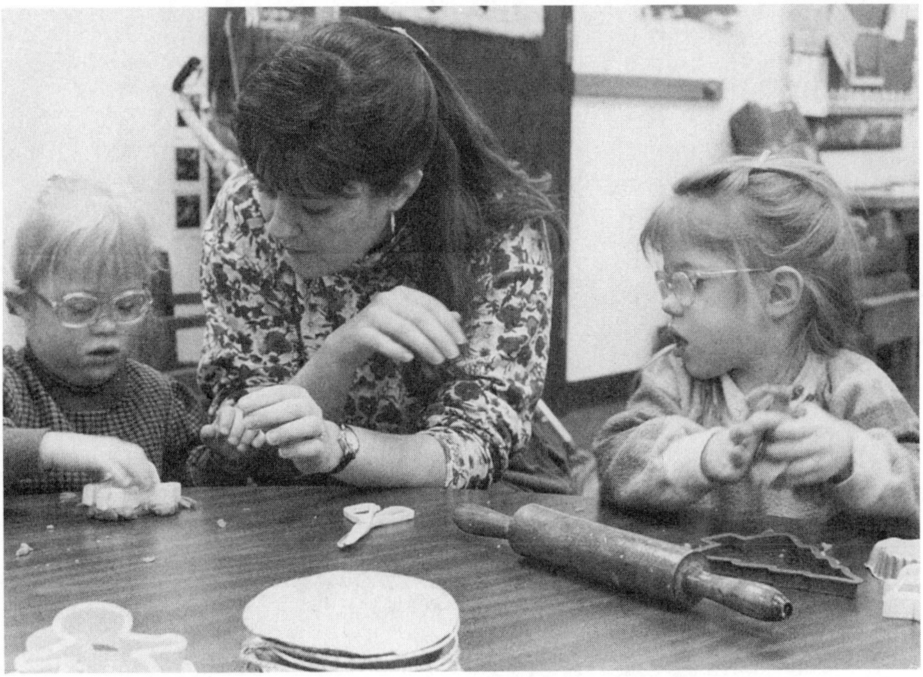

The opportunity to be nurturing within the teaching role motivates many toward early childhood education.

examined strategies for solving "routine" problems in the classroom. The strategies discussed were for those situations that could be resolved without undue difficulty, either immediately or with follow-up. Chapter 11 examines serious mistaken behavior, when strong emotions make the use of words to solve problems difficult.

CONDITIONS THAT MAKE INTERVENTION NECESSARY

Varying tolerance levels toward mild mistaken behaviors mean that teachers differ in responses to these situations. To maintain consistency in response to mild mistaken behaviors, teachers do well to link interventions to established guidelines, work to understand the child and the situation, and self-monitor moods and response tendencies. In contrast to mild mistaken behaviors, a large majority of teachers choose to intervene when:

1. children cannot resolve a situation themselves, and the situation is deteriorating;
2. one or more children cause serious disruption to the education process;
3. the danger of harm exists.

In the event of serious mistaken behavior, often two or all three of these conditions are present; virtually all teachers would then intervene.

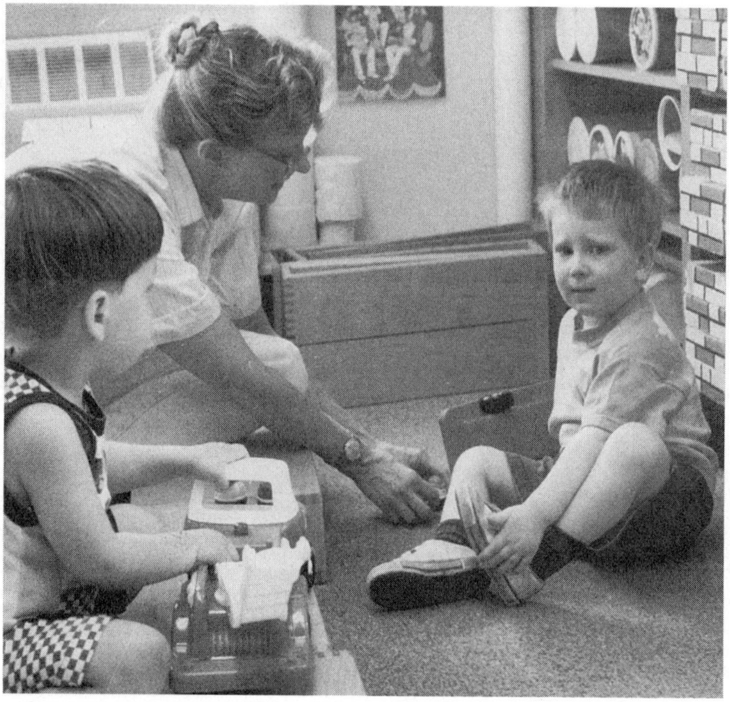

When children have lost control, the teacher uses a combination of intervention strategies.

Whenever possible, if the teacher can control the situation with intervention strategies discussed in the previous chapter—negotiation reminders, body language, humor, brief comments, inviting or requesting choices, describing situations, and directing behaviors—such strategies are desirable. They minimize classroom disruption, cause minimum shock to children, and restore equilibrium effectively. When children have lost control, however, the nature of the intervention becomes more involved. The teacher then uses a *combination of intervention strategies* for the purpose of resolving the conflict.

1. (Deteriorating situation): Nigel was in the space under a four-sided climber playing by himself. Dinee opened the door and started to come in. Nigel pushed against the door and said, "You can't come in here." Dinee pushed her way in, and the two were yelling at each other when the teacher arrived.

With firmness she said to both: "You are having a problem, so let's see if we can solve this problem, or you can play somewhere else." Nigel made a fist at Dinee, who hit his fist and then pushed him back. The loud voices got louder. The teacher, halfway in the door, put a hand on each child's shoulder and stated: "You have decided. Please separate, and we will talk about this later."

Dinee left, but Nigel lay down and began to cry. Outside the climber, the teacher sat by him for a bit and got him started on a favorite puzzle. Later, the teacher talked with the children about how they felt they might handle the problem "next time," and how they could be friends again.

2. (Serious disruption): Although the teacher had given a "five-minute warning," Randy was not ready to stop using the Legos as clean-up began. The teacher asked him to help put the Legos away, but Randy instead grabbed several loose ones and brought them to where he was building. The teacher went over to Randy and told him he could leave his structure for later, but he would have to put the new Legos away. Randy became upset and began to throw them. After ducking and bobbing, the teacher approached Randy, looked him in the eye and stated firmly, "Randy, I know you are angry, but Legos are not for throwing. Let's go sit so that you can cool down." She looked at the assistant teacher who nodded and took over supervising clean-up. The teacher took Randy's hand, and the two sat down. After he calmed down, the two talked about what happened and what he could do differently next time. At the end of clean-up, the teacher made sure that Randy successfully joined the next activity.

3. (Danger of harm): Darwin and Rita were painting on opposite sides of an easel. Darwin peeked around the side and painted some red on Rita's blue sky. Rita painted blue on Darwin's bare arm. Darwin dropped his brush and pushed Rita down. Rita yelled and while sitting began to kick Darwin's ankles. Looking furious, Darwin was in the act of pouncing when the teacher arrived and restrained him.

Darwin struggled with the teacher to get loose until he realized that he couldn't. After a few minutes in the teacher's "bear hug," with the teacher speaking soothingly to him, Darwin quieted down. When she felt she could leave him, the teacher tended to Rita, who was still sitting on the floor. She followed-up later with the children together. She asked each to explain what happened and how they felt. She let them know how she felt about the conflict, and got them to agree on a nonviolent course of action they could take next time.

In these three situations the teacher chose to resolve conflicts by nonpunitive intervention. In each case, the teacher worked to establish limits, order, reconciliation, and acceptable behavior alternatives for the future. During a conflict, all involved are at risk for psychological and physical harm. For this reason, crisis intervention is neither easy nor pleasant. When any or all three conditions are present—a situation deteriorates, serious disruption occurs, the danger of harm exists—intervention becomes necessary. Firm, friendly *nonpunitive intervention* is the measure of the value the teacher places in the guidance approach.

CRISIS MANAGEMENT TECHNIQUES

Crises are conflicts that get out of hand. Crises occur when emotions are running high, and the communication process is breaking down. In **crisis intervention,** the teacher makes a final effort to restore communication so that mediation can occur. If this is impossible, the teacher works to restore order, so that guidance techniques can be used when emotions have cooled down.

The three previously illustrated situations constitute typical early childhood classroom crises. Among the intervention techniques the teachers used were *commanding cooperation, separation,* and *physical restraint.* These procedures are fundamental **crisis management techniques** and each is discussed further.

Commanding Cooperation

In a guidance approach, the teacher matches the intensity of the intervention to the seriousness of the mistaken behavior. Chapter 10 introduced *giving choices* as a useful intervention procedure. At a prevention level, the teacher frequently works to *invite cooperation:* "I need some superstrong helpers to move the chairs." At a problem-solving level, the teacher *requests cooperation:* "As soon as the books are on the shelves and the blocks are in the box, we can go outside." At the crisis level, the teacher sometimes *commands cooperation:* "Brett, you choose: Use words to express your feelings, or go to another part of the room and cool down."

When commanding cooperation, the teacher is not making an ultimatum—"Either you shape up, or I will make you." Ultimatums set up adversarial relationships between teachers and children that undermine mutual trust (Greenberg, 1988). Instead, the adult requests children to choose a personal course of action and teaches them that they have some control in the situation. The child may not like the options, but the fact that he can choose retains dignity, in contrast to the "do it or else" alternative imposed by a threat.

Referring to Anecdote 1, Dinee and Nigel may choose to use words—the in-choice. In this case the communication process is restored and mediation becomes possible. If the children continue to use violence, they have elected to separate from the situation—the out-choice—their decision is respected, and the teacher later uses guidance methods to teach them more effective behavior alternatives.

The command for cooperation is a *method of first resort* among crisis techniques because it holds out the possibility of mediation to resolve the difficulty. This method

A common command for cooperation is that children discuss a conflict or play elsewhere. The teacher stands by to mediate to resolve the difficulty, or initiates a guidance talk later.

remains nonpunitive, however, only if the out-choice is a logical consequence of the behavior and if guidance is later offered. What seems a logical consequence to a teacher in the midst of a crisis may really be punishment, so the teacher should pose the "out" alternative with care.

For example, in a second grade situation a logical consequence of hitting while on the playground might be to sit and discuss how hitting made the other child feel and what could be done to help the child feel better, not to have in-school detention during recess for a week. In a preprimary setting, an out-choice for continued reckless play on a climber might be to go to a different activity; it would not be to stay off the climber for a week. A guidance talk that follows up by discussing consequences and teaching more acceptable behaviors are a key part of the procedure.

Some authors criticize the use of commanded choices, as by itself the technique does not help children realize the immediate and long-term benefits of mediation (Carlsson & Levin, 1992). Liedl, of the St. Philips School program, teaches children that if they choose to stay and mediate, they "keep their power" to be a peacemaker. If they choose not to use words, they lose their power—or rather, they give their power over to the teacher. (It's better, she emphasizes, for them to keep their power.) When one or both parties elect the out-choice, the teacher brings them together later, when feelings have cooled, and engages in a guidance talk. The follow-up is what keeps commanding choices in the "guidance camp." Notice, also that teaching management techniques like "keeping your power" outside of conflict situations assists children when crises occur, and is fundamental in crisis-centered guidance (Wittmer & Honig, 1994).

Separation

Separation from the group is the crisis intervention technique of next-to-last resort. Whenever possible, the teacher uses the least disruptive form of separation: diversion to an alternative activity in another part of the room—*redirection*. The teacher uses redirection when he decides not to mediate a problem. Even when separation is "only" redirection, the teacher still may opt to follow-up with a guidance talk to ensure that young children understand the events and maintain composure. Redirection is often used with preschoolers, especially ages three and younger, but it has its place with older learners as well.

In-room isolation—commonly known as the *time out*—occurs when a child is removed from a situation and placed alone in a separate part of the room, usually with no alternative activity. (Isolation in either a closed-off portion of the room or outside the room, unless in the company of an adult, is an inappropriate and even harmful intervention practice.) The time out has received criticism for overuse in early childhood classrooms (Betz, 1994; Clewett, 1988; Slaby et al., 1995). Introducing a note of practicality (maybe levity), Betz (1994), writes:

> I think that Time-Out should be used either for fairly serious matters, such as when a child is wildly out of control and repeatedly hurting others, or when a child has exasperated you beyond endurance and, if you *didn't* have the child take Time-Out, you very possibly would slug him. Time-Out should be thought of as a Last Resort (p. 11).

Actually, if a teacher is this upset with a child, the *teacher* may need a time out. But, Betz makes the point well: that putting a child on a "time-out chair" should not be an automatic occurrence, but reserved for serious situations. Traditionally, in-room isolation has been used for two distinct purposes:

- punishment for perceived misbehavior;
- a cooling-down time for when a child has lost control, before a guidance talk can occur.

In the past, insufficient distinction has been made between these two practices, with *time out* being the general term used. The distinction needs to be made clear.

The Time Out. In sports, a time-out is a break from the game for the purpose of substitution and strategy. For young children the time out should be a break from a tense situation for the purpose of regaining composure. In his clinical studies, Piaget (1960) has documented that young children—due to developmental egocentrism—have difficulty conceptualizing the intricacies of social situations. The ability of young children to "think about what happened" thus is limited, especially when put on a chair by themselves. During the time out, young children do not logically "analyze the consequences of their actions," even if directed to do so. Instead, they are likely to internalize the shame of being separated, while sometimes simultaneously relishing the negative attention received from the teacher. This developmental reality means that periods of isolation, without adult guidance at least as follow-ups do little to teach children "how to get along better." Even when considered a "logical consequence" by the teacher, the effect on the child is punishment.

As Clewett maintains (1988), isolation reinforces a teacher's sense of power by forcing conformity to his expectations. Isolation also pressures the child toward diminished self-esteem and negative feelings toward the teacher and the education environment (Clewett, 1988). **When isolation is used in retribution for unacceptable social activity, the separation becomes punishment and is discipline rather than guidance.**

Unless a child has lost control, mediation or one of the quick but nonpunitive interventions methods should be used. Separation before this point is often done for the teacher's convenience—to avoid the "bother" of mediation, or to rely on the "standard discipline practice" for when a child "misbehaves." In many classrooms the use of time-outs—meaning in-room isolation—is taken for granted. Teachers attest that it is successful in "getting a child to behave" at the time, but fail to notice that they have to use it several times a week with the child for this purpose.

The mark of an effective intervention technique is that it reduces the mistaken behavior. Ongoing use of the time out for one or a group of children indicates that the technique is not working (Slaby et al., 1995). In moving toward a guidance approach, teachers need to realize that methods sometimes taken for granted may be more punitive than commonly thought (Clewett, 1988). Teachers need to be professionals rather than technicians.

The Cooling-Down Time. Separation to help a child regain equilibrium is a logical consequence of loss of control. Often, the adult sits with the child during the cooling-down time. As the child regains composure, the adult talks with the child about what happened, what the child might do differently next time, how the child can help the other feel better, and helps the child rejoin the group. The difference between separation as punishment and separation as cool-down time is one of teacher disposition. The self-check for this difference is a straightforward question: **Am I isolating this child because he deserves to be punished or because he needs to regain composure?**

Classrooms using a guidance approach resort to the *time-out chair* seldom if at all (Clewett, 1988), and to *cooling-down times* only in the most serious situations. Guidance-oriented teachers start with developmentally appropriate, individually responsive programs that reduce the need for mistaken behavior. They prefer the intervention techniques discussed to this point, including mediation, requesting choices, and redirecting to alternative activity.

To distinguish further *cooling-down time* from *time out,* here are some additional considerations:

1. The use of a time-out chair or worse, a "naughty chair," institutionalizes separation as a form of punishment in the classroom. The chair becomes a place of negative value, and children made to sit on the chair are at risk of being stigmatized.
2. Instead of a designated chair, a child needing to be separated should go to an unused part of the room. Use of whatever quiet space is available helps keep the cooling-down time in perspective; it should be a special occurrence for which no institutionally designated chair or area is necessary.
3. Children need a cool-down time when they have lost emotional or behavioral control. Generally, an adult stays with a child while the child regains composure. Sometimes, if he believes his presence is reinforcing mistaken behavior, the teacher may have the child sit alone (Slaby et al., 1995). If the child is unaccompanied, the time of separation should be brief; a simple guideline is no more than one minute per year of age—i.e., three minutes for a three-year-old. If more time is needed, the adult should be there (Betz, 1994).
4. Routinely, at the conclusion of the separation, the teacher engages the child in a *guidance talk* that includes what the child might say or do differently next time (Slaby et al., 1995). Not a lecture, the teacher encourages the child to communicate about the situation. Part of the point of the conversation is empathy building, learning that certain actions hurt, and that hurting cannot happen "in this classroom." "I cannot let you hurt anyone, and I will not let anyone hurt you."
5. The guidance talk is one part of the *reconciliation* process at the conclusion of the cooling-down time. A second part is assisting the child to rejoin the group. Often, the teacher facilitates the transition by steering the child to a quiet activity alone or with one or two other children.
6. Reconciliation does not mean forcing a child to say that he "is sorry." Premature apologies contradict honest feelings and do an injustice to this important convention. Instead the adult may ask a child, when she

believes the child is ready, how the child feels he might make amends. If children are helped to understand their feelings and know that they are supported by the teacher, they will reconcile on their own—usually more quickly and fully than adults.

7. When it is part of the reconciliation process and not forced, *restitution* is a valuable part of reconciliation. With the teacher's assistance, a child might help clean up a mess that was made, rebuild a house that was knocked down, or get a wet towel for a bump on the head. Children can often think of ways to help another child "feel better."
8. Two common practices for concluding in-room isolation have been the use of a timer and the child's own judgment about when to rejoin the group (Slaby et al., 1995). In agreement with Clewett (1988), the cooling-down separation is a serious enough experience that direct teacher assistance is important for reconciliation.

Four kindergarten children were sitting down to "supper" in a housekeeping center. The pretend food was a large quantity of styrofoam "peanuts" used in packing. Mark, a developmentally delayed five-year-old, arrived to join the group. The table was too small and before Ina, the teacher, could arrive to mediate the problem, the children told Mark he couldn't play. Irate, Mark swept the bowl of "peanuts" on the floor and began to scream. He was in the act of dumping the four plates upside down when Ina arrived. She stooped, put her arm around Mark, and guided him to an unoccupied bean-bag chair. Sitting by him, Ina stroked Mark's head until he quieted down.

The teacher reminded Mark to come to her when he had a problem and told him the children felt sad about what had happened. She asked Mark what he could do to make things better. Mark said, "Pick up."

Mark and the teacher went over and helped the children who were already picking up the styrofoam. When they were done, Ina asked the children if Mark could join them for supper. "OK," said Shelley, "Mark can be the little kid." Shelley then measured carefully the "peanuts" they put onto his plate. Mark smiled at being included.

Physical Restraint

Physical restraint is part of an active intervention strategy to halt and discourage the continued use of aggression by a child. Some children experience aggression in their lives, and as a result of Level Two and Three needs together, use it against others. The payoff for aggression can be reinforcing for a child, and teachers must use words and actions to discontinue "an upward spiral of violence" (Slaby et al., 1995). The foundation of guidance is undermined if teachers allow children to hurt others. At the same time, the encouraging classroom promotes nonviolence in adults as well as children. The adult intervenes actively but neither punitively nor violently.

"Grownups as well as children are *never* allowed to hurt anyone in the classroom" (Slaby et al., 1995, p. 93).

The Crisis Prevention Institute (CPI, 1994) offers training "on how to use minimal-force restraint techniques that are appropriate, effective, and safe in given situations" (Slaby et al., 1995, p. 93). Especially with older children, CPI training is helping teachers learn to cope in violent situations. The following discussion of physical restraint, *the passive bear hug,* has been used by teachers of young children for many years.

Physical restraint is the crisis management technique of *last resort.* It is *not* any of the notorious methods of subtle or not so subtle corporal punishment used on children over time. Physical restraint is *not* paddling, spanking, slapping, ear pulling, hair yanking, back-of-the-neck squeezing, knuckle whacking, retribution child-biting, mouth taping, or binding to a chair. Neither is it pushing or pulling a child nor (in contrast to one author's view) hanging a child upside down (Cherry, 1983).

Physical restraint means holding a child, including arms, legs, and perhaps even head, so that the child cannot harm you, other children, or himself. Physical restraint is used when a child has lost control, physically and emotionally. A child in need of restraint may be attacking another child, the teacher, or another adult. The child may also be having a tantrum and showing such behaviors as hitting body parts against a floor or wall.

Once the teacher decides that physical restraint is necessary, the commitment is total. Quickly removing the child's shoes is a helpful survival strategy. Sitting down and clamping arms around arms and legs around legs is what physical restraint is about. Children generally will react strongly and negatively to being restrained. The teacher stays with it and often speaks soothingly to the child (Clewett, 1988). With many children calm words or even quiet singing or rocking helps; other children calm down more easily with silence.

With the realization that the teacher is providing needed behavioral and emotional controls, the child calms down. Gradually, the child finds the closeness comforting and, strange as it might seem, the passive restraint sometimes ends as a hug. (Who needs the hug more at this point is an open question.) If the child becomes able to talk about the event at the time, the teacher provides guidance. Otherwise, guidance talk is provided at a later time. After physical restraint, children (and adults) are drained. Helping the child into a quiet activity, like reading a book, promotes the reconciliation. A follow-up self-check by the teacher later in the day is needed: Did the teacher use a level of force necessary to prevent further harm and not cause more? Many programs have a written report system for when passive restraint is used. Supportive discussion with other staff members is also important.

For the third time Dean had his block structure knocked down. This time the child was Andy, and Dean began shouting. Dean threw blocks at Andy and then hit and kicked at him. Diane, the teacher, approached rapidly, said firmly "You're upset, Dean, but no hurting." When he began hitting out at her, Diane took hold of his arms and legs, and sat down on the floor.

Dean shouted for Diane to let him go, but she held on and began to say quietly, "Dean, I can't let you hurt anyone, and I won't let anyone hurt you. I am holding you so that no one will be hurt."

After struggling, Dean realized that the teacher would not let go and gradually became more quiet. Diane told him that it was no fun to have things destroyed by others and that he had a right to be upset. She encouraged him to next time use words and to come to her right away. After a few minutes, she suggested that Dean do some puzzles, which he did. Dean later asked to sit by Diane during snack—much to the teacher's relief.

Children show serious mistaken behavior when they cannot cope with trouble in their lives on their own. Indeed, any child is entitled to a "Level Three day" when nothing goes well and emotions run high. The crisis management techniques discussed here support children so that self-esteem is not further deflated by punitive teacher reaction. When serious mistaken behavior continues, however, crisis management techniques in themselves are not enough. A comprehensive strategy for addressing Level Three mistaken behavior is discussed later in this chapter.

WHEN TEACHERS FEEL ANGER

Because teachers are human, they feel anger. The source of the anger may be the children themselves—a child who manipulates or harms others—or a group that too many times fails to live up to expectations. The source may be beyond immediate teacher-child transactions, such as a parent who does not follow through, a fellow staff member who does not agree, or a friend or family member who lets us down. In 1972, Ginott pointed out that teacher preparation programs rarely educate about anger and how to handle it—a shortcoming still widely true today.

The teacher of young children may feel particularly guilty about anger—because consistent nurturing is such an expected part of this role. Yet, pre-kindergarten teachers no less than secondary teachers face anger within themselves. The issue is not feeling guilty about the reality of this emotion; the issue is how we manage the anger we feel.

Teachers generally can improve their management of anger through three steps:

1. monitoring feelings and making adjustments;
2. using safeguards when expressing anger;
3. practicing reconciliation.

Monitor Feelings; Make Adjustments

An effective anger management strategy begins before a crisis occurs. Teachers need to *self-monitor* moods and predispositions. Like children, all teachers are entitled to "Level Three days." For physical and emotional reasons, all teachers occasionally function at the survival level. Perhaps in the 21st century, more teaching contracts will include paid personal leave policies ("mental health days") to allow for this aspect of the human condition. In the meantime, teachers—both men and women—do well to prepare contingency plans for when they are emotionally or physically "down." The following coping strategies were suggested by participants in early childhood classes and teacher workshops in the upper Midwest.

1. Rather than show videos on a routine basis, a kindergarten teacher only uses them for two special purposes: to tie the video directly into the curriculum or to provide relief for the teacher. He talks regularly with the children about their favorite videos and for the second purpose always has a few favorites on hand.
2. A third grade teacher keeps a list of high-interest, largely self-directed activities to use when she is overtired or has a sinus headache.
3. Three first grade teachers have an agreement among themselves and with their rotating teacher aide, that for "special occurrences," the aide spends more time in a particular classroom. A Level Three day is an accepted "special occurrence."
4. In several preschool programs, teachers and aides work as "teaching teams," rather than in sharply defined professional and paraprofessional roles. As needed, one or the other adult can assume more leadership on a particular day.
5. In both preschool and elementary school classrooms, on Level Three days one member of a teaching team asks another to work with a child who shows frequent mistaken behavior. (By way of illustration, a kindergarten

A long-used coping strategy for down days is free time for children, outside when possible.

teacher states: "I have a good relationship with the special education teacher who works with three children in my room. Most days, I work fine with a particular 'active-alert' child. Once in a while, I rely on Jan to help with this child. We have become a real team.")

6. A first grade teacher, on days when he is overly tired, intentionally soft-pedals expectations for two children in his class, whom he otherwise "might come down hard on." (On these days he also fights the teacher's occupational hazard of hoping one or both of these children won't be in school—and the guilty feelings connected to this wish.)
7. A principal from the province of Ontario has a policy in her school that if any teacher ever needs a break, she will stop what she is doing and take over the teacher's class. She says it took a while for teachers to ask, but now she gets a request every week or two. She states the teachers like this policy—and teachers from other schools have asked to transfer to hers.
8. Teachers in a particular school have a buddy system. The system was set up carefully to match teachers who get along. If a teacher feels that a day will be challenging, the two might talk for a while before the children arrive or go for a walk off school grounds during a break.
9. The most frequent comment of workshop participants is that they let children, even preschoolers, know how they are feeling. In classrooms where concern for the well-being of all is modeled by the teacher, children respond in kind. Even three-year-olds have been known to tiptoe and whisper, " 'cause teacher's not feeling good."

Chronic problems with emotions that keep teachers from being at their best need attention. Just as it is important to understand the reasons for the behavior of children, it is also important for adults. Teaching is a difficult occupation. The teacher who seeks a friendly ear, counseling, or therapy to improve his work in the classroom is acting as a true professional.

Use Safeguards

By monitoring feelings and adjusting the program on Level Three days, the teacher reduces the risk of losing emotional control. But on *any* day, a teacher may become justifiably—or at least understandably—angry, even when teaching young children. Ginott provides guidance on the expression of anger (1972). His contention is that anger cannot always be controlled but that it can be managed. He states:

> The realities of teaching—the overloaded classes, the endless demands, the sudden crises—make anger inevitable. Teachers need not apologize for their angry feelings. An effective teacher is neither a masochist nor a martyr. He does not play the role of a saint or act the part of an angel. . . . When angry, an enlightened teacher remains real. He describes what he sees, what he feels, what he expects. He attacks the problem, not the person. He knows that when angry, he is dealing with more elements than he can control. He protects himself and safeguards his students by using "I" messages (pp. 72–73).

In his discussion, Ginott referred to the communication basic, "describe, express, and direct," introduced in Chapter 10. This safeguard steers the teacher toward the problem, rather than the child's personality. If two children are fighting, the safeguard might well result in the comment: "You are hitting and not using words. I do not like what I see. You will separate and sit down. Then we will talk." The teacher backs up the words by establishing physical proximity and indicating where the children are to sit. As soon as feelings have "cooled," he and the children use mediation and/or guidance talk.

I messages express strong feelings relatively nonpunitively and focus children on the teacher's concerns. Ginott discusses the use of *I* messages this way:

> "I am annoyed," "I am appalled," "I am furious" are safer statements than "You are a pest," "Look what you have done," "You are so stupid," "Who do you think you are?" . . . When Mrs. Brooks, the kindergarten teacher, saw five-year-old Alan throw a stone at his friend, she said loudly, "I saw it. I am indignant and dismayed. Stones are not for throwing at people. People are not for hurting" (p. 73).

Talking to the situation and not to the personality of the child is a most important safeguard. This "cardinal principle" pertains in many situations, but especially in the expression of anger. Ginott's contention is that when teachers express displeasure but still observe the safeguards that protect self-esteem, children listen. By using words effectively, teachers not only manage their anger, but model non-violent self-expression and conflict-resolution much needed in society.

Practice Reconciliation

Teachers, like children, make mistakes. For this reason as the leaders of the classroom, when teachers overreact, they need to model reconciliation (Gartrell, 1997). Under normal circumstances, children are resilient and bounce back (Hendrick, 1996). They also forgive easily, more easily than adults. Because teachers are important in their lives, children want to be on friendly terms with them.

Soon after a conflict, the teacher needs to reassure children that they are accepted for who they are and as members of the group. The importance of reestablishing relations is recalled by readers who can remember a conflict with a teacher when they were students. If on the following day, the teacher acted as if nothing had happened, the reader probably recalls a feeling of relief. If from that day on things never seemed the same, the year probably seemed a long one indeed.

Reconciliation is a matter of timing and inviting. No one is ready immediately after a confrontation to apologize and make amends. This is as true for children as it is for adults. Children may not be ready to reconcile with a teacher until they have had time to work through their feelings (Gartrell, 1987). After a cool-down time, reconciliation often occurs with the follow-up guidance talk. Children are ready to talk when they are not actively resisting the conversation. Sometimes, though, they will show reluctance, unsure of their standing with the teacher.

By the teacher's *inviting* reconciliation, children are more apt to oblige. The guidance techniques discussed in Chapter 7, including reflective listening and the compliment sandwich, are important. With young children, apologies, and acceptance of apologies, are often expressed nonverbally. A hug from a child says a lot, "Please forgive me" and "I forgive you" all at once.

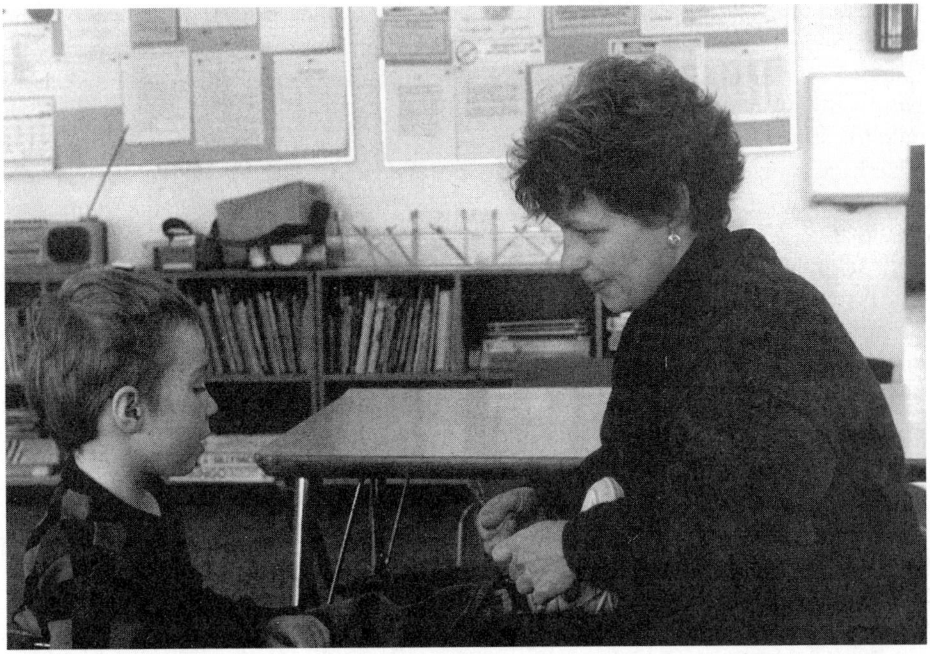

After a cool-down time, reconcilliation often occurs with the follow-up guidance talk.

R. J. was holding a door open for his first grade class while they walked to another room for a special activity. He began swinging the door toward children as they passed, making believe he was closing it. As Kaye walked by, R. J. lost his grip and the door banged into her, knocking her down. After tending to Kaye, the teacher looked for R. J., but he had disappeared. She asked an aide to take the class into the room for the activity and, getting more upset by the minute, went to look for R. J. She found him in the furthest corner of their classroom, looking anxious.

Teacher: (Loudly) You banged the door on Kaye, and I am really upset about it.
R. J.: (Crying) I didn't mean to.
Teacher: (Surprised at his reaction) What can we do about it?
R. J.: Say I'm sorry?
Teacher: All right. Anything else?

R. J. shakes his head no. The teacher decides not to pressure him. After helping R. J. feel better, she suggests that they join the group. When they sit down with the class, R. J. leans against the teacher. They both sit quietly for a short while.

A difficult challenge for any teacher is when he has overreacted and crossed the boundary between firmness and harshness, between guidance and punishment. The frailty of our humanness means that this sometimes happens. Because the skills of expressing strong emotions acceptably and getting along with others are difficult even for educated adults, teachers occasionally do express anger in ways that hurt.

Perhaps a first step in learning to recover from a bad episode is to recognize our feelings and forgive *ourselves*. Only then can we figure out how to make the best of the situation and to forgive the other. Thoughts in the middle of the night may be part of this healing process and talks with others important to us certainly are (Jersild, 1985). Children are forgiving and *need* us to be firm. If the undercurrent of our firmness is appreciation of the worth of each individual child, reconciliation offers the possibility of fuller understanding and more productive relations (Gartrell, 1987). As Ginott suggests in *Teacher and Child,* true reconciliation means change (1972). For professional teachers who care about young children, change means learning and growing.

STRATEGIES FOR WORKING WITH STRONG NEEDS MISTAKEN BEHAVIOR

Serious (Level Three) mistaken behavior is due to strong needs that a child feels, cannot meet, and acts out in relation to. The strong needs arise from physical or emotional factors, or a combination of the two. Often, the causes of strong needs mistaken behavior lie outside the classroom. Untreated *physical and health conditions* that bother a child are one source. To the list of long-standing health conditions, such as obvious physical disabilities, illness, hunger, and lack of sleep, teachers have seen an increase in less "traditional" conditions: attention deficit, hyperactive disorder, fetal alcohol syndrome, chronic allergies, abuse-related injuries and environmental illnesses, among others. Any of these conditions, undiagnosed and untreated, can cause the persistent behaviors, ranging from withdrawal to aggression, that constitute Level Three.

In recent years teachers have gone beyond the stereotype of "a bad home life" to address more openly the *emotional sources* of strong needs mistaken behavior of children in their charge. Due to life circumstances, for instance, some children show a fear of abandonment, more severe than that commonly felt by many young children. Other children may show the psychological effects of abuse: both victimization by the act and internalization of aggression as a relational style due to modeling of the act (Slaby et al., 1995). The difficulty these children sometimes experience in developing a conscience and empathy for others is a particular challenge for educators. Teachers are also seeing an increase of *post-traumatic stress syndrome,* due to violence perpetrated on children themselves or others in their presence. Once thought to affect mainly soldiers in war, experts now recognize that violence in families and neighborhoods can impact severely the sensibilities of young children (Rogers, Andre, & Hawley, 1996). Too often in our society, the effects of these traumatic conditions cause the continuing, extreme behavior that is characteristic of Level Three.

The teacher must react firmly to serious mistaken behavior, for the well-being of all concerned. Because young children who have problems easily internalize guilt, however, strategies for assisting them cannot be reactive alone. Discipline is not enough. Experts from many related fields have recognized that a comprehensive approach is needed with children having strong unmet needs. In the last twenty years, writers from the differing contexts of preschool, elementary, middle school, *secondary,* and special education have advocated a comprehensive or *collaborative* approach (Boyer, 1992).

At the preschool level, Head Start has given impetus to looking at children's behavior from an **ecological perspective** (Lombardi, 1990) that includes the social, cultural, economic, health, and behavioral circumstances affecting the family. The nursery school movement also has tended to view behavior from the broader child and family context (Moore & Kilmer, 1973). Such writers as Heath (1994), Curry & Arnaud (1995), Reynolds (1996), and Honig (1986) have recognized the importance of comprehensive strategies for addressing the behavior of young children having problems.

At the elementary/secondary levels, the Teacher Assistance Team procedure articulated by Chalfant et al. (1979) has become a widely accepted model "for within building problem-solving." Strengths of the model are its encouragement of teacher collaboration and nonjudgmental approach to the problems of children and teachers alike.

The Contribution of Special Education

Because of the nature of serious learning and behavior problems, special educators have developed systematic assessment, planning, and intervention strategies to assist children with disabilities. In use nationwide since the 1970s, the Individual Education Plan (IEP) is collaborative—in that it involves the input of a range of staff, as well as parents—and comprehensive, tailored to the complexity of needs identified through the IEP assessment.

Labeling or Diagnosis. Despite its promise, special education has suffered from an "image problem" that has worked against its effectiveness in the lives of young children. A widespread criticism of special education intervention is that children "must be labeled to be served." The intentions behind this sentiment are humane. Reacting to the idea that "labeling is disabling," the belief is that a child labeled with a behavioral disability probably will suffer more from a negative self-fulfilling prophecy than gain from the special education assistance.

The fallacy of this view lies in adults' inability to distinguish between the processes of **labeling** and **diagnosis.** A label is a judgmental shortcut that others use to put a child in a behavioral category: *hyper, rowdy, withdrawn,* etc. Labels do injustice because they blind adults to other behaviors and qualities of the child. By fixating on the labeled behaviors, the child becomes stigmatized and is undermined in the effort to grow and change.

Diagnosis is the process used by helping professionals to determine systematically the nature of a child's difficulty *to empower the child to overcome it.* Adults have the power to interpret diagnoses in different ways. A special education diagnosis only becomes detrimental when adults use the diagnosis as a label.

As an illustration, the difference is between a child who is labeled *hyper* by his teachers and a child who receives a diagnosis of having attention deficit-hyperactive disorder through a special education assessment. In the first case, teachers commonly use general isolation, enforced seat-work, and frequent time outs. The behavior does not change and remains disturbing to children and teachers alike. In the second case, the child receives counseling and perhaps diet restrictions or prescribed medications. The classroom staff, special education teachers, and parent(s) actively monitor the situation; and, in most cases the child's behavior changes. With the change, the label no longer fits and the child becomes more free to change and grow.

At its best, special education intervention involves close collaboration between classroom staff, specialists, parents, and the child (McCormack & Feeney, 1995). In such situations, adults work together to liberate children from the problems that result in Level Three mistaken behavior and the effects of consequent labels. The proactive approach to young children with problems used in the guidance approach builds from the special education experience.

Special Education and Guidance. Over the years, a problem in many schools has been denial of the precipitating circumstances that surround children who show Level Three mistaken behavior. Educators instead have tended to punish these children, thinking that what they need is strict control. In truth, punishment reinforces the negative feelings the children have about themselves and the world around them. Either immediately or later in life, the emotional difficulties and the acting-out behaviors often become worse.

In more fortunate circumstances, special education teachers are brought in, an assessment and IEP process are undertaken, and the downward spiral is lessened and hopefully halted and reversed. Following the special education orientation, practitioners of guidance hold that **children showing serious mistaken behavior need comprehensive assistance, not the stigma of a one-dimensional discipline approach.** In fact, an axiom of guidance is **the more serious the mistaken behavior, the more comprehensive the intervention program, and the more people likely to be involved in the solution.**

Many children experiencing conflicts in schools today do not meet the assessment criteria for a diagnosis of "emotionally/behaviorally disturbed." Clearly, however, these children need a comprehensive guidance program. The IEP procedure provides a model for addressing strong needs mistaken behavior. When classroom staff, parents, and other professionals collaborate, the groundwork is set for an effective problem-solving strategy for children who are having serious difficulties.

The Individual Guidance Plan

Children who show Level Three mistaken behavior pose the most difficult classroom challenges for teachers. A comprehensive strategy can be effective in addressing

An increasing practice is special education staff working alongside regular teachers in the classroom. Where staffing is adequate, inclusion allows service for many children with disabilities in the classroom.

serious mistaken behavior (Heath, 1994). Teachers do not need specialized licenses or multiple degrees to use the strategy.

The plan was introduced in Chapter 2 and discussed in Chapter 10. Of necessity, the **Individual Guidance Plan** (or IGP) starts with intervention to prevent harm and disruption. In addition the plan calls for learning more about the child, collaborating with all adults concerned, improving the level of teacher-child relations, and providing opportunities for the child to experience success. (A sample IGP worksheet is included in Appendix F.)

With due recognition to special education practice, the IGP uses the following six-step process:

1. *Observe Pattern of Mistaken Behavior*
   The teacher notices patterns of behavior that indicate trouble in a child's life. Any child is entitled to an occasional Level Three day. Patterns of atypical, extreme, or inappropriate behavior for more than a day or two, however, indicate serious unmet physical or emotional needs. The teacher observes when and how the mistaken behavior occurs.
2. *Use Consistent Guidance Intervention Techniques*
   The teacher responds consistently and firmly to the mistaken behavior, using guidance techniques. In a teaching team classroom, one teacher

may be assigned the lead to ensure predictable limits and consistent implementation of the IGP.

3. *Obtain Additional Information*
The teacher seeks to understand the child's behavior and the child more fully. Incidents of mistaken behavior are charted against days of the week, times of the day, and the daily schedule. Actions for gaining more information include talks with the child, discussions with staff, and a conference with the family.
4. *Hold IGP Meeting*
If the first three steps do not result in resolution of the problem, a meeting is held with parents, teaching staff, and other relevant adults. The team uses the problem-solving process outlined in Chapter 10 (p. 312). In developing the IGP, the team uses forms such as the worksheet included in Appendix F. The team involves the child in the IGP or shares the plan with the child.
5. *Implement Guidance Plan*
The team works together to put the IGP into operation. Consistent, nonpunitive intervention is part of the plan. A component of most plans is improvement in relationships between the child and adults. Another is adaptation of the program to increase the child's opportunities for success. Referral for assessment by special education or other professionals may be part of the IGP. (If special education services are warranted, an IEP may supersede the IGP). Counseling or other services also may be included.
6. *Monitor Guidance Plan*
The staff continues observations, reviews the plan, communicates with parents, and makes modifications as needed. If necessary, the staff holds follow-up IGP meetings.

Each of the following three case studies uses the IGP process differently. The first case study uses the IGP on an informal basis. In working with "Sherry" the staff did not follow the formal six-step procedure, but it did use a comprehensive guidance approach that reflected the steps. In the second case study, the teachers used the IGP more formally, and the steps were followed. The third case study follows the steps, but a telephone call was needed in place of the formal meeting. These cases illustrate the flexibility of the IGP procedure.

Case Study One: Guidance Plan Used Informally With Sherry, Aged Four

Sherry had few friends at the Head Start center. She occasionally joined children in the housekeeping area, but she stayed only for short periods before leaving to play by herself. Sometimes arguments precipitated her leaving; other times Sherry simply drifted off. The two teachers often had to coax her to stay on task during directed activities. Sherry got restless easily during large groups.

Sherry liked reading stories in small groups with a teacher. She also enjoyed small animal and people figures and engaged in extensive play with the figures. During

September, Sherry's first month at the center, the teachers had to talk with her privately several times about putting the figures in her jacket pockets to take home. The teachers discussed the problem in a staff meeting. They agreed that the mistaken behavior was a symptom of a larger problem, and rather than confront Sherry, they decided to try to learn more about her situation.

The teachers established that Sherry was the second youngest of nine children from a low-income family. One remembered from teaching an older brother that the father was a truck driver and was often away from home. The mother sometimes had seemed overwhelmed in the family situation and perhaps was a nonreader. To a large degree, the children had to fend for themselves.

The two teachers met with the mother, as they tried to meet periodically with each child's parents. The staff did not directly discuss their main concern, the fact that Sherry was taking things home from the center. They believed that the parents would react punitively to this information. Instead, they used a compliment sandwich, mentioning that Sherry really seems to like reading, playing "house," and using miniature figures.

They shared that they would like to see Sherry gain confidence in relating with other children because she tends to stay by herself. The teacher and mother discussed how the family could help Sherry gain confidence. The staff suggested that an older member of the family might begin reading to Sherry each day. The parent identified an older sister that Sherry was close to and said the sister could start the practice. The staff set up a system with the mother by which Sherry would take home a "special book" each day and return it the next.

The teachers commented that they also would begin to spend more individual time with Sherry, reading stories and having contact talks. They agreed the teacher would call the parent in two weeks to discuss Sherry's progress.

In a separate staff meeting, the teachers decided that one teacher would check Sherry's jacket at the end of each day. She would use guidance talks to reinforce that the figures are needed at the center, and compliment sandwiches to note Sherry's progress. One of the teachers hypothesized that Sherry might be taking things as a way of looking after herself, by "giving herself presents," as others didn't seem to give Sherry all the attention she needed.

Each day the staff informally noted how Sherry was doing and after a week agreed that she was building an attachment especially with one teacher. By two weeks, her "taking things" decreased, and Sherry seemed happier at the center. She shared with the teacher that her sister was reading her the books she took home, "and the other kids read 'em too." The teacher called the parent and expressed pleasure over the progress Sherry was making. The mother mentioned that she and her husband were trying to spend more time with the children; she commented that other children in addition to Sherry were enjoying the daily story time.

Case Study Two: Individual Guidance Plan with Gary, Aged Five

The playground supervisor reported to Ms. Martin, Gary's kindergarten teacher, that Gary "had a real chip on his shoulder." The supervisor had noticed that on more than one occasion when Gary thought someone was teasing him, he charged and pushed the child down. In the classroom, Ms. Martin noticed that Gary became restless easily and would actually need to pace for a while before he could settle down. Ms. Martin also noticed that Gary shied away from any kind of physical contact. Gradually, Gary's reactions to perceived challenges became more aggressive. On one occasion when Ms. Martin quietly asked him to resume his seat, Gary swept boxes off a shelf and sat under a table.

Ms. Martin began having daily contact talks with Gary. She used cooling-down times, but he reacted strongly to clear instances of isolation. On two occasions she had to restrain him in the isolation location. She felt that he was distancing himself from her despite her efforts to be nonpunitive.

Ms. Martin took two actions. First, she asked a special education teacher to observe Gary. During the observation, Gary had no difficulties. The special education teacher said she would come back another time.

Second, Ms. Martin called Gary's mom. Ms. Martin had met Gary's mom at the class orientation, and the two had talked. Gary's mom had said she was a single parent who was working at a liquor store and going to a technical college part-time. In the telephone call, Ms. Martin explained that she respected Gary's independent spirit, but that he was having difficulty managing his emotions. She asked if there were anything Gary's mom could share that would help her in working with him. Gary's mom hesitated then said that when Gary was four, he had been abused by her past boyfriend. Ms. Martin asked if she and the special education teacher could meet with the mom. Though reluctant, the mother agreed.

The mom did not show up for the first meeting. Ms. Martin called again, and the mom said she had to complete a late assignment for a class. The meeting was rescheduled after Ms. Martin emphasized that the meeting would only be about helping Gary. The meeting was held. Because of the abuse factor, Ms. Martin had reported the telephone conversation to the principal. The school social worker determined from Social Services that the abuse had been verified—it had been against both mother and child. At the meeting, the mother insisted that she did not want Gary to receive special education "testing" because she was afraid he would be labeled as disturbed. She said any informal support would be all right.

They agreed that a teacher aide would spend time with Gary each day. The mother was encouraged to seek counseling for her son through Social Services. The teacher would set up some "pace space" for Gary and a cubicle he could go to when he needed to be alone. The teacher suggested that when the aide was not present and Gary needed to, he could visit the school nurse, who was just two doors down from the class. The teacher and aide would work on helping Gary express strong feelings more acceptably.

The plan was put into place. Ms. Martin held a class meeting. She explained that sometimes children need special help to get along in school. She matter-of-factly mentioned that she and the aide would be working closely with Gary and sometimes they would do things differently with him. The teacher said that if the other children felt that they ever needed special help they should come and tell her; she would try to help them too. The children accepted the arrangement. Some of the children had been afraid of Gary, and the special assistance made sense to them.

Gary got so he liked both the teacher aide and the nurse. He developed enough trust in the teacher that he would come to her often when he was upset and verbally vent, which everyone thought was an improvement. He continued to pace and react violently at times when he felt threatened.

After two weeks, Gary stopped coming to school. The teacher tried to reach the mom by telephone, first at home, then at work and the college. She learned through the school social worker that Gary and his mom had left the community perhaps to escape from the boyfriend. Gary stayed on Ms. Martin's mind. One day after school a teacher called from another town. The teacher had Gary in her class, and the mom had told her she could call Ms. Martin for background. The two teachers kept in touch every week or so for the rest of the school year.

Case Study Three: Individual Guidance Plan with Wade, Aged Seven

After a few weeks of second grade, Wade began to have difficulties. He was in three fights in a week and showed inattentiveness toward most subjects in the classroom. The teacher, Mr. Harper, had to remind him to stay on task, and his homework assignments—a new happening for Wade—often went undone.

Two of the three fights occurred in the classroom. The first happened just as Mr. Harper returned to the classroom from lunch. The teacher quickly intervened. He described what he saw, told the two children how he felt about it, and separated them for a cooling-down time. He talked with each child, and then the two of them together. Wade felt that another boy had taken his "GT Racer," and a fight had resulted. The situation was resolved after Wade found his GT car in his desk. Mr. Harper similarly used mediation with the other fight that occurred.

Mr. Harper observed Wade and noticed that while Wade excelled in reading, he was having a difficult time with written assignments. Mr. Harper noted that Wade became frustrated quickly if he made a simple error. Small muscle control, particularly in penmanship, seemed to be a problem. In talking with Wade, the teacher learned that his older sister and brother teased him about "doing baby work" and "writing like a baby." From previous meetings with the parents, the teacher thought that his father might have inappropriately high standards for Wade as well. Because the source of Wade's unmet needs seemed to include his family, the teacher decided contact with the parents was important.

Wade's parents both worked, and setting up a meeting with them at the school proved difficult. Though not his preference, Mr. Harper decided to have a "two-part" meeting. Part one was with the student teacher and foster grandparent in Mr. Harper's class. Both shared concern about Wade's situation. They agreed that the foster grandparent and student teacher would have daily individual contact with Wade to improve his confidence and relations with him. At the student teacher's suggestion, the teacher agreed that they should do more open-ended art activities that didn't invite comparative attention to neatness. The team also came up with a few suggestions for Wade's parents.

Part two of the meeting was a telephone conversation with Wade's mom during her break at work. The teacher used a compliment sandwich, saying that Wade really liked reading and worked hard at tasks, but that lately he was showing quite a bit of frustration. Mr. Harper added that Wade seemed sensitive about his penmanship, and he was worried that some of Wade's assignments were not getting done for this reason.

Teacher and mom agreed that the family should be more encouraging toward Wade's written assignments. Mr. Harper suggested that new pencils with better erasers might help Wade to make corrections. Mr. Harper also mentioned some of the teaching team's ideas and got the mother's feedback about them. At the conclusion of the telephone call, the mother agreed that Mr. Harper would call with a progress report during the second week and that she and her husband would come in for a follow-up meeting in three weeks.

Wade came to school with the new pencils. He and Mr. Harper had a guidance talk about how the teacher, the family, and Wade were all going to work together to make school go better for him. He mentioned that Bill, the foster grandparent, and Kendra, the student teacher, would each be visiting with Wade to see how things were going. Kendra especially gave Wade lots of encouragement about his writing skills. The teacher asked for new pictures to hang on the "kids art" bulletin board each week. Bill got Wade to volunteer his fall collage and his "whatever you like to do outside in the fall" theme picture.

Mr. Harper provided private encouragement to Wade about his written assignments. Instead of stickers on his papers, the teacher gave more specific feedback in the form of written compliment sandwiches. On occasion, Wade still expressed his frustration graphically, but he used words and there were no more fights. Mr. Harper called the mom and shared his progress. The mother stated that she was working on the rest of the family to be more encouraging of Wade's efforts.

In the follow-up meeting with the mother and father, Mr. Harper remarked about the progress that Wade had made. He explained to the parents that Wade had high standards and had convinced himself that he could not meet them. The teacher commented that Wade did not respond well to classroom criticism and that instead he needed encouragement to succeed. For the father, who was concerned about "spoiling the boy," the teacher showed Wade's portfolio with sample assignments from early in the year and the preceding day. Dad could see a difference, and grudgingly agreed that the "positive approach" should be continued. Mr. Harper left the meeting feeling that progress had been made (and with an agreement that a special education teacher could be brought in to assess Wade's small muscle skills.)

IGP Afterthoughts

In these case studies, immediate intervention was given to address the mistaken behavior shown by each child. Beyond immediate intervention, however, the teachers recognized the mistaken behavior as symptomatic of larger problems in the children's lives. The *Individual Guidance Plan,* used informally or formally, allowed the teachers to learn more about the child. Such information is crucial if the teacher is to build a relationship and alter the environment in ways that allow the child to overcome mistaken behavior and to grow.

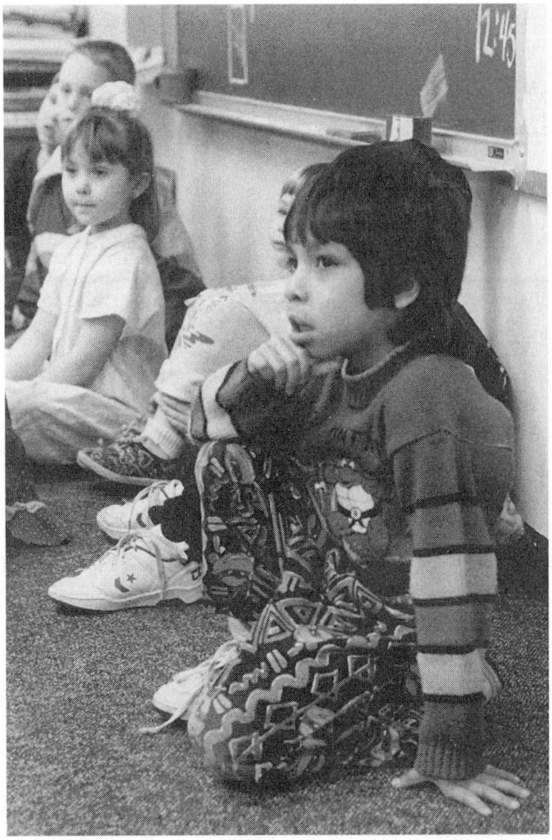

Teachers who use the guidance approach work to accept children and view them nonjudgmentally.

Teaching that uses the guidance approach can be difficult; it calls for teachers to go beyond their immediate feelings and reaction tendencies and to view children—and family situations—nonjudgmentally. Sometimes, as happened in Case Study Two, the IGP will not work out as a teacher would wish. We may not be able to change life circumstances for a child, but we can make the child's life a little easier. The professional teacher does not win every battle but learns as he tries and contributes to the life of the child, and sometimes the family, in the effort.

WHEN TEACHERS AND PARENTS DISAGREE

At one time or another, teachers and parents will have differences in viewpoints about program priorities, program content, teaching style, behaviors of the parents' own children, or the actions of other children. Boutte et al. (1992), Galinsky (1988), Lightfoot (1978), and Powell (1989) make similar points about such differences: They need not become **negative dissonances** but can serve as **creative conflicts,** which retain the possibility of being solved (Lightfoot, 1978).

Lightfoot distinguishes between these terms by maintaining that *negative dissonance* is the result of differences that alienate the parent from the teacher. In such cases, the teacher typically asserts the power of the educational institution over the parent, often on the basis of the parent's social or cultural background. Views, values, and communication styles of the parent are considered of lesser importance than those of the teacher, as an "official representative" of the school or center (Powell, 1989).

Creative conflicts arise from the diversity of life in a complex, pluralistic society in which the right of the individual to his own views is accepted (Lightfoot, 1978). The teacher who respects parents, whatever their background, realizes that differences in values or viewpoint need not terminate positive teacher-parent relations. The common ground of the child whose life they share makes differences an opportunity for creative communication, and possible resolution, not inevitably a point of division (Galinsky, 1988; Jacobs, 1992; Manning & Schindler, 1997).

Yet, the reality remains that some parents are difficult to communicate with, and many teachers feel under prepared for this part of the job (Boutte et al., 1992; Jacobs, 1992). The tendency to support the involvement of parents selectively, depending on the teacher's feelings toward them, leads to the "negative dissonance" that is important to avoid (Powell, 1989).

In the article, "Effective Techniques for Involving 'Difficult' Parents," Boutte et al. (1992) identify and provide suggestions for working with parents when conflicts arise. (See Recommended Resources.) Although responses differ whenever a parent

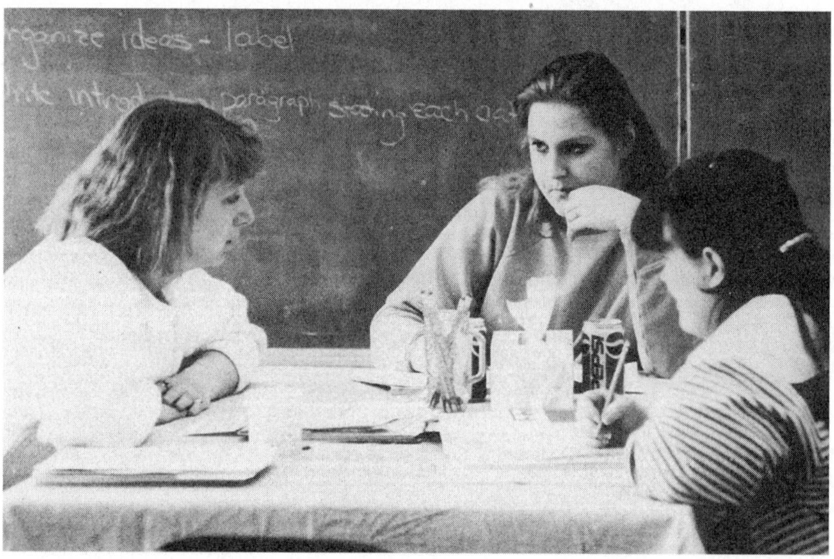

At one time or another teachers and parents will have differences in viewpoints. (Courtesy of Richard Faulkner, Family Service Center, Kootasca Head Start, Grand Rapids, Minnesota)

is antagonistic or unresponsive, teachers who find that they are in disagreement with parents engage in the basic negotiation process discussed in Chapter 10. Within this general recommendation, that teachers use the problem-solving inherent in negotiation, seven additional guidelines assist in a variety of situations when teachers and parents disagree.

Encourage Mutual Respect

Warren (1977) makes the case that parents who seem unworthy were once children whose unmet needs have prevented them from a healthy adulthood. The teacher who does not let personal judgments get in the way of involving parents in their children's education understands the importance of Warren's words.

Parents from backgrounds different than the teacher's have legitimate points of pride and values that their children share. Remaining open to learning about customs and lifestyles new to the teacher conveys respect for the family and the child.

At the same time, the teacher can take pride in being a professional and need not be defensive about educational practice that he knows to be appropriate. Regardless of differences in age or experience, self-respect is a right of the early childhood teacher. As a professional, the teacher uses appropriate practice in relations with parents, no less than with children. Appropriate practice means an invitation to parents to become involved and to collaborate in the education process of the child (Boutte et al., 1992; Rogers, Andre, & Hawley, 1996).

Model Reflective Listening

When parents feel strongly to the point of anger or confrontation, the teacher needs to listen, allow them to cool off, and not dispute or "block out" what they say (Boutte et al., 1992). To ensure the parent that the teacher is listening, he repeats the substance of what the parent has said, the basic element in reflective listening. The teacher is flexible about accepting specifics in the argument, but stops personal abuse, redirecting communication to the point of the meeting. Use of parents' ideas when deciding on follow-up shows that listening was at work. As part of the listening process, reiterating that everyone wants what is best for the child is important. Invitation for another contact in the future communicates that the teacher is serious about having parents involved. Parents who know they are being listened to become more likely to listen in return (Rogers, Andre, & Hawley, 1996).

Talk to Situations

In conferences the teacher should have specific information at hand about the child and the situation being discussed: observations, samples of the child's work, and written accounts of situations. The teacher describes events and does not judgmentally evaluate the child, the child's behaviors, or the child's family background. Citing a workshop she attended, Galinsky notes,

> Certain statements tend to create distrust and worry rather than an alliance. For example: If a teacher says, "Is something going on at home?" the parent may feel accused. Instead, try, "Did Arthur have a hard time getting up today? He seems tired" (1988, p. 11).

Basic guidance communication techniques like compliment sandwiches highlight progress and pose problems constructively. Honestly meant, open-ended questions

Honestly meant, open-ended questions make conversations with parents more friendly.

make conversations more friendly. A goal is to generate possible solutions to problems together, discussing the pros and cons of each (Rogers, Andre, & Hawley, 1996).

Invite Continued Involvement

For parents who are assertive, the teacher can work with these energies. Positive strategies include: providing current literature to discuss later, encouraging attendance at parent meetings, and seeking active involvement in the classroom. Such measures give the parent a respectful opportunity to learn more about, and contribute to, the program. As Boutte et al. state:

> Parents usually will feel less alienated and will be more willing to participate if they are involved more in the decision making regarding their children. All parents should be allowed to contribute to the program in some significant way (1992, p. 20).

In inviting continued involvement in the child's education, the teacher makes hypotheses about the level and type of involvement the parent may accept. He adjusts expectations as necessary to keep the communication going. The teacher who works around a point of difference and wins an ally has truly mastered the principle of "creative conflict" (Manning & Schindler, 1997).

Communicate with Staff and Consulting Professionals

If a teacher suspects a problem may arise, and certainly if a problem occurs, he should discuss the situation with other staff (Rogers, Andre, & Hawley, 1996). The communication may range from asking for information from a colleague who knows a parent to requesting that an administrator be present at a meeting. Venting to trusted others is also important, but communication about families needs monitoring to avoid the "teachers lounge phenomenon" (gossip). When the purpose is to improve relations with a parent, the communication marks the professionalism of the teacher. Beyond fellow staff, a consulting professional can also be a valuable resource (Manning & Schindler, 1997). In the complex world of today, teachers need collaboration to extend their ability to assist children, and their parents, to learn and to grow.

Switch to Mediation

Finally, in some situations attempted negotiation will not prove successful. In the event that parents become so upset that productive communication grows impossible, the teacher takes the initiative to bring in a third party. The circumstances of this realization might be in the midst of a conference, in which case the teacher terminates the conference on this note. The realization may be at the time a conference needs to be scheduled in which case the teacher communicates this preference to the parent. Whether the mediator is another teacher, center director, principal, or other professional, this strategy is important. A mediator helps ensure for all parties that the disagreement is not a "personal grudge" or a personality conflict. When emotions are high, the mediator can help teacher and parent focus on the facts and on the possibility of a positive resolution. Teachers sometimes feel that they are "failures" if they have to call on a third party. For the benefit of the child and relations with the family, this request can be among the most professional a teacher can make.

Collaborate for Safety

When dealing with serious family situations, the teacher needs to collaborate with colleagues for another reason: his own safety. In some circumstances, such as suspected child abuse, the teacher must by law report to authorities. As a result of involvement with a family, a teacher may possibly feel a need to assist in an emergency such as a battering or stalking situation.

The teacher is not a social worker, but is a member of a team of professionals helping the child and family. As soon as a problem begins to appear more serious than the teacher handles in everyday duties, he needs to cease being "the primary caregiver" and refer the situation to other appropriate staff and administration. Serious decisions regarding the health and safety of the child, or another member of a family served, must be made by a team led by an administrator. Communication with the family at this point is to come *not* from the teacher, but from the appropriate team leader (Manning & Schindler, 1997).

Sometimes, in an effort to save a child from harm, the possible wrath of a family member must be risked. From the beginning of the school year, the teacher works with the family to prevent creative conflicts from becoming negative dissonances. In the event of a deteriorating situation, however, the teacher collaborates with others to prevent standing out as a target. Whenever a teacher begins in a new school or program, he needs to take the initiative to determine the policy for handling serious situations. The teacher should discuss the policy with all parents as part of a parent orientation or "greeting meeting." The teacher should follow the policy, actively pursuing the assistance of other staff and administrators as necessary.

SUMMARY

What conditions make intervention necessary?

Three conditions make intervention necessary:

- Children cannot resolve a situation themselves and the situation is deteriorating;
- One or more children cause serious disruption to the education process;
- The danger of harm exists.

In these situations the teacher uses nonpunitive crisis management techniques in order to reestablish limits, accomplish reconciliation, and restore calm.

What are three methods of crisis management?

Commanding choices is the method of first resort because it holds out the possibility of mediation to resolve the difficulty. Not an ultimatum, the teacher uses the method to induce the child to mediate or choose an acceptable behavior alternative. When the child selects the "out-choice," the teacher follows-up with guidance.

Separation is the crisis intervention method of second resort. If mediation seems impractical, the teacher opts to redirect the child to a different location. If the child has lost control, the teacher uses a *cooling-down time,* as distinct from a time out. The teacher follows up with a guidance talk in order to help the child understand the situation, reconcile with the other, and become reunited with the group.

Physical restraint is the method of last resort. The passive bear hug communicates to the child that the teacher will reestablish limits. Physical restraint is exhausting but important to use with a child who has lost complete control. After the child has quieted down, the adult helps the child through reconciliation. The adult self-checks the level of force used in the restraint and discusses the event with fellow staff.

What techniques assist the teacher to manage personal feelings of anger?

An effective anger management strategy begins before a crisis occurs, as the teacher *self-monitors feelings* and *makes adjustments* in the program. Teachers do well to prepare contingency plans for when they are emotionally or physically "down" and are at risk for loss of control.

The teacher practices *safeguards* in the expression of anger. The teacher uses *I* messages that express feelings without humiliating others. He uses the describe-express-direct technique to address the problem without disparaging personality.

The teacher *practices reconciliation.* Teachers on occasion may over-react. For this reason, after a conflict, the teacher works to invite reconciliation. A first step is forgiving oneself for whatever happened. Then, the teacher works to reestablish positive relations with the child or group. Reconciliation initiated by the teacher testifies to the need of the professional to change and to grow, no less than the child.

What are strategies for working with Level Three strong needs mistaken behavior?

When working with children who show serious mistaken behavior, the teacher takes a comprehensive approach that is modeled after the special education *Individual Education Plan.* Either formally or informally, teachers use the *Individual Guidance Plan,* which has six steps:

- Observe the pattern of mistaken behavior;
- Use consistent guidance intervention techniques;
- Obtain additional information about the child;
- Hold an IGP meeting;
- Implement the guidance plan;
- Monitor the guidance plan.

The more serious the behavior, the more comprehensive the response, and often the more persons that need to be involved. Parents are central parties in the use of the IGP.

What are considerations when teachers and parents disagree?

At one time or another, teachers and parents will have differences. The teacher works to avoid having those differences become divisive. *Negative dissonances* occur when the teacher asserts the authority of the institution over the parent. Such division occurs most often when parents are of differing social or cultural circumstances than the teacher.

Instead, the teacher works to keep positive relations with the parent because the goal of each is the same, the best interests of the child. The teacher keeps in mind seven considerations for turning different viewpoints into *creative conflicts.* Based on a negotiation/mediation approach, the considerations are:

- encourage mutual respect;
- model reflective listening;
- talk to the specific situation;
- invite continued involvement of the parent;
- communicate with staff and other consulting professionals;
- switch from negotiation to mediation;
- collaborate for safety.

FOLLOW-UP ACTIVITIES

Note: In completing follow-up activities, the privacy of all involved is to be respected.

Reflection Activity

The reflection activity encourages students to interrelate their own thoughts and experiences with specific ideas from the chapter.

Identify a situation involving serious mistaken behavior shown by a child in a classroom you are familiar with. Referring to the chapter, what parts of the individual guidance plan approach did the teacher use in addressing the problem? What parts did the teacher not use? What would you do that is similar to what the teacher did to resolve the problem? What would you do that is different?

Application Activities

Application activities allow students to interrelate material from the text with real life situations. The observations imply access to practicum experiences; the interviews, access to teachers or parents. Students may compare or contrast observations and interviews with referenced ideas from the chapter.

1. **What conditions make intervention necessary?**
   a. Observe an instance when a teacher chose to intervene in a situation. How do the apparent reasons for the intervention correspond to the reasons for intervening presented in the chapter?
   b. Interview a teacher about the reasons he has for when to intervene. Compare the reasons with the reasons given in the chapter.
2. **What are three methods of crisis management?**
   a. Observe an incident when a teacher intervened in a crisis. Were the methods the teacher used any of the three mentioned in the chapter? Why or why not?

b. Interview a teacher about how he uses separation. Ask about this crisis intervention method and other methods when children's emotions are running high. How are the teacher's views similar or different than the text?

3. What techniques assist the teacher to manage personal feelings of anger?

Talk with two teachers about one of the following:

a. Adjustments they make on days when they are encountering physical or emotional difficulties.

b. How they manage angry feelings toward a child or a situation.

c. How they communicate with a child after they have intervened in a crisis situation when feelings are high.

How are their responses similar or different from each other? From the text?

4. What are strategies for working with Level Three strong needs mistaken behavior?

a. Discuss with a teacher how he worked with fellow staff, or other professionals, to help a child overcome Level Three (serious) mistaken behavior. Which steps of the IGP were formally or informally followed in the approach used?

b. Discuss with a teacher how he worked with a parent to help a child overcome Level Three mistaken behavior. Which steps of the IGP were formally or informally followed in the approach used?

5. What are considerations when teachers and parents disagree?

a. Interview a parent you are comfortable with and will give you open feedback. Reminding of the importance of protecting identities, talk about a time the parent disagreed with a teacher. Discuss whether the parent felt the disagreement got resolved successfully. Why or why not? What does the parent think a teacher should do to resolve a difference with a parent?

b. Interview a teacher about a time that he and a parent disagreed. Reminding of the importance of protecting identities, discuss how the teacher tried to resolve the disagreement. Did the teacher feel the effort was successful? Why or why not? What does the teacher think is important to successfully resolve a difference with a parent?

RECOMMENDED RESOURCES

Betz, C. (1994). Beyond time out: Tips from a teacher. *Young Children, 49*(3), 10–14.

Boutte, G. S., Keepler, D. L., Tyler, V. S., & Terry, B. Z. (1992). Dealing with difficult parents. *Young Children, 47*(3), 19–24.

Curry, N. E., & Arnaud, S. H. (1995). Personality difficulties in preschool children as revealed through play themes and styles. *Young Children, 50*(4), 4–9.

Heath, H. E. (1994). Dealing with difficult behaviors—Teachers plan with parents. *Young Children, 49*(5), 20–24.

Jacobs, N. L. (1992). Unhappy endings. *Young Children, 47*(3), 23–27.
Manning, D., & Schindler, P. J. (1997). Communicating with parents when their children have difficulties. *Young Children, 52*(5), 27–33.
McCormick L., & Feeney, S. (1995). Modifying and expanding activities for children with disabilities. *Young Children, 50*(4), 10–17.
McDermott Murphey, D. (1997). Parent and teacher plan for the child. *Young Children 52*(4), 32–36.

REFERENCES

Betz, C. (1994). Beyond time out: Tips from a teacher. *Young Children, 49*(3), 10–14.
Boutte, G. S., Keepler, D. L., Tyler, V. S., & Terry, B. Z. (1992). Effective techniques for involving 'difficult' parents. *Young Children, 47*(3), 19–24.
Boyer, E. (1992). *Ready to Learn.* Princeton, NJ: Carnegie Foundation for the Advancement of Teaching.
Carlsson-Paige, N., & Levin, D. E. (1992). Making peace in violent times: A constructivist approach to conflict resolution. *Young Children, 48*(1), 4–13.
Chalfant, J., Pysh, M., & Moultrie, R. (1979). Teacher assistance teams: A model for within building problem-solving. *Learning Disabilities Quarterly, 2*(3), 85–96.
Cherry, C. (1983). *Please don't sit on the kids.* Belmont, CA: David S. Lake Publishers.
Clewett, A. S. (1988). Guidance and discipline: Teaching young children appropriate behavior. *Young Children, 43*(4), 25–36.
CPI (Crisis Prevention Institute). (1994). *Managing the crisis moment* (catalog). Brookfield, WI: National Crisis Prevention Institute.
Curry, N. E., & Arnaud, S. H. (1995). Personality difficulties in preschool children as revealed through play themes and styles. *Young Children, 50*(4), 4–9.
Dreikurs, T. (1972). *Discipline without tears.* New York: Hawthorn Books, Inc.
Galinsky, E. (1988). Parents and teacher-caregivers: Sources of tension, sources of support. *Young Children, 43*(3), 4–12.
Gartrell, D. (1987). Punishment or guidance? *Young Children, 42*(3), 55–61.
Gartrell, D. (1997, September). Beyond discipline to guidance. *Young Children.*
Ginott, H. (1972). *Teacher and child.* New York: Avon Books.
Greenberg, P. O. (1988). Ideas that work with young children: Avoiding 'me against you' discipline. *Young Children, 44*(1), 24–29.
Heath, H. E. (1994). Dealing with difficult behaviors—Teachers plan with parents. *Young Children, 49*(5), 20–24.
Hendrick, J. (1996). *The whole child.* Columbus, OH: Merrill Publishing Company.
Honig, A. S. (1986). Research in review: Stress and coping in children. In J. B. McCracken (Ed.), *Reducing stress in young children's lives.* Washington, DC: National Association for the Education of Young Children.
Jacobs, N. L. (1992). Unhappy endings. *Young Children, 47*(3), 23–27.
Jersild, A. S. (1985). *When teachers face themselves.* New York: Columbia University Press.

Lightfoot, S. L. (1978). *Worlds apart: Relationships between families and schools.* New York: Basic.

Lombardi, J. (1990). Head Start: The nation's pride, a nation's challenge. *Young Children, 45*(6), 22–29.

Manning, D., & Schindler, P. J. (1997). Communicating with parents when their children have difficulties. *Young Children, 52*(5), 27–33.

McCormick L., & Feeney, S. (1995). Modifying and expanding activities for children with disabilities. *Young Children, 50*(4), 10–17.

Moore, S., & Kilmer, S. (1973). *Contemporary preschool education.* New York: John Wiley and Sons, Inc.

Piaget, J. (1960). *The moral judgment of the child.* Glencoe, IL: The Free Press.

Powell, D. R. (1989). *Families and early childhood programs.* Washington, DC: National Association for the Education of Young Children.

Reynolds, E. (1996). *Guiding young children: A child-centered approach.* Mountain View, CA: Mayfield Publishing.

Rogers, R. E., Andre, L. C., & Hawley, M. K. (1996). *Parents and teachers as partners: Issues and challenges.* Fort Worth: Houghton Mifflin.

Slaby, R. G., Roedell, W. C., Arezzo, D., & Hendrix, K. (1995). *Early violence prevention.* Washington, DC: National Association for the Education of Young People.

Warren, R. M. (1977). *Caring.* Washington, DC: National Association for the Education of Young Children.

Wittmer, D. S., & Honig, A. S. (1994). Encouraging positive social development in young children. *Young Children, 49*(5), 4–12.

12
Liberation Teaching

GUIDING QUESTIONS

As you read Chapter 12, you will discover answers to the following questions:

- **What is liberation teaching?**
- **What is the connection between liberation teaching and antibias curriculum?**
- **Why is liberation teaching important for guidance in the encouraging classroom?**
- **How does liberation teaching apply to relations with parents?**

In the "olden days" of teacher preparation, an instructor sometimes told education majors: "You can divide any class into three groups. The top third will learn even if they are not taught. The middle third will learn if they are well taught. The bottom third will not learn however they are taught." Today, this callous view of education is rejected by early childhood teachers.

Liberation teaching means that the teacher does not give up on any child. In Ginott's terms, the teacher who practices liberation teaching sees children beyond the frailties they may show (1972). The methodology of liberating teachers is developmentally appropriate, culturally responsive, and guidance-oriented. The teacher realizes that the child is an extension of the family system and works with the family to benefit the child.

As the capstone of Unit Three, Chapter 12 brings together the different strands of the guidance approach, that it:

- views human nature positively and builds self-esteem;
- prevents problems by accommodating the developmental and cultural characteristics of young children;
- builds the group spirit of the encouraging classroom;
- teaches children empathy and problem-solving skills;
- practices nonpunitive intervention to resolve difficulties;
- builds a team relationship with the parent and other adults.

The concept that integrates the strands of guidance in the encouraging classroom is liberation teaching.

LIBERATION TEACHING, WHAT IT IS

As introduced in Chapter 4, liberation teaching has its roots in the social psychology of the 1960s and 1970s. The term derives from such disparate sources as liberal Catholic theology and the writings of Faber and Mazlich (1974). Maslow (1962) provides a useful dynamic for the concept in his statement that all individuals have two sets of needs, one for safety and one for growth. To the extent that children feel that safety needs—security, belonging, self-esteem—are unmet, they are likely to feel stress and exhibit mistaken behavior. Personal development then becomes difficult. Unmet needs can be caused or aggravated in the classroom. In Maslow's terms liberation teaching is assisting the child to meet safety needs and empowering the child toward growth. Liberation teaching means extending the encouraging classroom environment to each child.

The work of other psychologists also applies to the liberation concept. In Piaget's terms liberation teaching is teaching for autonomy (Piaget, 1960; Kamii, 1984). In Elkind's refinement of Erikson's work, liberation teaching empowers the child to move away from shame, doubt, and inferiority toward initiative, belonging, and industry (1989). For Harlow, cited in Chapter 2, liberation teaching is assisting the child to rise from the social relations of survival and adjustment toward encountering. In the guidance theory of this text, children experiencing liberation teaching are apt to show Level One mistaken behavior rather than Levels Two and Three.

Parents and teachers may recognize liberation teaching as "plain old good teaching." The term *liberation* is useful because it identifies attributes of good teaching that are a part of the guidance approach. As well, it provides a goal for the use of guidance in the encouraging classroom.

Stigma or Liberation

To understand liberation, one must recognize **stigma.** In the classroom situation, stigma occurs when a teacher fixates on a vulnerability of a child and separates the child from the group. The separation at times may be physical, but at bottom is psychological, first in the mind of the teacher, then in the mind of the child and other children (Goffman, 1963). Thereafter for the child, full participation in the group becomes difficult. The effect is debasement of the self-concept of the victim and pressure on the group to condone and even support the act of stigmatization (Goffman, 1963).

Children most at risk for stigma are those who show chronic mistaken behavior. These are the children who need a positive relationship with the teacher the most, but often are the most difficult for the teacher to like and accept. There is an irony here. Young children at Level Three mistaken behavior are already victims of circumstances. (Children show serious mistaken behavior as a result of difficulty in their lives that is beyond their capacity to cope with and understand.) Through the mistaken behavior they show in the classroom they are vulnerable to further victimization by the teacher's act of stigma.

Mistaken behavior is a primary cause of stigma, but young children come into the classroom vulnerable in other ways.

1. Even when mistaken behavior is not the sole cause, *personality factors* can result in stigma. Children with unique temperaments, learning capacities, learning styles, verbalization abilities, experience backgrounds, or developmental characteristics can be a bother and even objectionable to some teachers. Likewise, children with a high need for attention or for independence may prove difficult for some teachers to accept.
2. Teachers also may react in a rejecting fashion to children with *physical vulnerabilities*. The "discomfort of association" or the inconvenience of additional needs cause some teachers to look on children having physical vulnerabilities with "quiet disfavor." A major group is children with disabilities:
   - established, such as a hearing loss or cerebral palsy;
   - recently identified, such as fetal alcohol syndrome, frail child syndrome, infantile crack addiction, or attention deficit/hyperactive disorder;
   - less easily diagnosed, such as allergies, or potential disabilities, like a child with a positive HIV diagnosis.

   Some teachers may also be discriminatory toward children who are of unusual facial appearance, short or tall of stature, underweight or overweight, or unclean. Gender differences, especially when manifested in exaggerated or nonstereotyped behaviors, sometimes "rub teachers the wrong way." Any of these physical vulnerabilities that a teacher finds

Gender differences that are expressed in nonstereotyped ways sometimes put children at risk for stigma.

inconvenient or displeasing can result in a child's being negatively separated from the group.

3. A third category of risk is the *social factor*. Increasingly even in traditional rural communities, children come from nontraditional family situations. Teachers uncomfortable with family backgrounds "out of the mainstream" may distance themselves from these children and their family members. Examples of social circumstances that put children at risk for stigma include:
   - income differences, when a family appears noticeably low income, or sometimes high income, to the teacher;
   - religious differences, when a family holds beliefs and/or regards holidays differently than the teacher;
   - family differences, when a family structure is troubling to the teacher by being out of the traditional marriage pattern (single parent families, foster families, two mom or dad families, etc.);
   - characteristics of family dynamics, when a teacher believes parenting behaviors to be suspect.
4. The fourth category is the *cultural factor*. Books and articles have been written about the importance of avoiding "culturally assaultive" classroom practices. (See Recommended Resources.) Educators now commonly understand that children and their families are at risk for stigma when

cultural differences are emotionally charged for the teacher (Rogers, Andre, & Hawley, 1996; Sturm, 1997). Works in the antibias literature (Derman-Sparks, 1989; York, 1991) suggest that teacher-denial in relation to cultural differences also constitutes stigmatizing behavior.

Stigmatized children are influenced toward perceiving the disparaged quality as central to their personalities (Goffman, 1963). In such cases self-esteem suffers and faith in one's potential diminishes. Whatever the child's behavior patterns, personality, physical condition, social background, or cultural heritage, stigmatizing teacher responses aggravate a child's need for safety, undermine the possibility of growth, and increase the likelihood of mistaken behavior.

Teacher Behaviors that Stigmatize

Similar to Purkey's concept of *disinviting* reactions (1978), stigmatizing behaviors by a teacher can be intentional or unintentional. Stigmatizing behaviors are those which:

- fixate on a vulnerability as a limiting factor in the child's development;
- establish psychological distance between the teacher and the child;
- tolerate or tacitly encourage stigmatizing responses by other children or adults;
- fail to alter the physical or social environment to include the child;
- stress competition and establish patterns of winning and losing (winners and losers) in the group;
- show preference for some in the class over others on the basis of social, cultural, academic, or behavioral criteria;
- ignore or disparage the background, lifestyle, and language of the family of a child;
- use forms of discipline that punish and fail to teach conflict resolution skills.

Teachers are apt to show stigmatizing behaviors especially if they feel marginal acceptance in the teaching situation. When support is inadequate, teachers are likely to find reasons that children do not "perform." If the reason is "the child's fault" or "the family's," then the teacher is "not to blame." Administration sensitivity to the difficulty of the job is an essential first step in assisting the teacher to overcome tendencies toward stigma. Support systems for teachers are important.

Liberating Responses

With the practice of liberation teaching, the teacher helps each child to feel accepted as a welcome member of the group. Supported through the encouraging classroom—children come to accept perceived vulnerabilities as a part of—but not dominating their identities. With acceptance assured through positive teaching, children become more understanding of the human qualities of others (Greenberg, 1992; Honig & Wittmer, 1996).

Liberating responses also can be unintentional or intentional. Liberating responses:

- show clear acceptance of the child as a worthwhile individual and member of the group;

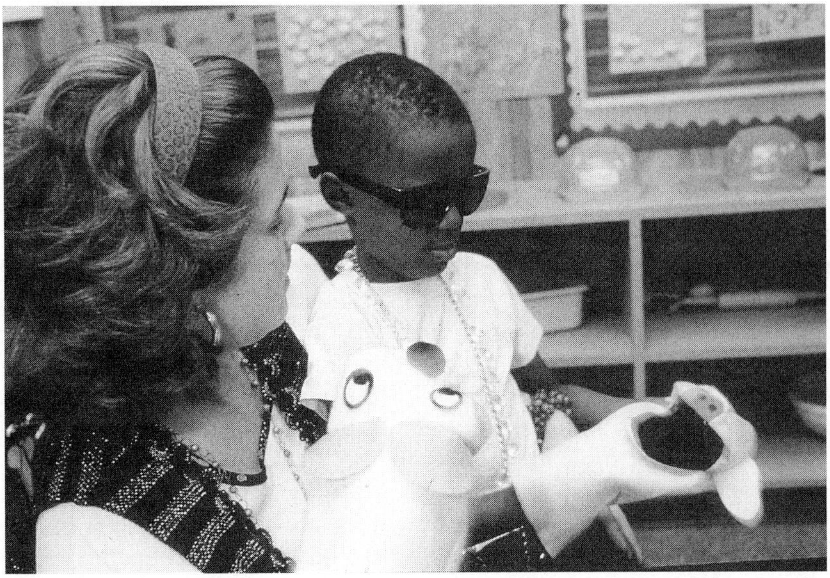

One way to encourage the acceptance of differing human qualities is through the use of puppets.

- empower the child's abilities;
- educate away from rejecting responses and toward empathetic responses;
- alter the physical and social environment so that all are included;
- facilitate cooperative and individual activities so that each child can experience success;
- appreciate the child's family background;
- sensitively incorporate elements of the child's family background and language into the program;
- use forms of discipline that guide rather than punish and that teach conflict management skills.

The teacher is effectively using liberation teaching when differing human qualities do not polarize the class, but instead they become opportunities for personal affirmation and mutual enrichment. The classrooms of liberating teachers are encouraging, caring communities.

LIBERATION TEACHING AND RESILIENCY

In an important article on *resiliency mentoring,* Weinreb (1997) points out that

> When children are faced with multiple issues such as family violence and substance abuse, compounded by the risks of living in poverty, they are more likely to be adversely affected; these issues intensify each other (p. 14).

In such children, factors of post-traumatic stress syndrome, suppressed conscience, and violence as modeled behavior combine to make the child susceptible to Level Three mistaken behavior and for stigma. In the face of this bleak prospect both for the child and the teacher, Weinreb (1997) reports consistent findings that some children "exposed to various forms of adversity grow up to enjoy productive, normal lives, even though some may suffer silent anguish and emotional wounds in some area of their lives." These children are considered *resilient,* in the definition of Werner and Smith, "the capacity to cope effectively with vulnerabilities" (Weinreb, 1997).

Three dynamics that promote **resiliency** seem to be personality factors in the child, characteristics of the family, and the social environment. Liberating teachers contribute to resiliency in relation to all three of these dynamics. Weinreb (1997) mentions that self-esteem and the ability to find meaning in activities and hobbies are two important personal characteristics that help children surmount adversity. In the encouraging classroom, the teacher empowers the child at risk for Level Three mistaken behaviors to experience success in classroom transactions.

Despite even the situation when a teacher builds positive relations with a child, she alone cannot turn around a child's life circumstances. This is a factor of discouragement and even despair for many early childhood teachers (Weinreb, 1997).

Sharon, a student teacher, developed a positive attachment with a child who previously had been unable to connect with other adults in the classroom. At the teacher's suggestion, Sharon spent contact time with Tyrell on a daily basis. After just a few days, the boy began to seek Sharon out and sit by her so she could recognize his accomplishments. On a Friday afternoon as dismissal approached, Tyrell unexpectedly hugged Sharon's leg and cried for her to take him home. Over the next few days, this behavior repeated itself. Sharon was bothered by the unknown circumstances that would cause Tyrell to express this need so strongly. She talked with the teacher and the principal about the child. Her student teaching ended a short time thereafter, but Sharon says Tyrell is not a child she will soon forget. She has kept in touch with her cooperating teacher since and always asks about him.

Teachers cannot become substitute parents or social workers for the children in their classrooms, but they can do their best in the classroom and work with others, including the parent as much as possible, to make home circumstances safe and secure. As schools and centers work more closely with other community resources such as neighbors and religious and community leaders, the social environments of children at risk can be improved. Weinreb (1997) comments that teachers: "Need to collaborate, cooperate and acquaint ourselves with other community efforts. Such collaboration, whether informal or formal, supports families, is cost-effective, and prevents burnout in teachers" (p. 18).

In a review of research about teachers' interactions with children, Kontos and Wilcox-Herzog (1997) conclude that "children exhibit higher levels of stress when teachers are harsh, critical and detached" (p. 11). In contrast, when teachers develop positive **attachments** with children, through sensitivity to their needs and consistent positive interaction with them, children's development, including **socioemotional development,** is enhanced. This finding dovetails with that of Weinreb (1997) that the single most important factor in the classroom is the early childhood teacher. By the practice of liberation teaching, the teacher provides a **protective buffer** that prevents the vulnerable child from being stigmatized and teaches the life skills that enable the child to overcome vulnerabilities. (To encourage resiliency, the teacher must help the child to meet *both* the need for safety and for growth.)

Weinreb points out that not all vulnerable children show resiliency. Moreover, as in the case of Tyrell, the limitations of classroom situations sometimes prevent the full provision of a protective buffer. Still, the practice of liberation teaching, in collaboration with others, increases this possibility. "Few studies have explored the role of teachers as protective buffers; those that do exist concur that teachers of young children can have an enduring and profound effect on the children they teach" (Weinreb, 1997, p. 19).

LIBERATION TEACHING AND ANTIBIAS CURRICULUM

Liberation teaching has much in common with the concept of **antibias curriculum.** As defined by Louise Derman-Sparks (1989), *antibias* means:

> An active/activist approach to challenging prejudice, stereotyping, bias, and the "isms." In a society in which institutional structures create and maintain sexism, racism, and handicappism, it is not sufficient to be nonbiased (and also highly unlikely), nor is it sufficient to be an observer. It is necessary for each individual to actively intervene, to challenge and counter the personal and institutional behaviors that perpetuate oppression (Derman-Sparks, 1989, p. 3).

Curriculum in this sense means that the antibias disposition is institutionalized in the educational program of the school or center. Derman-Sparks comments that antibias curriculum incorporates the positive intent and awareness of **multicultural education,** but avoids the surface treatment of other cultures—such as using the "Mexican Hat Dance" to "study" Mexico—which she regards as **tourist curriculum** (Derman-Sparks, 1989, p. 7). The author adds:

> At the same time anti-bias curriculum provides a more inclusive education: (a) it addresses more than cultural diversity by including gender and differences in physical abilities; (b) it is based on children's tasks as they construct identity and attitudes; and (c) it directly addresses the impact of stereotyping, bias and discriminatory behavior in young children's development and interactions (pp. 7–8).

A feature of antibias curriculum is its active involvement of parents in planning and implementing the program and its problem-solving approach to differences between parent and teacher (Derman-Sparks, 1989; Neuman & Roskos, 1994; York, 1991; McCracken, 1992; Wardle, 1992).

Liberation Teaching, An Additional Step

Liberation teaching is in harmony with the ideas of antibias curriculum. The basis of the antibias approach is the creation of an affirming environment in the classroom, in which children learn to appreciate others and themselves. This too is the goal of liberation teaching. Liberation teaching goes beyond the definition—though not the spirit—of antibias curriculum in one respect. Along with factors of race, gender, and disability, liberation teaching focuses on an additional element that leads to stigmatization in the classroom—behavioral and personality characteristics of the individual child.

According to a study by Bullock (1992), aggressive behavior is the most prevalent reason for stigmatization in the classroom. Children who are withdrawn and lack social skills also tend to experience the "passive oppression" of being ignored (Bullock, 1992). Though Bullock found differences for children "rejected" versus "neglected," his review of the research indicates that "many adolescents who drop out of school experience poor peer adjustments in their earlier years of school" (p. 93). Oppression as a result of cultural, physical, or *behavioral* factors is not acceptable in the guidance-oriented classroom. Liberation teaching seeks to reduce the effects of stigma, both to children oppressed by the mistaken behavior of others *and* to children showing the mistaken behavior themselves.

The Contribution of Antibias Curriculum

Just as guidance does, antibias curriculum gives power to liberation teaching. In the antibias view, the teacher is an activist who intervenes to halt discriminatory acts. In her discussion of the *power of silence,* Stacy York criticizes teaching practices that prevent open discussion of tacitly oppressive behavior:

> Teachers and schools create "no-talk" rules for classrooms. Controversial situations occur, and questionable things are said or done. A Euro-American child calls a Native American child a "dumb Indian." Three boys in the block corner won't let a Laotian boy join them. They chant, "Go away, poopy boy. You talk funny." Everyone in the classroom hears it and sees it. Children may even look at each other as the situation occurs, but nothing is said then or thereafter.
>
> Many times, people feel paralyzed and make no response. [Teachers] have told us that they fail to act because they are uncertain of the right thing to say; or they fear making a mountain out of a molehill; or because they feel they should not be influencing children with their ideas. But the silence only serves to reinforce the hurt, pain, fear, hatred, and distorted thinking (York, 1991, pp. 197–198).

York's examples illustrate the overlap of mistaken and stigmatizing behavior. In such situations, teachers need to intervene. Using nonpunitive, problem-solving techniques, they explain the unacceptable behaviors and teach prosocial alternatives. They may follow-up as well with a class meeting, a planned activity, or a discussion with a parent to reinforce the message that different human qualities are not to be feared or scorned, but learned from and understood. The activist message in

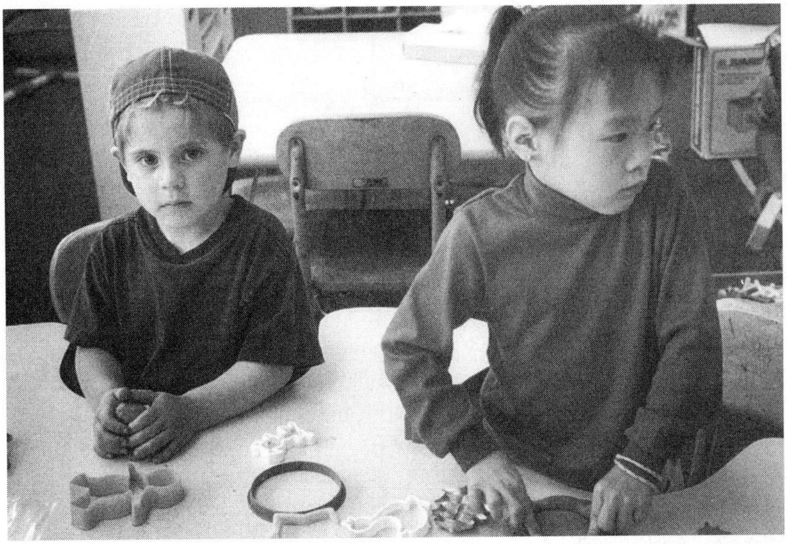

Oppression as a result of cultural, physical, or behavioral factors is not acceptable in the guidance-oriented classroom.

writings about antibias curriculum offers much to guidance discipline by empowering teachers to be liberating.

In a kindergarten classroom some boys were playing "fireman," using the climber for their station and the dramatic play areas for the "house on fire." Charlene asked to play, but was told, "You can't 'cause you're a girl. Only boys can be firemen." Charlene tried to get on to the climber anyway, but the boys pushed at her and began yelling.

The teacher intervened: "Hey, guys, do you remember our book about firefighters? Men and women can both be firefighters. That's why we call them firefighters instead of firemen. How can Charlene help you as a firefighter?"

The other boys didn't object when Steve said, "OK, Charlene, you can steer on the back." The teacher watched as the four got on their long wooden "fire truck" and "sped off" to the fire. Charlene turned a make-believe steering wheel in the back, helped to fight the fire, and even found a baby that needed to be saved. After the fire was out, the boys included Charlene on the climber fire station, " 'cause Charlene saved the baby."

That Friday a female firefighter, who was a friend of the teacher, visited the class. She arrived in street clothes and with the class's participation discussed, put on, and demonstrated her gear. No one commented the next week when Charlene and Della played firefighter with two boys.

LIBERATION TEACHING AND GUIDANCE

Traditionally, discipline systems have been used to support the content of the educational program. The purpose of the discipline system was to keep children in line so that the teacher could present the lessons without distraction. Guidance rises a notch above the usual support function. The reason is that the guidance approach actively teaches democratic life skills: expressing strong feelings in acceptable ways, cooperating with others, and resolving problems through the use of words. As the world becomes more complex and interconnected, these life skills are paramount. The skills learned in the encouraging classroom are the skills of social studies and the language arts, practice for life in a democracy.

Liberation teaching raises the importance of guidance further. Liberation teaching links the prevention of oppression occurring in mistaken behavior with the cultural and physical factors that also cause children to be stigmatized. If guidance encourages democratic life in the encouraging classroom, liberation teaching provides a foundation for that democracy in human relations—the appreciation of human qualities in the self and the other.

By empowering the child to overcome a vulnerability for stigma—and helping others to see the child as a worthwhile class member—the teacher models a precept of democracy: acceptance of the humanity of the other, with differing human qualities not a source of anxiety, but of affirmation. Human relations abilities are becoming ever more important in our culturally diverse society. Modern education serves no higher

Liberation teaching engenders an appreciation of human qualities in the self and the other.

purpose than to nurture this basic outcome. In the encouraging classroom through the use of guidance and liberation teaching, children learn human relations skills.

In a suburban first grade, Tom, a member of an all European-American class, approached his teacher, an African American. Without looking directly at her, but with some emotion, Tom declared: "Teacher, somebody's different in here."

The teacher responded, "Do you mean me, Tom? My skin is a darker color than yours and that's one of the special things that makes me who I am." Tom frowned and shook his head, but the teacher thought that her skin color was probably what Tom had on his mind.

The next day Tom's mother, an occasional classroom volunteer, called the teacher and said, "Annie, I just have to tell you what happened last night. Tom and I were in the supermarket when an African-American woman went by with a shopping cart. Tom turned to me and said, "Look, Mom, there goes a teacher."

Liberating teachers accept the child beyond the behavior. In refusing to demean, they model human relations and life skills that encourage the child to learn and to grow. Guidance, the encouraging classroom, and antibias curriculum infuse liberation teaching. Liberation teaching contributes an appreciation for the humanity of each child to the guidance approach.

LIBERATION TEACHING AND PEACE EDUCATION

The concept of peace education was discussed in Chapter 9. The goal of liberation teaching, to help the child at risk for stigma be liberated from vulnerabilities, is the goal for all children in peace education. When conflict occurs, teachers tend to regard children according to their role in it: *aggressor* and *victim*. A child who is seen as an aggressor is at risk for stigma because even if the teacher is able to control negative feelings, others in the classroom may avoid or reject the child (Bullock, 1992). Significantly, the child who is the victim is also at risk. Some children, perhaps victimized often in early childhood, suffer from low self-esteem and feel incapable in social situations. They may find themselves assuming a generalized "victim role" and continue to be a target of acting out behaviors by others.

Conflict management empowers children to overcome the labeling phenomena and find success in their efforts at peaceable communication. It allows children victimized in conflict situations to express their feelings, participate in an equitable resolution process, and achieve vindication. At the same time, the child who is growing in the ability to understand the perspectives of others is in a profound way being liberated from the vulnerability of the use of violence. Peace education, like liberation teaching, elevates all members of the encouraging classroom and teaches that mutual respect shows itself most fully in the peaceful resolution of social problems.

LIBERATION TEACHING AND PARENT INVOLVEMENT

The practice of liberation teaching means that the teacher accepts the fundamental connection between the life of the child and the family. The teacher works with and seeks to understand the family to benefit the child (Neuman & Roskos, 1994). The sections of previous chapters addressing parent involvement are based on this premise of liberation teaching. Liberation teaching with parents means that the teacher encourages the maximum involvement in the education of the child possible for each family. Over time, as trust builds between teacher and parent, parent involvement grows. Recapping information from previous chapters, a strategy for increasing involvement is suggested, using as reference points the following levels:

1. Sharing of information
2. Active involvement
3. Policy participation
4. Personal/professional development

Level One—Sharing Information

At the beginning of the school year, the teacher introduces parents as well as children to the program. The teacher becomes acquainted with each family and seeks ways to involve the family in the child's education. Families differ in the level of participation

Liberation teaching with parents means that the teacher encourages their maximum participation in the education of the child. (Courtesy of Richard Faulkner, Family Service Center, Kootasca Head Start, Grand Rapids, Minnesota)

that they are ready to accept (Coleman, 1997). Most families are at least willing to receive information. The teacher makes the most of this willingness, recognizing the two sources of information the parent will have: the teacher and the child.

On the teacher's part, she uses the methods of communication discussed in previous chapters—phone calls, happy-grams, orientation meetings, home visits, and parent conferences. The teacher works for three outcomes at this level of involvement:

- understanding by the parent that the teacher accepts and appreciates the child; ("joining" mentioned in Chapters 7 and 8);
- comfort felt by the parent in communicating with the teacher about family background, including information about the child;
- willingness on the part of the parent for increased involvement.

The child is the second source of information for the parent. If the child wants to come to school when sick, the foundation is set for further parent involvement. If the child does not want to come to school when well, participation beyond the passive receipt of information may be the best the teacher can expect. Through the foundation provided by a successful program for the child and active inviting by the teacher, parent participation is encouraged at additional levels.

Level Two—Active Involvement

The nature of active involvement will differ for each parent and with the program. Working parents may not be able to come into the classroom, except on a special occasion. They may be able to contribute materials, read or do other enriching activities with children at home, or arrange for a nonworking family member to attend the class. The use of a home-school journal—a running dialogue in writing between the teacher and parent—is a clear indication of active involvement with some parents who cannot participate with the group.

With parents who can come into the classroom, McCracken (1992) suggests a **tossed salad approach** in which parents from differing backgrounds add to the program in informal but important ways. Rather than focus on parent presentations around holidays or specific customs, parents interact informally with children and other adults—with friendships and discovered mutual interests providing incidental educational opportunities. As McCracken points out, when the families served are diverse, the tossed salad approach allows for multicultural education in a natural and supportive way. For such a program to work, parents must feel welcome and comfortable in the classroom—the job of the teacher, as leader of the teaching team (McCracken, 1992).

Another approach, a bit more formal, is to ask each family to have members come into class and share something of their heritage and their interests (Gestwicki, 1992). Every family would be asked, not just those with an "exotic" heritage, and the members could share anything that was important to them, such as a shared activity. The teacher might ask families who were comfortable with the idea to share at the beginning of the year. Use of the tossed salad approach would help other parents become used to the classroom before being asked to present. As mentioned, working parents might be able to have a nonworking member participate.

One method of parent involvement is to invite families to share with the class something of their heritage and interests. (Courtesy, *Bemidji Pioneer.*)

With planning and coordination, the teacher can provide follow-up activities for children around the topics of individual family visits. For instance, integrated curriculum activities could be set up around pets if one or more parents brought pets to share. One benefit of a family-share program is that it introduces cultural differences in functional ways for the children—even two Swedish American families would have different items and activities to share. A second benefit is that it allows each child to bridge the gap between home and school in personally satisfying ways. Some parents, who came only to share, might be encouraged to come back to the class at other times. A third benefit is the creation of a basis for an emergent social studies program across the year.

Level Three—Policy Participation

A third level of participation is in policy activities: program committees, advisory councils, policy boards. Some parents start at Level One, but prefer policy participation to educational participation. Each parent is different and progress to either Level Two or Level Three should be supported. The importance of policy participation is that it means the parent is taking a leadership role in the education of *all* children in the school or center. If the parent has begun at Level One and progressed to Level Three, the children, the program, and the parent all stand to benefit.

The model that Head Start has provided for encouraging low-income, often low-esteem parents, to become active participants in their children's education is one of liberation teaching on a broad scale (Collins, 1993). A single parent who over time comes to a meeting, volunteers in a class, gets elected to a policy council and positively influences program policy is what liberation teaching with parents is about. The gain in confidence levels in such parents is often impressive. The parents who says, "I sent my child and hoped that she would benefit, but I have benefitted as much or more," indicates liberation teaching at its best.

Level Four—Professional Development

One contribution of successful early childhood programs, and encouraging classrooms in elementary school, is parents who experience successful involvement and as a result prepare for and enter a professional field. Whether these parents become paid teacher assistants, family child care providers, Head Start staff, elementary grade teachers, special education teachers, or professionals in another field such as business or human services, the success of the parent involvement program for them cannot be denied. They began "only as parents" whom a teacher took an interest in, and over time improved life circumstances for themselves, their children, and their families.

(Journal of a graduate student) Margaret was a parent volunteer in the Head Start classroom I observed. (She had volunteered in the center previously.) A staff member said "Good morning" when Margaret arrived. "We are glad you could come today. How are you feeling?"

Margaret said, "My mouth is still sore, but it feels better than yesterday." (She had two teeth pulled.)

The teacher said, "If you don't feel well, Margaret, you can come in another day. Margaret indicated that she would stay. She hung up her coat and, without any direction from the teacher, went out to meet the second group of children who arrived on the bus. Margaret waited with the children while they hung up their coats, walked with them to wash their hands, and then sat down to breakfast with them. She reminded them how to open their milk and quietly asked Calvin to keep his feet still.

After breakfast, the teacher asked Margaret if she would like to play the alphabet fishing game that she brought. Margaret played the game with three children and had to ask four others to wait for a turn. The teacher came over to the table and said, "Margaret, the children are enjoying the game so much." Margaret smiled. Margaret then helped the children with brushing their teeth. The teacher asked Margaret if she could sit close to Ray during story time. She said, "He needs some extra attention today." Margaret sat down by Ray, and he crawled onto her lap.

Later, I interviewed Margaret and asked her what went into her decision to volunteer in the classroom. Margaret said, "At first, I volunteered because I wanted to make Alicia (her daughter) feel more comfortable. Alicia was with us most of the time and wasn't used to being with other groups of children without us. I felt more relaxed if I knew she was happy at school. Then I got used to being with the kids, and it was a lot of fun being with them, so I came back to volunteer. My hours changed, and I got put on part time, so I could volunteer more easily."

I asked Margaret what part the teacher played in her decision to volunteer. Margaret said, "On the first home visit, the teacher encouraged us to volunteer in the center, but she wasn't pushy about it. When I came into the center, I felt welcomed by the teachers. There was always a 'Hi' or 'Good morning.' The kids all said 'Hi' or gave me a hug. I felt like I was really contributing, giving more attention, and sometimes, like on the playground, making it safer for the kids. The teachers always thank me for helping out when I leave. When someone is appreciated, it makes them want to come back. If someone's not appreciated, they're not going to come back. Now, I know this is what I want to do. My family has seen a change in me. I'm starting college this fall to become a teacher. They weren't for it at first, but now they're all for it." Margaret paused, then added, "Just because the teacher got me to volunteer."

Many teachers in Head Start programs, as well as in other centers and schools, have success stories like this one with parents. The long-term societal benefits of early childhood education in the area of parent involvement have not been fully realized. In fact, measures of the success of early childhood education in general have perhaps focused too narrowly on the immediate measurable gains of children. When educators see the classroom more broadly, as an encouraging community involving parents no less than children, the full potential of guidance will begin to be realized.

SUMMARY

What is liberation teaching?

Liberation teaching is helping each child learn and grow, despite vulnerabilities that could lead to stigma. Psychologists such as Maslow, Piaget, and Erikson provide concepts regarding healthy development that are the outcomes of liberation teaching. The term *liberation teaching* is useful because it provides a goal for the use of guidance in the classroom.

To understand liberation teaching, one must recognize *stigma*. Stigma occurs when a teacher fixates on the vulnerability of a child and causes the child to become psychologically separated from the group. The effect of stigma is debasement of the self-concept of the victim and pressure on the group to condone and even support the act of stigmatization.

Because their behaviors make them easy to dislike, children most at risk for stigma are those who show chronic mistaken behavior. Children also are vulnerable for stigma in other ways: (a) Personality characteristics that "rub the wrong way" can cause teachers to show rejecting behaviors. (b) Physical vulnerabilities that put children at risk include gender differences, physical disabilities, or atypical physical characteristics. (c) Stigma due to social factors can result when atypical family situations cause discomfort in teachers. (d) Cultural factors are a fourth source of vulnerability, family backgrounds that cause distancing and discrimination toward a child or family.

Liberation teaching involves the mentoring of resiliency. Children who have suffered from violence often show the effects in Level Three mistaken behaviors. Teachers who develop positive attachments with such children assist them to overcome the adversities they have faced.

What is the connection between liberation teaching and antibias curriculum?

Antibias curriculum teaches alternatives to oppressive behaviors that perpetuate sexism, racism, and handcappism. Antibias curriculum incorporates the positive intentions of multicultural education but addresses more than cultural diversity by including gender and differences in physical abilities. Active involvement of parents in planning and implementing the program is a part of antibias curriculum.

Liberation teaching is in harmony with antibias curriculum, but goes a step beyond by addressing additional factors that lead to stigmatization: behavioral and personality characteristics. Liberation teaching holds that oppression as a result of cultural, physical, or *behavioral factors* is not acceptable in the encouraging classroom. The teacher protects from stigma both the child who is oppressed by mistaken behavior and the child who displays it.

Antibias curriculum empowers liberation teaching by casting the teacher in an active role in the face of mistaken behaviors. The teacher intervenes nonpunitively, explaining unacceptable behavior and teaching alternatives. She may follow-up as well with a class meeting, a planned activity, or a discussion with a parent to reinforce the message that differing human qualities are not to be feared or scorned, but learned from and understood.

Why is liberation teaching important for guidance in the encouraging classroom?

Guidance raises the matter of discipline a notch above its usual support function by teaching vital social skills important for life in modern society. Liberation teaching raises the importance of guidance further. Liberation teaching puts a premium on the acceptance of the humanity of the other, with differing human qualities a source of learning and understanding, rather than anxiety. Liberation teaching infuses guidance with a foundation in human relations. Peace education, like liberation teaching, elevates all members of the encouraging classroom and teaches that mutual respect shows itself most fully in the peaceful resolution of social problems.

How does liberation teaching apply to relations with parents?

The practice of liberation teaching means that the teacher accepts the fundamental connection between the life of the child and the family. The teacher encourages the maximum participation acceptable to each family, and over time, as trust builds, invites increased participation. The teacher encourages the parent to move from the sharing of information to active educational involvement to participation in program policy decisions to personal/professional development. The Head Start practice of empowering parents toward productive action provides a broad-based model for the practice of liberation teaching. Liberation teaching broadens the encouraging classroom to a community that includes children and adults together.

FOLLOW-UP ACTIVITIES

Note: In completing follow-up activities, the privacy of all involved is to be respected.

Reflection Activity

The reflection activity encourages students to interrelate their own thoughts and experiences with specific ideas from the chapter.

Referring to the text, identify a guiding principle important to you in the practice of

- liberation teaching;
- resiliency mentoring;
- antibias curriculum;
- peace education;
- levels of parent involvement.

Discuss the most important principles to you in your professional development.

Application Activities

Application activities allow students to interrelate material from the text with real life situations. The observations imply access to practicum experiences; the interviews, access to teachers or parents. Students may compare or contrast observations and interviews with referenced ideas from the chapter.

1. **What is liberation teaching?**
   a. Observe over a period of time a teacher who has been able to improve relations with a child whose behavior might be considered difficult. What have you observed the teacher do and say that seemed to contribute to the improvement? How has the child responded?
   b. Discuss with two teachers a "success story" each has had in helping a child to overcome vulnerabilities and succeed in the program. Reflect about what was common in the two teachers' approaches.
2. **What is the connection between liberation teaching and antibias curriculum?**
   a. Observe an instance or two where a teacher has intervened to halt acts of oppressive or stigmatizing behavior by one or more children toward another. How did the teacher intervene? Did the teacher respond to both the child/children who instigated the behavior and the

child/children victimized? What were the responses of the child/children involved? What connection between liberation teaching and antibias curriculum can you discern?

b. Talk with two teachers about an incident when each intervened to stop an act of oppression or discrimination. Analyze whether each intervention was guidance, liberation teaching, antibias activism, or a combination of the three.

3. **Why is liberation teaching important for guidance in the encouraging classroom?**
   a. Observe an instance of intervention when a teacher used principles of the guidance approach. Discuss the likely meaning of the experience for each child involved and for the teacher. Was liberation teaching at work? Why or why not?
   b. With teacher, discuss a child who was at risk for stigma as a result of her behavior. Ask the teacher about the approach she took to ensure that the child was included rather than stigmatized. What success or lack of it did the teacher believe resulted from working with the child? What were some of the teacher's reasons? How do the teacher's comments compare to ideas from the chapter?
4. **How does liberation teaching apply to relations with parents?**
   a. Interview a parent whom you believe to be participating successfully in a classroom or program. Ask what role the teacher had in helping the parent become a successful volunteer. Ask what the parent believes that she is gaining personally from the experience. Ask in what ways, if any, the experience has changed the parent's view of her personal development, education, or career aspirations.
   b. Discuss with a teacher a situation in which she helped a parent overcome initial reluctance to be involved and the parent ended up growing from the participation. Ask the teacher to reflect about the likely effect of the experience for the parent, the child, and the teacher.

RECOMMENDED RESOURCES

Boutte, G. S., & McCormick, C. B. (1992). Authentic multicultural activities: Avoiding pseudomulticulturalism. *Childhood Education, 68*(3), 140–144.

Bullock, J. R. (1992). Reviews of research: Children without friends. *Childhood Education, 69*(2), 92–96.

Clark, L., DeWolf, S., & Clark, C. (1992). Teaching teachers to avoid having culturally assaultive classrooms. *Young Children, 47*(5), 4–9.

Coleman, M. (1997). Families and schools: In search of common ground. *Young Children, 52*(5), 14–21.

Koeppel, J., & Mulrooney, M. (1992). The sister schools program: A way for children to learn about cultural diversity—When there isn't any in the school. *Young Children, 48*(1), 44–47.

McCracken, J. B. (1992). Tossed salad is terrific: Values of multicultural programs for children and families. In *Alike and different: Exploring our humanity with young children.* Washington, DC: National Association for the Education of Young Children.

Neuman, S. B., & Roskos, K. (1994). Bridging home and school with a culturally responsive approach. *Childhood Education, 70*(4), 210–214.

Weinreb, M. L. (1997). Be a resiliency mentor: You may be a lifesaver for a high-risk child. *Young Children, 52*(2), 14–19.

York, S. (1991). *Roots and wings: Affirming culture in early childhood programs.* St. Paul, MN: Redleaf Press.

REFERENCES

Bullock, J. R. (1992). Reviews of research: Children without friends. *Childhood Education, 69*(2), 92–96.

Collins, R. C. (1993). Head Start: Steps toward a two-generation program strategy. *Young Children, 48*(2), 24–33; 72–73.

Derman-Sparks, L. (1989). *Anti-bias curriculum: Tools for empowering young children.* Washington, DC: National Association for the Education of Young Children.

Elkind, D. (1989). *Miseducation: Preschoolers at risk.* New York: Alfred A. Knopf.

Faber, A., & Mazlich, E. (1974). *Liberated parents, liberated children.* New York: Avon Books.

Gestwicki, C. (1992). *Home, school and community relations: A guide to working with parents.* Albany, NY: Delmar Publishers.

Ginott, H. (1972). *Teacher and child.* New York: Avon Books.

Goffman, E. (1963). *Stigma: Notes on the management of spoiled identity.* Englewood Cliffs, NJ: Prentice-Hall, Inc.

Greenberg, P. (1992). Ideas that work with young children. How to institute some simple democratic practices pertaining to respect, rights, responsibilities, and roots in any classroom (without losing your leadership position). *Young Children, 47*(5), 10–21.

Honig, A. S., & Wittmer, D. S. (1996). Helping children become more prosocial: Ideas for classrooms, families, schools, and communities. *Young Children, 51*(2), 62–70.

Kamii, C., (1984). Autonomy: The aim of education envisioned by Piaget. *Phi Delta Kappan, 65*(6), 410–415.

Kontos, S., & Wilcox-Herzog, A. (1997). Teachers' interactions with children: Why are they so important? *Young Children, 52*(2), 4–12.

Maslow, A. H. (1962). *Toward a psychology of being.* Princeton, NJ: D. Van Nostrand Company, Inc.

McCracken, J. B. (1992). Tossed salad is terrific: Values of multicultural programs for children and families. In *Alike and different: Exploring our humanity with young children.* Washington, DC: National Association for the Education of Young Children.

Neuman, S. B., & Roskos, K. (1994). Bridging home and school with a culturally responsive approach. *Childhood Education, 70*(4), 210–214.

Piaget, J. (1932/1960). *The moral judgment of the child.* Glencoe, IL: The Free Press.

Purkey, W. W. (1978). *Inviting school success: A self-concept approach to teaching and learning.* Belmont, CA: Wadsworth Publishing Company, Inc.

Rogers, R. E., Andre, L. C., & Hawley, M. K. (1996). *Parents and teachers as partners: Issues and challenges.* Forth Worth, TX: Houghton Mifflin.

Sturm, C. (1997). Creating parent-teacher dialogue: Intercultural communication in child care. *Young Children, 52*(5), 34–38.

Wardle, F. (1992). Building positive images: Interracial children and their families. In *Alike and different: Exploring our humanity with young children.* Washington, DC: National Association for the Education of Young Children.

Weinreb, M. L. (1997). Be a resiliency mentor: You may be a lifesaver for a high-risk child. *Young Children, 52*(2), 14–19.

York, S. (1991). *Roots and wings: Affirming culture in early childhood programs.* St. Paul, MN: Redleaf Press.

Appendix A

The National Association for the Education of Young Children Code of Ethical Conduct

This Code of Ethical Conduct and Statement of Commitment was prepared under the auspices of the Ethics Commission of the National Association for the Education of Young Children. The Commission members were Stephanie Feeney (Chairperson), Bettye Caldwell, Sally Cartwright, Carrie Cheek, Josué Cruz, Jr., Anne G. Dorsey, Dorothy M. Hill, Lilian G. Katz, Pamm Mattick, Shirley A. Norris, and Sue Spayth Riley.

Preamble

NAEYC recognizes that many daily decisions required of those who work with young children are of a moral and ethical nature. The NAEYC Code of Ethical Conduct offers guidelines for responsible behavior and sets forth a common basis for resolving the principal ethical dilemmas encountered in early childhood education. The primary focus is on daily practice with children and their families in programs for children from birth to 8 years of age: preschools, child care centers, family day care homes, kindergartens, and primary classrooms. Many of the provisions also apply to specialists who do not work directly with children, including program administrators, parent educators, college professors, and child care licensing specialists.

Standards of ethical behavior in early childhood education are based on commitment to core values that are deeply rooted in the history of our field. We have committed ourselves to:

- Appreciating childhood as a unique and valuable stage of the human life cycle
- Basing our work with children on knowledge of child development
- Appreciating and supporting the close ties between the child and family
- Recognizing that children are best understood in the context of family, culture, and society
- Respecting the dignity, worth, and uniqueness of each individual (child, family member, and colleague)
- Helping children and adults achieve their full potential in the context of relationships that are based on trust, respect, and positive regard.

The Code sets forth a conception of our professional responsibilities in four sections, each addressing an arena of professional relationships: 1) children, 2) families, 3) colleagues, and 4) community and society. Each section includes an introduction to the primary responsibilities of the early childhood practitioner in that arena, a set of ideals pointing in the direction of exemplary professional practice, and a set of principles defining practices that are required, prohibited, and permitted.

The ideals reflect the aspirations of practitioners. The principles are intended to guide conduct and assist practitioners in resolving ethical dilemmas encountered in the field. There is not necessarily a corresponding principle for each ideal. Both ideals and principles are intended to direct practitioners to those questions which, when responsibly answered, will provide the basis for conscientious decision making. While the Code provides specific direction for addressing some ethical dilemmas, many others will require the practitioner to combine the guidance of the Code with sound professional judgment.

The ideals and principles in this Code present a shared conception of professional responsibility that affirms our commitment to the core values of our field. The Code publicly acknowledges the responsibilities that we in the field have assumed and in so doing supports ethical behavior in our work. Practitioners who face ethical dilemmas are urged to seek guidance in the applicable parts of this Code and in the spirit that informs the whole.

SECTION I: ETHICAL RESPONSIBILITIES TO CHILDREN

Childhood is a unique and valuable stage in the life cycle. Our paramount responsibility is to provide safe, healthy, nurturing, and responsive settings for children. We are committed to supporting children's development by cherishing individual differences, by helping them learn to live and work cooperatively, and by promoting their self-esteem.

Ideals:

I-1.1—To be familiar with the knowledge base of early childhood education and to keep current through continuing education and in-service training.

I-1.2—To base program practices upon current knowledge in the field of child development and related disciplines and upon particular knowledge of each child.

I-1.3—To recognize and respect the uniqueness and the potential of each child.

I-1.4—To appreciate the special vulnerability of children.

I-1.5—To create and maintain safe and healthy settings that foster children's social, emotional, intellectual, and physical development and that respect their dignity and their contributions.

I-1.6—To support the right of children with special needs to participate, consistent with their ability, in regular early childhood programs.

Principles:

P-1.1—Above all, we shall not harm children. We shall not participate in practices that are disrespectful, degrading, dangerous, exploitative, intimidating, psychologically damaging, or physically harmful to children. ***This principle has precedence over all others in this Code.***

P-1.2—We shall not participate in practices that discriminate against children by denying benefits, giving special advantages, or excluding them from programs or activities on the basis of their race, religion, sex, national origin, or the status, behavior, or beliefs of their parents. (This principle does not apply to programs that have a lawful mandate to provide services to a particular population of children.)

P-1.3—We shall involve all of those with relevant knowledge (including staff and parents) in decisions concerning a child.

P-1.4—When, after appropriate efforts have been made with a child and the family, the child still does not appear to be benefitting from a program, we shall communicate our concern to the family in a positive way and offer them assistance in finding a more suitable setting.

P-1.5—We shall be familiar with the symptoms of child abuse and neglect and know community procedures for addressing them.

P-1.6—When we have evidence of child abuse or neglect, we shall report the evidence to the appropriate community agency and follow up to ensure that appropriate action has been taken. When possible, parents will be informed that the referral has been made.

P-1.7—When another person tells us of their suspicion that a child is being abused or neglected but we lack evidence, we shall assist that person in taking appropriate action to protect the child.

P-1.8—When a child protective agency fails to provide adequate protection for abused or neglected children, we acknowledge a collective ethical responsibility to work toward improvement of these services.

SECTION II: ETHICAL RESPONSIBILITIES TO FAMILIES

Families are of primary importance in children's development. (The term *family* may include others, besides parents, who are responsibly involved with the child.) Because the family and the early childhood educator have a common interest in the child's welfare, we acknowledge a primary responsibility to bring about collaboration between the home and school in ways that enhance the child's development.

Ideals:

I-2.1—To develop relationships of mutual trust with the families we serve.

I-2.2—To acknowledge and build upon strengths and competencies as we support families in their task of nurturing children.

I-2.3—To respect the dignity of each family and its culture, customs, and beliefs.

I-2.4—To respect families' childrearing values and their right to make decisions for their children.

I-2.5—To interpret each child's progress to parents within the framework of a developmental perspective and to help families understand and appreciate the value of developmentally appropriate early childhood programs.

I-2.6—To help family members improve their understanding of their children and to enhance their skills as parents.

I-2.7—To participate in building support networks for families by providing them with opportunities to interact with program staff and families.

Principles:

P-2.1—We shall not deny family members access to their child's classroom or program setting.

P-2.2—We shall inform families of program philosophy, policies, and personnel qualifications, and explain why we teach as we do.

P-2.3—We shall inform families of and, when appropriate, involve them in policy decisions.

P-2.4—We shall inform families of and, when appropriate, involve them in significant decisions affecting their child.

P-2.5—We shall inform the family of accidents involving their child, of risks such as exposures to contagious disease that may result in infection, and of events that might result in psychological damage.

P-2.6—We shall not permit or participate in research that could in any way hinder the education or development of the children in our programs. Families shall be fully informed of any proposed research projects involving their children and shall have the opportunity to give or withhold consent.

P-2.7—We shall not engage in or support exploitation of families. We shall not use our relationship with a family for private advantage or personal gain, or enter into relationships with family members that might impair our effectiveness in working with children.

P-2.8—We shall develop written policies for the protection of confidentiality and the disclosure of children's records. The policy documents shall be made available to all program personnel and families. Disclosure of children's records beyond family members, program personnel, and consultants having an obligation of confidentiality shall require familial consent (except in cases of abuse or neglect).

P-2.9—We shall maintain confidentiality and shall respect the family's right to privacy, refraining from disclosure of confidential information and intrusion into family life. However, when we are concerned about a child's welfare, it is permissible to reveal confidential information to agencies and individuals who may be able to act in the child's interest.

P-2.10—In cases where family members are in conflict we shall work openly, sharing our observations of the child, to help all parties involved make informed decisions. We shall refrain from becoming an advocate for one party.

P-2.11—We shall be familiar with and appropriately use community resources and professional services that support families. After a referral has been made, we shall follow up to ensure that services have been adequately provided.

SECTION III: ETHICAL RESPONSIBILITIES TO COLLEAGUES

In a caring, cooperative work place human dignity is respected, professional satisfaction is promoted, and positive relationships are modeled. Our primary responsibility in this arena is to establish and maintain settings and relationships that support productive work and meet professional needs.

A—Responsibilities to Co-workers

Ideals:

I-3A.1—To establish and maintain relationships of trust and cooperation with co-workers.

I-3A.2—To share resources and information with co-workers.

I-3A.3—To support co-workers in meeting their professional needs and in their professional development.

I-3A.4—To accord co-workers due recognition of professional achievement.

Principles:

P-3A.1—When we have concern about the professional behavior of a co-worker, we shall first let that person know of our concern and attempt to resolve the matter collegially.

P-3A.2—We shall exercise care in expressing views regarding the personal attributes or professional conduct of co-workers. Statements should be based on firsthand knowledge and relevant to the interests of children and programs.

B—Responsibilities to Employers

Ideals:

I-3B.1—To assist the program in providing the highest quality of service.

I-3B.2—To maintain loyalty to the program and uphold its reputation.

Principles:

P-3B.1—When we do not agree with program policies, we shall first attempt to effect change through constructive action within the organization.

P-3B.2—We shall speak or act on behalf of an organization only when authorized. We shall take care to note when we are speaking for the organization and when we are expressing a personal judgment.

C—Responsibilities to Employees

Ideals:

I-3C.1—To promote policies and working conditions that foster competence, well-being, and self-esteem in staff members.

I-3C.2—To create a climate of trust and candor that will enable staff to speak and act in the best interests of children, families, and the field of early childhood education.

I-3C.3—To strive to secure an adequate livelihood for those who work with or on behalf of young children.

Principles:

P-3C.1—In decisions concerning children and programs, we shall appropriately utilize the training, experience, and expertise of staff members.

P-3C.2—We shall provide staff members with working conditions that permit them to carry out their responsibilities, timely and nonthreatening evaluation procedures, written grievance procedures, constructive feedback, and opportunities for continuing professional development and advancement.

P-3C.3—We shall develop and maintain comprehensive written personnel policies that define program standards and, when applicable, that specify the extent to which employees are accountable for their conduct outside the work place. These policies shall be given to new staff members and shall be available for review by all staff members.

P-3C.4—Employees who do not meet program standards shall be informed of areas of concern and, when possible, assisted in improving their performance.

P-3C.5—Employees who are dismissed shall be informed of the reasons for their termination. When a dismissal is for cause, justification must be based on evidence of inadequate or inappropriate behavior that is accurately documented, current, and available for the employee to review.

P-3C.6—In making evaluations and recommendations, judgments shall be based on fact and relevant to the interests of children and programs.

P-3C.7—Hiring and promotion shall be based solely on a person's record of accomplishment and ability to carry out the responsibilities of the position.

P-3C.8—In hiring, promotion, and provision of training, we shall not participate in any form of discrimination based on race, religion, sex, national origin, handicap, age, or sexual preference. We shall be familiar with laws and regulations that pertain to employment discrimination.

SECTION IV: ETHICAL RESPONSIBILITIES TO COMMUNITY AND SOCIETY

Early childhood programs operate within a context of an immediate community made up of families and other institutions concerned with children's welfare. Our responsibilities to the community are to provide programs that meet its needs and to cooperate with agencies and professions that share responsibility for children. Because the larger society has a measure of responsibility for the welfare and protection of children, and because of our specialized expertise in child development, we acknowledge an obligation to serve as a voice for children everywhere.

Ideals:

I-4.1—To provide the community with high-quality, culturally sensitive programs and services.

I-4.2—To promote cooperation among agencies and professions concerned with the welfare of young children, their families, and their teachers.

I-4.3—To work, through education, research, and advocacy, toward an environmentally safe world in which all children are adequately fed, sheltered, and nurtured.

I-4.4—To work, through education, research, and advocacy, toward a society in which all young children have access to quality programs.

I-4.5—To promote knowledge and understanding of young children and their needs. To work toward greater social acknowledgment of children's rights and greater social acceptance of responsibility for their well-being.

I-4.6—To support policies and laws that promote the well-being of children and families. To oppose those that impair their well-being. To cooperate with other individuals and groups in these efforts.

I-4.7—To further the professional development of the field of early childhood education and to strengthen its commitment to realizing its core values as reflected in this Code.

Principles:

P-4.1—We shall communicate openly and truthfully about the nature and extent of services that we provide.

P-4.2—We shall not accept or continue to work in positions for which we are personally unsuited or professional unqualified. We shall not offer services that we do not have the competence, qualifications, or resources to provide.

P-4.3—We shall be objective and accurate in reporting the knowledge upon which we base our program practices.

P-4.4—We shall cooperate with other professionals who work with children and their families.

P-4.5—We shall not hire or recommend for employment any person who is unsuited for a position with respect to competence, qualifications, or character.

P-4.6—We shall report the unethical or incompetent behavior of a colleague to a supervisor when informal resolution is not effective.

P-4.7—We shall be familiar with laws and regulations that serve to protect the children in our programs.

P-4.8—We shall not participate in practices which are in violation of laws and regulations that protect the children in our programs.

P-4.9—When we have evidence that an early childhood program is violating laws or regulations protecting children, we shall report it to persons responsible for the program. If compliance is not accomplished within a reasonable time, we will report the violation to appropriate authorities who can be expected to remedy the situation.

P-4.10—When we have evidence that an agency or a professional charged with providing services to children, families, or teachers is failing to meet its obligations, we acknowledge a collective ethical responsibility to report the problem to appropriate authorities or to the public.

P-4.11—When a program violates or requires its employees to violate this Code, it is permissible, after fair assessment of the evidence, to disclose the identity of that program.

The National Association for the Education of Young Children Statement of Commitment*

As an individual who works with young children, I commit myself to furthering the values of early childhood education as they are reflected in the NAEYC Code of Ethical Conduct.

To the best of my ability I will:

- Ensure that programs for young children are based on current knowledge of child development and early childhood education.
- Respect and support families in their task of nurturing children.
- Respect colleagues in early childhood education and support them in maintaining the NAEYC Code of Ethical Conduct.
- Serve as an advocate for children, their families, and their teachers in community and society.
- Maintain high standards of professional conduct.
- Recognize how personal values, opinions, and biases can affect professional judgment.
- Be open to new ideas and be willing to learn from the suggestions of others.
- Continue to learn, grow, and contribute as a professional.
- Honor the ideals and principles of the NAEYC Code of Ethical Conduct.

*The Statement of Commitment expresses those basic personal commitments that individuals must make in order to align themselves with the profession's responsibilities as set forth in the NAEYC Code of Ethical Conduct.

Appendix B

Sample Greeting Letters and Surveys to Children and their Families

SAMPLE INTRODUCTORY LETTERS TO CHILDREN AND THEIR FAMILIES

The following letters were composed by small groups of students in early childhood education classes at Bemidji State University. Many of the groups included experienced teachers. In a few cases the author combined wording from more than one letter. Readers may prefer some letters over others; the samples are intended to provide "starter ideas" for preparing introductory correspondence with families. Some letters were keyed into computers and included computer drawings, such as animals, to give them a friendly appearance. Stickers could also be used for this purpose.

To personalize the letters, the name "Shawn" is used for the child. The name given to the teacher is "Ann Gilbert." The university students recommend that the teacher locate and use the actual name of the parent or caregiver, rather than generic terms like, "Dear Parent(s)," or "To the Parent(s) of ____________." In the samples the name of a single parent, "Ms. Reno," appears. The school name, "Central," is used, though the program might be a prekindergarten center as well.

The sample letters are in four types:

1. Greeting letters to children
2. Greeting letters to families
3. Survey letters to help the teacher learn about the child and family
4. Survey letters to obtain information about how parents might be involved.

1. Greeting Letters to Children

These letters are sent together with letters to parents. Usually the correspondence would be mailed a week or two before the start of the program year. A day care program may modify the greeting to send as soon as a child begins attending.

Dear Shawn,

Welcome to our kindergarten class. I am excited about this year and have a lot of fun learning activities planned. I look forward to having you in our classroom and am sure we will have a successful year together.

Your teacher,

Ann Gilbert

(Froggy computer drawing)

Dear Shawn,

Hello, my name is Ann Gilbert. I will be your teacher this fall. I am very pleased to have you in our classroom. We will be doing many fun things this year. On the first day of school we are going to start talking about elephants. When you come to school the first day, I will have a picture of an elephant on my door so you know where to go. Be sure to let your family know they can visit our classroom anytime. See you soon!

Your teacher and friend,

Ann Gilbert

(Elephant computer drawing with the words, "See you at School"!)

Dear Shawn,

I was very happy to hear that you will be coming to my class this year. I know starting school can be a little scary, but you will be meeting new friends and doing many fun things.

Your mother told me she would like to come to our class with you. That is just great. If you like, you are also welcome to bring your favorite toy to play with during play time.

I am really looking forward to seeing you and your mother next week. This year is going to be great fun. I hope you are as excited to come to school as I am. A big welcome, Shawn.

Your teacher,

Ann Gilbert

2. Greeting Letters to Families

Greeting letters to families accompany the letters to children. They should let parents know they are welcome participants in their child's education. Often, the letters invite parents to "greeting meetings," "open house" class days, or introductory conferences—at home or school. Not all parents have an easy time with reading, and teachers need to be alert to this possibility. A transition meeting that includes last year's and this year's teachers or care givers can often provide helpful information about the child and family. **[Note: In some situations, it may not be advisable for teachers to give out their home telephone number, and some teachers may not feel comfortable doing so.]**

Dear Ms. Reno,

Welcome to the world of Central School! I am looking forward to having your child in our classroom this year. I am also very happy to welcome you into our classroom.

Room visits will be all of next week, and I would like to invite you to join us and learn about our "developmentally appropriate" classroom. Parents are always welcome in my class, and if next week is inconvenient, or there is anything you would like to talk with me about, my number at school is ____________. At home, you can call me anytime before ten at ____________.

Again, I am looking forward to working with you and your child throughout the school year.

Sincerely,

Ann Gilbert

Dear Ms. Reno,

Hi, I will be Shawn's teacher this year. I am pleased that Shawn is going to be in my class.

I would like to set up a time when we could meet sometime soon.

Whatever time is available for you, I'll be happy to set up a meeting. I could come to your home if that would be convenient. I would like to get to know the families before the school year starts. I will be getting in touch with you in the next few days to set up a meeting.

I look forward to getting acquainted with both you and Shawn.

Sincerely,

Ann Gilbert

Dear Ms. Reno,

Hello! It is the start of a new year and I'm excited about having Shawn in our classroom. This fall I have many activities planned, and I would like to invite you to come in and join us. Next week I am going to have two "greeting meetings" for parents to learn about our program. They will be in our classroom on Wednesday and Thursday evenings at 7PM and won't go over an hour. *Feel free to attend either evening.*

At the meetings, we will discuss the activities and projects your child will be doing and also talk about things that you can do to help at home and perhaps at school. I believe that parents are very important in children's education and want parents to feel welcome in our class.

If you cannot make it to either meeting or if there is anything else you would like to talk about, my number at school is _________. At home, you can call me anytime before ten at _________.

Feel free to stop by whenever you have time to visit the classroom.

Thanks,

Ann Gilbert

3. Survey Letters to Help the Teacher Learn about the Child and Family

Survey letters of this type help the teacher to better understand and work with the child and the family. Teachers who use surveys need to be careful not to give the impression of "prying." Instead, they need to convey that the information requested is optional and will help the teacher get acquainted with the child. **[Teachers might wait until after they have met families before asking parents to complete surveys.]** Some teachers prefer not to mail these surveys out at all, but have them completed at orientation meetings or use them to structure the initial parent-teacher conference.

A request for health information is included in some of the letters. This information usually is collected more officially by the school, or program, but sometimes immediate information about health situations can be important.

Dear Shawn and Family,

My name is Ann Gilbert. I am looking forward to this year and what it will bring. I would like to tell you a little about myself. I graduated from Bemidji State University with an Elementary and Early Childhood degree. I have a family of my own, and I am looking forward to sharing things about them with you.

In order for me to get to know you better, will you and someone in your family complete this "open letter"? It will be used to say "hello" to me and your classmates.

If there is anything else you or your family would like to tell me, please feel free to write on the back. You can return it in the addressed envelope.

Your teacher,

Ann Gilbert

Dear Teachers and Friends,

The long official name I was given when I was born is ____________________. But my favorite name I like to be called is ________________. I am __ years old. My birthday is ____________.

When I grow up I want to be __________________ ______________________________.
My favorite TV show, video, or book is ______________________________________.
Some things I like to do are ____.
My favorite food is ___________________. Something that makes me happy is _____________.
Something that makes me sad is ____________________________________.

I am excited to see you on the first day of school.

Your Friend,

____

(Please invite child to write name.
Any way s/he wants to is fine.)

(COMPUTER PICTURE LOGO)
School to Home Family News
Issue Number One, September, 19__/20__

To the family of ______________________________

This first issue of our class newsletter is a survey to help me get to know your child and the rest of your family better. It would be helpful if you fill out the information below and bring it to our first conference (already scheduled on __________________). The survey is optional, but it will help me to work with your child and also with a lesson we will be doing on "Ourselves and Our Families." We will be talking about the survey at our conference.

The name your child would like to be called at school

____

Your child's age ______ Your child's birthdate ______________________________
The people in your family are:
Name __________________ Relation to child ___________________________
Name __________________ Relation to child ___________________________
Name __________________ Relation to child ___________________________
Name __________________ Relation to child ___________________________
(If others, write on back.)
Home phone __________________ Emergency phone ______________________
Name and phone of emergency contact person________________________________

____

Any allergies or health concerns you want me to know about ____________________

____

____

Your child's:
Favorite toy ____

Favorite TV show, Video or Book ____________________
Special Pet(s) ____________________
Favorite story ____________________
Favorite things to do/play ____________________
Names and ages of special friends ____________________

____

Holidays your family does/does not celebrate ____________________

____

____

Please share any cultural or religious traditions that are important to your family

____

____

____

Please feel free to share anything else about your family that will help me to work with your child ____________________

____

____

____

4. Surveys about Parent Involvement

Surveys about parent involvement should also be done after the teacher has met the parent. Two ways to distribute the surveys are either at, or by mail after, the greeting meeting. The flyer "Suggestions for Parent Involvement" (Appendix D) might be sent with this survey.

Dear Ms. Reno,

Parent involvement is a special part of our program. Here is a menu of ways that parents can be involved, and they are all important. I invite you to participate in as many ways as you can.

I would be willing to:
Read a story to a small group ____ or the class ____
Make materials at home ____
Save materials at home ____
Share about my career with the class ____
Help with special occasions, parties, field trips ____
Share a talent or hobby ____
Share something of our family's cultural background ____
Help with small groups in centers/stations ____
Please comment on the choices you selected ____________________

____

____

__Right now, I can only help at home
__I can volunteer in the classroom. The time(s) best for me are ____________

Please feel free to visit the class any time you can. You do not need to sign up in advance. I will help you find activities that you are comfortable with. My telephone number at school is ____________.

Thank you,

Ann Gilbert

Dear Ms. Reno,

I enjoyed meeting you and Shawn at the Open House last Tuesday. I am happy to have Shawn in my class and am looking forward to an exciting year for all of us.

Children and parents alike really seem to benefit from working together in their children's education. There are many ways that parents and caregivers can be involved, and they are all important. I invite you to participate in any way you can.

Here are a few things that parents have done in the past. Please check any ways in which you would like to help:
__Share or read a story
__Help with small group activities
__Help with special events (field trips, etc.)
__Donate materials, such as buttons or milk cartons
__Talk about my job
__Bring snacks
__Other, I can help by ______________________.

I can:
__come in on a regular basis.
__come in once in awhile.
__not come in due to my schedule, but can help in other ways.
__not sure at this time.

Parents are always welcome to come into the classroom to visit or help out. Two great times to come in would be at either 10AM or 2PM when we have learning centers.

Please call me if you have any questions. My school telephone number is ___________________.

Just return this letter in the enclosed envelope. I am looking forward to a fulfilling school year for all of us.

Sincerely,

Ann Gilbert

Appendix C

Sample Brochure: The Education Program in Our Class

The following brochure was developed with input from undergraduate and graduate students in early childhood education at Bemidji State University. The brochure may be simplified or condensed and is often discussed at the greeting meeting.

PARENT'S GUIDE: THE EDUCATION PROGRAM IN OUR CLASS

Parents sometimes have questions about our education program. In our class, we use something called **developmentally appropriate practice.** This means that the teaching we do and the materials we use are tailored to the "age, stage, and needs" of each child in the class. Young children learn best when they have active, hands-on experiences that they can personally understand. In our class, we use practices that encourage problem-solving, cooperation with others, and individual expression. Children who become active, confident learners when they are young do better in school when they are older. Our program is designed to help your child learn that he can succeed at school.

This brochure tells about our education program. We go over the brochure during the greeting meeting with parents at the beginning of the school year. If you have questions or concerns, feel free to call me at home or school.

Parents are important in their children's education You are welcome to visit our classroom and become a part of our education program. You, your child, and I are all on the same team. We share common goals. I look forward to working with you this year.

Why Play Is a Daily Part of Our Program

As a parent you may ask how children learn while they are playing. Through play children learn things that cannot be easily taught. In play children are forced to use their minds. They make decisions and solve problems. They figure out how to make things work and how to put things together. They have experiences from painting to hammering nails to reading books that help them learn how to think. Play helps children to understand symbols—like designs and pictures—that are needed for reading, writing, and arithmetic. Science skills learned through play include observing, guessing what will happen next, gathering information, and testing their guesses. Children use words in their play to share thoughts and feelings, and so their language skills develop.

Through play children master control of their bodies. By playing with dolls or blocks or Legos, children are developing eye-hand coordination. By running and climbing and moving to music, they are developing large muscles and becoming physically fit.

They also learn to get along with others. Children have different ideas when they play. They learn how to listen to others' views, how to lead, and how to follow. They also learn to cope when things don't go the way they planned—for themselves or others. They learn how to solve conflicts with words rather than fists—a very important life skill. They learn to get along with others who have backgrounds different than themselves. Through play, children learn to control and express their emotions.

It is important for children to feel free to learn without fear of making errors. Play allows them to do this. (We have a saying in our class, "Mistakes are OK to make. We just try to learn from them.") Play is more than fun and games. It involves many types of learning and should be a part of every child's life—at school as well as at home.

Why Our Art Is Creative

Teachers in sixth grade would never give a class an essay to copy. They want children to do their own work. It is the same with art in the early years. A teacher who provides a model for children to duplicate encourages copying, and discourages children from thinking for themselves.

Nowadays teachers know more about the importance of art than they did when we were in school. Teachers know that even before children can read and write, they tell stories through their art. Art is the young child's essay, the young child's journal. If we ask a child to tell us about a creative picture, even if it doesn't look like "something" to us, the child often has a story about it. The making and telling of stories through art is important for the development of later skills in reading, writing, and self-expression. But this can only happen if the art is creative, if each child's picture is unique—truly the child's "own work."

Teachers who let children explore freely with materials are using art in a developmentally appropriate way. So are teachers who use spoken words rather than models to motivate children to draw their own pictures. Teachers frequently use themes to encourage creative art. Some popular themes are "what I like to do outdoors in the spring" and "who the people are in my family."

One of the things we now know about art is that children go through stages in their art development. Art that is creative, so that each child's work is accepted, lets each child work at his or her stage of development. Children develop important thinking skills, as well as eye-hand coordination, by doing creative pictures.

Though popular, coloring books and craft projects are *not* developmentally appropriate activities. They do not let young children work at their stage of development. Coloring in lines and copying crafts are easier for children in a later art stage that happens at about age seven. Children who are in earlier stages, such as the scribbling stage or the early picture stage, do not have the skills necessary for coloring in—or cutting out—lines accurately. Such experiences often lead to frustration and feelings that "I'm no good at art." We do not ask a kindergarten child to print like a third grader. For the same reason, we should not ask young children to work at a stage of art development that they have not yet reached. It is better for their development to give them blank paper and encourage creative pictures.

Please appreciate the original art work your child brings home from our class. Save samples and you will see your child's skills progress. Ask your children to tell you about their pictures. Enjoy their responses even if they tell you, "This is not a story to tell; it's a picture to look at." Your enjoyment of their creative art will help them gain ability to express their thoughts and feelings—important skills for school success. Their work will still be charming, and it will be *their own*.

Why We Use the Whole Language Approach

Whole language is an approach to teaching writing and reading. It is based on the idea that children learn language best by using all of its parts together. With whole language, children use all of their communication skills, speaking, listening, singing, art, and beginning writing and reading. In a whole language classroom there is less emphasis on drill of separate skills than in the past.

Here are some important whole language ideas so that you can see what it is all about.

1. Whole language surrounds children with the printed word through story books, labels of objects, lists of words and letters, and opportunities to write. Children learn to read by making sense of the pictures and printed words around them, including their own.
2. Children learn to write by using creative spelling and printing on a daily basis in their journals. With experience they eventually learn how to spell and write correctly, but we do not expect them to when they are young.
3. Writing by children helps them: learn thinking skills, develop their expressive abilities, develop a sense of "authorship," and practice writing mechanics. Important writing mechanics include sound-letter relationships, sentence structure, and the meanings of words.
4. Reading to and with children acquaints them with printed words, teaches children to love books and reading, and encourages positive attachments between adults and children.
5. Whole language stresses "parents as partners." By encouraging writing and reading in home and school, parents contribute to their children's "literacy development." The whole language team includes the parent, teacher, and child working together.
6. Whole language builds confidence, skill, and self-esteem. It is the "natural approach" to learning to read and write.

Why We Use Real Objects in Our Mathematics Program

Children are very quick at learning to count from 1 to 20 or even 1 to 100. Until they are older in second or third grade, though, they have a difficult time understanding what numbers stand for. They can hold up four or five fingers when you ask them how old they are, but don't really understand what "five years" means. (Ask them how old they think you or other people they know are—and enjoy their responses.) They can count twelve flowers on a worksheet perhaps, but not fully understand what the words "12 flowers" mean.

To help them build a concept of number, children need to sort, compare, match and count **real objects.** The objects provide a "concrete clue" as to what 12 objects really are and later what "12 take away 6" is. Manipulating objects encourages problem-solving and enhances logical thinking. The children will enjoy math and want to experiment more in mathematics.

In our class we begin by using materials that are familiar to the children. (Examples: buttons, keys, rocks, shoes, etc.) One way to get the children excited and involved is to have them bring sets of items from home. These materials will be used for motivation as well as tools for exploring and learning. (I will be talking more about how you can help your child develop a "collection.") When the children are comfortable with the materials in the lessons, they will have an easier time learning basic mathematics concepts. Skills that will aid them in mathematics later include forming sets, matching items, and understanding numeral to number correspondence (2 = **; 3 = ***).

We are very excited about our mathematics program. Through manipulating objects, children will have an easier time understanding and enjoying mathematics. (We want to prevent "math anxiety.") We would like to see all components of the education program be positive experiences for the children.

Why We Use a Guidance Approach to Discipline

Some forms of discipline may stop classroom problems temporarily, but they tend to have negative side effects. These forms of discipline often lower children's self-esteem, cause children to feel negatively toward school and learning, and lead to behavior or personal problems in the long run. Our class uses a guidance approach to discipline. This is what a teacher does who uses "guidance discipline." She:

1. Provides a developmentally appropriate program that encourages children to be active, involved learners.
2. Teaches children to appreciate themselves and others as worthwhile individuals.
3. Builds a group spirit in which all children know they are important members of the class.
4. Provides children with a few clear guidelines for behavior and a reliable classroom environment so that they can learn from their mistakes.
5. Guides children to use words to settle problems, as much as possible on their own.
6. Addresses problems directly, but respects the individual child by not embarrassing or humiliating.
7. Builds partnerships with parents, so that the teacher and parent can work together to help the child learn and develop.

If you would like more information about our guidance program, please feel free to get in touch. [The teacher may wish to provide other materials such as the position statement, **Developmentally Appropriate Guidance of Young Children,** by the Minnesota Association for the Education of Young Children—Appendix C.]

Why Parents Are Important in Our Program

As you may have figured out from the rest of this brochure, **parents are very important in our education program.** You are the first and foremost educator of your child. We both want the same thing for your child, that he has a successful, productive year in our class—one that will help your child become an effective learner and a happy classmate. To reach this goal, parents and teachers need to work together as a team.

Appendix D

Sample Flyer: Suggestions for Parent Involvement

Parents can participate in our program in many ways this year. Each parent's involvement will be a bit different. This pamphlet is to let you know about some of the ways. Remember, you are the first and foremost educator of your child. To whatever extent you can be involved, your child (and our whole class) will benefit.

PARENT'S GUIDE: BEING INVOLVED IN YOUR CHILD'S EDUCATION

At Home

1. Appreciate the work your child brings home. Talk with your child about what he is doing in school.
2. Read over the newsletters and notices your child brings home. Note special school events and suggested at-home activities.
3. Read with your child each day. Limit TV viewing and help your child find other activities. Model reading (and writing) in the home.
4. Talk with your child for a few minutes each day about anything he would like to talk about. Be a good listener.
5. Do activities with your child on a regular basis.
6. Save things that we could use in class. We have a need for everything from jars of buttons to items of clothing for "dress-up." Let me know about anything you think we might be able to use. I may ask in the newsletter or by the phone for special items from time to time.

With the Teacher

7. Feel free to call me. At school my telephone number is __________. Best times to reach me are __________. At home my telephone number is __________. Best times are __________. [Home number optional.]
8. I try to make a home visit to each family during the year. I will be contacting you to discuss whether this would be possible.
9. We have four regularly scheduled parent-teacher conferences during the year. These are very important for us to work as a team. If you can't make a conference, let's talk about another time or place that would be more convenient.

10. On occasion an additional parent-teacher conference may be necessary. I will contact you directly to arrange the conference and will let you know then what the conference would be about.
11. From time to time we have parent meetings, such as the Greeting Meeting. These are optional, but we would love to have you attend.

In the Classroom

12. Because I have an "open classroom" policy, you are welcome to visit any time. We have a special "parents' corner" set up in the room. You are welcome to just observe or to join in. I would be happy to talk with you about things you could do when you visit.
13. Help with special events. We sometimes have class parties, events, and field trips. Parents who can help at these special times are much appreciated.
14. Each week we invite a family to come in and share with the class something that is special to one or more family members. We invite all families to do our "Family Share" sometime during the year. Members can share something of their heritage, a hobby or special interest. I will be talking with you about this.
15. Another way to volunteer is as a Very Important Parent. VIPs come in on a weekly basis for a short period of time and help with such activities as learning centers or small group reading. We try to accommodate the schedules of anyone who would like to come in on a regular basis, but some times work better than others. Let me know if you would like to become a VIP. We'd love to have you do this.
16. Our program has committees, councils, and an Association. I will be talking about these at the Greeting Meeting. Your participation at this "policy level" will help make our total program run better.

As you can see, there are many ways you can be involved. Please fill out the Parent Survey to sign-up. Your involvement on our team will be much appreciated!

Appendix E

*Developmentally Appropriate Guidance of Young Children**

(Position Statement of the Minnesota Association for the Education of Young Children)

DEVELOPMENTALLY APPROPRIATE GUIDANCE OF YOUNG CHILDREN

A Position Statement of the Minnesota Association for the Education of Young Children

This position statement by the Minnesota Association for the Education of Young Children (MNAEYC) addresses developmentally appropriate guidance techniques for children aged birth to eight.

The importance of guidance techniques that are based on sound child development principles has been well established. Research on self-concept development and the self-fulfilling prophecy demonstrates the necessity of using guidance approaches that respect the course of child development and do not label children as behavioral failures.

This document is intended for use by administrators, teachers, providers and other caregivers of young children. The term "teacher" is used in a generic sense to refer to all adults who care for young children.

SUMMARY OF PRINCIPLES FOR DEVELOPMENTALLY APPROPRIATE GUIDANCE

Principle One

Children are in the process of learning acceptable behavior.

Principle Two

An effective guidance approach is preventive because it respects feelings even while it addresses behavior.

---

* Reprinted with permission of the Minnesota Association for the Education of Young Children.

Principle Three

Adults need to understand the reasons for children's behavior.

Principle Four

A supportive relationship between an adult and a child is the most critical component of effective guidance.

Principle Five

Adults use forms of guidance and group management that help children learn self-control and responsiveness to the needs of others.

Principle Six

Adults model appropriate expression of their feelings.

Principle Seven

Adults continue to learn even as they teach.

PRINCIPLE ONE

Children Are in the Process of Learning Acceptable Behavior

It takes individuals many years to learn appropriate ways to express strong emotions and interact appropriately with others. Young children are just beginning to learn these difficult personal and social skills. MNAEYC holds that teachers of young children should take a guidance approach that is educational in tone and responsive to the child's individual level of development rather than using punitive discipline.

Application Think of behavior traditionally considered "bad" or "rowdy" as mistaken. The behavior may be unacceptable, but it is the result of the child's developmental immaturity, of not yet understanding how to act "appropriately." In reinforcing reasonable limits, adults need to teach children "what to do instead," and not just "what not to do."

Examples Recognize that everyone makes mistakes: "We all spill sometimes, even teachers. The sponge is in the bucket. Let me know if you need help."

Reinforce limits and teach alternatives: "People are not for hitting. When you hit people it hurts them. Use your words when you are angry. Then people will know what you're upset about.

PRINCIPLE TWO

An Effective Guidance Approach Is Preventive Because it Respects Feelings Even While it Addresses Behavior

Most adults can remember instances of discipline in their childhood that caused pain and affected self-concept. The teacher may have thought that s/he was dealing only with "a problem of the moment," but the effects of the punishment stayed with the individual for years. An approach to discipline that is guidance rather than punishment-oriented respects the feelings and self-concept of the child, even while it addressed mistaken behaviors.

Application 2a. The adult structures the environment and sets expectations that enable children to succeed. Taking turns, sharing, losing at games, waiting for long periods, and sustained attention to teacher-led activities are difficult skills for young children. Teachers need to use developmentally appropriate practices to reduce mistaken behavior caused by a mismatch of the child and the educational program.

Example Teachers de-emphasize winning and losing in games and stress successful participation by all.

Teachers use open-ended art, rather than dittoes and product-centered crafts.

Teachers emphasize individual choice in learning centers and structure organized activities with children's attention spans in mind.

Application 2b. In group situations, the adult avoids discipline methods that publicly embarrass an individual such as writing a child's name on the blackboard or scolding a child in front of others. Instead, the adult uses problem solving strategies that show respect for the child's feelings while reinforcing limits.

Example Teacher to group: "As soon as we are all ready, the story can begin."

Teacher to aide (quietly): "Maybe you can sit by Sally and help her focus on the story."

Teacher to child: Teacher silently moves close to child who needs a reminder and then continues activity.

Application 2c. In individual situations, the adult accepts the child's feelings, addresses the child's behavior, and avoids references to the child's personality. The adult avoids labeling a child as a "trouble-maker" or "problem child."

Example "Mary, it's all right to be upset. Use your words to tell Jake how you feel."

"Larry, I know you're angry, but I can't let you throw blocks."

Application 2d. The adult recognizes that measures such as physically restraining a child or removing a child from the group are taken only when preventive and problem solving methods have not worked or when a child has lost control. Because these measures of last resort can be punishing for all concerned, the adult needs to help the child: reconcile with the adult, feel welcome in rejoining the group and learn more effective ways of expressing strong emotions. To reduce the punitive effects of "timeouts," they should be kept brief and be considered "cooling down times" that are followed up by discussion. The adult may want to stay with a child during a timeout.

Example "You need to use words instead of biting. You and I need to spend some time alone until you've calmed down. Then I'll help you figure out how to use the blocks with Carl."

"Nancy, we're glad you're ready to come to the art table now. We need some help with these paper chains."

Physical punishment is never appropriate Repeated use of timeouts, physical restraint or other crisis interventions with an individual indicate trouble in the child's life and a need to better understand the child. Repeated use of crisis interventions with a group indicates an over-reliance on them and a need to develop new guidance techniques.

PRINCIPLE THREE

Adults Need to Understand the Reasons for Children's Behavior

There are always reasons for children's behavior. Working to understand these reasons can assist the adult in helping the child. Although we can never know another person fully, we can increase our understanding and that effort in itself can lead to better relations and more mature behavior.

Application 3a. Children do things to see what will happen. Children learn from such actions, and from others' reactions. Sometimes "experimentation mistaken behavior," if harmless, should be ignored. If the adult decides to intervene, s/he should do so in a way that teaches the child about consequences and alternatives, but also appreciates the child's natural curiosity: the child's need to learn.

Example A child marks on a table. "Mary, you can color on the paper. Let's get some soapy water and wash the table nice and clean. Then we'll get some paper to use with those markers."

Application 3b. Children do things because they have been influenced by others to do them, either at home or in the classroom. With "socially influenced" mistaken behavior, the adult firmly but matter-of-factly reinforces a limit, but also teaches an acceptable alternative for next time.

Example Child says, "that damned kid makes me so mad." Teacher (hiding smile) responds: "Peter made you feel mad and you can tell him or me, but you don't need to call names. We'll get the message."

Application 3c. Children who show serious mistaken behavior almost always have trouble in their lives that is beyond their ability to understand and manage. Sometimes the trouble can be physical, such as a hearing loss. Other times, the trouble may be caused by a serious situation at home, center, or school. When a child shows rigid or exaggerated behavior, the adult should be alerted to the need for more information, especially if the behavior continues for more than a day or two. Observing and talking with the child can often add to an adult's understanding. Meeting with other staff can be helpful. A phone call or conference with parents may well be essential to better understanding the problem. Occasionally, consulting with an outside professional can help. When staff fully use their resources for understanding what is going on, an effective, coordinated plan for assisting the child is much easier to construct.

Example A teacher notices that a child shows uncharacteristic irritability especially toward the beginning and end of each week. Talks with a parent determine that the parents have separated and the child is living with the mother during the week and the father on the weekends. The staff works together with the parents to make the transitions more understandable and less traumatic for the child.

PRINCIPLE FOUR

A Supportive Relationship Between an Adult and a Child Is the Most Critical Component of Effective Guidance

Trust and acceptance are the prerequisite foundation of the relationship between an adult and a child. Not only do children learn about behavior from an adult, they also learn about themselves. It is generally understood that children who are labeled "behavior problems" tend to see themselves as the adult does and to show more mistaken behavior than before they were labeled. On the other hand, children who gain the understanding that they are valued and belong tend to develop positive self-concepts and have less need to act out against the world.

Application An irony of teaching is that the children who act the "worst" need a helping relationship the most, and are often the hardest to accept. Building relationships with such children is a challenge for the early childhood teacher and yet it is a critical task. In constructing productive relations with children who show troubling behavior, teachers need not "love" them, but do need to find ways to accept them as individuals and as members of the group.

Example The teacher talks with the child, the child's parents, other staff, and outside professionals to gain a better understanding of the child.

The teacher lists qualities of the child that she likes, appreciates, respects and can affirm. The teacher finds times during the day to focus positive attention on the child.

The teacher helps the child into activities where s/he can succeed.

REMINDER: An adult cannot build a supportive relationship primarily on acts of discipline.

PRINCIPLE FIVE

Adults Use Forms of Guidance and Group Management that Help Children Learn Self-control and Responsiveness to the Needs of Others

Children need to be able to decide between "right and wrong" not on the basis of fear of authority or peer pressure but on the basis of careful thought. The more we can help children to make thoughtful decisions in social situations when they are young, the more we are assisting them to become caring, responsible adults.

Application Children need many appropriate opportunities to solve problems, make decisions, and learn from their experiences.

Example Teacher to two arguing children: "You two seem to be having a problem. You can either work it out yourselves with words or I can help you. Which do you want?"

Teacher to child: "Karen, you choose. Let everyone have a turn or find an empty table and work by yourself."

PRINCIPLE SIX

Adults Model Appropriate Expressions of Their Feelings

As professionals, teachers make decisions about how to respond to behavior based on their judgments of the events at the time. Because we are human, sometimes we may jump in too quickly, over-react, show inconsistency, lose our tempers, or otherwise disclose our human frailties. Teachers who are professionals attempt to learn from their mistakes. They know that their job is challenging because young children are just at the beginning of learning very difficult social skills—skills that take into adulthood to fully master. They have accepted the fact that being a caring teacher is a life-long task.

Application When upset, teachers use methods to diffuse and express their feelings that do not put down the other person. They may pay attention to a "victim" first and talk with the child who did the hurting after they've cooled down. They may use *I* messages to describe their feelings rather than accuse and disparage the "culprits." They may firmly request more information before they make a hasty judgment. They may check themselves before responding to a child who is difficult for them to understand. Finally, they monitor their moods and feelings and are aware of their impact on teaching effectiveness.

Examples "Skip, I saw what happened. You need to wait here until I find out if Jenny is all right. We'll talk about it in a few minutes when I've calmed down."

"I am really bothered that the water got spilled out of the aquarium. We need to fill it up quickly and then we'll talk about what happened."

"When I see puzzle pieces dumped on the floor, I'm worried that we'll lose them and then we won't be able to do the puzzle anymore. Please tell me what happened."

PRINCIPLE SEVEN

Teachers Continue to Learn Even as They Teach

Application Teachers recognize that they are learners even as they are teachers.

Examples Teachers and caregivers should observe, and be observed by other professionals, in order to get feedback for personal review of teaching practices.

Teachers use collaboration with parents, staff, and outside professionals in order to continue learning about the children they work with.

Teachers read, attend courses, conferences, and workshops in order to update their store of ideas.

Teachers use observation and communication skills to learn from the best of all teachers, the children themselves.

REFERENCES

Bullock, J. (1988). "Understanding and altering aggression." *Day Care and Early Education*. Human Sciences Press.

Clewett, A. S. (1988). "Guidance and discipline." *Young Children*. NAEYC.

Elkind, D. (1982). *The hurried child: Growing up too fast too soon*. Reading, MA: Addison-Wesley.

Gartrell, D. (1987). "Punishment or guidance?" *Young Children*. NAEYC.

Ginot, H. G. (1972). *Teacher and Child*. New York: Macmillan.

Goffin, S. G. (1989). "How well do we respect the children in our care?" *Childhood Education*. ACEI.

Greenberg, P. (1988). "Avoiding 'me against you' discipline." *Young Children*. NAEYC.

Hendrick, J. (1988). *The whole child*. Columbus, OH: Merrill Publishing Company.

Kostelnik, M. J., Stein, L. C., & Whiren, A. P. (1988). "Children's self-esteem: The verbal environment." *Childhood Education*. ACEI.

Marion, M. (1987). *Guidance of young children* (2nd ed.). Columbus, OH: Merrill Publishing Company.

Stone, J. G. (1973). *What about discipline?* Cambridge, MA: Educational Development Center.

Warren, R. (1977). *Caring: Supporting children's growth*. Washington, D.C.: NAEYC.

Weber-Schwartz, N. (1987). "Patience or understanding?" *Young Children*. NAEYC.

APPROVED BY THE MNAEYC BOARD—JANUARY 30, 1988

DEVELOPMENTALLY APPROPRIATE GUIDANCE COMMITTEE:

Dan Gartrell, Author
Diane McLinn, Chair
Roz Anderson
Mary Holub
Vickie Iverson
Ginny Petty
Zoe Ann Wignall
Katie Williams

Revised by Dan Gartrell and Nancy Johnson—October, 1991
Designed by Michele Wolfel—(612) 483-4335
Printing by SPI Printing & Graphics

MNAEYC
1821 University Ave.
Suite 296-S
St. Paul, MN 55104
(612) 646-8689

Copies in booklet form are available by calling MNAEYC

Appendix F

Individual Guidance Plan Worksheet

INDIVIDUAL GUIDANCE PLAN WORKSHEET

Child's name___________

Initial Write-Up Date______

1. Noted Behaviors

Behavior Observed: Thoughts about Behavior:

2. Additional Information

Check procedures used. Then summarize information gained.

__Discussion with child. Date:____ __Discussion with parent. Date:____

__Discussion with other staff. Date:____ __Discussion with other professionals. Date:____

3. Cooperative Strategy Meeting **Date:**

Persons attending meeting:

Strategy to be tried:

4. Follow-up Meeting or Review **Date:**

Effort/progress shown by child:

Progress still needed:

Any change in strategy:

5. Summary of Results/Changes as of (Date)______

6. Summary of Results/Changes as of (Date)______

7. Summary of Results/Changes as of (Date)______

The use of a structured system may not be necessary with all children who show level three mistaken behavior. Still, some teachers find a set plan helpful. Appendix D includes an Individual Guidance Plan Worksheet. See the Instructors Guide for a full length form. The worksheet can be used without permission. The author does ask for feedback on its use by E-mail: dgartrell@vaxl.bemidji.msus.edu or by letter: Dr. Dan Gartrell, Professional Education Department, Bemidji State University, Bemidji, MN 56601.

Glossary

Adjustment relational pattern. The level of social relations in which priority is given to showing behaviors expected by significant others.

Anti-bias curriculum. An education program designed to prevent the development of bias in relation to racism, sexism, and children with disabilities.

Anticipatory set. A feeling of positive anticipation or motivation in children created by the teacher often in a large group setting toward a follow-up activity often done individually or in small groups.

Assertive discipline. An organized, "obedience-based" discipline system in which the roles of the student and teacher are clearly defined and the will of the teacher is to prevail.

Attachment. A relationship with an adult, when positive, is likely to result in enhanced self-esteem and receptivity to guidance in the child.

Authentic assessment. The use of tools such as anecdotal observations, check lists, and samples of children's work to assess children's progress while children are engaged in ongoing activities of the classroom.

Autonomy. Piaget's term for the ability to make ethical, intelligent decisions that balance others' viewpoints with one's own. Opposite of *heteronomy*.

Being direct. A firm intervention technique with mistaken behavior in which a teacher describes the problem succinctly, directs the child or children to an acceptable alternative behavior, and sometimes expresses the teacher's feelings toward the mistaken behavior.

Belonging. A basic need of children written about by Elkind as a co-definer of the period in early childhood of initiative versus guilt; failure to meet the need for belonging results in alienation (stigma).

Body language. Nonverbal language, such as smiles, eye-contact, and physical proximity used to support children and remind of guidelines.

Boisterous activity level. The level of play at learning centers that is very active and often loud.

Brevity. A quick, firm but friendly intervention technique in which a teacher uses concise language to reestablish limits.

Bucolic activity level. The level of activity at learning centers that is quiet, tranquil.

Buffer activity. An activity that uses time productively while waiting.

Busy activity level. The level of activity at learning centers that is bustling but not overly active or loud.

Character education. Education for which the outcome is an ability to make decisions that are ethical, intelligent, and socially responsive.

Child guidance. Leadership with children that models and teaches democratic life skills.

Child negotiation. The process whereby two or more children are able to resolve a conflict peaceably on their own.

Child-report. An alternate term for tattling by which children express concerns to teachers about perceived conflicts or emergencies.

Children taking charge. The capacity of children in a conflict situation to remove themselves from the immediate site and to negotiate a resolution.

Class meeting. A scheduled or unscheduled meeting of the teacher and the class to address business matters and matters of concern to one or more members of the group; other terms sometimes used with specialized meetings include *sharing circles* and *magic circles*.

Collaboration. Working in a team with others to solve problems and accomplish tasks that cannot be done on one's own.

Commanding cooperation. Firm direction by the teacher for a child to choose between two alternative appropriate behaviors, one of which may be preferred by the teacher, but either of which is acceptable.

Compliment sandwich. An encouragement technique that provides at least two acknowledgments of effort and progress accompanied by one request or suggestion for further progress.

Conditional acceptance. A classroom atmosphere in which students are aware that they will be accepted or rejected by the teacher on the basis of their performance academically and behaviorally, their backgrounds, or their personalities.

Conflict. A disagreement over an action one or more parties has taken, usually involving property, territory, or privilege; a mistaken behavior by a child or children, disagreed with by the teacher.

Conflict management. The ability to prevent and resolve disputes in a civil, peaceable manner.

Conflict management models. Defined procedures, sometimes involving lessons, verbal steps, and props, that adults and children use to management conflicts.

Conflict resolution. The ability to resolve disputes in a peaceable, civil manner.

Constructivist education. The concept that the child constructs knowledge through interaction with the social and physical environment, and the educational strategy that enables this learning process to take place.

Contact talk. Conversation between an adult and child for the purpose of sharing time together and becoming better acquainted rather than to accomplish an ulterior purpose.

Conventional discipline. The use of rewards and punishments to keep children under the teacher's control.

Cooling down time. A nonpunitive alternative to the time-out chair in which a teacher removes a child from the group and assists the child to regain control of her or his emotions.

Correction by direction. Intervention in which a teacher briefly directs a child to a guideline or appropriate behavior, rather than admonishes about a mistaken behavior.

Creative conflict. Disagreement with another that the parties believe can be resolved by negotiation and cooperative problem-solving.

Crisis intervention. Nonpunitive methods the teacher uses when a conflict has gotten out of hand; a first priority is ceasing a danger of harm or serious disruption.

Crisis management techniques. Guidance methods of last resort when a conflict has gotten out of hand such as commanding cooperation, separation, a cool-down time, or physical restraint.

Day clock. A particular kind of period chart that uses a "one-handed clock" to track routine time blocks in the daily schedule.

Describe without labeling. An intervention technique in which a teacher "gives words" to a conflict by addressing the situation and avoiding references to a child's teacher.

Developmental egocentrism. The inability of young children to understand the complexity of social factors in any situation and to see things from one's own perspective.

Developmentally appropriate practice (DAP). Educational practice that accommodates the development and individual needs of each child in the class.

Developmentally inappropriate practice. Educational practice that fails to accommodate the development and individual needs of each child in the class.

Diagnosis. Systematic assessment to determine the nature of a difficulty in order to empower the child to overcome it.

Differentiated staffing. Adults of differing educational and experience backgrounds working together as a teaching team.

Direct intervention. A sequence of responses to serious mistaken behavior that involves the teacher's describing what he or she sees, sometimes reporting feelings, and directing to alternative behaviors.

Discipline. Derived from the Latin term *disciplina* meaning teaching, instruction. In this progressive sense, synonymous with guidance. In its every day meaning, the use of rewards and punishments to keep children "in line." As a verb, "to discipline" commonly means to punish in order to bring under the teacher's control.

Discussing inclusively. During discussions, the ability to respond in an encouraging fashion to unexpected comments.

Disequilibrium. Piaget's term for when the individual experiences contradiction between perceptions and understanding.

Displeasure without insult. The use of self-report or *I* messages to explain, without character attack, strong feelings about a mistaken behavior.

Early Childhood. That period of childhood from birth to age eight.

Ecological perspective. A comprehensive viewpoint when working with children that encompasses the family's social, cultural, economic, educational, and behavioral dynamics.

Encounterer relational pattern. The most mature level of social relations; behaviors have less to do with expectations of others and more to do with the individual's effort to make meaning out of life.

Encouragement. Group- or individually-focused acknowledgment by an adult that recognizes progress and efforts and supports children's further efforts.

Encouraging classroom. A "community" classroom environment in which each child is empowered to feel a sense of belonging, self-worth and a capacity to learn.

Engagement. The total involvement of the child in the learning activity.

Equilibrium. Piaget's term for when the individual experiences harmony between perceptions and understanding.

Experimentation (Level One) mistaken behavior. Mistaken behavior that occurs as a result of involvement in or curiosity about a situation.

Extrinsic rewards. Recognition for achievements given by teachers that is outside the intrinsic value of the activity for the child; tends to build dependency rather than autonomy by discouraging personal assessment of the worth of own's efforts.

Family groups. A grouping system long used in early childhood that includes children of diverse ages and developmental characteristics in the same group, under the supervision of a primary caregiver.

Group management. Techniques used with the group to build the encouraging classroom by reducing the need for mistaken behavior in the group.

Grouping patterns. Various social arrangements of learners in an encouraging classroom, based on criteria such as interest and group dynamics rather than inferred ability level, frequently changing during the day.

Guidance. A way of teaching that empowers children to make decisions that are ethical, intelligent, and socially responsive. The teaching of democratic life skills.

Guidance approach. The use of guidance, distinct from discipline, to reduce the need for and resolve the occurrence of mistaken behavior in ways that are non-punitive and teach democratic life skills.

Guidance talk. A discussion with a child after an incident that helps the child understand how the other felt, what he or she might do to bring about reconciliation, and what acceptable alternative behaviors might be.

Guidelines. Agreements often made with the class that identify prosocial behavior; distinct from rules that tend to be stated negatively and lack specific direction to the life skills desired by the teacher.

Heteronomy. Piaget's term for being influenced in one's judgment by the authority of others—opposite of *autonomy*.

High-level mediation. Intervention by an adult to assist children to resolve a conflict, that calms children, helps them put the conflict into words, and assists them to reach a mutually acceptable solution.

Humor. A quality much appreciated by children that can both prevent and reduce the negative effects of mistaken behavior.

***I* message.** A communication technique in which one person reports perceptions and feelings to another in a straightforward but respectful manner.

Inclusion. The educational practice of including learners of diverse abilities and physical and behavioral characteristics in the classroom.

Inclusiveness. The ability of teachers to accommodate the expression of ideas by children when those expressions are not what the teacher expected.

Individual Guidance Plan (IGP). A strategy that is collaborative, systematic, and comprehensive to assist a child showing serious mistaken behavior; involvement of parents in the IGP process is a priority.

Industry. A basic need in the middle childhood period defined by Erikson, with inferiority resulting if the child is unable to meet the need.

Initiative. A basic need in the early childhood period defined by Erikson, with self-doubt resulting if the child is unable to meet the need.

Institution-caused mistaken behavior. Mistaken behavior that results from a mismatch of the educational program and a child's level of development and individual needs, a developmentally inappropriate educational program.

Integrated curriculum. Instruction that is interdisciplinary, interrelating separate content areas through thematic instruction.

Intentionality. When mistaken behaviors are done on purpose due to an error in judgment.

Intervention. Nonpunitive leadership shown by an adult when mistaken behavior occurs.

I to I. A conflict management model that emphasizes three rules: agreement to solve the problem; taking turns in speaking and listening; and respectful, truthful communication.

Inviting, requesting, commanding cooperation. A communication technique used by a teacher in which she or he uses different degrees of intensity matched to the situation in order to solicit cooperation.

Inviting cooperation. A friendly suggestion by a teacher that a child might choose to cooperate in a situation.

Joining. The teacher's establishing with parents that they are partners in working for the betterment of the child.

Labeling. Stereotyping of a child's character as a result of a pattern of mistaken behavior that the child may show.

Language arts focus. The time block set aside for integrated language arts instruction, typically including reading, writing, speaking, and listening.

Leadership communication. The cluster of communication skills used by a teacher with the group and the individual that encourage life skills and prosocial behavior.

Learned behavior. Behavior, including Level Two mistaken behavior, that a child is influenced by significant others to show.

Learning centers. Distinct areas within the classroom that provide a variety of related materials for children's use; other similar terms preferred by some professionals include: *learning areas, interest areas, interest centers*.

Level Three day. The kind of day any child or adult can have, when everything goes wrong; a "bad hair day" taken to the extreme.

Liberation teaching. The acceptance, support, and empowerment of children who might be singled out negatively from the group for physical, cultural, or behavioral reasons.

Life skills. Social skills needed for life in a democracy, including the ability to see another person's point of view, cooperate with others, express strong feelings in socially acceptable ways, and resolve problems through the use of civil words; difficult skills to learn, in the process of which children and adults make mistakes.

Logical consequences. Responses taken by adults that "fit" a child's mistaken act.

Low-level mediation. The level of conflict resolution in which children can calm themselves, define the problem, and reach a solution with minimum support and clarification by the adult.

Marginal mistaken behaviors. Milder mistaken behaviors that different teachers react to differently and that the same teacher might react differently to on different occasions.

Mediation. A conflict management strategy in which a third person, often a teacher, uses high- to low-level intervention to assist others to resolve a conflict.

Misbehavior. The conventional term applied to mistaken acts resulting in consequences that often include punishment and the internalization of a negative label, i.e., "naughty," by the child.

Mistaken behavior. Errors in judgment and action made in the process of learning life skills. Mistaken behaviors occur at three levels: experimentation, socially influenced, and strong needs.

Multicultural education. Curriculum and methods that teach children to respect and learn from points of uniqueness and commonality in various cultures; the celebration of cultural diversity for the commonality of human values that the respectful treatment of cultural differences engenders.

Multidimensional classroom. A classroom in which a variety of activities and grouping arrangements occur and the teacher is a manager of the daily program as well as a lead teacher.

Negative dissonance. A conflict with another that has gone past the point where it can be resolved by negotiation with another, and mediation is necessary if the conflict is to be resolved.

Negotiation. A process to resolve conflict used by two or more parties directly involved in a conflict.

Negotiation reminders. Statements that direct children to the negotiation process for resolving conflicts.

Nonverbal techniques. The use of body language, facial expressions, gestures, or physical proximity to keep learners on-task with a minimum of attention being drawn to the situation.

Peace education. The use of curriculum and teaching practice to empower children to learn and advocate peaceful alternatives to violence in daily life and the solving of social and environmental problems.

Peaceable classroom. A classroom environment based on self and mutual respect and the practice of preventing and resolving problems using friendly words.

Peace props. Objects such as puppets, the talking stick, talk-and-listen chairs, and the peace table that assist children to manage conflicts.

Peace table. A child-sized table with peace symbols on it that is reserved for peace education and planned and unplanned conflict management activities.

Peer mediation. A system of conflict management in which trained older children in a school mediate conflicts of their peers, frequently used in out-of-classroom situations.

Performance assessment. Assessment of children's efforts in selected tasks to determine performance in relation to identified outcomes; measures may include, but are not limited to, pencil and paper tests.

Period chart. A visual used to help children understand routine time blocks in the daily schedule.

Play. Self-selected, self-directed activity that is inherently pleasurable and through which the child "learns what cannot be formally taught."

Preprimary. Refers in this text to the kindergarten and prekindergarten levels.

Preventive guidance. Teaching practices in the encouraging classroom that prevent institution-caused mistaken behavior and reduce the need for mistaken behavior in general.

Private encouragement. Recognition of effort and progress directed by a teacher to an individual in such a way as to avoid singling out the individual in relation to the group.

Privilege. One of three common causes of mistaken behavior in early childhood classrooms, along with *property* and *territory*.

Proactive group management. Positive group management that reduces the need for mistaken behavior by building the encouraging classroom.

Problem puppets. A peace prop involving hand puppets used to instruct and resolve problems; also called *peace puppets* and *power puppets*.

Professional teacher. A teacher who does not depend on established routines and practices but takes a positive problem-solving approach responsive to the needs of children and the dynamics of the situation.

Property. The most frequent cause of mistaken behavior in the early childhood classroom; two other common causes are *territory* and *privilege*.

Protective buffer. Strategies used in liberation teaching to prevent children from being stigmatized by their vulnerabilities and to encourage toward resilience.

Public encouragement. Recognition of effort and progress directed by a teacher to the group without the singling out of individual group members.

Reconciliation. The process of positive resolution of an incident of mistaken behavior that might involve an apology, making amends, and/or reuniting with the group.

Reflective listening. A communication technique in which an adult repeats back or supportively acknowledges a remark, action, or implied emotion of a child.

Relational patterns. Levels of social relations shown by children; three relational patterns are survival, adjustment, and encountering.

Requesting cooperation. An intervention level of medium intensity in which the teacher communicates a clear expectation that the child will choose from among two or three acceptable options for behavior.

Resiliency. The capacity to overcome a vulnerability for stigma by meeting a need for safety, and so being able to engage in learning and personal growth.

Safeguards. Techniques for managing strong emotions to prevent harm to others, such as monitoring one's feelings, describing conflicts objectively, and expressing feelings nonpunitively (the use of self-report).

Scheduled class meetings. Meetings that are a part of the daily routine for discussing business, activities, and situations in a mutually respectful manner.

School anxiety. Stress felt by children as a result of routines, activities, or incidents at a school or center that are threatening or harmful.

Self-concept. The total collection of thoughts and feelings that an individual has at any point in time about who he or she is.

Self-esteem. The feelings one has about one's self at any point in time.

Self-fulfilling prophecy. The phenomena that persons who become labeled by others for particular behaviors come to see themselves as they are labeled and show an increase in the behaviors that others have come to expect.

Self psychologist. Psychologist who focuses on the developing self as the primary dynamic of human behavior.

Self psychology. A branch of psychology that focuses on the developing self as the primary dynamic in human behavior, with mental health being a function of continuing development and mental ill-health the result of obstacles to that development.

Self-report. The use of *I* messages to express strong feelings to others in a non-punitive way: "I feel upset when. . . ."

Sentence frame. A negotiation reminder in the form of a stock response that individuals use to de-escalate and resolve conflicts.

Sharing times. Times set aside during scheduled class meetings when members can express thoughts and feelings about a topic—often a "nonmaterialistic" alternative to show and tell.

Socially influenced (Level Two) mistaken behavior. Mistaken behavior that is learned behavior, a result of the intentional or unintentional influence of a significant other.

Social knowledge. Mental recognition of arbitrary sets of symbols (the names of "numerals") and behaviors (saying "please" and "thank you") common to a society.

Social problem-solving. The ability to manage and resolve problems and conflicts in peaceable ways.

Socioemotional development. The domain of human development that addresses the social and emotional dimensions together.

Starter statement. A statement of encouragement that acknowledges details and effort in children's work, such as "You are really working hard on that story."

Stickers and smiley faces. Rewards extrinsic to the effort of the child that tend to build dependence on the teacher rather than autonomy; if used at all, should be to celebrate the efforts of all rather than evaluate individual performance.

Stigma. The psychological and social process whereby an individual is negatively separated from the group for cultural, physical, or behavioral reasons.

Strong needs (Level Three) mistaken behavior. Mistaken behavior shows itself in extreme, inappropriate behaviors over time and is the acting out of strong unmet physical and/or psychological needs.

Survival relational pattern. The level of social relations children show when they experience the environment as a dangerous and painful place; behavior patterns are frequently inappropriate and extremely rigid.

Table talk. The naturally occurring conversing that occurs when individuals are seated around a table working on an activity.

Tabula rosa. The view that the mind and soul of the young child is a "blank slate, still to be written upon" by character shaping experiences.

Talk-and-listen chairs. A peace prop consisting of two chairs that children use to resolve conflicts; the children take turns in each chair until the problem is resolved.

Talking stick. A decorated stick passed from child to child, used to determine speaking order and facilitate the give-and-take necessary to resolve problems.

Teaching team. Adults of differing educational levels and experience backgrounds that work together as a team in the classroom.

Team-teaching. Two adults of similar educational backgrounds who share duties and tasks.

Territory. One of three common causes of disputes in early childhood classrooms, along with *property* and *privilege*.

Thematic instruction. Teaching that uses themes as the organizational unit of instruction, rather than the academic subjects taught separately.

Three levels of mistaken behavior. Mistaken behavior can be the result of experimentation (Level One), social influence (Level Two) or strong needs (Level Three).

Time confusion. The inability to understand time concepts in early childhood due to developmental factors.

Tossed salad approach. An approach to multicultural education in which adults of diverse backgrounds, usually parents, interact informally in the classroom community.

Tourist curriculum. The mistaken notion that by studying token facts about a culture, that may or may not be accurate, important instruction about that culture is occurring; for example, "Eskimos live in igloos."

Unconditional positive regard. Full acceptance of the child as a developing human being and member of the classroom group despite mistaken behaviors that the child may show.

Unscheduled class meetings. Meetings of each class called by the teacher (sometimes at the request of a class member) to discuss and find a resolution to problems and conflicts; guidelines for such meetings are that one person speaks at a time, and communication is to be truthful and mutually respectful.

Webbing. A visual brainstorming activity often done with the group in which content, learning activities, and sometimes teaching methods are generated for thematic instruction.

Withitness. The idea that the effective teacher is aware of the important dynamics of behavior in the classroom; that teachers have "eyes in the backs of their heads."

Index